The
Good Holiday
Cottage Guide
2006

The
Good Holiday
Cottage Guide

2006

Edited by
Bryn Frank

A reader told us recently 'When we did a recce of a house near Bristol before committing ourselves to a booking we noticed lots of little pairs of smart shoes tucked neatly under wardrobes and beside beds. We commented that there must be a family staying with lots of very tidy, very clothes-conscious children. "Oh, no," said the owners, "they're performing Snow White at the Theatre Royal, and we've got the seven dwarfs staying with us." '

An owner in Gloucestershire described a memorable February. He was discreetly requested by a woman due to arrive for a 'Valentine's Weekend' with her boyfriend if he, the owner, would sprinkle (real) rose petals over the four poster bed prior to their arrival. Which he did. But what really stayed in his mind was that after they left – the place was pristinely tidy – he discovered a pair of handcuffs attached to the bed – and no sign of a key...

The help of the following in preparing this guide is gratefully acknowledged:
Leyla Ali, Richard Bamforth, Carole Frank, John Harrison, Jan James, Nicky
Phillips, Paul Phillips, Debbie Richardson, John Ruler and Gillian Thomas.

Bryn Frank, Hertford, December 2005

© 2006 Swallow Press, PO Box 21, Hertford, Hertfordshire SG14 2DD.
Telephone 01438 869489. Fax 869589. ISBN 0-946238-26-X
www.goodcottageguide.com

email: bryn@goodcottageguide.com
or frank@cottageguide.demon.co.uk

Printed by Stephen Austin & Sons Ltd, Caxton Hill, Hertford SG13 7LU.
Telephone 01992 584955.

Distributed by Portfolio Ltd, Unit 5, Perivale Industrial Park, Perivale, Middlesex
UB6 7RL. Telephone 020-8997 9000. Fax 020-8997 9097.

Front cover

Top: Casa Fabia (Page 324: Tuscany Holidays);
Left: Box End (Page 50: Riverside Rentals);
Right: Macinnisfree Cottage (Page 97: Scottish Country Cottages).

Back cover

Top: The Barn (Page 244);
Left: Clydey Country Cottages (Page 145);
Right: Weavers Barn (Page 256: Discover the Cotswolds).

Please discuss...

The 2006 edition of the guide is the 24th. Set against the inexorable march of the internet, that probably means we qualify as 'survivors'. We do of course have our own website, which we think looks good and which we know to be effective (**www.goodcottageguide.com**), but even that tends to be a bit impersonal: our heart is really in the first-hand, personal visits to holiday cottages by which the guide made its reputation, in meeting owners and agents, and getting a healthy amount of feedback from readers. We enjoy the challenge of matching self caterers with 'the right property', generally know the locations, like to bring the various elements together. Keep those calls coming!

An interesting recent footnote from the owner of two Five Star cottages we feature relates to the internet. Along with perhaps ten per cent of owners with websites, she offers a virtual tour. But a downside, apparently, is that because holiday tenants have such an exact idea of what to expect when they arrive, she doesn't get so many 'oohs and aaahs' of appreciation. Also, we're told, arriving tenants can turn out to be too gimlet-eyed. A recent example: 'On your virtual tour the painting over the mantelpiece was of a nice seaside scene, now it's some silly modern abstract'.

Internet or not, some things *don't* change. A constant irritation for owners is holidaymakers arriving early, say at 3.15 pm rather than 4. As one owner in Norfolk said, 'it's like dinner guests invited for 7.30 pm arriving at 7.15 instead of the 'polite' 7.45'. And there's a possibly apocryphal account of a very early arrival in Derbyshire being handed a can of Johnson's 'Pledge' and being asked to give the furniture that last-minute spray and polish.

For other good ways to annoy cottage owners, see Page 270...

Approximately two thirds of the cottage owners featured in this guide accept dogs, and acceptance of dogs usually but not always means other pets too (a small number exclude cats). Most owners charge extra – usually between £15 and £20 per week per dog – for the inevitable extra wear and tear on properties, though this is without exception much less than kennels would charge. Please don't arrive with more dogs than you have permission to take, and please don't sneak a dog into a cottage where it's not welcome.

A number of owners we feature take great pride in paring their prices down to the minimum, for example where their overheads are low, and are happy to have their properties singled out as 'inexpensive'. Here is a short list of those who have asked to be included – not a comprehensive but, we think, a useful selection:

Please note:

A new cottage at *Little Boynes*, not yet seen by us,
is now available. See Page 254.

Bosinver Cottages and Lodges, featured by us for many years,
won the accolade of 'Self Catering Establishment of the Year'
in the Cornwall Tourism Awards for 2005. See Page 170.

Late amendments to Ballyvaughan, Page 284:
There is now only one apartment available, sleeping up to 3.
'Country houses' by the sea are no longer available.
Prices now €200 to €675

Late amendments to Delphi, Page 285:
All Boathouse cottages sleep 4, two in two twins, two in a twin
and a double. None have DVD players. Prices should be in
euros, not pounds.

Contents

Colour sections: Pages 193-200 and 233-240.

Walk the Line...

The Good Holiday Cottage Guide is happy to endorse twelve outstanding regional holiday letting agencies, who market themselves as 'Cottage Line'. See: www.cottageline.com (All except two are featured in this guide.)

Suffolk Secrets (Page 29)

'Whether you prefer villages or magnificent market towns, beaches or rolling countryside, Suffolk offers a wealth of ideas for the discerning holiday visitor. This agency (sister company to the well established and respected Norfolk Country Cottages) offers a quality selection of around 100 holiday cottages chosen for location and style.'

Suffolk Country Cottages, The Old Water Tower, The Common, Southwold, Suffolk IP18 6TB. Telephone 01502 722717. Fax 722323.

www.suffolk–secrets.co.uk   email: holidays@suffolk–secrets.co.uk

Norfolk Country Cottages (Page 40):

'Norfolk is a county of pretty, unspoilt rural villages, pretty countryside, sandy beaches, huge skies. There are miles of waterways on the Broads, seaside resorts and, of course, Norwich. In this fabulous region, the agency offers a huge variety of properties.'

Norfolk Country Cottages, Carlton House, Market Place, Reepham, Norfolk NR10 4JJ. Telephone 01603 871872. Fax 870304.

www.norfolkcottages.co.uk   email: info@norfolkcottages.co.uk

Northumbria Coast and Country Cottages (Page 91):

'Wild country, fabulous sandy beaches, the romance of the Scottish borders, the Roman Wall. These (and more) fall within the ambit of Northumbria Coast and Country Cottages. Their 200 or so properties are a great introduction to the far North Country.'

Northumbria Coast and Country Cottages, Carpenters Court, Riverbank Road, Alnmouth, near Alnwick, Northumberland NE66 2RH. Telephone 01665 830783. Fax 830071.

www.northumbria-cottages.co.uk   email: cottages@nccc.demon.co.uk

Discover Scotland (Page 18):

'A superb selection of cottages, houses and lodges in the hills and by the sea, amid glorious Scottish scenery and country unsurpassed for walkers (West Highland Way, Southern Upland Way etc). There are mountains to climb, forests to explore. About 250 properties to choose from.'

Discover Scotland, 27 King Street, Castle Douglas DG7 1AB. Telephone 01556 504030. Fax 503277.

www.discoverscotland.net   email: discover.scotland@virgin.net

Menai Holiday Cottages:

'*Superb cottages from simple to sumptuous in outstanding locations and settings. We only pick cottages we would holiday in ourselves. Delicious cooked meals delivered to cottages..*

Menai Holiday Cottages, 1 Greenfield Terrace, Hill Street, Menai Bridge, Anglesey LL59 5AY. Telephone 01248 717135.

www menaiholidays.co.uk
GHC@menaiholidays.co.uk

Toad Hall Cottages *(Page 208):*
'*Leafy lanes leading to hidden sandy coves, secret creeks where one can watch badgers and rare birds from one's secluded waterside cottage, outstanding sandy beaches, 'film-set' villages: these make this agency so successful. With properties on Exmoor, they have about 250 in total.'*

Toad Hall Cottages, Elliott House, Church Street, Kingsbridge, South Devon TQ7 1BY. Tel: 01548 853089. Fax: 853086.

www.toadhallcottages.com
email: thc@toadhallcottages.com

Salcombe Holiday Homes *(Page 209)*
'*At the southernmost point of Devon, between Plymouth and Torquay, the seaside town and sailing resort is known for its sheltered estuary, beaches and wonderful walks, watersports and fishing. There is a huge demand for holiday houses, and the agency looks after over 150 of the best.'*

Salcombe Holiday Homes, Orchard Court, Island Street, Salcombe, Devon TQ8 8QE. Tel: 01548 843485. Fax: 843489.

www.salcombe.com
email: shh@salcombe.com

Dartmouth Holiday Homes *(Page 214)*
'*Dartmouth is a pretty Devon town, home to the famous Naval College, at the mouth of the River Dart and very close to the sea. The estuary is a major sailing harbour, surrounded by beautiful National Trust sites and within a short distance of beaches and both Dartmoor and Exmoor.'*
Dartmouth Holiday Homes, 1a Lower Street, Dartmouth, Devon TQ6 9AJ. Telephone: Tel: 01803 833082 Fax: 835224

www.dartmouthuk.com
email: dhh@dartmouthuk.com

<u>*Dorset Coastal Cottages*</u> *(Page 223)*
'Over 100 lovely cottages (many thatched, most with open fires) in traditional villages near the magnificent Dorset World Heritage Coast, between Studland and Lyme Regis. They are available for weekly lets and short breaks year round (subject to peak time restrictions).
Dorset Coastal Cottages, The Manor House, Winfrith Newburgh, Dorchester, Dorset, DT2 8JR. Tel: 01305 854454. Fax: 854988.
www.dorsetcoastalcottages.com email: hols@dorsetcoastalcottages.com

<u>*New Forest Cottages*</u> *(Page 229):*
'William the Conqueror set aside the New Forest as his private deer hunting preserve, and many unique customs date back to this time. This incomparable countryside is home to ponies, cattle and other livestock roaming free. The 100 or so properties range from quaint thatched cottages with ponies grazing at the gate to comfortable modern townhouses.'

New Forest Cottages, 4 Quay Hill, Lymington, Hampshire SO41 3AR. Tel: 01590 679655. Fax: 670989.

www.newforestcottages.co.uk
email: holidays@newforestcottages.co.uk

<u>*Cottage in the Country/Cottage Holidays*</u> *(Page 266):*
'Specialising in Oxfordshire, the Cotswolds, Shakespeare Country and the Welsh borders, this agency has the advantage of personally knowing its 150 or so properties, easily accessible from London. Many enjoy pin-drop quiet in a tranquil part of England. Short breaks and pets are welcome in many.'

Cottage in the Country/Cottage Holidays, Tukes Cottage, 66 West Street, Chipping Norton OX7 5ER. Tel: 0870 027 5930. Fax: 0870 027 5934.

www.cottageinthecountry.co.uk
email: ghc@cottageinthecountry.co.uk

<u>*Freedom Holiday Homes*</u>*:*
'Freedom of choice throughout Kent and East Sussx from a superb range of quality cottages, barn conversions, oast houses, bungalows, apartments in rural, coastal or village locations. Pets welcome in many, short or long lets subject to availability, ideal locations for visiting the many castles, gardens, historic houses and picturesque villages in Kent and East Sussex.'

Freedom Holiday Homes, 15 High Street, Cranbrook, TN17 3EB. Telephone 01580 720770.

www.freedomholidayhomes.co.uk
email: mail@freedomholidayhomes.co.uk

THE COTTAGE COLLECTION

This fine collection of British properties has really made an impact in the last couple of years. You can check the availability of all the cottages on-line or speak to the Call Centre to book one without spending time contacting owners who may be full.

Impressively, Cottage Collection's Chairman Robert Dossor has doubled the choice in his portfolio in just two years, and created for the discerning holidaymaker a tempting choice of coastal or rural retreats where seclusion and privacy can easily be dovetailed with activities such as walking, climbing, horse-riding, fishing, golf or watersports, as well as visits to nearby attractions.

'Romantics' will be spoilt for choice, with everything from a coastal Cornish cottage to a delightful Derbyshire Peak District retreat (Churchdale Farm, in the Peak District Natonal Park, is a beautiful, quiet location). Or they can wake up in a castle in Wales: Snowdonia is just a stone's throw from Bryn Bras Castle, where there are six apartments available through The Cottage Collection.

Cottage accommodation that offers that great luxury of today, 'peace and quiet', can be pinpointed in The Cottage Collection's 2006 brochure. Properties are located in every Area of Outstanding Natural Beauty around Great Britain, and families, as well as other large parties, can be readily accommodated in a number of places.

With 'Pets Welcome' signs at most locations, and those with disabled facilities also in the portfolio, we suggest you send off for the 2006 brochure, or visit the impressive, inter-active website.

Spending time on The Cottage Collection's website brings one in touch with special offers, particularly off-peak promotions, which might include gourmet meals or cream teas on arrival – say, at Yapham Cottages, in Devon.

Brochure request line: 01603 724809 – or go to:
www.the-cottage-collection.co.uk

Bed and breakfast/hotel accommodation

We often receive requests from readers wanting somewhere to stay en route to distant cottages and for friends and family to base themselves for a night or two while visiting people staying in a holiday property. They are sometimes able to book in as 'extra people', but – as standards have improved and zed-beds are not so popular – not usually. So here below is some information (mostly in the owners' words) about self catering places linked with hotels and 'b&b'...

Gladwins Farm, Suffolk. See Page 32.
'Home-from-home farmhouse B&B in a typical Suffolk farmhouse; en-suite rooms, direct dial telephone, lounge area. £65 per night B&B for 2. Amid Suffolk's rolling 'Constable Country', with great views. Heated indoor pool, sauna, hot tub, tennis court. **'Visit Britain' Four Diamonds**. Contact: Robert and Pauline Dossor, Gladwins Farm, Harpers Hill, Nayland, Suffolk CO6 4NU. Telephone 01206 262261. Fax 263001. Email: GladwinsFarm@aol.com www.gladwinsfarm.co.uk

High House Farm, Suffolk. See Page 37.
'Beautifully restored 15th century farmhouse on family run arable farm. Featuring exposed beams and inglenook fireplaces, spacious and comfortable accommodation. Explore the heart of rural Suffolk, local vineyards, Easton Park Farm, Framlingham and Orford Castles, Minsmere, Snape Maltings, Woodland Trust and the Heritage Coast. B&B from £22. Reductions for children.' Contact: Mrs Sarah Kindred, High House Farm, Cransford, Woodbridge, Suffolk IP13 9PD. Telephone 01728 663461. Fax 663409. Email: b&b@highhousefarm.co.uk www.highhousefarm.co.uk

Layhead Farm Cottages, North Yorkshire. See Page 78.
'Enjoy peace and tranquillity in The Stables. A newly converted barn which is self-contained but close to our home. Two comfortable, tastefully decorated en-suite bedrooms for B&B – one twin, one double. Delicious Yorkshire breakfasts either cooked for you in the Stables kitchen or left for you to prepare yourselves. Local organic produce used, where possible. **'Visit Britain' Four Diamonds**. Contact: Rosemary Hyslop, Field House, Rathmell, Settle, North Yorkshire. Telephone 01729 840234. Fax 01729 840775. Email: rosehyslop@layhead.co.uk www.layhead.co.uk

Cressbrook Hall, Derbyshire. See Page 82.
'Perched high on the south facing Wye Valley, overlooking Cressbrook
Mill and adjacent to beautiful Monsal Dale, historic Cressbrook Hall
(circa 1835) is an impressive family residence standing in rural grounds.
Elegant en-suite B&B is offered in rooms with spectacular views around
the compass. Bakewell five miles, M1 20 miles.'
Cressbrook Hall, Cressbrook, near Buxton, Derbyshire SK17 8SY.
Telephone (01298) 871289. Fax 871845.
Email: stay@cressbrookhall.co.uk www.cressbrookhall.co.uk

Cote Bank Farm, Derbyshire. See Page 86.
'Wake to birdsong, stunning views and the smell of freshly baked bread.
The same care and attention given to guests in Cote Bank Cottages is
lavished on them in our farmhouse. Two doubles, one twin, all en-suite,
TV, tea/coffee trays. B&B from £33. Open March to November.'
Contact: Pamela Broadhurst, Cote Bank Farm, Buxworth,
High Peak, Derbyshire SK23 7NP.
Telephone/fax 01663 750566.
Email: cotebank@btinternet.com
www.cotebank.co.uk

Holmhead Farm and Guest House, Northumberland. See Page 87.
'This 19th century former farmhouse (AA/**'Visit Britain' Four Diamonds**.)
is within the Hadrian's Wall World Heritage Site, with panoramic views
over part of the Northumbria National Park. Stay at Holmhead and experience delicious food and comfortable ensuite bedrooms. No smoking;
tourist information; sightseeing planning – especially Hadrian's Wall.'
Tariff from £30.
Contact: Brian and Pauline Staff, Holmhead, Hadrian's Wall. Greenhead
CA8 7HY. Telephone 016977 47402.
www.bandbhadrianswall.com

Machrie Hotel and golf links, Isle of Islay. See Page 120.
'The "Machrie" lies close to its 15 self-catering cottages. Along with
11 twin rooms and five double rooms, it has two bars, a dining room, a
function room and a private dining room. The food is predominantly
local, with Islay beef, lamb and shellfish a speciality. Bar meals are
served both at lunchtime and in the evening.'
Contact: Machrie Hotel, Port Ellen, Isle of Islay, Argyll PA42 7AN.
Telephone 01496 302310. Fax 302404.
Email: machrie@machrie.com
www.machrie.com

Bailey Mill, Roxburghshire. See Page 123.
'Friendly farm holiday complex offering bed and breakfast at £25 per
person, per night or self catering courtyard apartments (short breaks
available). This is an ideal location for walking, cycling or horse-riding
through the beautiful Scottish/Cumbria border country. Guests are welcome to relax in our jacuzzi, sauna etc before enjoying
a drink and/or meal in our cosy bar.'
Contact: Bailey Mill, Newcastleton, Roxburghshire TD9 0TR.
Telephone: 01697 748617.
Email: pam@baileymill.fsnet.co.uk
www.holidaycottagescumbria.co.uk

Land Ends Country Lodge, Cumbria. See Page 126.
'Enjoy a real country experience at Land Ends. Our converted farmhouse
and barn are in 25 acres with lakes, pretty courtyard, fishpond. We have
ducks, moorhens, red squirrels, wonderful birdlife. All rooms en-suite.
'Visit Britain' **Three Diamonds.** From £30. Doubles, twins and singles.'
Contact: Barbara Holmes, Land Ends Country Lodge,
Watermillock, near Ullswater, Cumbria CA11 0NB.
Telephone: 017684 86438.
Email: infolandends@btinternet.com
www.landends.co.uk

Sutton Court Farm Cottages, Shropshire. See Page 247.
'Sutton Court Farm Cottages are also pleased to offer Bed & Breakfast.
You will be accommodated in one of our cottages and have full use of
all the facilities. Breakfast is offered in our 16th century farmhouse.
Prices £70 per double/twin room per night.'
Contact: Jane Cronin, Sutton Court Farm, Little Sutton, Stanton Lacy,
Ludlow, Shropshire SY8 2AJ.
Telephone 01584 861305. Fax 01584 861441.
Email: suttoncourtfarm@hotmail.com
www.suttoncourtfarm.co.uk

Delphi Lodge, Co Galway. See Page 285.
'You don't have to be a salmon fisherman to enjoy the exquisite and
peaceful surroundings at this well known but never overrun place (never
overrun because accommodation is limited). In addition to the
authentically restored, cosy cottages, there are twelve guest rooms. The
place is organised in house-party style, so there is no room service, and
guests generally eat communally in candlelight around a fine, huge dining
table. It's a bonus for lone travellers or people from overseas
wanting to make new friends.'
Contact: Peter Mantle, Delphi Lodge, Leenane, Co Galway.
Telephone 00 353 95 42222. Fax 42296.
Email: stay@delphilodge.ie www.delphilodge.ie

One of the best things about a holiday cottage: you can have a lie in!

Stop Press

Gattonside, near Melrose
Drumblair   map 4/153

Pleasantly located over the River Tweed from Melrose, with its historic abbey and excellent restaurants, is the attractive village of Gattonside and *Drumblair*, a detached bungalow. Nearby there's good walking (the Southern Upland Way passes close by), cycling, salmon fishing and golf, and there's an activity centre over the river. Edinburgh can be reached in an hour. Readers have spoken about the very comfortable accommodation and the excellent walking country around. The property **sleeps 4** in a bedroom (king size bed) with ensuite spa bathroom, and an ensuite twin room. There's double glazing and full gas central heating. The spacious sitting room/dining room has views of the Eildon Hills. The utility room houses a washing machine and tumble drier, and there's a store for bicycles or for drying outdoor gear. Well behaved dogs by arrangement. Bedlinen, towels, gas, electricity included. **'Visit Britain' Four Stars**. Cost: about £265 to £385. More details from Mrs J Stevenson, Camberley, Abbotsford Road, Darnick, Melrose, Roxburghshire TD6 9AJ. Telephone 01896 823648.

www.drumblairontweed.co.uk
email: jacky.stevenson@drumblair.freeserve.co.uk

There are views from the sitting room of the distinctive Eildon Hills...

It's low-key, quietly lovely country: a part of Scotland many visitors overlook.

Readers sometimes ask 'How are owners/agents chosen to be in this guide?' Most come via reader recommendations, occasionally from regional tourist boards. Others contact us directly.

Regular readers might spot cottages they have not seen for years: it could be that a cottage or group of cottages have been on a long let or have been marketed through an 'exclusive' agency, or that there has been a change of ownership: we may have dropped the cottages when they were under the previous ownership.

All the properties featured are visited, including those picked out within agency profiles, but occasionally a highly recommended cottage is only visited after publication...

Discover Scotland

This organisation has an impressive geographical spread that takes in the whole of Scotland. We already know many of the cottages. There is an exceptionally attractive colour brochure and a detailed website with online booking.

The agency has introduced many of our readers to peaceful, green and rolling Dumfries and Galloway: perhaps the 'best kept secret' in the country. Among places 'worth a detour' are the Rhinns of Galloway, the south west extremity of Scotland that terminates in the 200 feet high cliffs of the Mull of Galloway. From several high points, Ireland seems almost near enough to touch.

Outstanding places include the marvellously well situated *Fonthill*, **sleeping 6**, in Kippford, known for its sailing centre, and, in Rockcliffe, with a magnificent sea view, *Colbeine*, a family house of character. This also **sleeps 6**. Colleagues have also enjoyed a summer holiday in *Auld Schoolhouse*, Skyreburn, **sleeping 7**. They loved its quiet position, the burn running through the well kept garden.

Coleagues have stayed in The Auld Schoolhouse, just a short walk to a beach.

A Highland classic: Baile na Creige is just eight miles from Inverness.

We know several of the agency's properties on the Isle of Skye. One, Willowbank, is in the village of Broadford, on the main route from the mainland (via the bridge) to Portree. Outwardly pretty, inside it is a delight, with big rooms and views of the water. The big first floor sitting room is a particular joy. **Sleeps 8**.

Past the hamlet of Elgol itself, in an exquisite location with amazing views of the Cuillin Hills over Cuillin Sound, *Port Elgol Cottage* is also memorable for its cosy interior. Having visited it ourselves and met the owners, we can believe what they say about visitors spending 'most of their time looking out of the windows'! **Sleeps 4**.

Details of these and much more, and a good brochure, from Discover Scotland Ltd, 27 King Street, Castle Douglas DG7 1AB. Telephone 01556 504030. Fax 503277.

www.discoverscotland.net
email: discover.scotland@virgin.net

Interhome (Great Britain)

Widely known and admired for its huge but carefully monitored range of self catering accommodation in mainland Europe and elsewhere in the world, Interhome now has a healthy UK portfolio too.

We know a number of the properties on the company's books, and in other cases, even if we don't know the property we know the location. For example, just about two miles from one of our favourite places in west Wales – St David's – *The Pump House*, dating from 1899, is less than half a mile from a rocky beach and about a mile and a half from a sandy beach.

Sleeping up to 6, the two-storeyed house is also half an hour's walk from the quite delightful coastal-inlet village of Solva. Even *we* would put our walking boots on for that! Ref G6157/100.

In Grantown-on-Spey, in the north east corner of the Highlands, about 20 miles due south of Elgin, there is a fine apartment on the first floor of handsome 18th century *Speyside House*, set off grandly by an imposing clock tower. There are views from the apartment of the town square.

In Old Tolsey Cottage there's a chance to stay in the heart of Tewkesbury, with easy access to the Cotswolds and mid Wales.

Speyside House: a fine apartment in a grand mansion – a good base from which to explore Scotland's north east.

Sleeps 4 in a double bedroom and a sofa bed in the sitting room. Ref G8802/105B. (Our tip by the way for getting to this corner of Scotland is to fly to Inverness's Dalcross airport – quiet, rural and user-friendly – and hire a car.)

And to suit a good number of people we meet who like convenient town-based accommodation within a 'honeypot', mainly rural region, there's a most appealing half-timbered semi-detached town house (*Old Tolsey Cottage*) in the heart of Tewkesbury, in Gloucestershire. Thus well placed for exploring the Cotswolds, the property, which dates from about 1550, **sleeps 5**. Ref G3920/100.

But these amount to nothing more than a snapshot of what's available. Interhome has an extraordinary reputation for competitively priced accommodation and for efficiency – we hear from readers who use the company regularly, and say things like 'We are Interhome people'.

Telephone 020 8891 1294, fax 020 8891 5331, or see the Great Britain pages of the Interhome website: **www.interhome.co.uk**

(on line booking possible; short breaks available from March)

See also Pages 308 and 320.

Hoseasons Country Cottages*

The range of holiday properties on offer from this famous agency is impressive. Just for starters: thatched cottages, one-time barns, pubs, chapels, farmhouses, manor houses, converted watermills, schools, stables and coach houses.

Hoseasons have always been based in East Anglia, so it's not surprising that they offer a particularly good choice there. One of these is *Happy Days,* a stylish modern timber lodge (**sleeping 4**) beside the River Yare. Ref E2508. Readers also appreciate thatched cottages such as the pretty, Grade II listed *West Barton*, at Thorverton, near Exeter, in Devon. The beamed sitting room has a log fire, the dining hall has a woodburner and there's an Aga. **Sleeps 7** in two double bedrooms (one ensuite), a twin and a single. Ref E3072.

One of Hoseasons' grandest properties is *Ormathwaite Hall*, near Keswick, in the Lake District. Once home to the renowned Cumbrian

Ormathwaite Hall offers stylish living at the very heart of the Lake District.

Grade II listed West Barton is a cottage to fall for, very well located for touring.

doctor and scientist William Brownrigg, it's an 18th-century mansion (**sleeping up to 13**) in three acres of grounds, with glorious views of the Skiddaw mountain range. With an intricately carved oak staircase and features like an art deco bathroom, the houses oozes quality yet still feels like a comfortable family home. It has four double bedrooms (two with four-posters), a twin and a single. The grounds include lawned terraces, a walled kitchen garden, a cascading stream and woodland where deer and rare red squirrels can be seen. Ref E3157.

In Wales, *Globe House* is a Grade II listed building (**sleeping 10 to 12**) in the Pembrokeshire National Park. Just a short walk from a sandy beach, it's ideally placed for exploring the lovely coastal path and also for bird-watching as the cliffs are home to seabirds such as cormorants and ful-mers. Ref W7142.

If you fancy some monster spotting, one of the four *Loch Ness Cottages*, four miles from Drumnadrochit, would be ideal as they have a glorious panoramic view across the famous loch. Two cottages **sleep 2** in king-size four-posters and two **sleep 4**. Ref S4104, S4351, S4105 and S4077.

Details from Hoseasons Holidays, Lowestoft, Suffolk NR32 2LW. Telephone: 0870 534 2342. Fax 0870 902 2090.

www.hoseasons.co.uk

Ref C0003

Sykes Cottages*

This highly-regarded independent agency, based in Chester, has an impressive portfolio of over 800 properties throughout the UK, including the South West, Northumberland, Yorkshire, Wales and Shropshire. It has also recently and successfully expanded into Scotland.

It was started over 25 years ago by the mother of owner and managing director, Clive Sykes. Each cottage is personally inspected and carries either its local tourist board grading or the agency's own rating. Also, you can see what previous holidaymakers thought of each property by looking it up on the agency's website (www.sykescottages.co.uk).

Grove Cottage (Ref 1325) is at Brighstone, near Newport, on the Isle of Wight. Grade II listed, it sleeps four.

Badger Cottage (Ref 1037) is at St Issey, near Padstow, in North Cornwall. In a quiet rural location, it sleeps four.

People who appreciate properties with a bit of history to them will like the stunning Grade II listed *Station House* at Ruswarp (Ref 1220), a conversion of the Victorian station and station-master's house, just a mile from Whitby. Original features have been retained, and there's an Aga, a wood-burning stove, a stained glass window and a four poster bed. And it's lovely to explore the nearby coast and the moors.

For a 'last word in comfort' property, look no further than *The Retreat* (Ref 1239), on the outskirts of Mevagissey, in Cornwall. Overlooking fields leading to the famous Heligan Gardens, the property has a magnificent conservatory, four poster beds, underfloor heating and an open fire. But with the landscaped garden, the summer house, the children's activity area, BBQ and a private six-person hot tub, it's doubtful you'll spend much time inside, though the Eden Project, the glorious coast and Truro are in easy reach.

Sailors, and indeed anyone who loves the sea, will be delighted by *8 Seymour Court* (Ref 1288), a smart mews cottage on the edge of the water, with panoramic views over the harbour at Cowes, on the Isle of Wight. The cottage has been well-equipped, decorated and furnished throughout, with 'upside down' accommodation to make the most of the harbour views from the living room balcony. The pubs and restaurants of the town are just over the chain bridge, or one can explore the island's beaches, Italianate Osborne House, picturesque 'chines', and more!

Details from Sykes Cottages, York House, York Street, Chester CH1 3LR. Telephone 01244 356896. Fax 321442.

www.sykescottages.co.uk
email: info@sykescottages.co.uk

Stately Holiday Homes*

Among our very best discoveries of the last two or three years – including some visits – were the properties within the Stately Holiday Homes portfolio. As readers might have noticed, we're keen both on holiday houses of comfort and character and 'the stately homes of England' (as well as Wales, Scotland and Ireland). Courtesy of this splendid organisation and their impressive contacts the two elements come together delightfully.

Locations include, for example, Haddon Hall, in Derbyshire. Three miles from 'the big house' *Rock Cottage* – **sleeping up to 5** – is a fine, clean-

Essex is full of surprises: you can stay within the grounds of Castle Hedingham.

A classic rural scene, at Glanusk Park. Three super cottages are available.

cut, greystone house with a most attractive interior – it's interesting to note that so many of these estate properties are understated and easy on the eye, both inside and out. In a peaceful location (another big bonus) the house has **Four Stars** from **'Visit Britain'**.

Colleagues have already stayed at *Callander Cottage*, once a coach house to Shropshire's Combermere Abbey. Owner Sarah Callander Beckett is proud of her Scottish ancestry, and the cottage interiors have been professionally designed using touches of tartans in wonderful blues, reds and greens, all designed and woven in the Scottish Highlands. *Stapleton Cottage*, a few steps away, is thoughtfully adapted with disabled guests in mind, having a ground floor twin bedroom and ensuite shower. Both cottages are graded **Five Stars**.

Not yet seen by us, *Stone Lodge* is a Grade II beauty dating from about 1840. With pretty white-painted Gothic-style windows against the grey, it stands on the edge of the estate, on the Nantwich to Whitchurch road. **Sleeps 4**, but perhaps suits a couple better.

The 4500 acre Houghton Estate in Norfolk has been the home of the Marquesses of Cholmondeley since 1797. (The Queen, at Sandringham, is a next-door neighbour.) There are three cottages on offer: *The Water House* has a super walled garden, and *Bunker's Hill* is especially cosy in all weathers, with central heating as well as log fires. *See also Page 41.* We saw these during 2005, and loved them. We also visited *Snape Castle*, in North Yorkshire, and admired a warm and sympathetic conversion of a part of the main castle building. *See also Page 77.*

There are several Stately Holiday Homes properties in Scotland, Ireland and Wales. *Glanusk Park*, in the Brecon Beacons National Park, is very popular. Three traditional, stone-built cottages have stunning views over the estate and the Black Mountains. Each is single storeyed, fitting most harmoniously into its beautiful surroundings. *Library Cottage*, for example, has an especially impressive outlook, *Garden Cottage* has a memorable walled garden, and *The Kennels*, which is very quiet and peaceful, has a small stream running close. Garden ideally **sleeps 2** in a twin, but a single room is also available. The other two **sleep 4** in a twin and a double. All three have an open fire.

Among so many other good things, outstanding even in this exalted company, *Mead Cottage*, in the grounds of one of the most elegant, sumptuously comfortable manor-house hotels in Britain, is eye-poppingly 'last word'. It's in Castle Combe, one of this country's most photogenic, most

We have much enjoyed a stay in one of the so stylish, so lovingly tended Combermere Abbey properties. Three of them are available within the Stately Holiday Homes programme.

unspoiled villages. There is for example a charming and unusual divided 'double-living room' in which on one 'more formal' side there's a Scandinavian wood stove. The delightful small dining room used to be an ice house – but have no anxiety on that score: it has underfloor heating. **Sleeps 4** in great comfort.

Much less exalted than Castle Combe, but actually one of (much underrated) rural Essex's 'best kept secrets', the village of Castle Hedingham is dominated by the mainly 12th century castle. Within the castle grounds – accessed via a private gravel drive – *Garden Cottage* is a red brick, red tiled two-storeyed beauty **sleeping up to 5**.

A bonus here is that complimentary tickets are included for cottage guests to the popular jousting and 'medieval' events held at the castle.

Not yet seen by us but high on our schedule for 2006 is *Gilar Farmhouse*, close to the edge of the Snowdonia National Park.. This is a real one-off, a remarkable survivor (**WTB Five Stars**) from the past, full of original features: it dates back partly to about 1660 and has, among so many memorable features, a seven-foot-wide four poster bed.

In Ireland *Belle Isle Castle*, Co. Fermanagh, is perfect for larger groups. **Sleeping up to 14**, with seven bathrooms, the mansion stands in a 470-acre estate consisting of eight separate islands.

For the company's brochure, telephone 01638 674749; fax 663995.

www.statelyholidayhomes.co.uk
email: admin@shhl.co.uk

National Trust Cottages

When holidaying in a National Trust property it's a bonus to know that the rent you pay helps preserve Britain's heritage of great estates and glorious countryside. Over 330 properties are available, scattered across England, Wales and Northern Ireland. Furthermore, as you'd expect, the choice encompasses many unique buildings.

Each is helpfully graded with an Acorn rating which ranges from one up to five. This covers the environment, interior, housekeeping, facilities and the welcome offered in terms of a welcome tray, information folder and whether a staff member will be there to greet you personally.

Finding exactly what you want is further helped by a 'Quick Look' guide which lists cottages with specific attributes. These include those in which dogs are welcome, the quirky/unusual, the remote, the single-storeyed

The Birdcage, in Port Isaac, Cornwall is quite something. Sleeps 2 (small) people!

Mill Cottage is on the Blickling Estate, in Norfolk. Pretty as a picture, sleeping 6.

and ones suitable for accompanied wheelchair-users.

Among the many properties awarded the top 5-Acorn are two apartments (both **sleeping 3**) in the 400-year old Fountains Hall at Ripon in Yorkshire. *Proctor,* on the third floor, is furnished and decorated in the style of Charles Rennie Mackintosh; *Vyner,* on the secnd floor, follows the style of Edwin Lutyens. Ref 020016/7. Nearby, in the Studley Royal Deer Park, another 5-Acorn property, *Choristers' House* (**sleeping 10**) is available. Its has three double bedrooms and two twins. Ref 020022."

One of the 'quirky' category that particularly intrigues us is *Doyden Castle* (**sleeping 3**), which stands on the cliff-edge mid-way between Polzeath and Port Isaac in North Cornwall. Graded 4 Acorns, it's actually a small two-storey castellated folly rather than a real castle. With views of Lundy Bay, it was built in about 1830 by a local bon viveur for nights of feasting, drinking and gambling. Guests can drive to it via a cliff-edge track to unload, but cars have to be parked five minutes' walk away. Ref 011030.

Anyone who dreams of a romantic stay in a secluded thatched cottage would be enchanted by *Wood Cottage* (2 Acorns) at Durgan, beside the Helford estuary in south Cornwall. Originally an apple store, this tiny timber-built bungalow (**sleeping 2**) now has a cosy open-plan kitchen/dining/sitting room and double bedroom. The National Trust's Glendurgan Garden and Trelissick Garden are both nearby. Ref 011026.

Holidaymakers staying in *East Cottage*, near Dover, on the famous White Cliffs have an incomparable view of shipping passing to and fro in the Channel with (on clear days) the French coast. At the foot of the South

24

Foreland lighthouse, it's a former keeper's cottage (3 Acorns) which **sleeps 4** in two bedrooms – a double and a single. The lighthouse itself, no longer operational, is open to visitors on a limited basis. Ref 021003.

Close to another popular coast, *Mustard Pot Cottage* (**sleeping 4**) is on the Felbrigg Estate in Norfolk, about three miles inland from Cromer. In its own fenced garden at the end of a woodland track, it's a simple two-storey octagonal building (3 Acorns) with ground-floor extensions containing kitchen, bathroom, twin bedroom and a conservatory. What makes it special is the original part, with sitting-room (open fire) on the ground floor and above it, up narrow winding stairs, a double bedroom. Ref 010019. Three other cottages and two apartments (**sleeping 2 to 5**) are also available on the estate whose grand 17th-century house and grounds are open to the public on most days. Ref 010015/6, 010026, 010034/5.

Mortuary Cottage, near Barnstaple, is a really cosy hideaway for just two people.

Also for two is The Old Coastguard Station, in Yorkshire. Sea views assured!

For a really 'rustic' holiday amid wonderful scenery, *High Hallgarth* is a 17th-century stone cottage (**sleeping 7**) in a remote location overlooking Little Langdale Tarn, in the Lake District. As it has no bathroom and the toilet is an earth closet in an outbuilding, it is the sort of place children will find really exciting and remember all their lives. Ref 009002. A second picturesque cottage nearby, *Low Hallgarth* (**sleeping 4**), has the luxury of a shower and toilet! Ref 009003. The two properties (both graded 2-Acorn) share a telephone.

Murlough Gate Lodge, at Keel Point in County Down, Northern Ireland, is a charming stone cottage built in 1870 beside Dundrum Inner Bay, on the edge of the Murlough National Nature Reserve. It enjoys glorious views of the Mountains of Mourne, which provide some of the best hill-walking in Ireland. **Sleeping 4**, it has 4 Acorns. Ref 019014.

There is a user-friendly website where you can see all the cottages inside and out, check availability and book:

www.nationaltrustcottages.co.uk

Or call 0870 458 4411 for a brochure or 0870 458 4422 to book.

A voluntary contribution of £2 towards production, postage and packing of the brochure will be requested.

The Vivat Trust

We think this increasingly well-known charity does an admirable job in rescuing, restoring, letting and managing a range of historic buildings that in most cases are available for self catering holidays. These are well-cared-for properties that combine a feeling for the past with comfort and style.

After visiting several of the properties ourselves, we have not been surprised to get enthusiastic feedback fromreaders who've stayed in Vivat properties. One was much impressed by *The Cloister House*, at Melrose, in the Scottish borders. It is an elegant, early 19th century manse in the precincts of Melrose Abbey.

A highlight of journeys we recently made to Lincolnshire, Yorkshire and Lancashire was seeing the fascinating *Mill Hill Cottage*, a throwback to the 1750s. It's a rare survivor of the 'mud and stud' style, on the edge of a prettily situated Lincolnshire village.

Another little jewel of a cottage is *Church Brow*, on the outskirts of the small town of Kirkby Lonsdale, in Cumbria. It is eye-poppingly situated, on a steep bank above the River Lune, with panoramic views over the valley. Both outwardly and inwardly, three-storeyed Church Brow is pure delight, with an irresistible sitting room, with an open fire, that leads on to a formal garden terrace.

The geographical spread of properties could be the makings of a voyage of discovery for holidaymakers with an interest in history and architecture. To name several, there's the early 14th century stone-built *Chantry*,

Church Brow is one of our favourites: it's beautifully situated, full of character...

The Summer House is all that remains of a great country seat. Amazing views...

at Bridport, Dorset, a 17th century 'banqueting house' called *The Summer House*, and a 17th century 'gentleman's residence', *Stonegarthside Hall*, in Cumbria.

There are also two fabulous restored tower houses: *North Lees Hall*, at Hathersage, in Derbyshire, designed by the same architect as nearby Hardwick Hall, *Barns Tower*, in the Scottish borders, *Thistlewood Tower*, in Cumbria, and *The Tower of Hallbar*, in Lanarkshire.

Despite the seriousness of the purpose behind Vivat, there is nothing austere about the accommodation. The properties feel like lived-in homes, not museums, and for added comfort most have open fires or woodburners.

For an outstandingly good brochure contact The Vivat Trust, 70 Cowcross St, London EC1M 6EJ. Telephone 0845 0900194. Fax 0900174.

www.vivat.org.uk   email: enquiries@vivat.org.uk

East Anglia, East Midlands and The Shires

Hereward the Wake and his followers stood out against William the Conqueror for years from their marshy stronghold on the Isle of Ely, now in Cambridgeshire. This corner of England (though we're thinking more of Norfolk and Suffolk) still retains an air of 'apartness', and benefits from a degree of remoteness. But a maximum of three hours' drive from London or about two hours by train brings one into the best of the region. From Scotland, it takes about four, from the Midlands perhaps two. There are 'bucket-and-spade' family resorts with end-of-the-pier shows, the North Norfolk steam railway (with links to regional rail services). Roofs are thatched with Norfolk reed that lasts up to about 80 years. Churches the size of cathedrals dominate the skyline, meandering rivers are the haunt of wildfowl. Even if you are holidaying near the coast, visit Norwich: the cathedral, the castle, the open-air market. Even if you are staying in a self catering cottage, you can hire a boat on the Broads by the hour or by the day. To the west lie the prosperous farms of Leicestershire and Northamptonshire, underrated counties of golden limestone villages and elegant churches. To the north are the Lincolnshire Wolds and the haunting, flat fenland, and well into Lincolnshire are some of the finest sandy beaches in England, where without exaggeration you can be virtually alone during a sunny Bank Holiday.

Dalham Vale, near Newmarket
Jockey Cottage (map 1/1)

In the heart of a village close to the Suffolk/Cambridgeshire border, a few easy furlongs from horsey Newmarket, this most attractive and 'traditional' thatched cottage is well placed for exploring the best of rural Suffolk, a good part of Norfolk, Cambridge, Ely and the low key but fascinating Fen Country. Handy for a good village pub, it is one of those

Many years in this guide, lots of praise.

places that makes a really pleasant base to return to after touring (we have heard this from a number of overseas readers). Standing well back from the quiet road through this pleasant off-the-beaten-track conservation village, it has been tastefully and considerately restored and furnished. For example, there is a skilful blend of country furniture and top-notch contemporary soft furnishings, plus a new kitchen and a dishwasher. It has a woodburning stove in an inglenook fireplace, and **sleeps 4**. Remote control television. You'll find a welcome pack, a payphone and a garden.

Pets are possible by arrangement. Linen and towels are included. Cost: about £260 to £360. Weekend breaks are available from about £130. Further details from Richard Williams, Scorrier House, Redruth, Cornwall TR16 5AU. Telephone 01209 820264.
email: rwill10442@aol.com

Throcking, near Buntingford
Southfields Cottages

We've had a good number of calls from readers who have discovered and stayed in these cottages. It's rarely because they are in love with the delights of rural Hertfordshire (debatable), more often because the cottages are so well located for people who want to be within half an hour's drive of Cambridge and within reach – best by train, via Stevenage – of London. They are only occasionally available for holiday letting, but worth the effort. On a working (but not noisy or smelly) farm, well away

Charming and unpretentious. Falling into the increasingly rare 'traditional cottage' category, they are also inexpensive. Each sleeps up to 5.

from the main road, each of the semi-detached but private and self-contained pair enjoys good views and is pleasant and unpretentious.

Among the details that impressed us were bright, cottagey bedrooms, (plain white walls in most cases), some traditional knick-knacks, a sitting-out area at the rear. There is central heating, linen is provided and, although electric fires are installed, you can have usually have an open fire too. Not suitable for dogs. TVs.

Details from Mrs I Murchie 07913 480095.

Stoke Tye, near Dedham
Louie's Cottage   map 1/2

'Constable Country', a rural survivor in the face of relentless development on and around the Suffolk-Essex border, contains within its low hills and exceptionally fertile farmland some delightful surprises. The tiny hamlet that surrounds this classic thatched and 'pargetted' cottage (that is, adorned by traditionally intricate plasterwork) is one such delight. The house itself is used by the owners for their own holidays and weekends,

A classic thatched cottage: rural Essex is one of southern England's surprises...

and is suitably 'lived in', containing family antiques, charming knick-knacks, chintzy covered armchairs, a rocking chair and, for example, an upholstered window seat: very much our sort of place. We noticed an open fire, a separate study, a standard lamp, lots and lots of books – not just in one room but in several. There are two twin bedrooms with fitted carpets, chintz curtains, and – in one of those wide corridors that we partiuclarly like – even a Victorian rocking horse! **Sleeps 4**.

TV. Dogs welcome. No linen provided. Central heating throughout.

Details from 01438 869489.

Southwold and beyond
Suffolk Secrets*

We've been pleased to observe the gradual extension of the admirable Norfolk Country Cottages** into Suffolk, and during 2005 we spent some time looking at properties in and near Southwold that come under the umbrella of that part of their Suffolk operation known as 'Suffolk Secrets'.

Firstly, just inland from the daytime hustle and bustle of Southwold (at Reydon) we admired two absolutely pristine modern houses – many of our readers choose these in preference to 'olde worlde' properties. Finished to a very high standard, and both under the same discriminating ownership, *Field End* and *Cherry Trees* – respectively **sleeping 5 and 6** – are very quietly situated jewels, with a superb standard of finish both inside and out. They have off-road parking and for example (just the sort of detail we would have expected) king sized beds in each main bedroom. We thought the sitting room in Field End especially charming – spacious and nicely lit. It gives on to a south facing enclosed garden.

Almost close enough to the sea to try angling for fish, *Shrimp Cottage* is a pretty, pastel and white coloured 'bijou' delight, an absolute classic seaside cottage, complete with seasidey knick knacks and charming pictures. (We love one particular detail in the agency description: 'there's a sea view from the sitting room– even when you're seated'.) **Sleeps up to 4 'plus 1'** in two doubles and a small single – two rooms on the second floor via very steep, narrow stairs.

From a rear window of another property we were delighted to find ourselves gazing at one of the most famous views in Suffolk: Southwold across the marshes, hardly changed for a hundred years or more, an attractive skyline against a background of scudding clouds in a pale blue sky. *Blackshore Corner*, **sleeping 6** in three bedrooms and **'Visit Britain' Four Stars,** is a remarkable house, very close to the beach and next door to a pub of character. (On a summer day it's a bustling scene, but calmer and more beautiful 'after hours'.) The spacious sitting room is on the first floor to make the most of the *front* view of river and sea.

Details from Suffolk Secrets, The Old Water Tower, The Common, Southwold, Suffolk IP18 6TB. Telephone 01502 722717.

www.suffolk-secrets.co.uk email: holidays@suffolk-secrets.co.uk

** See Page 40

No 2, The Dunes, Thorpeness: a handsome base in a resort of character.

Garden House, Westleton: a pretty place in one of Suffolk's best loved villages.

Edwardstone, near Lavenham
Grove Cottages

During the last few years we've watched this charming, skilfully, lovingly converted group of 300-year-old cottages become established as one of the finest of its kind in East Anglia.

It's just two hours' drive from London (and therefore great for short breaks): but as you meander along West Suffolk's sleepy country lanes you might feel you are 200 miles from any big city. The location is ideal for walking, cycling (free bikes), exploring the beautiful River Stour on canoes (for hire), horse-riding, golfing, touring and 'pubbing'.

We have admired and noted so many good things. Such as charming 'ragged' walls, an original bread oven in *The Bakery*, original brick walls, wooden floors, beams. Plus personal touches such as fresh flowers, locally hand-made soaps, fridges stocked for you with the makings of a full English breakfast, a communal fridge-freezer.

We met several guests enjoying the afternoon sun in the beautiful orchard garden. They were planning a barbecue – barbecues are provided, as well as a party-sized barbecue with refectory tables – and had enjoyed the owners' home produced honey. One couple spoke of the friendly welcome they'd had from owner (and film director) Mark Scott, as well as that from his dogs and ducks.

Early in 2005 we called again to see *Don's Barn*, a most sympathetic conversion **for a couple only** – a five feet wide bed: excellent – of a property that dates from the early 1700s. There's period furniture and – a joy – a big log fire. **'Visit Britain' Four Stars**.

If you can drag yourself away from all this you will not want to miss picture postcard Kersey and a remarkable throwback to the medieval age,

With a great commitment both to the history of the properties and to 21st century comfort, these are very special.

All the (very pretty and cottagey) main bedrooms have five-foot beds, and four of the five cottages have an open fire.

preserved-in-aspic Lavenham. Bury St Edmunds and Cambridge are an easy meander (avoiding main roads) and Norwich is not a lot further.

Sleep from 2 to 6. TV, stereo, CD player, selection of music and books. Spacious power showers, no baths. Finest cotton linen and towels provided. Pets welcome. Non-smokers or very considerate smokers preferred. 'Visit Britain' **Four Stars**. Cost: about £193 to £853. Details and a brochure from Mark Scott, The Grove Cottages, Priory Green, Edwardstone, Suffolk CO10 5PP. Telephone 01787 211115. Fax 211220 or 211511.

www.grove-cottages.co.uk   email: mark@grove-cottages.co.uk

Woodbridge and around
Suffolk Cottage Holidays *

On a bright early-summer day in 2005 we renewed our acquaintance with this much admired medium-sized local agency, and saw a couple of properties we'd not seen before. Among these was chic, stylish *Bala Cottage*, at Felixtowe Ferry – a passenger ferry still runs, *after hundreds of years*. This is the oldest part of Felixstowe (fishing boats, yachts, two good old pubs, excellent walking routes): full of character. The cottage has spectacular views across the River Deben and part of the coast. **Sleeps up to 8.**

When we first saw Rose Cottage we asked 'Is it for sale?' It's that appealing.

Rosecot is in Peasenhall, one of our favourite, deeply rural Suffolk villages.

Across the Deben, in Bawdsey, but on a quiet country lane, *East Lane Cottage*, **sleeping 8**, is much bigger than it immediately appears. It's a classic 'roses round the door' rural delight, with a charming garden.

The first thing we said when we saw *Rose Cottage*, in a memorable location also overlooking the River Deben was 'is it likely to be for sale at any time?' and they smiled: 'that's what everybody asks'. It's that appealing – not just the exceptional location even in East Suffolk terms – but full of light, character and comfort inside. **Sleeps 10.**

In Woodbridge itself, in an enviable situation near the centre of the town, *34 Brook Street* is also close to the famous quay and tide mill. This is a real charmer, much more spacious than you might think, occasionally used by the owners themselves (always a good sign). In brief, an inspiring example of how a traditional and rather historic house of character has been adapted to suit the needs of 21st century self caterers. Not only is there private parking but even space for your own dinghy. **Sleeps 6.**

Among other notable places (but we hear from several sources that there are no duds) was *Valley Cottage*, Ramsholt. This would really suit people who like to be away-from-it-all, though against expectations there's an outstandingly good pub on the water's edge just a couple of hundred yards away (but the cottage is very well hidden from prying eyes and the summer pub crowd). **Sleeps 4.**

An excellent brochure/details from John and Lizzie Hammond, Suffolk Cottage Holidays. Telephone 01394 412304. Fax 412309.

For details of the sister company, Big House Holidays, see www.bighouseholidays.co.uk

www.suffolkcottageholidays.com
email: john@suffolkcottageholidays.com

Dedham Vale, near Nayland
Gladwins Farm Cottages

Though it is deeply rural, Gladwins is easily accessible – less than two hours' drive from London, less than three from Birmingham. Guests are very well placed for exploring east and west Suffolk and, say, the Norfolk border and Norwich.

The extraordinarily well situated group of cottages has consistently high standards and excellent facilities, and we have seen for ourselves the warm welcome from the Yorkshire-born owners, the far-reaching country views, the splendid indoor pool, and, of course, the goats and the pigs!

All but three properties face on to a courtyard. *Chelsworth Cottage*, **sleeping 8**, is very private and has spectacular views over the Vale of Dedham, an Area of Outstanding Natural Beauty. It has a four-poster bed, TV and ensuites in *all* bedrooms, a log burner, central heating and stereo. And it even has its own hot tub!. A particular bonus is that it has a specially adapted ground floor twin room for disabled people. Most recently available, **sleeping 6**, *Wiston Cottage* has three en-suite rooms, all with their own TV, its own garden and the same impressive views. Pets are welcome here.

Hadleigh **sleeps 4/5** and is attached to the owners' home; *Constable* **sleeps 6**, *Gainsborough* and *Dedham* both **sleep 4**, *Lavenham* **sleeps 4 'plus 1'**, *Melford* **sleeps 2** in a four poster 'for that special occasion' and also has its own hot tub. *Kersey* **sleeps 2 plus 1**. All could be described as 'little showhouses' with their cosy, comfortable interiors, woodburners, modern pine, good fitted carpets and local pictures. (There's another hot tub adjacent to the pool buildings for all the other cottages to share.)

There is access to 22 acres, an air-conditioned pool and sauna building, an adventure playground, an all-weather tennis court and a trout lake.

Excellent facilities and an outstanding situation in Constable Country'...

Interiors have been sympathetically done: this (appropriately!) is 'Constable'...

Dogs welcome, except in Lavenham, Hadleigh and Chelsworth. Small-screen TVs/video players. Cost: £240 to £1790. **Sleep 2 to 8**. Open all year; short breaks. Gainsborough and Wiston are suitable for accompanied disabled visitors.

Further details from Pauline and Robert Dossor, Gladwins Farm, Harpers Hill, Nayland, Suffolk CO6 4NU. Telephone Nayland 01206 262261, fax 263001. Bed and breakfast is also available.

www.gladwinsfarm.co.uk   email: GladwinsFarm@aol.com

Brundish, near Framlingham
Potash Barns

We've rarely come across such a deeply rural, family-orientated arrangement of cottages. Children love the Hebridean sheep, the ducks and the goats, as well as a variety of hens that, when given the chance, can be as mischievous as puppies.

It was colleagues searching for a Suffolk venue for a family weekend of twelve people who first discovered the newly-converted Potash Barns, near Brundish, not far from the Norfolk border.

Of the three cottages, which we ourselves visited in 2005, *Cartlodge* is free-standing and just a step away from the other two, *Old Oak* and *Goat Willow*. These two are linked via a large central hall with sofas and a fireplace: ideal when renting both cottages.

Each cottage has a different layout, incorporating two bedrooms, a comfortable living room, and a well-equipped kitchen. The decor is both stylish and rustic, with solid wooden beams, elm or terracotta floors, and high quality fittings. The solid wood kitchens all have large fridges, dishwashers, ranges and porcelain sinks.

We admired the magnificent flower arrangements in each cottage, and the fresh, top quality organic veg and groceries that owner Rob supplies win accolades too. He can also arrange for a meal to be waiting in the oven. Each cottage has an outdoor eating area with BBQ, and there's a separate games room with table tennis, table football and a variety of games.

The cottages each **sleep 4 or 5** plus two on double sofa beds in each living room. The master bedroom at Old Oak has a huge glass skylight, enabling you to lie in bed and gaze at the stars. Cart Lodge is laid out on one floor, and has a walk in shower as well as a bath – useful for less mobile guests. Each has TV, video, DVD, washer and dryer, bath and power shower, a CD player, books and games, a woodburner and central heating. All three cottages are **'Visit Britain' Four Stars**. Children have their own play area with swings and trampoline. Most pets can be accommodated in Cart Lodge. Cost : about £250 to £665.

Details from Rob Spendlove, Potash Farm, The Street, Brundish, Suffolk, IP13 8BL. Telephone 07747 038386. Fax 01379 384819.

www.potashbarns.co.uk
email: enquiries@potashbarns.co.uk

We were wowed by the rural location, the animals, the easy-going comfort...

Colleagues still enthuse about a stay they arranged for a group of friends.

33

Woodbridge, Orford and around
Mrs Jane Good (Holidays) Ltd *

This family run, long established agency must have the most exquisitely situated offices we know: right by the yachting marina and The Quay that are a major draw in Woodbridge, which is certainly one of the most attractive market towns in England.

It's a fitting base for an agency with (in many cases) exceptionally well situated properties – a number of them of great character – that deals exclusively with rural and coastal Suffolk. Regular readers will know how highly we rate it: it is thoroughly reliable and features a notable number of classically pretty and highly photogenic cottages.

The Nest at Badingham is neat, tidy, and absolutely 'just so', with every single detail taken care of ...

Ivy Lodge, close to the Tunstall Forest, near Orford and the coast, is an intriguing and skilful conversion.

Appropriately, Mrs Jane Good (Holidays) Ltd have a number of properties very close to the water in Woodbridge itself.

Among several holiday homes on the agency's books in the town is *No 12 St John's Terrace*. Near the centre of town, with a neat garden, it has been lovingly restored. Close to the fine parish church (one bedroom overlooks it), it **sleeps 4** and is just three minutes' walk from the charming, effectively pedestrianised Thoroughfare, at the heart of the town. Another well presented (and Grade II listed) terraced cottage in Woodbridge – **sleeping 3** – is *Treetops*.

One of our favourite small towns in the whole of Suffolk is Orford, nicely 'on the way to nowhere', and happily the agency has a number of properties there. These include, on a quiet private track near the quay, *No 6 Coastguard Cottage*s. From the rear bedroom – the Victorian terraced cottage **sleeps up to 4** – there are glimpses of the River Alde. The cottage has central heating *and* an open fire. Also in Orford, a recent addition to the Jane Good portfolio is *Oxo Cottage*, **sleeping 8**, which 'oozes period charm' and also has the bonus of inglenooks and a big garden.

Among a sprinkling of gems in inland Suffolk, we are fond of *The Nest* at Badingham, just a short distance from the A1120 Yoxford to Stowmarket road. Absolutely pristine and lovingly cared for, this little semi-detached cottage has retained a number of original features. **Sleeps 4**.

Between the villages of Brandeston and Cretingham, about five miles from the historic market town of Framlingham (do see its famous castle, where Mary Queen of Scots was a prisoner), is *The Potash*, a detached, mainly 16th century, thatched house. There is a large garden and views over fields and the upper reaches of the River Deben. Original features such as exposed beams and wooden floors add to the character, and the spacious sitting room has a wood-burning open fire and a grand piano! **Sleeps 8** in two doubles and two twins.

Within striking distance of famous Aldeburgh, and of the 'heritage coast', heaths, forests, rivers and bird reserves, *Ivy Lodge*, on the outskirts of Tunstall, is a most interesting and comfortable folly, which was originally a gatehouse for Rendlesham Hall, that is bigger than it first appears. **Sleeps 4 'plus 2'**.

Just two miles north of Aldeburgh lies Thorpeness, which we know well: a charming seaside place, created as a holiday resort by the Victorians. *Westdene* is a very handsome half timbered house **sleeping up to 8**. It is

Westdene, at Thorpeness, is just five minutes from a super shingle beach. Most usefully, it sleeps up to eight.

Treetops (on the right) is a Grade II listed cottage in easy reach of so-pretty Woodbridge town centre.

accessed via a little-used unmade track, and has an open fire. Also in Thorpeness are two very substantial houses that will suit birdwatchers. *Bittern* and *Crossing Cottage* respectively **sleep 10** and **8**. Bittern is a handsome family house on the banks of the Meare, has a private jetty, is adjacent to the golf club and is notable among other things for a full size snooker table; there is easy access from both properties to the RSPB's North Warren bird reserve, and in fact Crossing Cottage is within it. That bright, modernised house **sleeps 8** and is very family-orientated.

We are fond of the wooded landscape around Eyke, just four miles from Woodbridge, where people seeking absolute peace and quiet who also like the idea of being close to wildlife will appreciate *Stone Hall*. **Sleeping 4**, it is very much a traditional cottage, up a long drive and with an open fire.

We like the agency's handy A5 brochure detailing all the 75 or so properties on their books, and the star rating each cottage gets: a very honest assessment in our experience, from five stars for 'excellent' to one for 'basic'. Even most of the expensive properties are sensibly priced, and many that we know to be perfectly acceptable and big enough for a family are only a little over £300 a week during high season. Dogs are welcome in about half the properties – unusually (in almost every case) at no extra charge.

For a copy of the brochure (always a good read) contact Penny at Mrs Jane Good (Holidays) Ltd, Little Bass, Ferry Quay, Woodbridge, Suffolk IP12 1BW. Telephone/fax: 01394 382770.

www.mrsjanegoodltd.co.uk   email: theoffice@mrsjanegoodltd.co.uk

Hacheston, near Woodbridge
Lodge Cottage

An extremely comfortable 'Colonialstyle' property – albeit thatched – with decking and a verandah. There's access to seven acres (which dogs are welcome to enjoy too!) and an open-air pool.

With the bonus of the handsome riverside market town of Woodbridge just ten minutes' drive away, distinctive Lodge Cottage – we try to avoid the word 'unique', but it may apply here! – stands close (but with ample privacy) to the owners' substantial country house. 'B and B' is also available in the main house. We arrived to see the cottage in the summer of 2005 as it was being spruced up by a team of cleaners in readiness for new arrivals. We admired the very spacious and stylish (triple aspect) sitting room/dining room – easily roomy enough for a convivial evening with visiting friends, and loved the way the well lit, very comfy bedrooms are a few steps down on a lower floor: a rather cosy arrangement. Guests have use – shared with the owners – of the heated outdoor swimming pool, the gardens and the paddocks. There is even a small football pitch! **Sleeps 5 'plus 1'.**

Details from English Country Cottages, Stoney Bank Road, Earby, Barnoldswick BB94 0AA. For bookings, telephone 0870 192 1066. You can also 'dial a brochure': 0870 192 0391. **www.ecc2006.co.uk**

Bruisyard, near Framlingham map 1/9
Margaret's Cottage

Cosy and warm, with a shared swimming pool and a games room with snooker. A fine base from which to enjoy mid- and coastal Suffolk.

On a warm afternoon in August we turned off a little used country lane to a haven of peace that has been created from the coach house, stables and outbuildings of nearby Cransford Hall – *see also the opposite page.* We loved the combination of tall, shady trees and manicured gardens, and much admired the Edwardian walled garden that originally belonged to 'the big house'. Effectively one wing of the owners' substantial house, Margaret's Cottage is a real charmer. We loved the light, bright, spacious lemon-coloured main bedroom, the deep terracotta armchairs and the green sofa in the spacious sitting room, the well equipped solid oak kitchen, the wood-stove that guarantees a cosy autumn or winter break. There's an exceptional shared games room, with the joy of a full size snooker table, and access to a shared open-air heated pool. **Sleeps 4** in a double and a twin. Cost: about £350 to £650. Not suitable for pets; no smokers. Linen and towels included. Details from Mr and Mrs Roberts, The Clock House, Bruisyard, Saxmundham, Suffolk IP17 2EA. Telephone 01728 663512, fax 663301. **email: cherianroberts@yahoo.co.uk**

Bruisyard, near Framlingham
The Clock House

It seems that every time we think we know 'every stick and stone' of rural Suffolk we come across another hidden gem. Thus via narrow, leafy, silent lanes a few miles to the north of ancient Framlingham we happened on a quartet of cottages – three of them handled by English Country Cottages (long a leader in the field of rural properties of char-

The pool is just one of the attractions here.

acter) in well-wooded grounds and set off by manicured gardens. It's a fine combination of the sociable sort of place to make new friends (say around the neat, heated open air pool or in the excellent games room, which is graced by a super full sized snooker table). *The Pottery* (**sleeping 6**) and *The Foundry* (**sleeping 4**) are two separate halves of a substantial single-storeyed property in a tucked-away woodland setting; *Gardener's Cottage* (**sleeping 3**) is separate, in a corner of the rare Edwardian walled garden that originally belonged to 'the big house'. A nice touch: home cooked gourmet meals can be delivered to your door.

Details from English Country Cottages, Stoney Bank Road, Earby, Barnoldswick BB94 0AA. For bookings, telephone 0870 192 1066. You can also 'dial a brochure': 0870 192 0391. **www.ecc2006.co.uk**

Cransford, near Framlingham
Wood Lodge   map 1/8

Tucked away, and really quiet, this spacious cottage is a long-time favourite of ours. We recently took a detour from the historic castle town of Framlingham for a revisit, and met cottage guide readers sunning themselves in the big lawned garden. We like the deep armchairs, the big wood stove guaranteed to create a warm and cosy atmosphere, off which the

A readers' favourite for many years...

central heating runs, its masses of space, its character, its history (it dates from about 1800), and its attractive pictures. It even boasts a complete Encyclopedia Britannica 'of a certain age'! The kitchen is well equipped, and includes a dishwasher, the dining room is inviting, bedrooms are spacious. **Sleeps 8** plus cot. **'Visit Britain' Three Stars**. TV and DVD/video, stereo and CD player. Dogs by arrangement. Free logs. Cost: £250 to £650. Linen and towels for hire. 'B & B' available. Details from Tim and Sarah Kindred, High House Farm, Cransford, near Woodbridge, Suffolk IP13 9PD. Telephone 01728 663461. Fax 663409.

www.highhousefarm.co.uk
email:Woodlodge@highhousefarm.co.uk

37

Wortham, near Diss
Ivy House Farm

A much-liked set-up, on the rural edge of a Suffolk village by the Norfolk border.

Pleasantly situated on the edge of the 2004 'Suffolk Village of the Year' (very close to the Norfolk border), these are inviting – but not twee – and spacious. Positioned well back from a quiet road, there are three cottages in a row, a detached cottage and, across the yard, a historic Suffolk 'long house'. The fine detached modern cottage, built to high specifications, is designated as the owners' retirement home. **Sleeps 6.** The three places opposite (not uncomfortably close) have mainly open plan living areas and comfortable bedrooms. Each **sleeps 4.** The 'long house' is packed with character: we've long admired a cosy kitchen, an inglenook log fire in one sitting room, a superb dining room, spacious bedrooms (the 'master bedroom' is triple-aspect), good views from most bedrooms. **Sleeps up to 10.** The leisure centre has a pool table and a full-sized snooker table, and there's an excellent indoor swimming pool. Dogs welcome. Linen and towels included. TVs, videos, CD players. Cost: £238 to £1465. Details: Paul and Jacky Bradley, Ivy House Farm, Wortham, Diss, Norfolk IP22 1RD. Telephone/fax 01379 898395.

email: prjsbrad@aol.com
www.ivyhousefarmcottages.co.uk

Cranworth, near East Dereham   map 1/19
Holly Farm Cottages

A bonus: golf, fly fishing and coarse fishing are all very close at hand...

We first saw these absolutely pristine, newly available semi-detached cottages on a hot mid-Norfolk afternoon when the only sound was the buzzing of bees. Just a few yards from the owner's house they are nevertheless very private, overlooking fields. Everything is done to very high standards, and it is typical of the conscientious owner that she offers a choice of feather/down or more conventional duvets, or even sheets and blankets. Each is a mirror image of the other but *Cottage No 1* has a king sized bed and *Cottage No 2* has zip-link twins which can make a lovely 6 ft double. Each also has a sofa-bed in the uncluttered, maple-floored sitting room. Kitchens are excellent, and of course brand new, and the quietness of the location is a tonic. Children will love the small flock of Soay sheep and their own pets are welcome. There's a paddock for a visiting horse or pony. Linen/towels included. Cost: about £180 to £375. Details from Jennie McLaren, Holly Farm, High Common, Cranworth, Norfolk IP25 7SX. Telephone 01362 821468.

www.hollyfarmcottages.co.uk email: jennie.mclaren@btopenworld.com

Norfolk, countywide
The Great Escape Holiday Company*

Run by the extraordinarily energetic and enthusiastic Marion Rose-Cartwright, 'The Great Escape Holiday Company' has made a notable name by concentrating on places of style, most of whose properties are used from time to time by the owners themselves.

We have looked at a number of the places they have on their books. Norfolk has an especially wide range of cottages and houses of character, and this is reflected by what's available through the agency.

The Dovecote at Docking is just ten minutes' drive from the sea, but nicely inland for peace and quiet. It's a place for a large family to get together and to get away from each other when togetherness palls. With a very big living room, an excellent, very modern kitchen and masses of space everywhere, this listed building is exceptional. It overlooks open fields, there's free use of a tennis court, a games room with table tennis, deep, squishy armchairs and much more. **Sleeps 11**, plus two cots.

Another one to note is *Holly Lodge*, another high ceilinged, recent restoration and extension of an old building, surrounded by open countryside and in its own third of an acre, highly recommended for a family or large-group to get together well away from city cares. The master bedroom may be the biggest any of our inspectors have seen on their travels! **Sleeps up to 12.**

Hidden away from public gaze, though in the centre of the village of Snettisham and in fact one of its oldest properties, 250-year-old *Stratheyre Cottage* has so much going for it: ancient beams, a pretty garden and a log fire. **Sleeps 4 'plus 1'.** There's a famous pub a few yards away.

Beam Cottage, on the quayside at Burnham Overy Staithe, an especially charming location even in North Norfolk terms, is on three floors (always appealing) and has fabulous estuary views. Bring your binoculars! It has a woodburning stove, and **sleeps 7**.

Properties of great character in North Norfolk, with some impressive interiors.

Homes from home: pretty as a picture, both inside and out.

Further details/brochures from Marian Rose-Cartwright, The Great Escape Holiday Company, The Granary, Docking, Norfolk PE31 8LY. Telephone 01485 518717. Fax 518937.

www.thegreatescapeholiday.co.uk

email: bookings@thegreatescapeholiday.co.uk

Norfolk and beyond
Norfolk Country Cottages*

With about 300 properties covering the whole of Norfolk and North Suffolk, this hugely successful letting agency is based just off the well-preserved market place of the attractive small town of Reepham (visitors are welcome in the office).

We have visited a number of pin-drop-quiet cottages in deeply rural inland corners of the county and some cosy and convenient cottages (and more modern houses) in the much sought after family resorts of the north coast.

Among the latter, there are such places as *12 Cliff Drive*, Cromer, which **sleeps 10** and is superbly located just a few minutes' walk from the pier,

Claremont House is a splendid family house at much-sought-after Blakeney.

Meadowsweet is, indeed, 'sweet'. It is at Coltishall, which is handy for Norwich.

the beach, the boating lake, the shops and more. Also on the coast, at Blakeney, *Claremont House* is a fine Grade II listed house **sleeping 8**. It is jjust a short walk from the quay, and would surely make a great place for one of those memorable seaside family holidays.

Among others, we have also had good reports of *Lyons Green* at Little Fransham, a lovely spacious country house in an idyllic position at the end of a private lane. **Sleeping 7** in four bedrooms and overlooking its own beautiful grounds (including two lakes where fishing may be available), it is an ideal base to relax and enjoy the views from the large conservatory.

We have seen several properties just inland from some of England's best sandy beaches, including *Lodge Cottage*, a fine Victorian gatehouse in the historic village of Salle, and *Jotts Cottage*, a sensitively converted old dairy and milking shed at Bawdeswell.

At Coltishall, prettily situated on the River Bure, *Meadowsweet* is a detached 200-year-old gem fronting on to the river and **sleeping 4**. A four person dinghy is available for the use of guests.

Details/brochure available from Norfolk Country Cottages, Carlton House, Market Place, Reepham, Norfolk NR10 4JJ. Telephone 01603 871872. Fax 870304.

You can check property details and availability online at:
www.norfolkcottages.co.uk
email: info@norfolkcottages.co.uk

Houghton Hall, near Sandringham
The Water House, South Lodge, Bunkers Hill

Though we know Norfolk well we hadn't previously visited Houghton Hall, which stands in many-acred splendour about seven miles from Royal Sandringham and about fifteen from the north coast at Holkham, Brancaster and Burnham. With two long established holiday cottages and one (as pretty a gatehouse as you'll ever find, on the edge of the 'estate village') only recently available, this

Bunker's Hill is an absolute delight...

is a peaceful and rather romantic holiday base. Most of the time cottage guests will feel they have the vast estate, the woods and the herds of deer to themselves: delightful. The cottages themselves are real charmers. While 'bijou', recently available *South Lodge*, **sleeping 4**, is a gem, we'd find it hard to decide – for peace and quiet and a memorable escape from everyday cares – between *Bunker's Hill* and *The Water House*. These respectively **sleep 4** and **5**. Among many memorable features we appreciated comfortable, understated, 'cottagey' interiors, a sense of colour in the design – we love the painted wooden furniture – the 'country antiques', the well chosen lamps and pictures, the rugs – all combined with a feel for history.

For contact details, see the Stately Holiday Homes feature on Pages 22–23.

Castle Acre, near King's Lynn
Peddars Cottage   map 1/22

This delightful Norfolk base is a long time favourite of ours. With lots of space, it is in a village of great character that is however never overrun with tourists. Fitting well into its historic surroundings (see our photo!) the house had a makeover during 2004 that included a refurbished and much admired honey-coloured bathroom and shower and a redecorated

Castle Acre is just off the beaten track, and this too makes a delightful base...

main bedroom, with new soft furnishings. The cosy interior incorporates an open fire, repro oak furniture, a traditional 'cottage suite', old local prints, a modern fitted pine kitchen. There are attractive table and standard lamps and lots of books. There are carpets virtually throughout. TV. One pet possible. Garage. Linen and towels included. **Sleeps 6** in a double, a twin and an adult-sized two-bunk-bedroom. Cost: £300 to £350. Details: Mrs Angela Swindell, St Saviour's Rectory, St Saviour, Jersey, Channel Isles JE2 7NP. Telephone 01534 736679. Fax 727480.

www.castleacre.org
email: jsyedu71@localdial.com or **info@castleacre.org**

41

Burnham Thorpe
The Corner Pightle

Among all the peaceful, unspoilt villages of rural North Norfolk we have a special fondness for Burnham Thorpe – birthplace of Lord Nelson. It's very close to Burnham Market, but half-hidden away. We recently visited this traditional, very cosy, rather rambling house in pristine flint set off prettily in white and with

A classic Norfolk country cottage situated – better yet – in a famous village.

one of those pantiled roofs that add so much to the charm of the region. about 20 minutes' drive from, say, Hunstanton and just about three miles from the famous sands at Holkham. **Sleeping up to 6** in four bedrooms, overlooking the village green towards a pub named after local-boy-made-good Lord Nelson, it has so many good things going for it, such as a safely enclosed south-west facing garden, a wood-burning stove, a downstairs bedroom for convenience, a number of original beams. As with the Hunstanton properties in the same ownership (see Page 56) it is sympathetically lit, comfortably furnished and full of tender loving care. Linen and towels included. Not suitable for dogs. Cost: about £350 to £750.

Details from Nicky and Angus Runciman, 8 Luard Rd, Cambridge CB2 2PJ. Telephone 01223 246382.

www.sunnyhunny.com email: angusrunciman@hotmail.com

Brancaster Staithe/Burnham Market
Peartree Cottage map 1/24

Peartree, **sleeping 6**, is a real beauty. Stylishly decorated and furnished, with a woodburner, it has fabulous rear views over an inspiring coastal panorama. The 'nautically-themed' main, third-floor double bedroom – king sized bed – has a telescope trained on the more distant muddy creeks and sailing boats! Not suitable for pets. Comfortable, newly available *Walnut Cottage* is a desirable

Peartree is a fine house with great views, light and bright and partly open-plan...

arable-farm property on the outskirts of Burnham Market, in easy reach of beautiful beaches and bird watching country. There's a large enclosed garden with off-road parking and boat space. **Sleeps 5**. One well-behaved pet is welcome. The main rooms overlook the farm and the horse paddock.

TV/video; Walnut has DVD too. No smoking. Linen and towels are included. Short breaks are available. Cost: (Peartree) about £350 to £975; (Walnut) about £250 to £625. Details from Suzy Lyles, Muckleton Farm, Burnham Market, King's Lynn, Norfolk PE31 8JT. Telephone 01485 518318/518340.

www.peartreecottages.co.uk email: peartreecottage@farming.co.uk

Brancaster
Sussex Farm Holiday Cottages

In one of the most idyllic locations in the whole of Norfolk, only minutes from some memorable beaches and bird-haunted marshes, these are also deep in the country. Within the pretty, quiet and leafy enclave of cottages are the detached *Park Drive, The Pheasantry* and *One Hundred Acre*, and the semi-detached *Apple Tree* and *Beech Tree*, **sleeping 10, 8, 7, 8 and 8** respectively. They are spacious and full of character. Two

In this delightful spot one is both deep in the country and near the sea.

of these are suitable for people of limited mobility. We have always found the cottages clean and tidy, with original features that add to the charm, with 'cottagey' doors, good carpets, microwave ovens, radio cassette players, televisions and videos. All have dishwashers and large freezers. All have central heating *and* open fires (logs included). Linen and towels included. Dogs (one per property) welcome. Cost: about £460 to £1100. Short breaks welcome. Details and a good brochure from Sue Lane, 4 Stiffkey Road, Warham, Wells, Norfolk. Telephone 07885 269538 (mobile). Fax 01485 210261.

www.tbfholidayhomes.co.uk email: info@tbfholidayhomes.co.uk

Blakeney
Jenny's Cottage   map 1/28

This is a little jewel at the heart of miraculously unspoilt Blakeney. It is one of the most loved places on the North Norfolk coast, notable for the beauty of the tidal shore, the walks to Blakeney Point, the birdlife, boat trips to see the seals. Comfortable holiday cottages are hard to come by here, but happily this is a small-scale, Grade II listed, flint and tiled gem (dating from 1839), with a pretty courtyard garden that in summer overflows with hollyhocks. In the heart of the village, near a welcoming pub and a well stocked shop, it is ideal for a couple with a small

A rare chance to stay in the centre of famous Blakeney.

child (a double and small single). It's full of charm and comfort: a wood burner in an inglenook fireplace, well arranged lighting. Though space is limited, the main bedroom, via steep and narrow stairs, is quite a good size, and there is even a bath in which serious walkers can ease their aching bones. We thought this would make a good and inexpensive base for a winter holiday. Well behaved dogs are welcome. Linen and towels can be hired. TV. Non smokers only. Cost: about £200 to £350. Details from Simon Flint, Sherwood, Sandy Lane, South Wootton, King's Lynn, Norfolk PE30 3NX. Telephone 01553 672208.   **email: Simon@flint2.fsnet.co.uk**

Brancaster Staithe
Vista Cottage/Carpenter's Cottage

Even in the context of the glorious, much-loved North Norfolk coast these two cottages are notable for their 'tender loving care' and their memorable location.

In both *Vista* and *Carpenter's* you can almost reach out and touch one of the most beautiful coastlines in Britain. To be exact, you can walk down the cottage gardens right on to the salty marshes and join the coastal footpath, or make your way somewhat more directly towards the water.

From the back windows of both the properties in the ownership of the Smith family, muddy inlets dotted with yachts and fishing boats snake as prettily as in any sailor's favourite picture out towards the North Sea. Bring your binoculars!

Being on the A149 Cromer to Hunstanton coast road (mostly local or day time traffic) they are not remote or irritatingly difficult to find after a long journey. There is a patio with a gas barbecue, and two good pubs nearby.

Vista has a big garden, unforgettable views out to sea and (it's not always the case with coastal properties) immediate access to the water. It's also very cosy...

Carpenter's (also with some marvellous views) is a pretty 'upside down' cottage for 2.

In Vista Cottage, **sleeping 6**, we met a family who were enjoying spending time in a 'family-friendly' kitchen/diner with original stone flags and excellent fittings, such as washing machine and dishwasher. There is a very cosy sitting room with open fire. On the first floor, via a steep staircase, there is a double, a twin and a bunk bedded room (adult sized). The house is well carpeted and there is plenty of heating.

Next door is Carpenter's Cottage, set back from the road by a small, safely enclosed courtyard. In the owners' family for over a hundred years, it is a delightful 'upside down' house with a sitting room/kitchen/diner on the first floor and a very cosy, 'compact' double bedded room on the ground floor. The original fireplace has been restored: a lovely focal point on an autumn or spring evening, and there is a well planned window seat from which to enjoy those fabulous views. **Sleeps 2**.

Dogs are welcome in both. Linen and towels are included. Cost: approximately £210 to £750. (Pro-rata off season short breaks are available, for a minimum of three nights.) TVs. **'Visit Britain' Three Stars**: we'd have thought Four.

Details from Mrs G J Smith, Dale View, Main Road, Brancaster Staithe, King's Lynn, Norfolk PE31 8BY. Telephone/fax 01485 210497.

South Raynham, near Fakenham
Idyllic Cottages@Vere Lodge

Located most peacefully in rural North Norfolk, Jane Bowlby's creeper-clad, part Regency, part-Georgian home is the focal point of a clutch of comfortable cottages, each with its own individual character, amid lovely, wooded, undulating countryside.

It's a thoughtfully run, caring, tranquil place in which to enjoy a self-catering holiday. We have long rated it one of the very best set-ups we know – not just in Norfolk but in England as a whole.

Over many years we have visited and revisited the individual cottages, of which there are now fourteen, and found their advertising slogan – 'Peace, Beauty, Excellence' – more than justified. We have also stayed in three different cottages.

There is a magic to this place which even the detailed and colourful brochure fails to capture. Children relish the eight acres of freedom, the company of new friends, the daily feeding-round of the many tame animals and birds. Parents can relax, knowing their young are safe and happy.

Vere Lodge is ideally placed for exploring. Vast sandy beaches backed by sand-dunes or pinewoods are barely twenty minutes away, as are coastal resorts which range from the picturesque to the larger, more commercial holiday centres. Within easy reach are dinosaur parks, steam-engine exhibitions, stately homes such as Holkham and Blickling, and scores of other

Vere Lodge is a place for all seasons.   *Rose Cottage is handsome and relaxing.*

attractions: one of our own favourites is the steam museum at Thursford.

An impressive leisure centre is the icing on the Vere Lodge cake. There's a large, very warm covered pool (36 feet by 18), with a shallow end with steps for children, and a slide.

There's a sauna, solarium, games room with table tennis and pool table, and a centrally heated lounge looking on to the pool. Doors open on to two grass and paved sun patios, so that on hot summer days this effectively becomes an open air pool.

There's also a small shop, a launderette and a range of home-cooked frozen foods. If you *are* considering a break between, say, October and March, you'll find the pool as warm then (80° plus) as in high summer, and all the other facilities are available.

Which brings us to the cottages themselves and details of the accommodation. A good lot of thought and effort has been given here to providing those

45

little touches – good pictures, stylish flower arrangements, pretty ornaments – which help to set Vere Lodge out of the ordinary. Not surprisingly, Vere Lodge enjoys a high English Tourism Council grading.

Secret Garden and *The Robin's Nest* are two spacious single-storey cottages built on what was once the kitchen garden to Vere Lodge. We thought them delightful, noting especially masses of space and privacy, deep sofas, good carpets, a combination of character and comfort. Both are extremely quiet and secluded with about half an acre each of garden, mainly lawn, surrounded by high flint walls. They **sleep 6** in three bedrooms – one double, two twins – and have an impressive lounge with an open fire. They are approached via Church Lane, a narrow and barely-used lane which forms the southern boundary to Vere Lodge and leads only to the tiny church and former rectory. On the other side of the lane lie the leisure centre and the seven acre grounds of Vere Lodge with all their amenities.

The other properties are more part of the Vere Lodge 'family'. *Apple Cottage* is a spacious and entirely self-contained ground-floor apartment, plush and comfortable, which faces on to a large landscaped courtyard. Suitable for retired couples, young couples with a baby, or the elderly or partially disabled. **Sleeps 3**. *Dahlia* and *Thyme* are two cottages which face west over fields of corn or bright yellow mustard. They therefore enjoy not only lovely views but also all the afternoon and evening sun. This is particularly true of Thyme, an 'upside-down' cottage, with a large upstairs living room, while Dahlia has the advantage of an upstairs en-suite bathroom. **Both sleep 6**. Both have their own sitting-out patios.

Apple, suitable for the partially disabled.   *Children and animals are welcome here.*

The Dolls House is a small, simple 'budget' cottage, the ground floor of which was once a part of a gun room. Complete with huge doll, it looks out over lawns to the horseshoe of beeches and flowering cherries beyond. It is warm, comfortable and compact. **Sleeps 4**. *Dove Cottage* is furnished to a standard not generally found in a holiday cottage. It has panoramic views of the grounds, woods, and surrounding countryside from the upstairs living room which opens on to its own completely private roof-terrace. We very much like the cool, soft, grey blue ambiance, and the open fireplace. **Sleeps 2 plus 2**. *Garden Wing* is undoubtedly the most popular of all the cottages: ground-floor throughout, it is especially suitable for the disabled. The large and elegant sitting-room looks out over the croquet lawn to woodland beyond. **Sleeps 4**. *Lavender Cottage*, large and west facing, once housed coaches and a harness room. It is a long raised-level cottage, outside which is a large terrace screened by a conifer hedge, with a flight of steps leading up to the front door.

It's furnished in log-cabin style, but to standards such as original log-cabins never enjoyed with, for example, carpets on polished wood floors. **Sleeps 6**. *Possum's*, once a full-size billiard-room, is a spacious and unusual apartment called after Miss 'Possum' Smith, who cared for the Bowlby children for over thirty years. Tall Georgian windows face on to formal yew-hedges and flower borders flood-lit by night. **Sleeps 3**. *Pump Cottage* was purpose-built and 'incorporates the lessons learned from 25 years' experience of self-catering'. All the accommodation is on the ground floor and is suitable for the elderly or partially disabled. Open fireplace here too. **Sleeps 2**. *Rose Cottage*, the largest of all the cottages, is south-facing and therefore very sunny, with its own private walled garden. It is bright and airy, with deep, comfy armchairs and sofa, an open fire and a downstairs shower and loo. **Sleeps 7**. *Rowan* and *Honeysuckle* are an identical pair of 19th century cottages. An unusual feature is the central fireplace, raised for the protection of young children, with a log-burning fire facing into the lounge and behind it an electric fire to warm the dining room. Both are furnished in 'country-style', with a raised south-facing terrace in front of each.

Among the many things they do so well at Vere Lodge are short breaks in autumn, winter, spring or early summer. To enhance that 'baby it's cold outside' mood, several cottages have open fires. Better yet, prices even in these very comfortable properties for a three-day break – starting or finishing on any day of the week – can be as low as £17.00 per night per person (6 persons), which includes the use of the leisure centre.

Vere Lodge is something of an animal sanctuary, too, delightful for young

Lavender Cottage once housed coaches.

The most popular cottage is Garden Wing.

children. At feeding time (9.00 am daily) there are freshly-laid eggs to be gathered, often from under an indignant hen. In the centre paddock, tame and gentle miniature Angora goats stand on their hind legs against the fence awaiting their turn, while Mingo the donkey, and Toby the docile pony, await theirs.

Children will also love the Enchanted Wood. We certainly do, but we won't spoil the surprise!

Dogs are welcome, and remote-control videos, televisions and clock radios are standard throughout. Details and a copy of an impressive full colour brochure from Vere Lodge, South Raynham, near Fakenham, Norfolk NR21 7HE. Telephone 01328 838261. Fax 838300.

www.verelodge.co.uk

email: major@verelodge.co.uk

Bylaugh, near East Dereham
Bylaugh Hall Cottages

Deep in rural Norfolk, Bylaugh lies in a beautiful valley amid unspoiled farmland unaffected by major roads. Here the restoration of a fine country house is hand in hand with the creation to a very high standard of several substantial self catering properties. We are bowled over by the quality of the work, the atmosphere and the enthusiasm of the owners. A flex-

A fabulous base from which to explore deeply rural inland Norfolk...

ible arrangement means large groups can stay here, yet smaller parties have privacy. We can hardly do justice to the range and quality of accommodation: it is essential to send for a brochure or to look at the website for details, for example, of *The Courtyard Mews*, *The Front Mews*, *The Coachman's Lodge*, *The Stables*, *The Smithy*, *The Brewery* and, separate from the others, *The Manor*, a superb modern house that sleeps from **12 to 15 people**. Among many good things is the splendidly restored Orangery, a super party and small-conference venue. Individual houses **sleep up to 18** and multiples can accommodate groups of up to 80-plus.

Details from Bylaugh Hall, Bylaugh, East Dereham, Norfolk NR20 4RL. Telephone 01362 688121. Fax 688167.

www.bylaugh.com   email: info@bylaugh.com

Tunstead, near Wroxham   Colour section A, Page 1
Old Farm Cottages   map 1/34

In the summer of 2005 we revisited (via quiet, ever more rural country lanes) these beautifully converted and painstakingly run former barns. They make a fairly central point in rural Norfolk from which to explore the Broads – Wroxham, for example, is close – the exquisite North Norfolk coast, the more family-orientated east, the city of Norwich itself, and even

Peaceful Norfolk is all around, but the coast and the Broads are handy...

more beyond. A number of readers have commented on how much they enjoy the covered indoor pool at the end of a day's touring. This excellent pool is set off nicely by a gym, a spa, a solarium and a games room. Each of the six properties has its own enclosed patio and barbecue. There's a high degree of privacy in these spacious, pristinely cared-for conversions, but children also have the chance to make new friends. **Sleep 2 to 6**. Linen included, towels for hire. Dogs welcome in most. Cost: from (short breaks) £252 to (full weeks) £465 to £867. **'Visit Britain' Four Stars**.

For details, telephone 01692 536612.

www.oldfarmcottages.com
email: mail@oldfarmcottages.fsnet.co.uk

Horning, near Norwich
Ferry Marina Cottages

We revisited on a summer Saturday in 2005, just as this busy and popular development of holiday properties was being made ready for new arrivals.

We were there mainly to check out an ongoing upgrading of the longer-established properties and – more interestingly – to see a clutch of quite superb, spacious, sumptuously comfortable houses (they are grander than 'cottages'!), each with its own private mooring on a spur of the River Bure. We were impressed by the expensive fittings, the excellent lighting, the warm carpeting. Notably, all the spacious sitting rooms are on the first floor, so as to take advantage of the views over the marina.

In the upgraded established properties, where we've always noticed a good degree of privacy, easy-on-the-eye blues set off uncluttered interiors. (We were also impressed in one property by the sight of housekeepers making up beds with 'sheets and blankets' instead of duvets, as requested by guests.)

A huge part of the ongoing appeal of the cottages is the 'instant access' to the Norfolk Broads from them all. During several summer visits we too have enjoyed the breeze off the water! All the Ferry Marina houses and apartments are on the water, all have their own mooring and some have garages and balconies. We looked at four or five types, which vary in size, and were impressed. They all have views of cruisers and yachts, and it's not only in the new places that you can choose to have your own mooring. (It's nice to hire a day launch or picnic boat, from two hours up to a week-hire, depending on the season.)

There's a leisure centre 'on site', with an indoor pool, spa bath, sauna, steam-room, sunbeds, plus a games room, with pool, table tennis and more.

Reliably comfortable bases from which to enjoy a very popular part of the Broads.

You are virtually on the main River Bure, with a super indoor swimming pool...

The village of Horning lies at the heart of the Norfolk Broads, but retains its character. Best of all worlds, perhaps: Ferry Marina is at the far, more rural end of the village (a ten minute walk from the centre, where there are pubs and good local shops). There's also a big 'family' pub right on the water a short stroll from the houses: delightful on a summer evening.

Sleep 2 to 8. TV. Linen provided, but not towels. Dogs welcome in some units (extra charge). Out of season reductions on boat hire. Details from Ferry Marina Cottages, Ferry Road, Horning, near Norwich NR12 8PS. Telephone 01692 630392/fax 631040.

www.ferry-marina.co.uk   email: sales@ferry-marina.co.uk

Horning (Norfolk Broads)
Little River View

Of all the bustling villages that are a focal point for visitors to the Norfolk Broads (it's not all lonely creeks and wildfowl-haunted marshes), our own favourite is Horning. And at its very heart, opposite a 100 year old pub of character and handy for a range of village shops, stands a pretty, charming cottage that – always a good sign – is occasionally used by the owners themselves. We noted two comfy, deep sofas in the very cosy sitting room, a 'proper' bath in the (downstairs) bathroom, a spacious double and twin bedroom on the first floor, an inviting kitchen/diner. This is one of those places in which the owners' concern for their guests' com-

As neat and pretty a cottage as we've seen in East Anglia.

fort is apparent, with, for example, books, games, information folders, etc. Note too that landlubbers may hire a day boat nearby to get a flavour of life on the Broads. This is a rarity in such a sought-after location! **Sleeps 4**. TV/video/DVD. River views. Not suitable for pets. Cost: about £219 to £539. Short breaks. Linen, towels and gas/electricity included. No smoking. Details from Victoria Free. Telephone 07801 288822 or 07759 125919.

www.littleriverview.co.uk   email: info@littleriverview.co.uk

---

Horning (Norfolk Broads)
Riverside Rentals

Any thatched cottage in Norfolk will be sought-after by self-caterers. Put it right by the water in the Norfolk Broads, and people will go into raptures. *Box End* (**sleeps 6 'plus 2'**) and *Willow Fen* (**sleeps 6 'plus 2'**) are two thatched beauties (Box End is pretty enough to feature on our cover!) within a quartet of properties in the same ownership; the other two are *Willow Lodge* (**sleeps 8 'plus 2'**) and *Little Wiluna*, which is a

Delightfully, all the properties enjoy substantial riverside frontages...

smaller property within the grounds of Wiluna, a fine, imposing riverside property. Add to all their considerable charms the fact that the three principal properties have substantial river frontages, moorings – day boats can easily be hired locally – and gardens, and that they all have light, bright airy rooms, and you have places 'worth the detour'. Also, pets are welcome by arrangement in the three biggest properties, and each has bath *and* shower.

Linen is included. TV and DVD. Cost: about £215 to £1450. Details from Grebe Island Leisure, Wiluna, Ferry Cott Lane, Horning, Norfolk NR12 8PP. Telephone/fax 01692 631549.

www.riverside-rentals.co.uk
email: riverside@riverside-rentals.co.uk

Clippesby (Norfolk Broads National Park)
Clippesby Holiday Cottages

There are three excellent *Pinelodges* in a woodland setting, with country views and a wheelchair ramp to the sun deck (**sleep 6**). We also like the quiet bungalows that overlook fields (two **sleep 4**, two **sleep 6**), and saw two larger cottages (each **sleeps 8**) along with some recently converted two-storeyed *Clocktower Apartments* (**sleeping 4**) with first-floor sundecks looking on to well tended gardens.

In the country but not far from the sea...

There's a heated open air pool, grass tennis courts, a bar/restaurant serving evening meals, play areas, a small shop and café and an 18-hole mini-golf course. (Tucked away among trees in a different landscaped area is a **'Visit Britain' Four Star** touring park, with the David Bellamy Gold Award for Conservation.) TVs, central heating and bed-linen; some have open fires too. **'Visit Britain' Four Stars**. Cost: from £299 to £949, including bed-linen and electricity. Colour brochure: the Lindsay family, Clippesby Hall, Clippesby, Norfolk NR29 3BL. Telephone 01493 367800; fax 367809.

www.clippesby.com or **www.discoverthebroads.com**
email: holidays@clippesby.com

Overstrand, North Norfolk   map 1/31
Danish House Gardens

A superb location! During a 2005 visit to North Norfolk we checked out this absolutely pristine, modern, two-bedroomed, detached bungalow, very quietly situated at the end of a residential cul-de-sac. Only about 100 metres from the clifftop, not only does it have fine sea views, it's within easy walking distance of Overstrand's fine sandy beach and

Easy living in this understandably very popular part of North Norfolk...

promenade. Golfers with a recognised handicap might wish to enjoy the adjacent Royal Cromer Golf Club: those who think this game 'just spoils a good walk' have easy access to Cromer, Sheringham, Blakeney, Mundesley, Norwich and Great Yarmouth. The comfortable, centrally heated bungalow was completed in 2004. It is furnished to a high level, with a full range of new facilities and equipment and has **Four 'Visit Britain' Stars**. Well behaved dogs are welcome. Cost: about £200 to £500.

Details from Paul and Christine Walker, 17 Rook Tree Lane, Stotfold, Hitchin, Hertfordshire SG5 4DL. Telephone 01462 731357. Fax 731357.

www.overstrand-holiday.co.uk
email: info@overstrand-holiday.co.uk

Hunstanton, Brancaster and beyond
Norfolk Holiday Homes*

So many of our readers have discovered the inspiring, uncrowded county of Norfolk through this agency, which has featured in our guide every year without a break since our first edition in 1983. We have never once had any kind of complaint, have visited and revisited many times and have never seen a dud. This would be admirable in a private cottage set-up – in an agency of any size it is a remarkable accolade.

Norfolk Holiday Homes specialises in the north west corner of the county: fine sandy beaches, tranquil villages, lonely church towers, the traditional seaside resort of Hunstanton, excellent bird watching and much more.

During a recent visit we were very impressed by *Courtyard Cottage* and *Norfolk House* in the quiet, just-inland village of Docking. With lots of evidence of the absolute dedication of the owners, far beyond the normal requirements, and their good taste and an eye for detail, the **Five Star** property (you can take them as one or separately) is, simply, stunning. **Sleeping respectively 5 and 4**, together they make a memorable holiday home **for 9 people**.

There are several properties in Old Hunstanton, which has all the advantages of a slightly old fashioned seaside atmosphere with easy access not only to a glorious sandy beach of its own but also to the bright lights of the lively 'family resort' of Hunstanton-proper, with its new pier. There are clean, bright modern houses (which always have a certain following) and others with a more 'cottagey' style.

Spindrift for example, is literally a minute's walk from the beach, and also pubs, restaurants and shops. There is a pretty, enclosed courtyard garden as a bonus, and the property **sleeps 5 'plus 1'** (there is a king size double in the main bedroom). *Sandbanks* is a superb, large, detached family residence (**sleeping 8,** on the outskirts of the town in a very desirable area, yet within easy reach of the cliff tops and the beach). There are rural views from the front and distant sea views from the rear first floor rooms.

Norfolk House has one of the most stylish interiors we know. Yes, of course, it has Five 'Visit Britain' Stars.

The Old Coastguard Lookout is an extraordinary place: you'll have to get your booking in early!

Ashdale House is an exceptionally comfortable detached house tucked away in quiet surroundings, but still close to the beach, golf course and other holiday amenities. The garden is fully enclosed and there is ample parking. Furnished to a very high standard throughout, the property offers spacious accommodation **for 7 people**.

Finally, but still only scratching the surface, *The Old Coastguard Lookout,* overlooking the clifftops near the lighthouse, has been thoughtfully restored since it was built in 1906 as a Marconi Wireless Station. It has associations with both World Wars, was once a maritime museum and spent its 'last years' as the Coastguard Lookout. It has unique accommodation on three storeys, and enjoys superb, uninterrupted panoramic views of the Wash and the coast. **Sleeps 3**.

Linzel Cottage is a superb, 17th century, chalk and brick cottage just off the village green at Thornham, which has been tastefully restored to a very high standard to reveal its original beauty and charm. **Sleeping 6**, the accommodation incorporates a galleried hall and landing, bathrooms with cast iron baths, Yorkstone flooring and terracotta floor in the kitchen plus a multitude of other interesting features. Not to be missed! The nearby pond – full of greedy ducks – is an added bonus for children.

Near Pentney, eight miles south of King's Lynn, is *Fairywood Cottage* (**sleeps 4**), secretly tucked away overlooking farmland and woods, with tracks running through – ideal for dog-walking, and dogs are indeed welcome here.

It's worth remembering – especially if you don't already know Norfolk – that even a cottage that on the map appears to be well inland is probably just a few minutes' drive from the coast. Some coast! The wide sandy beaches, typically set off by pine trees, are remarkable, but everyone comments on how quiet they are even at the height of the season.

There is lots going to appeal to the whole family: children will especially like the entertainments at Thursford, the North Norfolk steam-railway, and the narrow gauge railway that puffs through idyllic, unspoiled pastureland between Wells-next-the-Sea and Walsingham.

Dogs are welcome in over half the properties on the agency's books, and several cottages have open fires, which can be the makings of an autumn or winter break. Also, short breaks and discounts may be available. All properties are inspected and graded by 'Visit Britain', and a number have ground floor accommodation suitable for disabled people.

Ashdale House, in Old Hunstanton, is exceptionally comfortable. It is close to the beach and the golf course.

Linzel Cottage at Thornham is one of our own favourites. Overlooking the village green, it sleeps six 'plus baby'.

An exceptionally good brochure, fully illustrated in colour, is available from Sandra Hohol, Norfolk Holiday Homes, 62 Westgate, Hunstanton, Norfolk PE36 5EL. Telephone Hunstanton 01485 534267/fax 535230.

www.norfolkholidayhomes-birds.co.uk
email: shohol@birdsnorfolkholidayhomes.co.uk

Norfolk Coast
Sowerbys Holiday Cottages*

We've a very high regard for this medium-sized agency of about 80 properties, based in widely admired Burnham Market. During 2005 there were some delightful additions, such as *Avocet House* in Titchwell (**sleeps 13**), an outstanding brick and flint house; *Coastguards' Cottage* in Thornham (**sleeps 10**), in an idyllic position; *Seven Edges* in Brancaster (**sleeps 10**), a wonderful family home

Hilltop, sleeping 4, is a 'traditional' gem.

in a quiet lane; *La Hat House* in Old Hunstanton (**sleeps 8**), a renovated light and spacious three-storey house with direct access to the beach and a short walk from the golf course. There are three apartments in *The Granary* at Wells, with stunning panoramic views. (All the cottages mentioned have exceptional sea and/or marsh views.) Also new are *Hope Cottage* in Holme (**sleeps 2**), a perfect hideaway for two, and *Fern Cottage* in Burnham Market (**sleeps 6**), a stunning three-storey Georgian cottage right on the village green. Details from Sowerby's Holiday Cottages, Market Place, Burnham Market, Norfolk PE31 8HD. Telephone 01328 730880, fax 730522.

www.sowerbysholidaycottages.co.uk
email info@sowerbysholidaycottages.co.uk

Wiveton, near Blakeney
Bones Cottage map 1/38

During a 2005 visit to the north Norfolk coast we made sure to revisited this charming place, **just for 2 people**. In a blissfully quiet and peaceful place, it is only about ten minutes' very pleasant walk from the hauntingly beautiful saltmarshes at Cley and twenty minutes from the quay at exquisite Blakeney. There is also a good pub just a short walk away. The owners' home (bed and

Private, inexpensive, close to one of the best parts of the coast. One reader called it 'a little piece of old England'...

breakfast also available) is adjacent, but the cottage feels very private. There is a neat, small, rather cosy kitchen/diner, a shower-room and, in short, a charming atmosphere. Among other details we liked the big window that seems to light up the whole cottage. It looks on to the front garden and gets the sun all day long. Altogether, we thought *Bones* would make an excellent base from which to enjoy the coast, and it is inexpensive. Bed-linen is provided.

Small TV. Not suitable for dogs. Cost: about £230 to £300. Further details from Mrs Stocks, Bones Cottage, Hall Lane, Wiveton, Holt, Norfolk NR25 7TG. Telephone 01263 740840.

Holt
No 6 Carpenters Cottages

Very conveniently situated, this most attractive flint and pantiled terraced cottage lies close to the centre of Holt, a small Georgian town of considerable character. There are good pubs and restaurants, two department stores, antique shops and two fish-mongers – good for local crabs! But best of all is the easy access to the

A cosy, very convenient town house that is only minutes away from the exceptional North Norfolk coast.

coast (delightful Blakeney is only about ten minutes away) and to such attractions as Felbrigg, Blickling and Holkham Hall. There's a well-equipped kitchen and a bright and cheerful sitting/dining room, informal, comfortable and altogether inviting, opening on to a secluded walled garden area. The cottage is often used by the owners themselves, and its good standards reflect this fact. We spotted well chosen local pictures, books, including a number about Norfolk, board games and puzzles. The cottage **sleeps 3** in a good-sized twin room and a smallish single.

Cost: about £160 to £340. Small, well behaved dogs are welcome. Further details are available from Mrs Sally Beament, 36 Avranches Avenue, Crediton, Devon EX17 2HB. Telephone 01363 773789.

email: sallybeament@hotmail.com

Holt   map 1/41
Sunnyside Cottage

In a quiet mews in the handsome town of Holt, just a fifteen minute drive from the North Norfolk coast, this quite excellent and reasonably priced cottage is pleasantly tucked away, light, bright and spacious. Dating from the 1880s, it is furnished to a high standard in Victorian style but with modern comforts. We endorse the enthusiastic comments sent in by some of our readers: 'Beautifully furnished and equipped'...'immaculate and spotless'...'excellent colour schemes' ...'beds made up with excellent linen – better than I have at home!'...'gorgeous, polished wood floors'. The

A very special place indeed, with the rare advantage of being in an inland town with easy access to the coast.

owners have spent much time working to make Sunnyside Cottage the welcoming haven it is.

Sleeps 5 in a double and two other bedrooms. TV, video, radio, CD player, books and games. Heating, electricity and bedlinen included, but bring your own towels. Stay for as short or long a period as you wish. Cost: reasonable, from under £200 to £380 per week. Not suitable for pets. Details from Michael Drake, Broadland House, Station New Road, Brundall, Norwich, Norfolk NR13 5PQ. Telephone/fax 01603 712524.

email: michael.drake@ukgateway.net

Hunstanton
Northernhay/Highland House

Northernhay is one of our own all-time seaside favourites, a super family house in the 'traditional' resort of Hunstanton: amusement arcades, fish and chips, children running free on a super sandy beach. Parts of the town are quite chic, with good golf, cosy pubs and fine family houses that have easy access to the sands. A spacious

Northernhay is one of the handsomest houses in what is known affectionately as 'Sunny Hunny' – see website details...

and sunny Edwardian villa within a cliff-top conservation area, Norrhernhay has lots of original features, a conservatory and some bedrooms from which you can see the sea. Most usefully **sleeping 10** in four double bedrooms and a children's double-bunk room, it has a neat garden and secure parking for two cars. *Highland House*, with gardens front and back, is equally full of character and style. Also **sleeping 10** (in six bedrooms: two doubles, two twins and two singles) it combines a number of original features with modern comforts, such as a part-'island' kitchen with glass-fronted cupboard doors and two sumptuous family bathrooms. Linen and bath towels are included. Not suitable for pets. Cost: £375 to £875. Details from Nicky and Angus Runciman, 8 Luard Road, Cambridge CB2 2PJ. Telephone 01223 246382.

www.sunnyhunny.com   email: angusrunciman@hotmail.com

Ringstead, near Hunstanton   map 1/46
Pickles Patch/Tumblers

We have had so many enthusiastic reader reports about these properties during the fifteen years they've been featured in our guide. (We remember turning up one hot August day and chatting with regular visitors to *Tumblers* sunning themselves outside 'their' cottage.) In both cottages interiors are spacious and welcoming, with deep sofas and armchairs, fine pictures, pretty curtains, good fitted carpets, all helping to make them real

A super village location (but quiet), with a good pub nearby, and especially lovingly cared-for interiors and gardens.

'homes from home'. Specifically, Tumblers **sleeps 4 'plus 2'**, *Pickles Patch* **sleeps 6 'plus 2'**. The village itself is quiet, but with the traditional resort of Hunstanton and sandy beaches a short drive away.

TV and video; barbecue and garden furniture; linen and towels included, plus 'light and heat'. Dogs by arrangement. Guests can also enjoy a garden of about an acre. Cost: about £350 to £750. More details from Margaret Greer, Sedgeford Road Farm Holiday Cottages, Ringstead, Hunstanton, Norfolk PE36 5JZ. Telephone 01485 525530 or 525316.
email: Ringstead.Gallery@btinternet.com

Norfolk – countywide
Countryside Cottages*

Is this the best of both worlds? This family-run business takes in both the glorious North and West Norfolk coast as well as the tranquil interior of the county. It has on its books some of the most eye-catching properties in this miraculously unspoilt and uncrowded corner of England. It includes snug and romantic retreats and quiet hideaways such as the Old

Owl Cottage is a North Norfolk classic, fitting so well into its surroundings.

Bakehouse at Bale, **sleeping 4**, and beach-side houses such as *Smugglers* at Thornham, which commands breathtaking views and **sleeps up to 10**. Also at Thornham, *Admiral's Lodge* **sleeps up to 9**. A good proportion have open fires or woodburning stoves, and notable views. Some accept dogs. Staying in any of the personally selected, exceptionally stylish cottages is such a civilised way to plan visits to Norfolk's historic houses, market towns, salt marshes, pine fringed sandy beaches and idyllic rural villages.

For further information contact: Countryside Cottages, 5 Old Stable Yard, Holt, Norfolk NR25 6BN. Telephone 01263 713133. Fax 711877.

www.countryside-cottages.com email: ccottages@dialstart.net

Wells next the Sea
Chantry   map 1/47

With easy access to some of the most beautiful parts of the North Norfolk coast, 'Wells' is a small family resort with real character and lots to do. In the heart of the town, but tucked well away from sight and much bigger inside than one would imagine, as well as more imposing from the outside, we thought this delightful: not a show-house, but a practical and welcoming family home on three storeys. It has bags of character, and has been most sympathetically renovated and upgraded by the owners. We liked so many things: the small enclosed 'courtyard' garden, with many flowers and shrubs, the sense of history (it dates in part

Notably quiet, though it's in the heart of the little town...

from the 17th century), the impressive amount of space – a lovely big landing, bathroom and dining room, for example – the original details, such as a rare brass *single* bed in one room, plus some old pine.

Duvets or blankets available. **Sleeps up to 7**. Not suitable for pets. Linen and towels by arrangement. Cost: approximately £200 to £500. Details from Mrs V Jackson, 3a Brickendon Lane, Brickendon, near Hertford, Hertfordshire SG13 8NU. Telephone/fax 01992 511303.

Norwich
Dowager's Cottage (The Old Rectory Hotel)

Within the mature garden of this highly regarded country house style hotel, this inviting cottage looks directly on to the heated outdoor pool (summer months), enjoys the advantages of self-contained living and immediate access to the hotel and its award-winning restaurant. Just for 2 (double bedroom), we thought it particularly cosy, with a combined sitting room/dining room, compact but fully fitted kitchen, bathroom with

Just two and a half miles from Norwich, but seemingly out in the country...

bath (shower over) and downstairs cloakroom. Most usefully, there's a direct dial link to the hotel; you can also use the wireless broadband connection. **Sleeps 2**. Weekly bookings: Saturday to Saturday. Non-smoking. No children (under 18) or pets. Cost: about £255 to £350. Gas central heating (included). English breakfast and dinner can be booked in the hotel. Shorts breaks available October to March. Details from Chris Entwistle, The Old Rectory, 103 Yarmouth Road, Thorpe St Andrew, Norwich NR7 0HF. Telephone 01603 700772. Fax 01603 300772.

www.dowagerscottage.co.uk
email: enquiries@oldrectorynorwich.com

Norwich   map 1/48
The Moorings

Norwich is a visitor-friendly city, and the Norfolk Broads are a must-see for people holidaying in the county. So the idea of a detached riverside holiday cottage just five miles by road from the city centre and a leisurely 50 minutes via the River Yare is something of note. For a four-berth cabin cruiser – a first for

We'll see this in 2006, and hopefully 'test drive' the cabin cruiser too!

us – *comes with the property*. The cottage, not yet seen by us, only became available in the autumn of 2005, and, being used from time by the owners (always a good indicator) is especially comfortable. For example, the master bedroom has a king-sized bed, there is an open fire in the sitting room and a pool/snooker table in the games room, There are fine landscaped gardens, with a barbecue terrace overlooking the River Yare and secluded rear garden complete with open air hot tub. Plus – of course – the joy of that easy-to-handle cabin cruiser.

Sleeps up to 10. Not suitable for pets. Linen/towels included. Widescreen TV/VCR/DVD/Sky. Also Playstation 2.

www.bythebroads.com   email: ask@bythebroads.com

Cambridgeshire/Lincolnshire/ Nottinghamshire

In our opinion these three counties represent one of eastern and middle England's best kept secrets. We're fond of Cambridgeshire (that exquisite 'city within a university', the vast skies above the Fens, the stark beauty of Ely cathedral), Lincolnshire (the endless sandy beaches, its own great cathedral at Lincoln, the usually deserted Wolds) and Nottinghamshire (deep, dark Sherwood forest, grand stately homes, memories of perhaps our finest novelist, D H Lawrence). Indeed, one of Lawrence's childhood homes is, against all the odds, available as a holiday home. In this corner of England, very soon after you leave main roads you are surrounded by quiet, rural, low key landscapes dotted with small market towns and sleepy villages. We think of Stamford, and marvellous Burghley House on its outskirts; of the genteel but not stuffy little town of Woodhall Spa, of climbing to the top of Boston Stump for marvellous panoramic views. On the coast, 'bracing' Skegness has a certain chic, and the RSPB reserve at nearby Gibraltar Point has an unforgettable atmosphere.

Denton, near Stilton (Cambridgeshire)
Orchard Cottage map 1/49

People who appreciate the classic picture-book country cottage will find this idyllic. Full of character and style (it's well out of earshot of any main roads, but easy to get to), it combines a powerful sense of the past with lots of comfort and warmth. It's like something from an idealised landscape painting by artists of 'the Norwich School'. In a historic part of 'the Shires' (peaceful stone villages, pubs with log fires,

Well away from main roads but actually quite accessible and not remote, this is one of our all-time favourite finds...

perhaps the ghostly echo of a hunting horn), Orchard is a rare example of a sympathetically converted 18th century cottage. In a half acre garden (with croquet), opposite a farm, with fields on three sides and farmland views, it is used from time to time by the owner herself, and is well planned, very comfortable and, in brief, a highly desirable holiday base. Much of the furniture is antique, and even the large bathroom has Victorian fittings; there is an open fireplace in the sitting room and a well appointed kitchen of character which leads into a conservatory. With a deep pond in the garden, this is unsuitable for small children. Dogs accepted by arrangement with the owner. **Sleeps 6**.

Linen and towels are included. Also a plentiful supply of wood and coal. Cost: about £350 to £850. Further details from Jenny Higgo, 22 Stocks Hill, Manton, Oakham, Rutland. Telephone 01572 737420.

www.higgo.com/orchard

email: orchard@higgo.com

Welton-le-Wold, near Louth
Stubbs Cottages

We've stayed in one of the Stubbs properties, namely *Foreman's Cottage,* and it has become a real favourite. **Sleeping 7**, it is located on a high lying part of the family farm, and has fine views. It's spacious and warm, and although it's a not a traditional roses-round-the-door place, it's really 'nice to come home to'. All the Stubbs cottages, in this guide without a break for over 20 years, have a lasting reputation for being clean, nicely situated and *very rea-*

Foreman's Cottage, deep in the Lincolnshire Wolds, is warm, comfy and surprisingly spacious. And as with all the Stubbs cottages, it is reasonably priced.

sonably priced. They are located in the hilly, wooded Lincolnshire Wolds (where good self-catering accommodation is rather thin on the ground). Among other properties there is, in the nearby off-the-beaten-track village of Welton-le-Wold, *The Old Schoolhouse*, **sleeping 6** and dating from the 19th century. Dogs are welcome. Cost: (approximately) £250 to £375.

A useful sketch map of Lincolnshire (so you don't miss the best beaches and resorts) is incorporated in the details, available from Margaret Stubbs, C V Stubbs and Sons, Manor Warren Farm, Welton-le-Wold, near Louth, Lincolnshire LN11 0QX. Telephone/fax 01507 604207.

Fulstow, near Louth
Bramble and Hawthorn

We revisited in 2005 and appreciated, as we have for many years, the 'tender loving care' these charming single storeyed cottages exude. This part of Lincolnshire is a place of vast skies and near-empty roads, and there's easy access to the green and

Deep in the country but handy for the sea.

rolling Wolds. These (**map 1/58**) are just 20 minutes from the sea, and there's a water-sports centre a mile away. Both *Bramble* and *Hawthorn* overlook a paved, gravelled 'courtyard'. There are good-sized open plan sitting rooms with cosy coal-effect fires, spacious bathrooms, and well designed bedrooms (each has a double and twin, though Hawthorn can take 2 extra on a double sofa-bed, therefore **sleeping up to 6**). You'll find fresh flowers, a welcome tray and chilled wine. The 'Information Centre' stocks maps, books and guides, with a video library. Linen and towels included. Non smoking. Children over ten welcome. Not suitable for dogs. Cost: from about £160 for a three-night break to £370 per week, high season. Details: Cheryl and Paul Tinker, Waingrove Country Cottages, Fulstow, near Louth, Lincolnshire LN11 0XQ. Telephone: 01507 363704.

www.lincolnshirecottages.com
email: ptinker.tinkernet@virgin.net

Langwith, near Mansfield
Blue Barn Cottage

This delightful family house on a mixed 450-acre farm near historic Sherwood Forest is a great favourite of ours. (It has featured in this guide for many years, and we know a family of nine who have holidayed here *ten times*.) It's close to the farmhouse at the end of a mile-long track from the village, yet very accessible, being only 15 minutes' drive from

This quiet and spacious house is one of our personal long-term favourites...

the M1 (junction 30). A cosy sitting room – all is very quiet here – with TV leads on to the dining room. Upstairs there is a double bedroom, a family room with a double and two singles, a twin room with cot and a small twin room, all opening off the landing. **'Visit Britain' Three Stars**. There is a large garden and barbecue. Cost: from £450, which includes all linen, towels, central heating and a 'welcome pack' of provisions. There is a big kitchen/breakfast room with Rayburn, electric cooker, microwave, fridge, and an extra downstairs toilet/shower. Not suitable for dogs.

Further details, together with a colour leaflet, from June Ibbotson, Blue Barn Farm, Langwith, Nottinghamshire NG20 9JD. Telephone/fax 01623 742248.

email: bluebarnfarm@supanet.com

Norton Junction, near Daventry
The Old Tollhouse map 1/63

We hadn't realised how this would capture the imagination of readers. Said one, from Harrogate 'this amazing property is unforgettable for anyone who is interested in canals and canal-boats'. For the former toll-keeper's cottage stands virtually on an island on the Grand Union Canal. It is well situated for canalside walks and a visit, for example, to the excellent British Waterways Museum at

If you like being around canal boats but find living on them a bit of a hassle, this might be just the place for you...

Stoke Bruerne. Specifically, there is one small double bedroom, an open fire (an initial supply of coal provided), a garden with garden chairs, an open plan sitting room with a dining and kitchen area. A pay phone is available. There is a pub within 250 yards and a shop a quarter of a mile away. **Sleeps 2.** One pet is welcome: your dog will love the towpath walks! Short breaks available. Ref 1056.

Further details available from Country Holidays, Spring Mill, Earby Lancashire BB94 0AA. To book, telephone 0870 192 1040. Brochures: 0870 607 8514.

Live search and book: **www.country-holidays.co.uk**

Yorkshire and The Peak District

Among a mass of tourist board statistics we read some years ago, one detail remains in our head. Of all the English counties, it's Yorkshire whose inhabitants are most likely to holiday within their own county boundaries. The county's pride in its history and its landscapes is infectious. There's ancient York itself, and comparatively unsung East Yorkshire, embracing such little known places as the quiet village of Lund and elegant Beverley. There are the renovated mills and industrial museums of West Yorkshire – whose rugged countryside has a charm of its own. And there are of course the better-known Yorkshire Dales and the North York Moors, as well as the North Yorkshire coast.

From the North York Moors, narrow roads lead to secret seaside resorts such as Robin Hood's Bay. Nearby Whitby and Scarborough have their own character, but the real pleasure is seeking out little-known sandy coves and silent valleys among the dales and moors.

The best of Derbyshire and Staffordshire is contained within yet another National Park: the Peak District National Park is the longest-established in Britain, and attracts more visitors than any other, but on the whole this region's gritty but picturesque villages and great houses are little known among southerners.

Bulmer, near York
Ashwall House   map 3/62

This is extraordinary. It's rare that we would describe a property as being 'in a class of its own', but this qualifies. A quiet no-through-road leads from the picturesque village of Bulmer, just three miles from Castle Howard, to this palatial, no-expense-spared house with stunning views. We have enjoyed a memorable stay here, and revelled in the blissful silence, the spacious rooms, the handsome main staircase, the dining hall

This is outstanding, and sensibly priced. It's quiet, and interiors are exquisite.

set off by glorious floor-to-ceiling windows, the inviting drawing room. A large conservatory/games room has a three-quarter sized snooker table and other games. This memorable property **sleeps up to 12 people** in five bedrooms, with four bathrooms. One ground floor bedroom and bathroom is suitable for wheelchair users. The charming garden incorporates a small ornamental lake with a gazebo-style bridge to an island. This property is perfect for family gatherings, reunions and special occasions. Catering can be arranged so there is no need to cook if you don't want to. Quality towels and linen are of course included, and the house has, of course, **Five 'Visit Britain' Stars**. Cost: from £900 to £2200 per week. For short breaks and weekends, see the websites:

Telephone 01845 597614 .

www.ashwallhouse.co.uk or **www.house-parties.co.uk**

York
City Breaks*: York City Centre

This is a small but unique collection
of properties in the centre of one of
England's finest and most historic
cities, which is a particular pleasure
to explore after hours, when most
day visitors have gone. There is
superb modern accommodation, all
of it with the enviable luxury of private parking, most of it with those
so-desirable river views. They range
from one bedroom **for 2** to five bedrooms for **up to 10**. All are furnished

A typically comfortable apartment in a highly sought-after location...

to either **Four or Five Star** standards, and are between five and ten minutes' walk to the city centre. All properties are privately owned, and
meticulously maintained by their caring owners. You may view all the
features of each of them at **www.city-breaks.net** (other properties in and
around York and Harrogate, and also Central London, can also be viewed
on this website).

Prices range from £295 per week for **2 people** up to £1090 **for 10**.

For short break details, see the website. All prices include linen and fuel,
and most include towels. Telephone 01845 597614.

York map 3/69
York Lakeside Lodges

We love the fact that you are just two
miles here from the historic heart of
ancient York but seemingly in the
country. It's a well planned, tranquil
place, in which fourteen Scandinavian
timber lodges stand (with a high
degree of privacy) on the fringes of a
large lake jumping with coarse fish.
The fishing is one of the charms of

Perhaps 'the best of both worlds': handy for central York, but feeling very rural.

the place: another is its location, with coaches going to the York centre
every ten minutes, and a nearby 24-hour Tesco's. Four lodges are **'Visit
Britain' Five Stars** (very private, with fine views): two with one bedroom, one with two bedrooms and one with three bedrooms; the others
are **Four Stars**. Winner of a Yorkshire White Rose Award for tourism,
and equipped to high standards, all are well insulated and double glazed:
good for autumn and winter breaks. Options include one, two and three
bedroom detached lodges, one bedroom semi-detached lodges, and one
and three bedroom cottages at the rear of the owners' house. **Sleep 2 to 7**.
Cost: £205 to £710 (and an admirable £98 for a two-night break in winter). Dogs welcome. Brochure from Mr Manasir, York Lakeside Lodges,
Moor Lane, York YO24 2QU. Telephone 01904 702346. Fax 701631.
www.yorklakesidelodges.co.uk email: neil@yorklakesidelodges.co.uk

Burnt Yates (Nidderdale), near Harrogate
Dinmore Cottages

We have stayed in the smallest of these three cottages, tucked away close to the owners' house at the end of a neatly maintained private lane. Each (even that smallest one) is spacious and well-cared-for, with many excellent details such as wood burning stoves, tidy flower borders, attractive pictures and old prints, and always-useful Ordnance Survey maps. Plus peace, quiet and privacy with-

Many years in the guide, never anything but praise. Well off a main road, but conveniently located, these are excellent.

out isolation. Converted from 17th century farm buildings in the landscaped grounds of the owners' fine country house, they are handy for exploring the whole of North Yorkshire and its historic towns, houses, gardens, and abbeys.

Sleep 2 to 5. 'Visit Britain' Four Stars. One is popular with disabled visitors. Linen included. TVs, videos, microwaves. Not suitable for dogs. Cost: about £240 to £580; short breaks from £150. Major credit cards accepted. Details from Alan Bottomley, Dinmore House, Burnt Yates, Harrogate, North Yorkshire HG3 3ET. Telephone/fax 01423 770860.

www.dinmore-cottages.co.uk
email: aib@dinmore-cottages.freeserve.co.uk

Brompton-by-Sawdon, nr Scarborough
Headon Farm Cottages

We get a buzz from following the no-through-road to this group of cottages, much loved by our readers. Converted from 19th century farm buildings round a courtyard, Headon Farm Cottages (**map 3/76**) are handy for Scarborough and the Moors. *Byre* for example has a kitchen/diner and lounge/diner with plush sofa and chairs, from which open stairs lead

Big bathrooms, good beds, lots of books and pictures. Horse-riding a speciality...

up to a double and a twin bedroom with cot. *Barn* is similar, also with patio doors to the courtyard from the kitchen. *Stables* has space, a beamed lounge, an open staircase off the hall leading to a light landing, a double overlooking the courtyard, a large beamed twin. *Farm House Cottages* have beamed lounge/diner/kitchen (open fire if desired), a double, a twin and a bathroom. All **sleep 4**, plus Z-bed on request in Byre and Stables. Well-behaved dogs welcome: two per cottage. Short breaks from £80. TV/video. Linen and towels provided. Cost: about £190 to £400. Details: Clive and Denise Proctor, Headon Farm Cottages, Wydale, Brompton-by-Sawdon, North Yorkshire YO13 9DG. Telephone 01723 859019.

www.headonholidaycottages.co.uk email: headonfarm@supanet.com

Glaisdale Head, near Whitby
Wheelhouse

What an exquisite location! We've seen some places in our time, but this one really stays in the memory. We visited in 2004 and after a leisurely tea on the terrace could hardly tear ourselves away. Within a small hamlet in the lee of Glaisdale Moor and Egton High Moor, this charming cottage has stunning views across the head of the valley and to the escarpments of the moors above. But it's not remote: Whitby is just 12

This is a marvellously well situated cottage, with exceptionally kind and welcoming owners living next door...

miles away, Pickering 15. Close by is a station on the ultra-scenic railway line which runs to Whitby. Within the North York Moors National Park, the cottage has its spacious sitting room and kitchen upstairs (microwave and washing machine) to take advantage of those views. There is a multi-fuel stove in the sitting room. Downstairs are two double bedrooms (one has a four-foot bed) and one single, plus a large bathroom. There is a terraced patio garden and parking for two cars. **Sleeps 5.** Small dogs are welcome by arrangement. Heating, linen and towels included.

Cost: about £250 to £375. Details from Colin or Mary Douglass, The Wheelhouse, Glaisdale, Whitby YO21 2QA. Telephone 01947 897450.

Whitby and Sleights map 3/98
White Rose Holiday Cottages

New last year in the historic, lively town of Whitby were the *Harbourside Apartments*, conveniently situated on Whitehall Landing. There are also apartments (**just for 2**) close to the swing bridge. Both locations are ideal for shops, pubs and the beach. *Garden Studio*, close to the park, **sleeps 2**. Less than three miles from busy Whitby, the village of Sleights is ideally situated for 'coast and country'. Within the village – one of our own favourites in this part of Yorkshire – 'White Rose' have three

All three courtyard cottages are nicely maintained and very comfortable...the owners really do 'aim to please', and the number of return visits is extremely high.

cottages in a courtyard known as Garbutts Yard; there are two bungalows and, new for 2006, a smart dormer bungalow. All the properties are kept to a very high standard, and are **'Visit Britain' Three/Four Stars.** TVs. Weekend breaks. Linen and towels included. Cost: about £250 to £1250. Details/brochure from June and Ian Roberts, Greenacres, 5 Brook Park, Sleights, near Whitby YO21 1RT. Telephone 01947 810763.

www.whiterosecottages.co.uk email: enquiries@whiterosecottages.co.uk.

Beadlam, nr Helmsley
Townend Cottage

A much-loved cottage from which to explore the North York Moors and beyond.

During its *21 years* in our guide, this charmer of a cottage has been consistently popular with readers. A wing of the owner's 18th century farmhouse, conveniently just off the main road that runs through the village, it stands on the edge of the North York Moors and is less than an hour from Scarborough and York. The cottage is comfortable and full of character, and with its Baxi open fire, notably cosy in winter or during those worthwhile autumn breaks. There are good beds, a fine kitchen and bathroom, and all is tastefully decorated and furnished, with double glazing, and gas fired central heating. Some internal stone walls are a feature, and there are oak beams to add character. We like the wide staircase and the big main bedroom.

'Visit Britain' Four Stars. TV/Video/DVD/CD. **Sleeps 4**. Cost: about £190 to £350. Dogs and other pets are welcome. Details from Mrs Margaret Begg, Townend Farmhouse, Beadlam, Nawton, York YO62 7SY. Telephone 01439 770103.

www.visityorkshire.com   email: margaret.begg@ukgateway.net

'In Brief'...

At **Easingwold, near York**, *Tudor House* is within walking distance of the often unfairly overlooked but actually very attractive centre of this partly Georgian town. A Grade II listed building, Tudor House usefully **sleeps up to 8,** and makes a good jumping-off point from which to explore much of the best of North Yorkshire, and is a pleasant cross-country jaunt from Castle Howard...

Also in **Easingwold**, *Orchard Cottage* (yes, it does overlook an orchard!) has two sitting rooms, though it only **sleeps 4**. It is a light and bright conversion of a former granary, set well back from the road and with the advantage of a big garden...

Details from Blakes Country Cottages, Spring Mill, Earby, Barnoldswick BB94 0AA. To book: 0870 192 1022. Brochures: 0870 241 7970.

Live search and book: www.blakes-cottages06.co.uk

Harrogate, The Dales and around
Harrogate Holiday Cottages*

We like staying in Harrogate. Lively and attractive in its own right, the famous town has the advantage of easy access to much of the best of Yorkshire: York itself, the North York Moors, the Dales and even the coast.

From extremely comfortable apartments in the town centre to cosy cottages in the heart of the Yorkshire Dales, this agency – which we have known for several years – makes genuine efforts to 'match the client with the property'.

Among places readers have recommended or we have seen are *Crimple Head Mews*, in the country village of Beckwithshaw but just a five minute drive from Harrogate, with a four poster bed and the use of a hard tennis court (**sleeps 5**).

In the town centre of Harrogate there are swish apartments with iron bedsteads and stainless steel kitchens ideal for the businessman and holidaymaker alike, as well as more traditional properties and some handsome Edwardian houses.

The company also operates beyond Harrogate, in and near such places as historic Knaresborough – known for its castle and Mother Shipton's Cave – in which several properties are offered overlooking the lovely River Nidd and Gorge. There are also places at Bedale and Ripon and in surrounding pretty villages such as Bishop Monkton.

There are several properties in Nidderdale, an 'Area of Outstanding Natural Beauty', and in the pretty Dales village of Darley, one of Yorkshire's 'best kept' villages.

About half the properties on the organisation's books accept pets, and several encourage short breaks.

Further details of any of these and an extremely stylish brochure are available from Harrogate Holiday Cottages, Crimple Head House, Beckwithshaw, Harrogate, North Yorkshire HG3 1QU. Telephone 01423 523333. Fax 526683.

www.harrogateholidays.co.uk

email: bookings@harrogateholidays.co.uk

This handsome family house, just ten minutes' drive from Harrogate, welcomes pets, and sleep up to seven people...

The original milkmaids would not recognise this one-time milking parlour, sleeping just two people...

Ebberston (near Scarborough)
Cliff House

We are full of admiration for the immense energy and style with which Simon Morris has turned Cliff House's properties into some of *the very best in Yorkshire*. The four acres of land, with the walled garden, an amazing pyramid-shaped treehouse, the secret wooded gardens and the trout pool, are a source of fascination. (Youngsters love the toddlers' play area and the animals.) There is a covered, heated pool with a jacuzzi, a hard tennis court and a big games room with table tennis, pool, and darts.

Cliff House stands conveniently on the A170 – though in several cottages you'd hardly know the road is there – and is only about ten miles inland from Scarborough, with the North York Moors on the doorstep.

Lilac **sleeps 4** in a downstairs twin with en-suite toilet and handbasin, and a first floor double room. There's a downstairs kitchen/diner with open fire; upstairs lounge with garden views, and bathroom. *Maple* with its own small courtyard, **sleeping 6** and suitable for people of limited mobility, has a downstairs en-suite twin, as well as two first floor bedrooms and bathroom. *Beech* (**sleeping 5**) has a downstairs twin room and bathroom, kitchen/diner and lounge with big picture windows enjoying excellent views, a single and a double room upstairs. *Pine* and *Willow* (**sleep 4**) are

A fine arrangement of houses, handy for the moors and the seaside.

There's a high standard of furnishing, comfort, and attention to detail.

'upside down' cottages with bathroom, toilet and two bedrooms on the ground floor; beamed lounge/diner/kitchen (with open fire) taking advantage of first floor views. *Holly* **sleeps 6** in a double and two twins, and is quietly situated near the gardens. Its lounge has an open fire and picture windows; there is a dishwasher. *Apple* (**sleeps 2**) is converted from the laundry and apple store of Cliff House and has a beamed lounge and kitchen/diner, with double bedroom – overlooking gardens and apple trees – and bathroom upstairs. *Pear* also **sleeps 2** (**plus 1** in a pulldown bed) and we found it altogether individual and charming, light and interesting. A beamed kitchen/diner leads to the lounge and on into a beamed double bedroom with high sloping ceiling, overlooking the gardens.

'Visit Britain' Four Stars. TVs and videos. Dishwashers in Holly, Beach, Maple and Lilac. Linen, towels, heating included. 'Sorry, no pets.' Cost: £215 to £975. Brochure from Simon Morris, Cliff House, Ebberston, near Scarborough, North Yorkshire YO13 9PA. Tel 01723 859440. Fax 850005.

email: cliffhouseebberston@btinternet.com
www.cliffhouse-cottageholidays.co.uk

Scarborough/Scalby
Wrea Head Country Cottages

These skilfully converted farmhouses have been a favourite among readers of this guide for many years, *and we have never had a complaint.*

At the end of a quiet lane, only a short drive from Scarborough (you can see its ruined castle on the headland), the cottages are exceptionally well placed for enjoying both seaside and countryside.

The mainly south-facing, well cared-for properties have been national winners of the then ETC's "England for Excellence" Award for Self-

Children love to stay here, and to get to know the horses and the teddy bears!

A fine pool, sauna and jacuzzi bring something special to these cottages.

Catering Holiday of the Year. They were also *three time* winners of the 'White Rose Award' as the Yorkshire Tourist Board's Self-Catering Cottages of the Year.

There are nine in all, of differing sizes, with well-tended gardens. Most have sea views. On the edge of the North York Moors National Park, only an hour from York, this is an ideal location to explore villages and market towns, the Heritage Coast and neighbouring forest drives. There's a sauna and an indoor heated pool with a jacuzzi at one end. This sends small waves down the pool to the delight of young children, who also have their own Teddy Bears Cottage, a two-storey wooden playhouse complete with Father Bear, Mother Bear and Baby Bear upstairs in bed and its own fenced garden and picnic area. Older children will enjoy the unusually well-equipped adventure playground.

Hay Barn Cottage (**sleeps 8**) particularly impressed us with its clever design whereby sitting room, dining room and kitchen are separate but linked. There are well-chosen fabrics throughout (bedrooms in particular with their pretty duvets, curtains and table lamps are charming). Kitchens are modern, mostly with dishwashers, and overhead beams add character. All have TVs and DVDs, full gas central heating and **Four 'Visit Britain' Stars**. Ample parking, laundry room, library (DVDs, books and games); telephone and barbecues are available. No pets, no smoking. Open all year. Cost: from £265 to £1460 (includes indoor pool, gas and electricity, linen and towels). Good value special breaks in winter, ie four nights for the price of three.

Further details from Steve and Sue Marshall, Wrea Head House, Barmoor Lane, Scalby, Scarborough, North Yorkshire YO13 0PG. Telephone Scarborough 01723 375844. Fax 352743.

www.wreahead.co.uk   email: ghcg@wreahead.co.uk

69

Wrelton, near Pickering
Beech Farm Cottages

These are winners in every sense. Their quality is reflected in the fact that they have won the (then) English Tourism Council's prestigious 'England for Excellence' award and, in 2002, *for the fourth time*, the Yorkshire Tourist Board's 'Self-Catering Holiday of the Year' award.

In a quiet village on the edge of the North York Moors, the cottages are ideally situated for the many attractions of North Yorkshire – moors, dales, forests, coastal walks, abbeys, castles, historic buildings, seaside resorts, steam railway across moors, historic York, market towns and small villages.

The cottages are in a peaceful and pretty courtyard opening on to fields. This is effectively a hamlet in its own right in which every house is a haven of comfort.

There is a good range of accommodation to choose from. The six larger cottages are rated **Five Stars** by **'Visit Britain'**, the highest quality rating possible. *Beech Royd* and *Tanglewood* both **sleep 4**. *Columbine* and *Bracken Brow* **sleep 6**. For larger groups *The Farmhouse* (a listed building) and *Shepherd's Lodge* both **sleep 10**. They are well equipped, including dishwashers, videos and digital TV. There are also two charming little detached **Four Star** cottages, *Fat Hen* and *Dove Tree,* that **sleep 2 or 3**.

There is an excellent indoor pool and sauna. Children love the play area, the animals (including two 'lovable' llamas) and the paddock. Included are electricity, gas (the cottages have gas central heating and double glazing and are cosy for winter), linen, towels, and the use of the swimming pool.

Effectively a hamlet in its own right, in which every house is a haven of comfort.

The accommodation is great, and the indoor swimming pool is a huge bonus.

Guests can be certain of a warm welcome, and appreciate personal touches, such as fresh flowers and a home-made cake on arrival. We've met the owners, who take pride in ensuring everything is just right.

Open all year, with short breaks outside the school holidays. Details from Pat and Rooney Massara, Beech Farm, Wrelton, Pickering, North Yorkshire YO18 8PG. Telephone 01751 476612, fax 475032.

www.beechfarm.com
email: holiday@beechfarm.com

Ruswarp, near Whitby
Danby and Goathland Cottages

Much as we like Whitby, we prefer at the end of the day to leave the holiday crowds to their own devices. Our preference when visiting this resort that's both a working fishing port and a traditional family resort is to go inland a bit. Ruswarp (pronounced 'Russup') fits the bill anyway as it is a charming place in its own right, close to the pretty River Esk, popular on holiday weekends for its miniature railway and for boating but never overrun, and well placed for excursions into the North York Moors.

Better yet, this enclave of stone-built, handsomely tiled cottages is well away from the road and quite private. From the gardens there are moorland views (to reach the cottages you climb for about two hundred yards, past a handy golf course).

These are reasonably priced, very well situated and popular cottages...

...with especially spacious sitting rooms just made for happy family holidays.

Known as Heron Cottages, most of the little group are holiday homes, but private and nicely self contained, with a children's play area and attractive field and woodland surroundings. *Danby* and *Goathland* are adjacent, and are similar inside. We revisited recently, remembering how impressed we'd been on our first visit by the roominess of the cottages: each has a spacious open plan sitting room giving on to a back garden that can be a late-afternoon sun trap.

We noticed comfortable sofas, round dining tables, big and deep cupboards, an attractive combination of stone and exposed beams, well fitted kitchens, books and board games. Danby **sleeps 6** in two doubles and one single/bunk bedded room, Goathland **sleeps 5** in a double, a twin and a single.

TVs. Linen but not towels included. Not suitable for dogs or other pets. Cost: about £270 to £500. Weekend breaks.

Details from Mr and Mrs Greendale, Pond Farm, Brantingham, East Yorkshire HU15 1QG. Telephone 01482 666966. Or from Mr and Mrs Holgate, Nunthorpe, Godmans Lane, Kirk-Ella HU10 7NX. Telephone 01482 654917.

paul.greendale@genesisIT.co.uk
www.heronholidaycottages.co.uk

Robin Hood's Bay
Farsyde Farm Cottages

Superbly located on Yorkshire's spectacular 'Heritage Coast', these cottages are close to the much loved old
fishing village of Robin Hood's Bay,
one of the most attractive places in
North Yorkshire. (Whitby's just six
miles away.) You can walk to the village and beach in a few minutes. The
beach is partly sand, with rock pools.
Mistal Cottage, where we've stayed,

*There are marvellous views, and the
ambiance is much appreciated by readers.*

is outstanding, and deserves its **Four 'Visit Britain' Stars**. **Sleeping 4**
(non-smokers, please), it has a large living room with marvellous views.
The small indoor swimming pool (in a log cabin) is for the private use of
Mistal occupants, and Farsyde's fine horses are for guests to ride. The
four smaller, **Three Star** Mews cottages look over shared gardens
towards the moors. There's a skilful use of space. Gardens have patios,
and lawns with garden furniture. This is a farm with *real animals (*large
and small*)*, including Paddington, the Newfoundland. Short breaks available October to June. Cost: about £170 to £620. Details/brochure from
Victor and Angela Green, Farsyde House, Robin Hood's Bay, Whitby,
North Yorkshire YO22 4UG. Telephone 01947 880249. Fax 880877.

www.farsydefarmcottages.co.uk email: farsydestud@talk21.com

Draughton, near Skipton   map 3/93
Grange Farm Cottages

In quiet but not remote Draughton,
these attractive cottages, which we
saw in 2005, were created from a
former farmhouse, and are rare
examples of 'traditional cottages':
cosy, more 'old world charm' than
designer-converted. They have beautiful views across the valley to
Bolton Abbey, with its ruined priory
and woodland walks. Within twelve

Large groups can rent all the cottages...

miles are Haworth, the steam trains of the Yorkshire Dales Railway and
Worth Valley Railway, and the Pennine Way. *Delph House* has a stone-
flagged kitchen floor, many exposed beams, a woodburner and a four
poster bed. **Sleeps 10** in three doubles and two twins. *Garden Cottage*
sleeps 4 in two bedrooms, one with a four poster and one twin. *Grange
Farm House* **sleeps 6** in two doubles and a twin; it, like both the others,
enjoys original features such as beams and a stone-flagged floor.

Refs B5065/ND52/ND51. Details from Blakes Country Cottages, Spring
Mill, Earby, Barnoldswick BB94 0AA. To book: 0870 192 1022.
Brochures: 0870 241 7970.

Live search and book: www.blakes-cottages.co.uk

Kettlewell
Fold Farm Cottages

Kettlewell is one of the most sought-after villages in Yorkshire, and at its heart, superbly well situated, this is a quartet of traditional, quiet, thick-stone-walled, warm and comfortable cottages next to the friendly and hospitable owners' farm. We revisited in 2005, and found everything 'just

Right in the heart of the village, with the big advantage of private off-road parking.

right'. Not surprisingly the level of repeat visitors is exceptionally high. We have met several, revelling in the well cared for interiors, the deep carpets, the good quality lined curtains, the books, the table lamps, the antique or 'country' furniture. Beds are excellent, and original features have been retained. The location is super for exploring the Yorkshire Dales National Park, with Malham Cove and Tarn and Great Whernside nearby. **Sleep 2 to 4**. **'Visit Britain' Four Stars**. TV. Linen and towels provided. Dishwashers in all but *Buttercup*.

Small dogs are welcome by arrangement, but one cottage is totally pet and smoking free, and smoking is discouraged in all the others. Private off-road parking. Cost: approximately £180 to £440. Details from Mrs B Lambert, Fold Farm, Kettlewell, near Skipton, North Yorkshire BD23 5RH. Telephone 01756 760886.

www.foldfarm.co.uk   email: info@foldfarm.co.uk

Settle   map 3/117
The Folly

We'd been longing to see this locally famous place, and we did so in the autumn of 2005. At the heart of the Yorkshire Dales, in the middle of famous Settle, The Folly has the distinction (*very* rare among holiday cottages) of being Grade I listed. Built in

A rarity: a Grade I listed holiday property.

1679, part of it now belongs to a building preservation trust, and houses a local museum. The entire ground floor of the North Range has been painstakingly restored and makes an absolutely top-drawer holiday apartment **for 2** (with a **Five Star 'Visit Britain'** grading). It is so steeped in history that guests step back in time as well as into style and comfort. A splendid virtual tour of the interior (at **www.the-folly.co.uk**) brings the whole place alive, whereby one can appreciate the balance between 21st century comfort and the preservation of original features. Settle is a gem. It's also the start of the Settle-Carlisle railway.

Note: the owners will pick up guests who arrive by train in their gleaming maroon-coloured 1914 Model T Ford!

Details from **www.the-folly.co.uk**

Buckden, near Skipton
Dalegarth and The Ghyll Cottages

One of our longest-serving inspectors chose to spend a family holiday at
The Ghyll in 2005 – an accolade in itself. She was delighted by the place,
and especially by one of its most-loved features. For at the rear of the trio
of cottages, dropping down at a steep angle, is as pretty a bubbling beck
as you'll ever see in the Yorkshire Dales. Because of the way the land lies
and the situation of the cottages, this feels almost like a private enclave.

Featured by us *without a break since 1983*, both the Dalegarth and The
Ghyll properties have **Four 'Visit Britain' Stars**, the latter Disabled
Category 2. Better yet, we weren't surprised Buckden were runners up in
2004 in the Yorkshire Tourist Board's White Rose Award for self catering
excellence. This tribute came from a reader a couple of years ago: '(It
is)...the best self catering we have rented by far...a high standard of fit-

*A neat cluster of purpose-built traditionally styled houses with superb facilities. The
warm, covered pool, and the adjacent solarium, are irresistible, and the whole place is
surrounded by the unspoilt beauty of Upper Wharfedale.*

tings and furnishings, extremely well maintained by the owner on site, for
whom nothing is too much trouble...We are visiting in October for the
sixth time...'

Lonely roads that go deep into wild country are pleasant enough for the
tourist, but when such roads combine scenic beauty with ease of access it
is twice as nice! The B6160, which runs from near Skipton, through
Upper Wharfedale, to the heart of the Dales, is one of those roads.

A few yards off it, on the south side of the small village of Buckden, in
what was once the kitchen garden of a great house nearby, *Dalegarth* consists of a neat cluster of eleven purpose built, traditionally styled stone
houses grouped around a dog-leg cul-de-sac. They are modern, neat and
tidy, and fit very attractively into the landscape.

During a recent visit we met regular visitors relaxing in their spacious sitting rooms (all are on the first floor) and enjoying woodland and hill
views – this is fine walking and touring country. Serious walkers used to
aching limbs should note that seven of the cottages (there are two types)
have small sauna rooms.

The cottages, which are **ideal for 4 but can sleep 6** (two bedrooms, plus
bed-settee in lounge), have excellent bathrooms, state-of-the-art kitchens
and large, most comfortably furnished lounges with TV and natural stone
fireplaces. They are classified as 'type A' and 'type B' and are identical
except that 'type A' have a sauna in the bathroom, breakfast bar in the

kitchen, patio-style windows leading out on to a balcony from the lounge and an en suite shower, toilet and vanity unit in the master bedroom.

Dalegarth has an impressive indoor swimming pool, plus a solarium and games/exercise room and an exceptionally attractive terrace to sit on after your swim and admire the scenery. Also, there is a full linen service and a well-equipped laundry room that incorporates a large communal freezer.

David and Susan Lusted live in one of the houses and keep these warmly carpeted, superbly-equipped properties clean and efficiently run.

The three *Ghyll Cottages* were designed specifically for those with mobility problems. Built in natural stone, set in secluded landscaped grounds to the rear of the village of Buckden, in a quiet, sunny location, they share the leisure amenities of Dalegarth, less than two hundred yards away.

Each of the cottages has a covered loggia leading to an entrance porch which opens into a large lounge/dining room, off which is a fully-fitted and extremely well-equipped kitchen, including microwave, dishwasher

The Ghyll represents a considerable investment in thought and comfort. It enjoys a regular following.

View of The Ghyll's garden: how could you resist a ramble in the hills? Even on a Bank Holiday you can easily escape.

etc. A double bedroom, thoughtfully provided with versatile 'zip link' beds, a spacious ensuite bathroom with spa bath, walk-in shower, etc, completes the downstairs, with another double bedroom and bathroom upstairs (one cottage has two upstairs bedrooms). The south-facing lounges offer direct access to sunny patios and every property has remote control TV and audio centre, video and video library, central heating and a full linen service. Main bedrooms have TV and radio. Wheelchair-bound people staying there have told us that The Ghyll has it 'just right' and could not be faulted for the facilities.

The Lusteds have a policy of welcoming inspection during changeover periods. No dogs at The Ghyll (except guide dogs) but a small dog at Dalegarth is possible by arrangement. Some cottages are 'non-smoking'. Cost: about £378 to £620. Special winter mini-breaks. Details and colour leaflet from Mr and Mrs D Lusted, 2 Dalegarth, Buckden, near Skipton, North Yorkshire BD23 5JU. Telephone/fax 01756 760877.

Disabled readers should note that some while ago The Ghyll Cottages were chosen as national winners by the Holiday Care Service, at the World Travel Exhibition in Earls Court, London.

www.dalegarth.co.uk
email: info@dalegarth.co.uk

Reeth and Healaugh
Swaledale Cottages

Featured every year in this guide since it was first published in 1983, these cottages make a splendid base from which to explore the still miraculously unspoilt Yorkshire Dales. They are just a 20 minute drive from one of our favourite towns in the north of England – Richmond.

Two properties – *Thiernswood Cottage* and *The Bothy* – are within the wooded grounds of Thiernswood Hall, which is, delightfully, approached by a tree-lined drive a third of a mile long. With an open fire in the sitting room, Thiernswood Cottage is a really inviting place 'to come home to' after, say, walking in the Dales. It is deceptively spacious, with a well equipped kitchen, dining room and cosy sitting room with open fire, two charmingly co-ordinated bedrooms – one double, the other twin bedded, both with en-suite bathroom. **Sleeps 4**. Cost: about £208 to £492.

The Bothy is tucked away, and is **ideal for 2** – indeed, for honeymooners! It is a charming conversion of tack rooms above the old stone stable block of Thiernswood Hall, and, being out of sight of the big house, especially private. There are splendid rural views from the sitting room. Cost: £170 to £342.

Linen and towels are included in Thiernswood Cottage and The Bothy; with heating included in Thiernswood Cottage from the end of October to the end of April.

In the village of Healaugh is a four bedroomed listed cottage called *Swale View*. Once the village inn, with many old features retained, it has an open fire in the sitting room. The main bedroom has a four poster double bed and ensuite bathroom. **Sleeps 6**. Cost: about £251 to £562.

Swale View used to be the village pub, and retains several original features, including – our favourite! – an open fire.

Thiernswood Cottage is 'deceptively spacious' and also has an open fire. It fits prettily into its wooded suroundings.

Short breaks in all cottages, £135 to £195. A dog is welcome in Swale View. All have gardens, off-road parking and great views. **'Visit Britain' Four Stars**. Details from Mrs J T Hughes, Thiernswood Hall, Healaugh, Richmond, North Yorkshire DL11 6UJ. Telephone 01748 884526.

www.swaledale-cottages.co.uk
email: thiernswood@talk21.com

Sedbusk, Bainbridge, Hawes, West Burton
Clematis, Well, Shepherd's and Fell View Cottages

Our readers have really taken to *Shepherd's Cottage*, **sleeping 6**, a feather in the cap of Anne Fawcett, whose old stone built cottages are all in picture-postcard locations. We've had so many compliments over the years, especially about this spacious Grade II listed stone cottage, about a mile from Hawes. Built in 1633, it's notable for its original mullioned windows and cosy farmhouse kitchen. There are three character bedrooms –

Clematis has inspiring views, and is a house of great character and history.

two doubles and a twin. *Clematis*, perched on a bank in the sleepy hamlet of Sedbusk, enjoys spectacular views. It has big rooms – notably the welcoming sitting room. **Sleeps up to 7**. In West Burton, 17th century *Well Cottage* **sleeps 4** (a twin and a double), with a pretty walled garden. Overlooking the green in attractive Bainbridge, *Fell View* **sleeps up to 6** in two doubles and a single. It has an open fire and an Aga. Each cottage is **'Visit Britain' Four Stars**. Linen/towels included. Central heating/electricity included. Dogs welcome. Cost: about £175 to £675. Details: Anne Fawcett, Mile House Farm, Hawes in Wensleydale, North Yorkshire DL8 3PT. Telephone 01969 667481. Fax 667425.

www.wensleydale.uk.com

email: milehousefarm@hotmail.com

Snape, near Bedale   map 3//105
The Undercroft (Snape Castle)

You'd hardly believe you're just 20 minutes' drive from the busy A1 as you approach the tranquil parkland which adjoins the village of Snape. The most imposing building by far is Grade I listed Snape Castle (*re*-built between 1420 and 1450!), whose most famous one-time resident, Catherine Parr, was to become Henry VIII's last wife. Providing a rare chance to stay (in 21st century comfort!) surrounded by so much history,

Cleverly combining history and comfort.

The Undercroft is a beauty: spacious, thoughtfully lit, lovingly restored, warm (there's a wood stove, plus underfloor heating) and altogether inviting. We especially liked the deep sofas, the super, separate big shower and the neat stone stairway up to the small twin room, and noted that the good-sized downstairs double makes the property accessible to people with limited mobility. **Sleeps 4**. No smoking, no pets.

For contact details, see the Stately Holiday Homes feature on Pages 22–23.

Rathmell, near Settle
Layhead Farm Cottages

Perhaps the most memorable thing among many delights of this informal grouping of cottages at the end of a private lane off a quiet, unclassified country road (though it's by no means remote) is the 'peace, perfect peace'. Also notable are the spaciousness of the cottages, the considerable comfort and the good degree of privacy.

Readers have spoken of a 'really friendly welcome' at these old stone barns, converted to create cosy, comfortable, spacious, well equipped cottages, in which original oak beams and exposed stonework have been retained. On the site there is a games room with pool and table tennis, and a children's adventure playground. Also, there are plenty of walks following tracks and lanes on the farm straight from the cottage doors.

Marshfield **sleeps 6** in three bedrooms, including an innovative galleried master bedroom overlooking the open plan lounge. *Cobblestones* and *Craggs Barn* both **sleep 5** in one double plus a single bed, and one twin-bedded room. A bed settee can add **an extra 2**. *Mickelden*, the newest property on the scene, is actually two separate apartments **sleeping up to 6** and **up to 5**. But they can be taken together to accommodate **up to 11**.

The 18th century traditional *Farmhouse*, also **sleeping 10** in five bedrooms, has been carefully renovated to provide comfortable accommodation for larger groups of family or friends. Additionally there is *The Stables*, **sleeping 6** in one double and one twin, both en-suite (with a chair bed in each). This doubles for bed and breakfast, cooked in your own kitchen and using local produce.

With uninterrupted views over farmland, guests are well placed to explore this interesting part of the Yorkshire Dales. The well preserved market town of Settle is only three miles away, and there is superb walking and caving. Slightly further afield is Skipton, and the Lake District is within striking distance.

A wide range of home cooked frozen meals, jams, and free range eggs are available for purchase. All cottages are **'Visit Britain' Four Stars**. Pets are welcome by arrangement. Cost: from £250 to £795. Details/colour brochure from Rosemary Hyslop, Field House, Rathmell, Settle, North Yorkshire BD24 0LA. Or see the outstandingly good website. Telephone 01729 840234. Fax 940775.

www.layhead.co.uk email: rosehyslop@layhead.co.uk

We really like this arrangement of well cared for, warm and cosy cottages...

...not only for its own sake but also for the quiet but handy-for-touring location.

Stanbury, near Keighley
Sarah's Cottage

This was a real find for us: modestly priced, very comfortable, located in a most interesting and attractive part of West Yorkshire – a really worthwhile find on a bright, breezy day. It has easy access to invigorating country walks, and among much else the Keighley and Worth Valley (Steam) Railway, the Brontë Parsonage at Haworth. There is a well planned small garden, with a bird feeder that

Very modestly priced and lovingly cared-for by the owner – who lives next door.

attracts 'all sorts' and a garden seat from which to enjoy the view, an exceptionally comfortable deep-carpeted ambience, absolute cleanliness. We especially liked the table lamps, the main bedroom with its picture windows, the neat kitchen/diner. There is a small second bedroom with adult-sized bunks and an upstairs bathroom with a power-shower over the bath. There is also a garage. Not surprisingly, this is **'Visit Britain' Four Stars**. One well behaved dog is possible. Television and video. Linen and towels included. Cost: about £130 to £260. Further details from Brian Fuller, Emmanuel Farm, 101 Stanbury, Keighley, West Yorkshire BD22 0HA. Telephone 01535 643015.

email: brian.fuller2@btinternet.com

Luddenden Foot, near Hebden Bridge
Stanbury, near Haworth   map 3/101/108

It was a reader who'd attended a wedding locally who first recommended these to us. Semi-detached *Greystones Farm Cottage* is at Luddenden Foot, near Hebden Bridge. Adjoining the owner's house, it is just half a mile from a pub, has good views, a wood-burning stove, and a bathroom with a bath *and* a separate shower. **Sleeps 4.** Ref 13082. *Lower Height Cottage* is a thought-fully converted 400-year-old barn a

Greystones Farm Cottage is a good base from which to explore West Yorkshire.

short walk from one of the most celebrated places in West Yorkshire – Top Withens Barn, described in 'Wuthering Heights'. Delightfully access is via a moorland track, and there are memorable views. **Sleeps 2** in a twin. Ref 80015.

Details from Country Holidays, Spring Mill, Earby, Barnoldswick, Lancashire BB94 0AA. For bookings, telephone 0870 192 1040; brochure line 0870 607 8514.

Live search and book: www.country-holidays.co.uk

Derbyshire
Peak Cottages*

The quality of the properties on this agency's books impresses us greatly: nothing is mediocre. Recommended new places on their books that we'll want to see include, for example, *Clematis Cottage*, at Baslow, and a charming conversion at Uppertown, near Bonsall, called *Brocliffe Cottage*.

Next spring we'll look at the 'delightful' one-bedroom properties in rural surroundings at Biggin Grange (on the edge of Wolfescote Dale): *Cheese Press Cottage*, *The Old Farrowings* and *Courtyard Creamery*.

Ashford Barns are, for example, in an ideal location in the heart of the Peak District National Park, in a rural spot but in walking distance of three popular villages (Ashford in the Water, Little and Great Longstone). A short walk takes one into Monsal Dale, where fishing permits are available. This is a high-quality two and three bedroom conversion with en suite bathrooms and internal links for when both properties are taken together. A further barn here provides accommodation all on one level.

Dealing almost exclusively in Derbyshire, this organisation has a reputation for offering top quality cottages, and has recently celebrated its tenth anniversary. Its well-thought-out brochure is outstanding. It gives full details of each property together with **'Visit Britain'** star ratings and use-

Mulberry Cottage (not featured) is in Barlow, and has super views.

Taddington Barns: 'character accommodation, with a heated indoor swimming pool'.

ful information such as the distances to the nearest grocery shop, post office and railway station.

There are about 175 cottages altogether, ranging from converted barns to spacious country houses. Such as *Reuben's Roost*, *Bremen's Barn* and *Hopes Hideaway*, which have top-quality accommodation. You can also enjoy rural tranquillity at *Rewlach Chapel*, Reepsmoor, near Longnor. In addition, *Taddington Barns* have recently been completed to provide character accommodation in rural surroundings, with the added advantage of a heated indoor swimming pool. Cost: about £125 to £1000.

The Peak District is good 'short break' country (lots to see and do, easy to 'get away from it all') and a wide range of Peak Cottages properties offers short breaks.

Details/brochures: Colin MacQueen, Peak Cottages, Strawberry Lee Lane, Totley Bents, Sheffield S17 3BA. Tel 0114 262 0777. Fax 0114 262 0666. For information about on-line booking, a range of photos and details of the availability of the agency's 180 or so properties:

www. peakcottages.com   email: enquiries@peakcottages.com

Great Hucklow, near Castleton
The Hayloft

Just finding this charmer was a pleasure in itself. We drove through countryside criss-crossed by dry stone walls and set off by cloud-scudding skies, then turned off the A623 towards an attractive stone-built farm. The first floor conversion provides comfortable accom-modation (on one side, it overlooks the tidy farmyard and the valley beyond, on the other, higher and wilder country: every room here has a good view). There is a pleasant, good sized sitting room with open fire, well chosen rugs on a polished wood floor, a comfortable deep sofa, a grandfather clock and other antique pieces. The kitchen/diner is well

At the end of a no-through-road, walkers will love this.

appointed, the bathroom is spacious and warm, and there are two twin rooms. The owners' pretty and safely enclosed garden is freely available to guests.

TV. **Sleeps 4**. **Four 'Visit Britain' Stars.** Linen and towels. Dogs wel-come. Cost: £140 to £357. Details from Mrs M Darley, Stanley House Farm, Great Hucklow, Derbyshire SK17 8RL. Telephone 01298 871044.

email: margot.darley1@btinternet.com

Hartington   map 3/122
Hartington Cottages

The village of Hartington is one of the most sought-after in the Peak District: pubs, tea-shops, antique shops, excellent walking from the village centre. Also at its heart are three outstanding cottages. One, the inspiring *Knowl Cottage*, overlooks the village and is reckoned to be between 500 and 700 years old. It

Knowl Cottage – a Peak District gem...

has that magical combination – lots of original features (such as a part of the original cruck beams) and a powerful sense of history, plus masses of 21st century comfort. Combining both elements is an open fire in a hand-some inglenook fireplace. Not surprisingly, the cottage (**sleeping 6**, with three ensuites) has **Five 'Visit Britain' Stars**. The other two cottages here, *Manifold* and *Dove*, side by side, are tucked away in a private little enclave just behind Knowl. Expensively converted from an old barn, they each have **Four Stars**. Dove **sleeps 2**, Manifold **2 'plus 1'**.

Details from Patrick and Frances Skemp, Cotterill Farm, Liffs Road, Biggin-by-Hartington, Buxton SK17 0DJ. Telephone 01298 84447.

www.hartingtoncottages.co.uk
email: patrick@hartingtoncottages.co.uk

81

Cressbrook, near Bakewell
Cressbrook Hall Cottages

On a bright recent autumn day we travelled through dramatic and craggy scenery close to the very heart of the Peak District National Park to revisit Cressbrook Hall, half hidden away in glorious parkland. Here, *Hall Cottage* and *Garden Cottage* (each **sleeps 4 'plus 1'**, with the option of a reserve twin room) are private and self contained. We have always liked the cottages 200

We really like the comparatively little known location, a very good touring base.

yards away – especially the spectacular view of the Wye Valley enjoyed by *Lower Lodge, Rubicon Retreat* and the adjacent *Hidesaway*. **Sleeping 6**, this is suitable for wheelchairs. *Carriage Cottage* **sleeps 8/9**. Two bathrooms. Wheelchair-user-friendly. Well behaved dogs are welcome. Recently added are *High Spy* and *Top Spot*, adjacent, **sleeping 11** in five ensuite doubles and an ensuite single, all on the ground floor.

B and B available in The Hall. TVs. Linen included. Cost: £115 to £895. Details: Mrs Hull-Bailey, Cressbrook Hall, Cressbrook, near Buxton. Telephone 01298 871289; fax 871845. Freephone 0800 358 3003.

www.cressbrookhall.co.uk   **email: stay@cressbrookhall.co.uk**

Offcote, near Ashbourne
Offcote Grange Cottage Holidays   map 3/121

Here are two quite exceptional properties. Close to the edge of the Peak District National Park, each **sleeps up to 14** (plus two cots). And both have received the huge accolade of **Five Stars** from **'Visit Britain'**. But these are details that don't convey their no-expense-spared style and their huge appeal. *Hillside Croft* is a handsome stone-built Grade II listed country house in six acres. Dating from 1709,

Hillside Croft is an outstanding house.

on three floors, it has two log burners, impressive ancient oak beams, a magnificent kitchen, dining room and sitting room, and wide, shallow stairs that will suit the elderly and children. *Billy's Bothy* is a super brick-built conversion in peaceful pastureland. Among many good things it has oak floors, underfloor heating in the ensuite bathrooms and brass and cast-iron beds, an exceptional farmhouse kitchen. And late in 2006 it will even boast a sauna and small gym. Not suitable for pets, no smoking. Quality catering can be arranged. Details from Pat and Chris Walker, Offcote Grange, Offcote, Derbyshire DE6 1JQ. Telephone 01335 344795 Fax 348358.

www.offcotegrange.com
email: enquiries@offcotegrange.com

Darwin Lake, near Matlock
Darwin Lake Cottages

Only about ten minutes' drive from Matlock, in a secluded location by a lake and within a peaceful forest setting, this is a group of extremely comfortable, spacious properties of permanent home standard. We have recently met readers who'd enjoyed a family reunion here, for Darwin Lake lends itself very well to large-group bookings. But there is flexibil-

We have stayed in one of these spacious, expensively appointed properties.

ity too, and along with the large three bedroomed detached cottages there is also a terrace of two-bedroomed cottages. Most bedrooms in each of the cottages are ensuite, decor is pristine, kitchen-diners 'have everything'. Pedestrian walkways allow for a good degree of contact with the lake, of which the holiday cottages have superb views. Videos/TVs/CD-players. Linen, towels and electricity are included. Dogs are accepted in two of the cottages. **'Visit Britain' Four Stars**. Cost: about £270 to £995; short breaks usually available. Open all year. Details/brochures from Nikki Manning, Darwin Lake, The Lodge, Jaggers Lane, Darley Moor, near Matlock, Derbyshire DE4 5LH. Telephone/fax 01629 735859.
www.darwinlake.co.uk
email: enquiries@darwinlake.co.uk

Bamford (Hope Valley, near Bakewell)
Shatton Hall Farm Cottages   map 3/128

Since we first featured it, about 20 years ago, we've thought of Shatton Hall Farm as a haven of peace and tranquillity. A mile from the main road, up a well surfaced lane, it is memorable for way-marked walks through woodland. *Orchard Cottage* and *The Hayloft*, recent barn conversions, are next door to each other, have beamed living rooms furnished

In this guide for many years, and lots of very enthusiastic reports from readers...

in old pine, and cosy coal-effect gas fires. *Paddock Cottage*, down the yard and with a wood burning stove, is the perfect winter retreat, for a short break or longer. A well behaved dog is allowed there, as there is a fenced car park to this cottage. All the cottages **sleep 4** in two double bedrooms (one is a twin room) plus sofa-beds in Orchard and Hayloft. Recently renewed kitchens and bathrooms helped these thoughtfully planned cottages to achieve a **'Visit Britain' Four Star** rating. Cost: £275 to £450. Open all year. Details: Mrs Angela Kellie, Shatton Hall Farm, Bamford, Hope Valley S33 0BG. Telephone 01433 620635. Fax 620689.
www.peakfarmholidays.co.uk
email: ahk@peakfarmholidays.co.uk

Knockerdown (Carsington), near Ashbourne
Knockerdown Farm Cottages

We like the way this arrangement of former farm buildings, several with panoramic views, is geared to families. For example, two units (*Bruns* and *Sabinhay*) interconnect to provide extra-large accommodation.

During our most recent revisit we looked at the newly available *Farwell*, usefully **sleeping 6 'plus 2'** – the 2 in a comfortable and private ground floor bedroom. It is spacious, uncluttered, expensively fitted out: well recommended. And we've stayed in *Middleton*, a neat two storeyed cottage with a twin and a double bedroom and a good use of the available space.

Our main purpose was to visit nearby Chatsworth House and Haddon Hall, but we discovered what a useful touring base Knockerdown makes for other places, with the Dales on the doorstep. Carsington Water (all kinds of water sports, and cycle trails) is a few minutes away on foot. There are the eerie caverns of the High Peak to visit – in one, you can even take an underground boat trip – and Alton Towers.

Guests appreciate the excellent indoor, warm pool and leisure centre. It's a pleasant place to make new friends, but also quiet and private. There is an exceptional adventure playground, and three acres for children to romp in.

We have stayed here ourselves, and appreciated the tidy, unfussy interiors...

...as well as the excellent swimming pool: it was very warm on a chilly autumn day.

All the cottages, from one that **sleeps 2** to two that **sleep 10**, with fourteen others in between, **sleeping 4** plus cot **and 6** plus cot, are quite private. We noticed plain white walls, oak beams, pine fittings, good quality carpets, some exposed interior stone walls. Nearly all the cottages have an open plan arrangement of sitting room, dining room and kitchen. We applaud the 'instant heat' convector heater/storage radiators.

Videos, TVs. Video library. All linen and towels are included. No dogs. **'Visit Britain' Three/Four Stars**. Cost (including electricity): about £288 to £1849 weekly, with short breaks usually available (open all year) from about £196.

Further details and a good brochure can be obtained from Tina Lomas, Knockerdown Farm, near Ashbourne, Derbyshire DE6 1NQ. Telephone/fax 01629 540525.

www.derbyshireholidaycottages.co.uk
email: info@knockerdown-cottages.co.uk

Eyam/Hope
Dalehead Court

The news from the ownership of these excellent properties (in two separate locations) is that a rather special small property became available at Hope in the late spring of 2005. **Sleeping just 2** in a 'super king size' double convertible to twins, it has been done to **Five Star** specifications, and, usefully for people with limited

Derbyshire has great appeal, and all these superbly maintained cottages make a fine base.

mobility, is all on one level. Also at Hope are *Stables*, **sleeping 2**, and *Granary* and *The Lime Loft*. Each **sleeping 4**, they are by a tumbling river and private and pleasantly 'cottagey', though with a degree of spaciousness not always associated with cottages.

A private courtyard in the heart of Eyam, one of the most historic Derbyshire villages, with ample private parking, is the location of one of the two cottage-groups in the same ownership. All three at Eyam are finished expensively, with style. *Pinfold Barn*, **sleeping 6**, is an 'upside-down' house with an inviting first floor sitting room, three cosy bedrooms, a stunning 'undersea' bathroom, a separate shower and the main bedroom en-suite. *The Captain's House*, **sleeping '4 plus 1'**, is a Victorian beauty, with a big sitting room, surround-sound cinema TV and a twin and a king-sized double bedroom. Attractive, stylish *Pinner Cottage* **sleeps 2**, also in a king-sized bed. **'Visit Britain' Four and Five Stars**. Dogs welcome in Pinner.

Cost: about £190 to £440. Linen and towels available (free for two-week stays). Details from Mr and Mrs D Neary, Laneside Farm, Hope, Derbyshire S33 6RR. Telephone 01433 620214.

www.peakdistrictholidaycottages.com email: laneside@lineone.net

---

Biggin-by-Hartington (High Peak)
Cotterill Farm Holiday Cottages map 3/134

This is a focal point within the most impressive part of the Peak District, and it is always a pleasure to turn off a road, well away from traffic, on to a long private farm drive to see these three skilful conversions. *Dale View* is an 'upside down' cottage to take advantage of the views (it has a shower, not a bath), and the more conventional *Liff's Cottage* enjoys views of Liff's Hill, two miles away. Each **sleeps 4** in a double and a twin. *The Dairy* is a **2-person** property of great charm, its one (double) bedroom within a gallery overlooking a big living room. A wood-burner is a feature, and there is a spacious bathroom. All are **'Visit Britain' Four Stars**. *The Milking Parlour* **sleeps 3**, and is on the ground floor, without steps.

Linen, electricity and heating are included. Non-smoking. 'Sorry, no pets'. Cost: about £220 to £450, depending on which cottage and when. Details from Frances Skemp, Cotterill Farm, Biggin-by-Hartington, Buxton SK17 0DJ. Telephone 01298 84447.

www.cotterillfarm.co.uk email: enquiries@cotterillfarm.co.uk

Chinley, near Buxton
Cherry Tree Cottage/The Old House

In the course of their 24 years in this guide we've never had anything but wholehearted praise from readers both for owners Pam and Nic Broadhurst and for their properties. It's a marvellous record.

Their two cottages are full of comfort and character, with great attention to detail. *Cherry Tree Cottage* **sleeps 6**. It overlooks the children's picturebook farmyard (little ones can feed the ducks and hens, and older ones are welcome to play more or less at will on the farm). We remember Cherry Tree's big dining room, and readers have written to say: 'The cottage was perfect – we felt at home and relaxed the moment we stepped through the door' and 'so sad to be leaving such great accommodation'.

There's an open fire (plus central heating throughout), fresh flowers, rugs, comfy armchairs and sofas, oak beams, antiques, lots of nooks and crannies, good paintings, excellent views, children's games and toys, comfortable bedrooms. The kitchen (with most attractive tiling) has a dishwasher and microwave. These are probably the best equipped farm-based cottages we know, with shaver points, electric blankets, rotary whisks, coffee filter machines, barbecues.

The more recent property is a historic and intriguing cottage dating from abut 1560, **sleeping 2** and appropriately called *The Old House*. You descend most cosily from a bedroom with a five foot double bed and inspiring views of the Blackbrook Valley, into a lower-level sitting room with antique oak furniture and inglenook fireplace with log burner.

Cherry Tree (on the right) quickly became a firm favourite among our readers, being extremely well equipped, cosy and comfortable.

The Old House is full of history, a most unusual property for just 2 people, who'll love (as we did) the antique oak and the inglenook fireplace with its log burner.

Situated as they are in the Peak District National Park (but only a mile from the village), the cottages make a fine base from which to explore the area. It is, by the way, easy to get here by train.

Both are **'Visit Britain' Four Stars**. Cost: about £230 to £600. Dogs are welcome. TVs/videos.

Further details from Mrs Broadhurst, Cote Bank Farm, Buxworth, via Whaley Bridge, High Peak, Derbyshire SK23 7NP. Telephone/fax 01663 750566.

www.cotebank.co.uk   email: cotebank@btinternet.com

Northumberland and Durham

Although the busy A1 trunk road offers tantalising glimpses of the Northumberland coast, with an occasional distant sight of possibly the best beaches in England, drivers rushing through should try to get further inland to experience the county at its best. This most northerly of all the English counties embraces a wide variety of countryside, much of it impressively 'wild and woolly' and some world-class castles: Alnwick, Warkworth, Lindisfarne, Dunstanburgh and Bamburgh. And if you venture into the Cheviot Hills, which beautifully straddle the English-Scottish border, you can be virtually alone except for curlews and skylarks even on an August Bank Holiday. Much further south, we are especially fond of the Tyne Valleys (North and South), and the Roman Wall country. That is well trodden, but little known are the beautiful windswept moors that characterise the three-way border between Northumberland and Durham and Northumberland and Cumbria. County Durham is in fact one of 'England's best kept secrets', not just for its deep, dark green river valleys, its stone villages set off so effectively by flowers, but its great castles (Barnard Castle is very impressive, as is the nearby Bowes Museum) and the historic city of Durham – a castle and a great, sombre cathedral. And one of the best family days out in the north of England is the Beamish Open Air Museum – full of nostalgia for mums and dads, full of things to amuse and educate children.

Greenhead (Hadrian's Wall)
Holmhead Cottage   map 3/136

You could hardly find somewhere closer to the Roman Wall to stay in than this. (To avoid the crowds, you could visit early or late.) Adjoining the owners' home-cum-guest house, single-storeyed Holmhead Cottage has an open plan sitting room/kitchen/dining room, a twin and a double bedroom, all on the ground floor. There's central heating from the adjacent house (adjusted as required), electricity inclusive, hi-fi and CD player, washing machine, dishwasher, microwave, TV, video. All linen and towels. Private walled garden. Shops, swimming, tennis, riding just three miles away; a pub, a bus stop and a cafe are just half a mile away in the village. Golf is just 500 yards away. Short breaks. Non-smokers only. Not suitable for dogs. Payphone. Note: the Roman Wall visitor centres are open all year: the cottage owner is an expert on the subject. Cost: about £259 to £398. Details from Pauline Staff, Holmhead Guest House, on Thirlwall Castle Farm, Hadrian's Wall, Greenhead-in-Northumberland, via Brampton CA8 7HY. Telephone/fax 016977 47402.

Ideally placed for exploring 'the Wall', and very comfortable in its own right.

www.holmhead.com
email: via website

Wycliffe, near Barnard Castle
Boot and Shoe Cottage

We like this very much. With the dark waters of the Tees flowing just feet from the cottage (trout fishing by arrangement), and access via a private lane along the river, the cottage – once used by a cobbler – is idyllic. With the considerate owners living next door, you won't feel isolated, but can unwind in privacy. Among features we approve of: deep sofas, an open fire, old beams, some antique furniture. There is a safely enclosed front garden, and French windows lead out to the back garden and a barbecue area, with steps down to the river bank. TV. Not suitable for dogs (but kennels on site). Linen, towels, coal, logs provided. Welcome hamper, frozen meals to order. **'Visit Britain' Four Stars. Sleeps 4** (but, with one 2'6" bed, just three adults), plus an optional double **for an extra 2**. Cost: £190 to £380. Short breaks from £190. Details/brochure from Rachel Peat, Waterside Cottage, Wycliffe, Barnard Castle, Co Durham DL12 9TR. Telephone 01833 627200.

An especially warm, inviting sitting room, and a delightful location...

www.bootandshoecottage.co.uk email: info@bootandshoecottage.co.uk

---

In brief...

County Durham can seem like the poor relation when seen against glorious, romantic Northumberland, but it has its moments. We're big fans of the three-way meeting of counties (that is, Durham, Cumbria and Northumberland) close to the rather windswept, ancient, hillside town of Alston, just inside the Cumbrian border. Along the South Tyne Valley, near Haltwhistle – nothing to do with the railway that links Carlisle and Newcastle, and which used to be the starting off point of a branch line to Alston – we love the self catering and B and B at *Bastle House*, Slaggyford, and, closer to Haltwhistle itself, the neat cottages at Common House Farm (details of the above from 01438 869489, or from **frank@cottageguide.demon.co.uk**.

In County Durham, in a good position from which to fan out and explore the South Tyne and the Roman Wall country, as well as much of the best of this 'Cinderella' of a county, *The Stables* and *The Byre* at Wolsingham, near Tow Law, are on a working farm but cosy and comfortable – we know and recommend them.
Telephone 01388 527248.

**www.greenwellfarm.co.uk
email: greenwell@farming.co.uk**

Akeld, near Wooler
Akeld Manor and Cottages

One of our readers wrote to say she'd not expected to find a place quite so comfortable and with such extensive facilities on the edge of the 'wild and woolly' Cheviot Hills – some of the least known stretches of wild countryside in England. Better still, some of the finest and least-crowded beaches in Britain are little more than half an hour's drive away.

The 'great comfort' involves interiors five-star hotels would be proud of, with deep carpets, subtle lighting that can add so much to the ambiance of holiday cottages, solid, handsome beds (five-feet wide in some cases), expensive fabrics, excellent insulation, last-word kitchens.

These are eight very sympathetic conversions of one-time farm buildings within 36 acres of the Northumbria National Park, and each one feels private and self contained. They range from a one bedroomed cottage **sleeping just 2, plus baby**, to four cottages that **sleep 4** and three that **sleep 6** (one of those actually **4 'plus 2'**). All have baths, and almost all have shower too.

We visited early on a Sunday evening and admired an indoor leisure centre being much appreciated by families who had been out and about during the day: a warm and inviting pool (which we could happily have plunged into after a day on the road), an antique full-sized snooker table (which might also have side-tracked us), a gym, solarium and games room.

Very sympathetic conversions, with sumptuously comfortable interiors...

...plus an up to the minute indoor leisure centre that is a huge attraction in itself.

To complement the excellent accommodation and leisure facilities, there is a tremendous selection of home made meals for guests who occasionally tire of self catering. Quality and prices are exceptional.

There is huge demand among readers of this guide for larger properties, and the splendid *Akeld Manor* can certainly oblige. For the main house of the original estate, **sleeping up to 15**, is a real showpiece. We have too little space to detail all its charms, but there is for example a games room with pool table, a five-foot four poster in one bedroom, a private walled garden, two open fires. Short breaks. Not suitable for pets. Resident on-site staff. Linen included but not towels. Cost: about £269 to £891. Akeld Manor about £924 to £2109. Details from Pat and Sian Allan, Shoreston Hall, Shoreston, Seahouses, Northumberland NE68 7SX. Telephone 01665 721035. Fax 720951.

www.borderrose-holidays.co.uk   email: allan.group@virgin.net.co.uk

Harehope Hall, near Alnwick
Cresswell Wing/Sawmill

Deep in rolling farmland, with views of the Cheviot Hills, Harehope Hall is an imposing mansion, and guests in *The Cresswell Wing* (it is on three floors) have a substantial part of it to themselves, so anyone who appreciates high ceilings, big windows and easy-going, traditional comfort will love it. We like the spacious drawing

Pleasant accommodation, a fine estate...

room with its deep sofas, the open fire (lit when we last called), the big bedrooms – including two atticky ones that would suit children – the 'country antiques'. **Sleeps 8** in two twins and two doubles. (Extra beds available, if needed, plus cot.) Central heating. Most recently available is *Riverview*, **sleeping 6**, adjacent to *Sawmill Cottage*, on a corner of the estate. **Sleeps 4**. These are splendid: better yet, they can be booked together by large groups. They are indeed next to a working sawmill. Linen/towels included. Dogs *and horses* welcome. Note: a speciality here are carriage driving/riding holidays, using the lanes of the estate (but bring your own horses/carriages!). TV. Cost: about £200 to £550. More details from Alison Wrangham, Harehope Hall, Harehope, near Alnwick, Northumberland NE66 2DP. Telephone 01668 217329.

email: john@wrangham.co.uk

Shilbottle, near Alnwick
'Shilbottle'   map 3/142

This arrangement of properties is one that our readers seem to love, not least because glorious sandy beaches and historic Alnwick are only three miles away. We've long admired the all-inclusive facilities: the gymnasium, indoor pool, sauna, steam room, sunshower, tennis-court, games room, adventure play-ground, cricket and golf nets, sports

Featured in this guide for over 20 years.

field and coarse fishing. Riding lessons and hacks are available at Town Foot, with beauty therapists to pamper one. There's a 17th century farm-house **sleeping 12** with five bath/shower rooms, three-bedroom chalets with en-suite facilities and open plan living/dining rooms, cosy cottages, and a flat **sleeping 2**. All have full central heating and wood-burners. Some are smoke- and pet-free.

'Visit Britain' Three to Five Stars. TV/DVD/video. Dogs are welcome by arrangement. All linen, electricity, logs and gas included. Cost £135 to £1580. Details from Mrs C M Stoker, Town Foot Farm, Shilbottle, Alnwick, Northumberland NE66 2HG. Telephone/fax 01665 575591.

www.villagefarmcottages.co.uk   email: crissy@villagefarmcottages.co.uk

Alnmouth, Bamburgh and around
Northumbria Coast and Country Properties*

There's one cottage on their books that seems to us to sum up the appeal of this agency, which we know from our correspondence has introduced so many readers to the special magic that is Northumberland.

Sandpiper is at the heart of the little known but most appealing seaside village of Low-Newton-by-the-Sea, close to a charming and unpretentious pub, and just yards from the water's edge. **Sleeping 6**, it is a listed 18th century, one-time fisherman's cottage of character, with a log-burning stove. Dogs are welcome.

At High-Newton-by-the-Sea, *Snook Point* is an extremely comfortable single-storeyed house with sea views. Among others by the coast, there are several properties in famous Bamburgh (best known for its castle and its sandy beach), all of whose sitting room windows face the North Sea. And there are cottages of great character in Seahouses, Beadnell, Embleton and Craster.

This hugely respected agency covers one of the three or four most scenically impressive corners of England, and is based in pretty, unspoilt Alnmouth. We visited three of the cottages in the village itself: all three a delight! If you should book either of the two old 'smugglers' cottages' in Victoria Place (one is almost *on* the beach) or tucked away *Estuary View* (on three floors), you are in for a treat.

We like the atmosphere of old railways and especially old railway stations, and the agency has a real winner on its books. This is – yes – *The Old Station House*, at Low Akeld, near Wooler. It has been superbly preserved and restored and **sleeps 8/9**.

The brochure for the agency's 200-or-so properties carries a colour photo of each. As well as such highly rural but not remote cottages mentioned above, they include town properties in famous and handsome Alnwick and several in Warkworth (as with Alnwick, the town embraces one of northern England's most famous castles). Another example is the *Old Lifeboat Cottage*, **sleeping just 2**, right on the waterfront and shoreline of the River Tweed estuary at Berwick-upon-Tweed. An amazing location.

Details from Northumbria Coast and Country Cottages, Carpenters Court, Riverbank Road, Alnmouth, near Alnwick, Northumberland. Telephone Alnmouth 01665 830783/830902. Fax 830071.

www.northumbria-cottages.co.uk email: cottages@nccc.demon.co.uk

Glebe House, Bamburgh (not featured) is part of a handsome old vicarage. Sleeps 8.

Estuary View – and yes, the view from the house is as good as you'd hope!

91

Bamburgh, near Belford/Holy Island
Outchester and Ross Farm Cottages

With **Four 'Visit Britain' Stars** apiece, these make stylish and very comfortable holiday homes from which to explore the spectacular Northumberland coast. At *Outchester Manor* there are eight superb properties. We're not surprised they were recent winners in the 'Pride of Northumbria' awards! **Sleep from 2 to 6**. At Ross, there are cottages both in the peaceful hamlet and down the

Everything is stylish and full of character.

lane to the sea. Spacious *Sandpiper* and *Oystercatcher* have charming sitting rooms. Each **sleeps 4 to 6,** but can combine to **sleep 12**. Newly available next door is *Skylark*. Also **sleeps 4 to 6**. Along the sea lane, *West Coastguard Cottage* has a cosy, smallish sitting room, a separate dining room, great upstairs views. *East Coastguard Cottage* is similar (each **sleeps 2 to 4**). *Coastguard Lodge,* **sleeping 2 to 5**, is a gem: a neat garden, a fine sitting room, an expensive kitchen. Outchester cottages cost about £225 to £670, the Ross cottages about £260 to £670. Not suitable for pets. Linen/towels included. Details/brochure: Mrs J B Sutherland, Ross Farm, Belford, Northumberland NE70 7EN. Telephone 01668 213336. Fax 219385.

www.rosscottages.co.uk email: enquiry@rosscottages.co.uk

Rothbury map 3/140
The Pele Tower

High above Rothbury, though on account of trees out of sight of the town, this is a two-storeyed cottage of great character (some cottage – it is a 19th century extension to the original tower), lovingly cared for by owner David Malia, who lives in 'the big house' next door. Full of history

This is a Five Star beauty, with a kind, painstaking and dedicated owner...

and 21st century comfort, the Grade II* listed, 14th century pele tower really is 'something special'. There are stone flags in the excellent modern kitchen, every labour saving device imaginable, video and digital satellite TV. CD/tape hi-fi, 'Play Station 2' entertainment system, a woodstove, extra TVs in bedrooms, teasmade, whirlpool bath and shower, mountain bikes and more. Unsurprisingly it has been shortlisted in the 'England for Excellence' awards and is a former 'Winner of the Lionheart Award: Most Popular Self Catering Accommodation'.

Sleeps 4 in a double room and a twin room. **'Visit Britain' Five Stars**. Unsuitable for pets or smokers. Cost: about £250 to £640. Details from David Malia, The Pele Tower, Whitton, Rothbury, Northumberland NE65 7RL. Telephone 01669 620410. Fax 621006.

www.thepeletower.com email: info@thepeletower.com

Bowsden, near Bamburgh/Holy Island
The Old Smithy

Though it's in a very peaceful rural location, it's only five miles from the exceptional Northumberland coast (don't miss Holy Island). When we first called however at this very inviting detached cottage conversion, tucked away but not isolated, we met a couple happy to stay put: the woodburner was warming the cottage, and they were ensconced in the welcoming kitchen/diner. Adjacent to that is a cosy sitting room (a former smithy) with a deep sofa/armchairs, attractive stripped pine, rugs, books, well chosen pictures, and other stylish things. This room overlooks the south facing *Warm and very well planned.*
walled garden and the Cheviots. We liked the skilful conversion, with two bedrooms downstairs and one upstairs, the bathroom with shower, a loo on each floor, the central heating that's complemented by the woodburner. This is a traditional farm: natural calf rearing, summer-grass-fed lambs, free range chickens. **Sleeps 6**, plus cot. TV. Dogs welcome. Cost: £220 to £530. Details from John and Mary Barber, Brackenside, Bowsden, Berwick-on-Tweed, Northumberland TD15 2TQ. Telephone 01289 388293.

www.brackenside.co.uk
email: john.barber@virgin.net

Mindrum, near Cornhill-on-Tweed   map 3/150
Briar Cottage

This is only just inside Northumberland, so close to Scotland that you can almost hear bagpipes and see mating haggis. It's a well-cared-for cottage in very pleasant countryside. We've stayed, and remember such details as a log and coal fire lit ahead of our arrival. There are good-sized rooms: from the front window of one *Consistently popular with our readers...*
we watched cattle on the hills. Used from time to time by the owners, and thus with all the essentials, the cottage has a twin and a double, a good sized bathroom with shower. Small front garden. Large enclosed lawned gardens to side and rear, including a paddock with picnic bench. Private parking. The area is good for touring, with Scotland and the Cheviots so close, and the coast half an hour away. Dogs welcome. TV/video/DVD. Linen, fuel, oil central heating, electricity included. Cost: £210 to £425.

Details from Northumbria Coast and Country Cottages, Carpenters Court, Riverbank Road, Alnmouth, Northumberland NE66 2RH. Telephone 01665 830783/830902. Fax 830071.

www.northumbriacottages.co.uk   email: cottages@nccc.demon.co.uk

Beal, near Holy Island
West Lodge/The Stables/The Coach House/Bee Cottage

We think we'd put Holy Island second to the Roman Wall among our Northumberland 'must-sees'. So the location of *Bee Cottage* (**sleeping 4**) is all the more amazing: it has a memorable panoramic view from most rooms of Holy Island, accessible via the causeway at low tide. Close to the owners' farmhouse, it has a nicely lit sitting room with a log stove, a modern kitchen, a smart bathroom, a double and a twin. On a grander scale,

Everything here is aimed at the highest standards. See Colour section A, Page 2.

West Lodge, Stables and *The Coach House* (**sleeping respectively up to 8, 6 and 9 people**, are recent additions to the Nesbitts' 'family' of cottages. They are beauties: masses of space, grand sitting rooms, sumptuous bedrooms, super ultra-modern kitchens. You'll not get lost, as West Lodge, Stables and Coachhouse are in fairly close proximity to the A1. TVs. Dogs welcome. **'Visit Britain' Four/Five Stars**. Linen/towels provided. Cost: £270 to £1200. Details from Jackie Nesbitt, Bee Hill Properties, Beal, near Holy Island, Berwick-on-Tweed, Northumberland TD15 2PB. Telephone 01289 381102. Fax 381418.

www.beehill.co.uk   email: info@beehill.co.uk

Belford, near Holy Island   map 3/156
Bluebell Farm Cottages

The large village of Belford, once a stage-coach stop between York and Edinburgh, is full of history and low-key charm. Tucked away off one of the roads leading out of the village, we discovered this enclave of six stone and pantiled farm-building conversions. Neatly within what is effectively a hamlet in its own right, and **sleeping from 2 to 6**, each is *admirably spacious*, with big windows, lots of light and a good degree

We really liked these unpretentious cottages, and their convenient location. Single travellers, by the way, are 'very welcome' here...

of privacy. We noted deep sofas and armchairs, patios with picnic-benches and access to barbecues, in the case of *Farne*, *Lindisfarne* and *St Abbs*, backing on to a little burn. (There is a caravan park in the same ownership, out of sight of the cottages, though there is a shared reception office.)

TVs. Linen, towels, gas central heating and electricity included. Short breaks available. Pets by prior arrangement. Cost: about £160 to £450. Details from Phyl Carruthers, Bluebell Farm Cottages, Belford, Northumberland NE70 7QE. Telephone 01668 213362 or 0770 333 5430.

email: phyl.carruthers@virgin.net

Scotland

We're not averse to sailing round the Greek islands, but we'd say that on a sunny autumn day Scotland's Inner Hebrides could be the most beautiful place in Europe. Just for starters: the ever-changing colours of the Cuillin Hills on Skye, absolute peace and quiet on half inhabited islands, an old-fashioned courtesy and integrity among most people one meets. Readers describe idyllic cottages from where they have explored lochs, glens and burns, mountains, forests and off-shore islands. The north-east of the country has one of the greatest collections of castles in the world, and you can follow a 'whisky trail' to some well-known distilleries. World-famous too are some of the golf courses, such as the Open Championship course at Carnoustie, and the course at St Andrews. For skiers, Glenshee and Aviemore are Scotland's main resorts, but we would say the mountains and hills are even more impressive in spring, summer and autumn. We are keen on the strange 'lunar landscapes' of the wild country to the north of Lochinver, on the Trossachs, and the rolling brown moors of the Border country that is thick with ancient castles and abbeys.

Stop Press: see page 18 for details of a well situated, comfortable bungalow near Melrose, called Drumblair, and sleeping 4.

Duns   map 4/154
Duns Castle Cottages

A reader from Reading who stayed here in 2004 said 'It was magical!' And certainly, the idea of staying within or in the grounds of castles appeals greatly. Each property here has its own character, is very private but benefits greatly from the situation – either close to the grand Gothic-fantasy of a castle or on a slightly more distant corner of the

A super base for exploring the Borders, interesting in itself, and only – for example – about an hour from Edinburgh.

estate. We remember the charming *Pavilion Lodge*, a 'folly' gatehouse, a cosy nest **for 2**, with a romantic turretted bedroom reached via a winding stair, and an open fire (the only one that has an open fire, though some others have coal-effect gas fires). *St Mary's* is a rambling family house **sleeping 11** that may be joined to *Coach House* (**sleeps 3**) behind. *The White House*, **sleeping 6**, is private and comfy, *Azalea Cottage* is elegantly furnished and is located above the lake. *Carriage Mews*, **sleeping 5**, forms one wing of the attractive courtyard. Note: the seaside is only 20 minutes away, Edinburgh about 40 – an easy drive in both cases.

TVs. Linen included, towels available (extra charge). Cost: about £195 to £1180. Details from Mark Slaney, Duns Castle, Duns, Berwickshire TD11 3NW. Telephone 01361 883211; fax 882015.

www.dunscastle.co.uk
email: info@dunscastle.co.uk

The National Trust for Scotland
Holiday Accommodation Programme

We could happily devote a month to visiting some of the most mouth-watering of The National Trust for Scotland's holiday properties.

We are hoping to see a particular rarity on the glorious Isle of Skye. This is *Beaton's Croft*, a traditional croft house, internally reconstructed for the sake of comfort but with the original ambience retained. **Sleeping 2** (with – of course! – a peat fire) it is at Bornesketaig, and has fabulous views across to the Outer Hebrides.

Consider fabulously situated *Mar Lodge*, on Royal Deeside. We know the place and if we had to choose one great estate – there are over 77000 acres of it – that encapsulates the romance and beauty of mainland Scotland, this might be it. All five of the elegant apartments are graded **Four Stars** by **'Visit Britain'**, and three of them have the advantage of access via the impressive main entrance. One of them, *Bynack* is notably roomy, and **can sleep up to 15** (though it is available to smaller groups).

Most recently, during a journey through the east of Scotland, we saw the first floor apartment (**sleeping 4**) at *St Andrew's House*, built in the 17th century as an overflow for courtiers attending royal visitors to the Falkland Palace next door. It is in the heart of the attractive little town.

And between Perth and St Andrews, we found two attractive little bungalows (**sleeping 4 and 5**) in the extensive grounds of the *Hill of Tarvit* mansion, built in 1904. A spacious, elegantly furnished apartment (**sleeping 4**) with views over farmland is also available on the second floor.

We also visited Culzean Castle (pronounced 'Cullane'), a magnificent building on the Ayrshire coast, and were impressed by the spacious, high-ceilinged *Brewhouse Flat*, in the west wing, and by *Royal Artillery Cottage*, that forms part of the courtyard next to the castle. Being on the cliff edge, it has impressive sea views. Each **sleeps 4**.

One of the 'attractive little bungalows' in the grounds of the Hill of Tarvit mansion.

This is Steading Cottage, in the grounds of (and facing) Craigievar Castle.

One can also stay in the most attractive detached cottages in the grounds of picturesque Craigievar Castle. Both **sleeping 4**, *Kennels Cottage* and *Steading Cottage* are only about a hundred yards from the fabulous castle. For a copy of the irresistible brochure contact Holidays Department, The National Trust for Scotland, Wemyss House, 28 Charlotte Square, Edinburgh EH2 4ET. Telephone 0131 243 9331. Fax 0131 243 9594.

www.nts.org.uk email: holidays@nts.org.uk

Scotland-wide
Scottish Country Cottages*

Of all the glossy annual brochures that cross our desk, the one that has most often had us booking cottages for ourselves is that from Scottish Country Cottages. The combination of stunning holiday properties and glorious scenic photography that puts those properties into their geographical context is memorable.

For example, in a part of Scotland most outsiders don't know – the Ayrshire coast – *High Mains Cottage,* at Ballantrae, is an attractive traditional cottage, well modernised (but still with an open fire) with panoramic views. **Sleeping up to 6**, it has a big garden and is quietly located. A sand-and-shingle beach and a pub serving food are just a mile. Ref UPC.

There's another part of this beautiful country that's better known by Scots – especially Glaswegians! – than others, and that is 'The Trossachs'. Just

Dalvanie Mill, Glenisla, near Blairgowrie (not featured) sleeps up to six. Ref S33.

An unforgettable location, and three cosy cottages that are 'just for two'.

200 yards from the focal point that is Loch Katrine, *The Old Smiddy* is a fine property with loch views and a woodburner. **Sleeps 6**. Ref UYA.

A couple of years ago we heard from Buckinghamshire-based readers who stayed in *Macinnisfree Cottage*, on the Isle of Skye. **Sleeping 7**, this looks on to an extraordinary panorama that takes in some of western Scotland's most-loved coastal landmarks and seascapes. Ref SBC.

Any of the cottages on the Ardmaddy Estate, about twelve miles south of Oban, brings together history and fabulous views. There are four extremely well converted cottages, the biggest of which (in terms of accommodation) is *The Stables*, **sleeping 8 'plus 2'**. Ref SBZ.

One of our favourite parts of Scotland is the Kintyre peninsula, and we are very pleased to single out three extraordinary cottages, **each for 2**, once used by lighthouse keepers of the now-automated lighthouse on Davaar Island, near Campbeltown. (Refs SEE/SED/UMG.)

Just ten minutes from Edinburgh, and steeped in history, *Liberton Tower* is amazing, a 15th century castle keep that combines period features such as tapestry wall hangings, rugs on a stone floor and an open fire with modern comforts. It has spectacular views. **Sleeps 4 'plus 2'**. Ref UKH.

Details and brochures from Scottish Country Cottages, Stoney Bank, Earby, Colne, Lancashire BB94 0AA.

Booking line: 0870 192 1028. 'Dial-a-brochure': 0870 608 6519.

www.scottish-country-cottages06.co.uk

Straiton, near Maybole
Blairquhan

In the wooded valley of the Water of Girvan, with panoramic views of mountains, lochs, rolling hills and tumbling rivers, this is, simply, a beautiful place. And we've noticed over more than twenty years how the Blairquhan estate seems to appeal particularly to our sort of reader. We like the fact that there are no rules about where you may go on the estate.

McDowall is one of several charmers on this lovely estate. Note that the upstairs twin room has views of the gardens. Note also: there's a downstairs double bedroom.

Cuninghame is a fairly recent conversion, with masses of character. Stay here and you'll experience the fabulous walled garden!

We know all seven properties. *Cuninghame*, converted in 1995 from the original potting shed and bothy and situated on the wall of the glorious walled garden which was a riot of colour when we visited, has a living/dining room/kitchen with woodburner, French windows and a huge arch-to-floor window; downstairs are two twin bedrooms and bathroom; upstairs a further twin room and a spacious playroom. *McDowall*, also a former bothy and on the garden wall, has a kitchen/living room with sofa bed and a double bedroom downstairs; upstairs is a twin room overlooking the gardens. *Kennedy Cottage* forms one side of a courtyard which is part of Blairquhan Castle and has stone carvings dating to 1575. *McIntyre, Farrer* and *Wauchope* are apartments in the former coachman's house and stables; we especially liked the former, **sleeping 6**, with a large upstairs kitchen/living/dining room that has glorious views.

During 2004 Wauchope was greatly enlarged. Downstairs, it has a large living room, an adjoining dining room and kitchen, and a bathroom. (There are two divan beds in the living room.) Upstairs, there are four bedrooms with twin beds, and a second bathroom.

Bishopland Lodge, tucked away on its own, has exceptional views towards the castle and of the Girvan Valley. The peace of it struck us – not a sound except for the sheep! Throughout we noted excellent carpets and rugs, pretty drapes and duvets, attractive pictures and posters, useful bedside and standard lamps.

All have oil central heating. Prices are from around £197 in winter to £603 in summer. Details from the Blairquhan Estate Office, Straiton, Maybole KA19 7LZ. Telephone 01655 770239, fax 770278.

www.blairquhan.co.uk
email: enquiries@blairquhan.co.uk

Blairgowrie, near Pitlochry
Ardblair Castle Cottages

It's an idyllic scene. In the lea of a picture-book castle, with ginger-haired Highland cattle grazing in the grounds, the two cottages are as 'Scottish' as you will get. They are easily accessible, not uncomfortably remote, and the kind, laid-back welcome is bonus. We've had many enthusiastic reader responses over the years.

The location is one of the best possible Scottish touring bases, three minutes' drive from the 'gateway-to-the-Highlands' town of Blairgowrie, but in fine (rolling and wooded rather than bleak) rural surroundings.

The 19th century, white timbered coach house and stables that stand in the grounds of the castle have been converted by Mr and Mrs Blair Oliphant into two very well-equipped, extremely comfortable, painstakingly cared-for self-catering units. The open plan kitchen/living room, the tidy looks of the units, with their fitted neutral carpets (tiles in the bath-

An unusual example of Scottish weatherboarding, behind which is an extremely comfortable and informal base from which to explore central Scotland.

A typical sitting room at Ardblair: neat, easy-to-look-after, unfussy and yet perfectly comfortable. 'Nice to come home to' after a day's touring...

rooms and kitchens) and simple pine furnishings, all lend a certain stamp of quality. *We have never, in seventeen years, had a reader-complaint.*

Among the things people remember are good books to read, a particularly attractive set of carved dining chairs in the *Coach House* and a delightful arrangement of dining table and benches in *The Stable*. The Stable has two bathrooms and **sleeps 9** in twin and triple-bedded attic rooms with sloping ceilings and Velux windows, plus four wee ones in an adult-sized bunk-bedded ground floor room. Though if all nine were in residence space might be tight. The Coach House **sleeps 5** in a double and triple-bedded room.

Guests can enjoy the family's 800 acre farmlands, whose livestock includes the beautiful Highland cattle, geese and occasional visits from a local herd of deer. Another advantage here is the well recommended Recreation Centre in Blairgowrie.

Not suitable for dogs. Open all year (night storage heating, TV, double glazing). Cost: a *very reasonable* £230 to £395. Linen provided.

Details from Mr Blair Oliphant, Ardblair Castle, Blairgowrie, Perthshire PH10 6SA. Telephone/fax Blairgowrie 01250 873155.

Balquhidder
Rhuveag

This is one in a thousand. Overlooking Loch Voil, near the village of Balquhidder, this beautifully situated house is almost surrounded by a mass of trees, azaleas and rhododendrons. We have seen it, and would love to stay one day: used frequently by the owners themselves, it is warm and very comfortable, with log fires, a

One of our all-time favourites in Scotland, both for character and location.

Rayburn in the kitchen, and a clothes drying room, as well as central heating. Though rural and 'traditional', there is nothing primitive about the cottage: in a splendid kitchen it has a dishwasher, washing machine, ceramic hob and more. It **sleeps 8**, and has three reception rooms (one of which, with TV, can double as a bedroom). The house gets water from a burn which flows through its six acres; there is splendid walking, as well as fishing, sailing and windsurfing. You can hire boats, and even learn to water ski on Loch Earn, at the end of the glen. There is a renowned farmhouse-pub, half a mile up the road, with a superb licensed restaurant.

Dogs are welcome, but this is sheep country, and they must be well controlled. Linen and towels are not available. TV. Cost: about £350 to £475. Details from John and Vanda Pelly, Spring Hill, East Malling, Kent ME19 6JW. Telephone 01732 842204, fax 873506.

Kirkmichael, near Pitlochry   map 4/166
Balnakilly Highland Cottages/Log Cabins

Perthshire – so much more accessible than, say, the western Highlands, is hilly, green and beautiful. These cottages (unpretentious, comfy, quiet and full of character: **Colour section A, Page 3**) are on a 1500-acre estate. You could be 'miles from anywhere', but you're not in fact remote. There are four properties, one of them the traditional stone *Loch Cottage*, two of them Norwegian log cabins, the fourth a two storeyed timber building, finished to a good standard, called

Interior of Rowan, a substantial two-storey timber building that offers traditional 'cottagey comfort'...

Rowan Lodge. We have always especially liked Loch Cottage, newly refurbished in 2005, which all but opens right on to the water.

Sleeps 4, 5 or 6. There's ski-ing in the area in season, and good walking, shooting and fishing are all readily available – on the estate and elsewhere. Dogs are welcome. Linen is provided, towels are available for hire. TV. Cost: £190 to £400. Details from Mr and Mrs Reid, Balnakilly Estates, Kirkmichael, Perthshire PH10 7NB. Telephone or fax 01250 881356.

www.balnakillyestate.co.uk   email: balnakilly@hotmail.com

Ecosse Unique*

We have never, in 24 years, had a whisper of a complaint about this agency, which has about 300 properties spread all over Scotland, from the beautiful Border country to Orkney. In a sense, the organisation was a 'founder member' of *The Good Holiday Cottage Guide*!

Most properties, such as *Old Hyndhope*, **sleeping 6**, splendidly situated on a Selkirkshire hilltop, are in peaceful rural or coastal locations. Or, for stimulating city breaks, where apartments often have the edge over hotels, you could consider 17th century *Peffermill House* (**sleeping 6/7**) in Edinburgh, or one of the agency's rather elegant properties in Glasgow.

Among the many beautifully situated properties on the agency's books is Achduart, sleeping 6 and overlooking the tranquil Summer Isles. It is four miles from Achiltibuie.

Balvarran Mill borders the River Ardle near popular Pitlochry – fishing is included! This is one of a number of intriguing properties we will see for ourselves during our 2006 visit...

There are idyllic cottages in Highland Perthshire, such as *Balvarran Mill* (**sleeping 4**) near Pitlochry, near Loch Tay, and, in the hills of a private country estate near Dunkeld, the spectacularly positioned *Keeper's House* (**sleeping 6/7**).

There are also a number of excellent cottages round Loch Ness, such as *Bunloit Farmhouse* (**sleeping 5**), where the view is simply jaw-dropping.

On the ever-romantic islands of Skye, Mull and (just off the mainland near Kinlochmoidart) the privately owned Eilean Shona, there are excellent shoreline cottages (of all sizes) in locations to die for, while on the mainland there are many traditional and cosy Highland cottages set amid equally stunning scenery. Check out, for example *Bunallt Eachain* (**sleeping 6**) and *Achleek* (**sleeping 5/6**) on the shores of Loch Sunart, or *Achduart* (**sleeping 6**) which overlooks the lovely Summer Isles, off the west coast.

Do request their brochure: Ecosse Unique Ltd, Lilliesleaf, Melrose, Roxburghshire TD6 9JD. Telephone: 01835 822277. Fax 870417.

Or check their web sites:
www.unique-cottages.co.uk and **www.uniquescotland.com**
email: reservations@uniquescotland.com

Dunning, near Perth
Duncrub Holidays

One of our readers told us what an excellent focal point Duncrub makes for exploring Perthshire. She had stayed in one of the two much-admired 19th century chapel apartments, a ten minute walk from the conservation village of Dunning (it's easy to locate: only just south of the A9 trunk road). *The Tower House* (**'Visit Scotland' Five Stars**), the

Chapel House incorporates original features (as does The Tower House)...

ultimate romantic hideaway **for 2**, has an open plan kitchen/dining/sitting room on the ground floor and, via a narrow stone spiral staircase, an upper floor double bedroom (five foot bed) and bathroom. *Chapel House* (**Four Stars**) in part is modern, incorporating parts of the original chapel. It **sleeps 4** in an ensuite twin and upper floor double bedroom and bathroom. Visitors can enjoy a game of badminton and table tennis in the nave of the chapel. Linen and towels are included. TVs, videos, central heating, washer/dryers. Well behaved dogs are welcome in Chapel House. No smoking. Cost: about £320 to £550. Switch/Solo/Access/Visa/Mastercard. Details from Wilma Marshall, Duncrub Holidays Ltd, Dalreoch, Perth PH2 0QJ. Telephone 01764 684100. Fax 684633.

www.duncrub-holidays.com   email: ghc@duncrub-holidays.com

Tomich, near Cannich
Tomich Holidays   map 4/168

This is a memorable corner of the Highlands, and the group of traditional stone and slate courtyard cottages – a snug and cosy Victorian dairy and six two-storeyed timber chalets – is a delight. The cottages have memorable panoramic views (among the best in this guide) and

Even in Highland terms, a lovely place...

are **'Visit Britain' Four Stars** (the other properties are **Three Stars**). The Victorian dairy is a stone-built cottage, part of a Grade II listed building. A short stroll away, among trees, are the timber chalets, private but not remote, within 100 yards of another. Each is roomy, simple and 'practical', but comfortable, with balconies for wildlife spotting, birch trees and grassy banks. Most are booked by guests returning for 'endless walks', the cycling, the wildlife, the quiet, and the lovely indoor pool. Tomich is a beautiful stone-built place, preserved as a conservation village. Surrounded by imposing hills, it and the estate are a tourist flagship. Dogs welcome. TV/videos. **Sleep 4 to 6**. Cost: £205 to £570. Details from Tomich Holidays, Guisachan Farm, Tomich, By Beauly, Inverness-shire IV4 7LY. Telephone 01456 415332 or fax 415499.

www.tomich-holidays.co.uk   email: admin@tomich-holidays.co.uk

Aviemore
3 Dalfaber Park

With a **'Visit Scotland' Four Star** grading, this place has so much going for it, not least the all-year-round appeal of Aviemore (ski-ing, walking, golf, fishing, lots of children's activities, the Cairngorm Mountain Railway). And this well appointed newly built house is in a quiet location in walking distance of

Conveniently placed for the fast A9 and thus for travelling further afield, to Inverness and points north-west and east.

all the main attractions. **Sleeping up to 8** – three doubles and a twin – in comfort, it's spacious and uncluttered with, for example, a good sized sitting room with an open fire for which coal is supplied, and which complements the full oil-fired central heating, a stylish black leather suite, a smart dining room with doors to the garden, and one of the double bedrooms usefully on the ground floor. The first floor 'master bedroom' is ensuite. There's a garage and off-road parking. Not suitable for pets.

Linen and towels are included. Cost: from about £460 to £800 (more for Christmas/New Year). Details from Emma Cleverdon, 3 Dalfaber Park, Aviemore, Inverness PH22 1QF. Telephone 020 8900 2866. Fax 2983.

www.dalfaberpark.com
email: info@dalfaberpark.com

Lochaline (Morvern)
Shore Cottage   map 4/183

The location is quite stunning, even in Scottish terms. Even better: one of our favourite short ferry crossings in the whole of Scotland operates from close to this charming substantial property that was originally an inn (built 1846). The ferry is however infrequent, and doesn't operate particularly early or late, so disturbance

An enviable location on the Morvern shoreline, with inspiring views...

should be minimal. This is one of our favourite corners of the whole country, and we suggest that if you are visiting the Isle of Mull you contrive to take the 'long route' from Oban on one leg of the journey and this less well known five minute crossing on the other. The walking (and strolling!) is marvellous, traffic a rarity.

Specifically, the house **sleeps 6**, has a bathroom with bath and shower, an open fire and a large enclosed garden. In living here you will no longer be required to provide refreshments for passing travellers, but you will find a pub 600 yards away. Ref 16444.

Details from Country Holidays, Spring Mill, Barnoldswick, Lancashire BB94 0AA. To book: 0870 192 1040. Brochures: 0870 607 8514.

Live search and book: www.2006country-holidays.co.uk

Scotland-wide
Large Holiday Houses*

This is an extraordinary organisation, which has been a holiday and special-occasion inspiration to many readers (and others!). For example, when we turned into the Newmiln Country Estate and saw the 18th-century mansion (**sleeping 16/20**) ahead of us, we immediately realised why 'celebs' and wedding parties love taking it over. The sumptuously-furnished house, eight miles north of Perth, feels like a real home, and the 700-acre estate with tennis court and children's play-area offers complete seclusion. For those who don't want to self-cater, Elaine McFarlane, the resident owner, is happy to arrange the services of a top chef.

Newmiln is one of over a hundred impressive properties (**sleeping from 7 to 37**) spread widely over Scotland that are on the books of Large Holiday Houses, run by Wynne Bentley, who founded it in 1997. Her base, *Poyntzfield House*, a Grade A listed Georgian mansion (**sleeping 16 plus 4 under-10s**) near Inverness, is among them. She certainly offers a compelling combination: the romance of great houses and castles, marvellous locations and the huge appeal of properties where extended families or groups of friends can stay together. Several are historically important, such as the 11th-century *Dairsie Castle* (**sleeping 8/13**) in Fife, close to St Andrews, and cliff-top *Craighall Castle* (**sleeping 10**) in Perthshire.

Calgary Castle, which enjoys one of the best views on Mull, facing sandy Calgary Bay beyond meadows framed by woods, is more modern, having been built in the 18th century as a laird's house. Despite its tower and mock battlements, it has a comfortable, lived-in atmosphere.

We had a delightful stay, ten miles south of Oban, at the secluded *Bragleen House* (**sleeping 7/8**) at the end of a five-mile lane beside Loch Scammadale. The owner, who built it in 1996, ready for his retirement, has combined luxury with comfort – spacious rooms, deep sofas, double-glazing and a fitted kitchen complete with bread-maker. After a morning walk up the sleepy glen at the back, we strolled later in the day down to the loch to see a perfect sunset reflected in the still water.

Details and a copy of the brochure (one of the best we've seen) from Wynne Bentley, Large Holiday Houses Ltd, Poyntzfield House, Poyntzfield, Dingwall, Ross-shire IV7 8LX. Telephone 01381 610496. (She also has large properties in France : see Page 298.)

www.LHHScotland.com   email: LHHS@LHHScotland.com

Lickleyhead Castle, Aberdeenshire. Family owned, never a ruin, it retains much of its original medieval atmosphere. Sleeps 14.

Drumrunie House, Braemar. A great 'good four star' family house, with super gardens and stunning views. Sleeps 12.

Scotland-wide
Little Holiday Houses*

As you might expect from the people behind the splendid Large Holiday House (opposite page), their new portfolio of smaller properties includes only places of character, many of them superbly well located.

Those locations alone make this a must-send-for brochure, as the quality of much of the photography is outstanding. For example, *Woodlands* (**sleeping 10 'plus 2'**) is a roomy and very comfortable modern house that sits at the foot of the Kintail mountains and is close to Loch Duich. Well situated for keen walkers it does (of course) have an open fire!

If you appreciate fine period houses for themselves you will probably like *Lochnagarry*, at Golspie in Sutherland. **Sleeping up to 10**, it is notable for elegant, high ceilinged rooms. There is a Rayburn and an open fire.

Almost any rural property on the stunningly beautiful west coast will appeal to readers of this guide. For example, *Clachan Garden*, near Ullapool, is a top notch property in a fabulous setting, located within one of our favourite features – a walled garden.

Culkein, equally memorable and pristine, is perched on the shores of Eddrachillis Bay, north of Lochinver, and underneath magnificent and famously photogenic Suilven mountain. It has an especially inviting and stylish sitting room, with an open fire. This and Clachan Garden **sleep 9** and **7 'plus 1'** respectively.

Too often overlooked by visitors to Scotland, the peaceful, fertile Black Isle (the original of the 'black' has nothing to do with colour) is also a useful jumping-off point for seeing much of the far north. **Sleeping 6**, the *West Wing* of Poyntzfield House – see also the opposite page – is a part of the fine Georgian mansion that is normally rented out as a whole by large groups but at quieter times of the year gives smaller parties the chance to experience the splendid ambience. There's a super farmhouse kitchen, a snooker room with a *full size table,* a large grassy area for outdoor games.

Details and a copy of the brochure (one of the best we've seen) from Wynne Bentley, Little Holiday Houses Ltd, Poyntzfield House, Poyntzfield, Dingwall, Ross-shire IV7 8LX. Telephone 01381 610496.

www.LittleHolidayHouses.com
email: LHH@LHHScotland.com

Smartly on parade: handsome Clachan Garden is on the shores of Eddrachillis Bay, beneath Suilven mountain...

The School House, Glenfinnan, is on 'the 'Road to the Isles'. With a cosy woodburner, it's rather romantic. Sleeps 8.

Glen Strathfarrar, Struy, near Beauly
Culligran Cottages

These are great favourites among 'cottage guide' readers. Situated on a Highland Nature Reserve, but not really remote, and close to a salmon-rich river on a sporting estate, Frank and Juliet Spencer-Nairn have five properties. Better yet, guests have the delicious freedom of the metalled but private road leading into the hills. Four are Scandinavian chalets, quite spacious, with picture windows,

This is one of the best places in Scotland to observe wildlife in its natural habitat.

sleeping up to 7; the other is a characterful, traditional cottage with a blend of 'antiquey', solid and modern furniture – including the obligatory stag's head! It has one double and two twin bedrooms, a good fitted kitchen, and is in a superb location (well off the Beauly to Tomich road) without seeming isolated. Bikes for hire. No TV. Trout and salmon fishing in the Rivers Farrar and Glass. Guided tours of Frank's deer farm. Dogs welcome. Cost: about £169 to £469. Details from Frank and Juliet Spencer-Nairn, Culligran Cottages, Glen Strathfarrar, Struy, near Beauly, Inverness-shire IV4 7JX. Telephone/fax 01463 761285.

www.farmstay-highlands.co.uk/culligran
email: juliet@culligran.demon.co.uk

Dalcross, East Inverness
Easter Dalziel   map 4/189

This neat and tidy, notably well cared for trio of traditional, stone built cottages makes an exceptionally good base from which to explore the whole of the north, east and west of Scotland. Unpretentious but comfortably furnished, they are surrounded by a large grassy area, with a pretty heather garden to the front and panoramic views of the surrounding

Always a warm and friendly welcome, and unfussily comfortable cottages...

countryside. On a working farm with beef cattle, sheep and grain, the jewel in this particular Scottish crown is *Birch*, at one end of the three adjoining properties. It is thickly carpeted, comfortably furnished, its pale green soft furnishings and deep-pile carpets easy on the eye. There's an appealing separate dining alcove. **Sleeps 6**. *Rowan* and *Pine* (**sleeping 4 and 6**) are a little more old fashioned but comfortable, warm and cottagey. They are reasonably priced, and open all year. **'Visit Scotland' Three/Four Stars**. TV. Dogs welcome. Linen and towels included. Cost: about £135 to £430. Details from Mr and Mrs Pottie, Easter Dalziel Farm, Dalcross, Inverness IV2 7JL. Telephone and fax 01667 462213.

www.easterdalzielfarm.co.uk   email: ghcg@easterdalzielfarm.co.uk

Rural Retreats*
Newtonmore/Loch Lomond/Dumfries

Rural Retreats have virtually become a household name among holiday cottage enthusiasts. The name is associated with high standards of comfort, properties of character and highly desirable locations – which in Scotland means very highly desirable locations indeed!

We are especially fond of the little-known country north of Dumfries, where Rural Retreats have four properties on the superb green, rolling 3300 acre Crofts Estate. One of these is *Marwhirn Cottage*, **sleeping 4**, beautifully located half a mile down a private drive. It has an especially inviting, charmingly lit sitting room, with an open fire.

Among several superbly well situated properties is *Borenich*, near Pitlochry, very close to (though not quite in sight of) Loch Tummel. **Sleeping 6**, with a zip-link double bed in the main bedroom, it has an open fire and stands within an acre and a half of its own grounds.

Sitting room of Borenich, a super, detached, recently refurbished property near the popular town of Pitlochry.

Lochenkit, near Dumfries, lies on a private estate, and sleeps up to eight people in comfort and style...

In the Highland village of Newtonmore, situated in the new Cairngorm National Park and thus well placed for walking, is stone-built, detached, 100-year-old *Woodlands Cottage*, **sleeping 5/6**. This charming cottage has a woodburner in the especially handsome sitting room, a private enclosed garden and the River Spey is an easy ten minute stroll away.

Just a mile from the western shores of Loch Lomond, *The Carriage House* is a spacious, detached, Victorian stone property **sleeping 4**. Originally a coach house on a small country estate, it has been brought up to modern day standards and now boasts a very large sitting room (open fire), a second reception, a master bedroom (6ft bed) with an ensuite bathroom, and a double room (5ft bed) with ensuite shower-room.

Lochenkit is a 19th century farmhouse on a private estate. Refurbished to high standards, it **sleeps 8** in great comfort. It is on the edge of the moors, with delightful walks. There's a large farmhouse kitchen with an Aga, a sitting room with a log fire, one king-size bedroom with ensuite bathroom, one double and two twin rooms.

Details and a copy of the organisation's impressive brochure from Rural Retreats, Draycott Business Park, Draycott, Gloucestershire GL56 9JY. Telephone 01386 701177, fax 701178.

www.ruralretreats.co.uk   email: info@ruralretreats.co.uk

107

Kinlochlaggan, near Newtonmore
Ardverikie Estate Cottages

The beautiful Ardverikie Estate, rising above and around Loch Laggan, is a kind of microcosm of the extraordinary Highlands. The estate even embraces a substantial sandy beach that is just one bonus for city dwellers escaping to one of the characterful cottages tucked away in the heart of, or on the edge of, the Estate.

It's well away from any town, a real tonic for people wanting to get away from city cares, but it's not actually in the back of beyond.

We have visited and revisited all of them and found a range of sizes and different degrees of seclusion as well as different styles of interior. If you prefer family furniture to MFI and care more about seeing a deer, a hare or a pine marten while you are doing the washing up than about dishwashers and deep-pile carpets, these could be for you. All the houses except *Pinewood*, incidentally, have open fires with free firewood.

Most recently available is *Rowan Brae*, **sleeping 6** and quietly situated close to the water and good walking. We admired the special character of *Ardverikie Gate Lodge* – a listed building this, by a road, best suited to a couple plus, say, one friend or relative. The spiral stair is excellent and fine prints and a particularly good bedroom enhance its appeal further. Pinewood has an especially cosy dining room, gets lots of sun and is indeed among the trees. Not a luxury item but, we thought, welcoming and comfortable. **Sleeps 4**.

Ardverikie specialises in the larger house – near the old farmsteading, *Gallovie Farmhouse*, with a five-oven Aga, is a world away from the average estate cottage. It can **sleep up to 13**! Try it if you are looking for atmosphere, lots of rooms (including a separate TV room). There's an enclosed mature garden. *Inverpattack Lodge*, standing on its own on a hillside overlooking the road with good views, **sleeping up to 12**, has a huge family sitting room, a big dining room and farmhouse kitchen.

A real selling point of a holiday at Ardverikie is access for cottage tenants during much of the year to the many square miles of the private estate.

Gate Lodge absolutely sets the mood as you approach this memorable place...

Inverpattack sleeps twelve, with masses of space and even more 'character'.

Cost: about £393 to £1450: not expensive if you consider how many the larger properties sleep. Details from Mrs Desiree Bruce, The Estate Office, Kinlochlaggan, Inverness-shire PH20 1BX. Telephone 01528 544322.
www.ardverikie.com email: bookings@ardverikie.com

Attadale, near Lochcarron

In 2005 we took a train from Kyle of Lochalsh to Inverness, passing the tiny station halt ('by request only') that serves the glorious Attadale estate. The line and its surroundings got us reaching for our index of superlatives: 'unforgettable scenery'..'a blissful escape from the everyday world'...'exceptional even in Highland terms'...

By road, the A890 must surely be one of the most scenic routes in the Highlands, especially where it veers westwards from the Ullapool/ Inverness road, and then arrives at Kyle of Lochalsh, across the water from Skye. With panoramic views at every turn, it surely underlines one's belief that Scotland is one of the most beautiful countries in the world.

Across the loch from the elongated, pretty, white-painted village of Lochcarron you take a private drive; with the single track railway and the loch behind us, we reached the owners' impressive mansion, and from there drove out into the estate, passing the beautiful gardens that are open to the public, and finally reached several of the cottages. Guests have complete access to the estate, famous for its wildlife and its natural beauty, except from 15th August to 15th October when they are asked to keep to the paths while deer are being culled. Loch fishing up in the hills is available, and following a seven year restocking programme, sea trout and salmon have returned to the River Carron: day tickets are available.

The cottages offer that magic formula: complete harmony with their surroundings, and all the 21st century comforts that self-caterers increasingly demand. Prettily pale against the looming green hills, usually with just the sound of bleating sheep and perhaps a rushing burn to interrupt the blissful silence, they are most attractively and thoughtfully fitted out. We noticed open fires or wood stoves, good beds, lots of lamps, upholstered cane armchairs, many very attractive pictures (some by the owners' daughter, who is a painter). Here was a delightfully lit alcove in which to snuggle up with a book, there a cosy and congenial juxtaposition of dining room and kitchen. All the cottages are **'Visit Scotland' Four Stars**.

Such a romantic, 'away from it all' location, with comfy estate cottages...

...in complete harmony with their beautiful and unspoilt surroundings.

Sleep 4 to 8. Well behaved, sheep-respecting dogs welcome. Linen and towels provided. No TV reception. Cost: from £265 to £465. Details and colour brochure from Frances Mackenzie, Attadale, Strathcarron, Wester Ross IV54 8YX. Telephone/fax 01520 722862.

www.attadale.com
email: cottages@attadale.com

Glen Coe
Glen Coe Cottages

The location is amazing: you couldn't find accommodation much closer to the mysterious and famous glen than in one of these three neat, tucked away pebbledash bungalows in their leafy enclave overlooking the River Coe. You first turn off a minor road that snakes uphill towards dramatic Glen Coe, then you cross a cattle grid and pause beside the mirror-like Torren lochan (featured in the latest Harry Potter adventure, 'The Prisoner of Azkaban' – filmed in Glencoe). After this you continue along a track to the three cottages. They have featured here for *twenty-two years*, and we have never had a complaint. They combine mod cons with just a hint of the outdoor life – the setting is beautiful and not remote and you do not have to have climbing boots to enjoy it. Fishing is available in the owners' two trout lochs and in the river that flows prettily past the doorstep.

A high standard of comfort is achieved despite the comparatively small size and open plan nature of the single-storey buildings. All the cottages have underfloor heating, fired by an eco-friendly woodchip boiler, and dishwasher, and a shared laundry room for those damper days – for this is

The river and the dramatic glen are near: one is memorably 'close to nature'.

The cottages are 'compact', but well planned and notably warm all year round.

'outward-bound country'. There's a large drying room in the laundry building, a TV/video in each cottage, a payphone and internet access.

All three cottages have a good degree of privacy, because they separately face the river through big picture windows and do not look directly at each other. The River Coe is very well fenced off from the properties and there is no danger to little ones. There is a lot of pinewood, well fitted kitchens and sitting-cum-dining rooms.

This is an excellent base from which to tour not only the wild landscape of Glen Coe and Rannoch Moor but, being close to the Corran Ferry, it is quickly accessible to the Morvern and Ardnamurchan peninsulas and, beyond them, the Isle of Mull. Fort William is half an hour to the north.

Sleep 6 to 8, or the whole place can be taken over by a group of **up to 24 people**. Scottish Tourist Board's Gold Award for Environmental Management; member of ASSC. **Three 'Visit Scotland' Stars**. Dogs welcome. Discount for couples-only, children under two free, cots and highchairs included free. Cost: up to a maximum of £695, weekend booking at £98 per night. Details from Victoria Sutherland, Torren, Glencoe, Argyll PH49 4HX. Telephone 01855 811207. Fax 811338.

email: victoria@glencoe-cottages.com

Arisaig, near Mallaig
Arisaig House Cottages

We stayed here in 2005. Better yet, we went by train, and loved the fact that we needed to ask the driver to stop especially for us at what is all but Arisaig House's own little railway station.

It's very special in all sorts of ways, both for itself and for its location. Built as a grand private house in 1864, rebuilt after a fire in 1937, used by the SOE during the Second World War and later opened as a luxury hotel by the Smither family, Arisaig House is a solid stone building occupying a marvellous hillside setting with views to the sea. When the Smithers decided to retire they moved into the main part themselves, leaving four attractive houses on the estate available for holiday lets (**two sleeping 8, one 6 and one 3**), together with two apartments (**sleeping 4 and 2**). All have been decorated and furnished to the same rigorously high standard that won the hotel many accolades. A first for us was to see that the three principal houses each have a computer giving internet access.

Largest of the houses is *The Bothy,* which has two double bedrooms, two twins, two bathrooms and a piano. We particularly admired the terrace outside the lounge, as it runs all along one side overlooking the gardens

The setting (on the magical 'Road to the Isles') is wooded and utterly peaceful...

...and every one of the properties is reliably stylish and very comfortable.

with the sea beyond. *The Courtyard Apartment*, the smallest property (**sleeping 2**), has a lovely mountain view.

The legendary 'Road to the Isles' north to Mallaig (nine miles) passes the main entrance, so guests can easily take a boat trip to Skye or the smaller islands. To the east a fast scenic road leads through the mountains to Fort William (35 miles), and the top-class nine-hole Traigh golf course is only six miles away. On the estate itself, a new all-weather tennis court has been built in the walled garden, and there is a games room with table-tennis, pool table and exercise machine. Mountain bikes are available for hire, and a ten-minute walk takes you direct to a small, sandy beach.

The Arisaig website shows up-to-the-minute availability and all the accommodation can be booked on line (5% discount).

Details from Andrew Smither, Beasdale, Arisaig, Inverness-shire PH39 4NR. Open all year. Some short-breaks are available. No pets. Linen and towels included. Cot and highchair available. **'Visit Scotland' Three/Four Stars**. Telephone 01687 462686.

www.arisaighouse-cottages.co.uk
email:enquiries@arisaighouse-cottages.co.uk

Aultbea, near Gairloch
Shore Croft

It's a beautiful part of Scotland: in a peninsula overlooking Loch Ewe, only yards from a pebble beach, and just 20 minutes' drive from charming Gairloch, this fine architect-designed house has the further advantage of memorable views. **Sleeping up to 8** in great comfort, Shore Croft has accommodation on two floors. Downstairs there's a very large kitchen/dining room with dishwasher, range cooker,

The house is quite an attraction in itself, and the location sets it off beautifully...

a large American fridge freezer and microwave. There is a dining table seating eight and French doors opening on to decking with garden furniture and a barbecue, a large sitting room with open fire, satellite TV, DVD and music system, plus a cloakroom. Upstairs, the master bedroom has an en-suite shower room and separate dressing room; there are three further twin bedded rooms and a family bathroom.

Open all year. Cost: about £480 to £950 per week (Christmas and New Year prices on application). Dogs welcome. No smoking. Contact Hilary Cowan. Telephone 0151 494 1488.

www.shorecroft.co.uk
email: hilary.cowan3@btinternet.com

Achnamara, near Lochgilphead
The Bothy   map 4/206

Many of our readers love properties without mains electricity (mostly for nostalgic reasons), along with seclusion in a beautiful and private place; *The Bothy*, **sleeping 4**, might suit them. On its own in 45 acres of mixed woodland, it's adjacent to over a mile of coastline, with a private jetty, slip and boathouse suitable for small boats. There are woodland walks and

The owners' house: Millstone on the right.

stunning views. Boat trips can be arranged. This well built log cabin (**'Visit Scotland' Four Stars**) is warm and cosy, with a woodburning stove that heats the water, so a hot bath is easy. There are two bedrooms: one double (large), the other bunk bedded (small). Bedlinen and towels provided. The sitting room and kitchen are open plan and have double-glazed windows.

NB A second property, *Millstone Cottage* (**sleeping 4**, attached to the owners' house – see photo) is also available.

Details from The Cottage Collection, 17-23 Ber Street, Norwich NR1 3EU. Telephone 01603 724809.

www.the-cottage-collection.co.uk
email: bookings@the-cottage-collection.co.uk

Strontian, by Acharacle
Seaview Grazings

For about twenty years now, this harmonious, easy-on-the-eye arrangement of Scandinavian log cabins has proved to be the makings of a
delightful getting-to-know-the-Highlands experience for cottage guide
readers. And many of these have become regulars at Seaview Grazings:
70% of bookings are repeats, with many weeks sold out months in
advance. When we last visited, the Hanna family who run it were awaiting the arrival of a family who have been coming here for a fortnight's
holiday *three times a year for seventeen years*.

The eleven-acre site has fourteen cabins (**sleeping 4 or 5**) on a lightly
wooded hillside facing the loch. Built of real pine-logs, they are available
throughout the year, being of permanent-home standard with double-glazing, modern kitchens and full bathrooms, all now with over-bath shower.
Each feels private, but many guests like the fact that there are neighbours
(and the owners) near at hand. Shops and pubs are only a mile away.

All the cabins, which are regularly refurbished, have large windows to
make the most of the lovely views, yet they have a really warm atmosphere inside, with full central heating. The fully-fitted kitchens have four-
ring electric cookers, washing machines, fridge/freezers, microwaves and
roomy cupboards.

Boat-hire can easily be arranged locally, as can loch fishing – for begin-
ners as well as more experienced anglers – up in the hills. The area is also
excellent for all grades of walking. 'Wild glens, peaceful woodlands,
beautiful coastal walks and mountain challenges – at the end of a week
we'd experienced only a fraction of what was on offer', wrote one reader.

Yet another extraordinary location on the west coast of Scotland! Quite amazing...

Each of the log houses feels private and self contained, but there's no isolation.

Motoring from Strontian is a joy too. We ourselves arrived after a visit to
Mull via the 19-mile drive from the pretty ferry crossing at Lochaline.

Blankets/duvets, linen, towels, electricity included. Children's cots and
highchairs available free of charge. Three cabins have two bedrooms
(double and twin), the others have three (double, twin and single). Cost:
from about £250 to £610. Some short breaks available. Details from John
Hanna, Seaview Grazings Holidays, Strontian, by Acharacle, Argyll PH36
4HZ. Telephone 01967 402191.

www.seaviewgrazings.co.uk
email: gareth@seaviewgrazings.co.uk

Carbost/Staffin

Among a good clutch of properties on Skye in the hands of the ever more interesting and go-ahead Welcome Cottages organisation are two that both retain a lot of their original character and are in scenically impressive locations. Just a hundred yards or so from the sandy bay at Carbost, a few miles north of Portree at the head of Loch Snizort Beag, an unpretentious but comfortable single-storeyed property (Ref W7725) has an open fire and excep-

This Staffin property is within easy striking distance of the ferry (from Uig) to the Outer Hebrides – a delightful trip to 'a different world'.

tional views even for Skye. **Sleeps 4 'plus 2'**. Further north, at Staffin (Staffin Island is famous for its birdlife) is a handsome, traditional croft-house (Ref W4138) that makes a comfortable holiday base. **Sleeping 4**, it has panoramic views, a woodburning stove and is handy for visiting impressive Dunvegan Castle.

For availability and bookings, contact Welcome Cottages, Spring Mill, Earby, Barnoldswick, Lancashire BB94 0AA. Telephone (brochures) 0870 192 0809, 0870 336 2825 (bookings). Properties in France are also available: see Page 299.

www.welcomecottages.com

Stein (Isle of Skye)
The Captain's House

Any part of Skye is worth a visit, but we do appreciate the more out-of-the-way places. Such as the quiet, pretty, waterside village of Stein **(map 4/203)**, where nothing is out of place within its row of white houses. They incorporate one of the best pubs and one of the best seafood restaurants on the island. The hand-

The Captain's House is an excellent property, a great place from which to explore the whole of Skye...

somest house of all, known for its ground floor art gallery and craft shop, is The Captain's House. The first and second floors of this make up a spacious holiday house (self-contained, private and quiet). We liked the big sitting room, the deep sofa and armchairs and the Victorian tiled open fire. The large kitchen/breakfast room overlooks the loch, as do all but one of the rooms in this appealing property; off it there's a separate dining room. There are two large bedrooms, one double and one twin. **'Visit Britain' Three Stars**. **Sleeps up to 4** (cot available). Non-smokers preferred. Linen, not towels, included. Dogs by arrangement. Cost: about £205 to £355. Details from Mrs Cathy Myhill, The Captain's House, Stein, Waternish, Isle of Skye IV55 8GA. Telephone 01470 592223/592218.

www.the-captains-house.co.uk   email: cathy@the-captains-house.co.uk

Isle of Skye
The Old Mill/Tigh Anna

Skye has long been a favourite among readers who like to escape the rat-race and get 'back to nature', especially for hill walking. We like to take trips into the Cullin Mountains and to the Outer Isles. These two extremely comfortable, well equipped traditional properties are ideal holiday bases. Surrounded by mountain and coastal scenery,

Tigh Anna has fabulous views of the Outer Hebrides: try to build in time to make the ferry crossing during your stay.

The Old Mill is a conversion of a former mill. At the northern end of Skye, ten miles from Uig (ferries to the Outer Isles), it **sleeps 6** in two doubles and two singles. Shops and a safe, sandy beach are only about six miles away.

Tigh Anna, at Dunvegan, enjoys wonderful sunsets and spectacular views over the sea to the Outer Hebrides. It is a renovated, traditional croft cottage situated only a mile from the white beaches of Loch Dunvegan. There's an open fire in the sitting/dining room, a double, a twin and a single bedroom (thus **sleeping 5**) and a garden.

Details from **frank@cottageguide.demon.co.uk**

Telephone 01438 869489.

Isle of Mull (Carsaig)   map 4/200
Pier Cottage/The Library

Even in Mull terms – it's a very laid-back place – you get a real 'end of the world' feeling as you approach these two remote cottages, a few yards above the rocky shore on the island's south coast. Access is along a four-mile narrow wooded lane off the single-track 'main' road: *one of the most scenic we've ever driven.* The single-storey stone *Pier Cottage*

Marvellous, we thought, for autumn and winter breaks. Weekends may be available. (This is Pier Cottage.)

has a verandah where we found two happy visitors watching out for otters and seals over a late breakfast. None appeared while we there but as a consolation they gave us bunches of delicious grapes from the prolific vine that covered the ceiling. Wood-panelling inside Pier Cottage (**sleeping 3/4**) gives it a cosy feel and there are masses of books. *The Library* – built originally to house more of the owner's books – is a roomy, open-plan log-cabin (**sleeping 4/6**) up the terraced garden. An unusual feature is a small plunge-pool in the shared rock-garden. Cost: £295 to £495. Details from David McLean, The Oasis, 181 Lyham Rd, Brixton, London SW2 5PY. Telephone 020 8671 6663. Mobile (part-time) 07980 504355.

email: dhmclean@tiscali.co.uk

Dervaig (Isle of Mull)
Penmore Mill

Even during its first year in the guide
we had happy reader reports about
this. An old watermill (**sleeping 8/9
people**) just outside the village of
Dervaig – famous for the tiny Mull
Little Theatre – was imaginatively
converted by Pat and Iain Morrison,
who live in the house behind. We
guessed Pat is an artist: the bathroom is a pale turquoise, and each

*Mull is 'a different world', and this is a
superb base from which to explore it...*

bedroom, two doubles (one downstairs), a twin and one with bunks, features its own colour scheme set off by pine floors. A long pine table is the
centrepiece of the fitted kitchen – fridge-freezer, washing-machine, dishwasher, microwave, double-electric oven – which has a terracotta tiled
floor with cosy underfloor heating and a farmhouse atmosphere. It leads
into the sitting room with its log-effect stove and deep sofas. A sheltered
patio-deck makes a pleasant sitting/eating area. Iain runs the island's
Turus Mara boat trips, so most guests go to see Fingal's Cave on Staffa
and to the Treshnish Isles, home to a colony of puffins. Cost: about £500
to £850. Details from Pat Morrison, Penmore Mill, Dervaig, Isle of Mull
PA75 6QS. Telephone/fax 01688 400242.
email: info@turusmara.com www.mull-self-catering.co.uk

Isle of Carna
Isle of Carna Cottage

This really is one to note, a rare
chance to stay on the beautiful 600-
acre, traffic-free island of Carna, in
the middle of Loch Sunart, in the
Western Highlands (**map 4/212**). It's
situated between the peninsula of
Ardnamurchan to the north and the

This cottage really is one in a thousand!

remote hills of Morvern to the south. Wild flowers abound; the 550 ft
rocky peak offers spectacular views; and there are many rocky inlets and
beaches ideal for watching wildlife: seals, herons, cormorants, eagles,
buzzards, porpoises, otters, foxes and red deer live here. Originally a
shepherd's bothy, the cottage is a cosy, well equipped, tranquil base for
trips on or off the island. There's no electricity: cooking is by means of a
bottled-gas stove, lighting by gas or candle, plentiful heating/water by a
Parkray Anthracite stove, open fire and closed stove, Calor gas fridge. A
16 ft boat with outboard engine supplied; caretakers contactable by radio
at any time. Cost (including boat): about £525 to £775. Dogs welcome.
Linen supplied, but not towels. **Sleeps up to 8,** with two adult sized bunk
beds. Details from Timothy and Sue Milward, Pine House, Gaddesby,
Leicestershire LE7 4XE. Telephone 01664 840213. Fax 840660.
www.isleofcarna.co.uk email: timothy@timmilward.wanadoo.co.uk

Three Mile Water (Fort William)
Druimarbin Farmhouse

One of our all-time favourites in Scotland, this fine, pleasantly rambling family house – just three miles south of Fort William – has marvellous views of Loch Linnhe. We appreciate the home comforts, the character and the location: excellent for touring. Reached via its own drive, and on the edge of woodland, it **sleeps up to 7/8** (in comfortable beds) – though the handsome dining

This is a warm and comfortable base for a family holiday in the Highlands, with many gratifying reader reports...

table will actually seat 12. There is an open fire (logs are supplied) in the drawing room, which is graced by fine paintings, antique furniture, comfortable sofas, old fashioned armchairs. There are lots of good books, the odd bit of tartanry to remind you you're in the Highlands, a very well equipped kitchen, a payphone, Ordnance Survey maps.

TV, video and DVD. Bedlinen included. Walk-in drying room. Dogs possible by arrangement. Cost: £700 to £800 per week. Further details are available from Mrs Anthony German-Ribon, 57 Napier Avenue, London SW6 3PS. Telephone/fax 020-7736 4684.

www.coruanan.co.uk   email: germanribon@postmaster.co.uk

Arduaine, near Kilmelford   map 4/209
Arduaine Cottages

Bring your binoculars. Better yet, bring your easel and your paints, so as to capture the sparkling water, the bright white yachts, the view of low-slung small islands. This and more is what you'll see from *The Chalet* and *The Post House Cottage* (both recently refurbished, the latter a semi-detached property adjacent to the owner's house). The Chalet **sleeps 2 'plus 2'**, with an open plan sitting

Even in lovely West Coast terms, this is a memorable location.

room/kitchen, double sofa bed and a dining table placed by a big picture window to take advantage of the marvellous view of Loch Melfort, across the road. The separate bedroom has twin beds. The Post House Cottage has a large kitchen/diner, plus picture-windowed sitting room, and **sleeps up to 5** in two bedrooms, one with a king sized double also placed to enjoy the view, the other with a double and a single. The cottages are garden-fronted. TVs and videos. Dogs and other pets welcome. Linen and towels included. Cost: from about £150. Details from Julie Rowden, Arduaine Cottages, Arduaine, by Oban, Argyll PA34 4XQ. Telephone 01852 200216. Mobile 07767 695088.

email: arduainecottages@aol.com

Achahoish, near Lochgilphead
Ellary Estate Cottages

Ellary is a world apart. Of all the places we've featured over the years, it stands out as a haven of quiet and calm, an antidote to stress. Don't be daunted by the map: we promise you that the journey warrants the effort! For one reaches Ellary via one of the most beautiful lochside roads we know even in the west of Scotland (hardly any traffic) and it is one of those places that *guarantees* 'peace, perfect peace'.

The 15,000 acres on the sumptuous promontory between Lochs Sween and Caolisport, in Argyll, belong to the Ellary estate, an ancient family property that is partly farmed (predominantly sheep) yet mostly left wild for recreation purposes. Guests are welcome to wander where they will.

An Ellary Estate holiday is for people who thrive on a day's tramping through woods and hills. Those seeking laid-on entertainment and nearby clubs should look elsewhere. Even the nearest shop is 20 minutes' drive!

No-one can guarantee that you'll see otter, deer, eagles, peregrines, wildcats or any other estate residents, but they will certainly tell you where and when to look. Apart from walking on the wild side you can take to

In any of these exquisitely situated cottages, you will feel a million miles from everyday anxieties.

The location is everything. It is a rare pleasure to take in the scenery from these wide verandahs.

the loch waters, though bathing does tend to be a chilling experience. There are several lovely beaches of white sand and Ellary has proved to be very popular with sailors who bring their own dinghies (the Ellary people will help you launch your vessel). There is also fishing – trout from the lochs and salmon and sea trout in Lochead Burn. Four of the self-catering units are ranch-type chalets, simply-built wooden structures with wide verandahs overlooking the loch. The cottages are mostly of stone, once the homes of estate workers, and each one has its own particular charms. *The Lodge*, most recently available, is a particular joy: we loved the spiral staircase! There is an open fire as well as night storage heaters, a double room and two twin rooms.

All this adds up to a peaceful retreat that is also suitable for energetic families, to which many of our readers return year after year.

Sleep 4 to 8. Cost: about £215 to £550. Pets usually possible by arrangement. Details from The Estate Office, Ellary, Lochgilphead, Argyll PA31 8PA. Telephone 01880 770232 or 770209. Fax 770386.

www.ellary.com
email: info@ellary.com

Scotland-wide
Blakes Country Cottages (Scotland)*

Though they don't have a separate brochure for Scotland, Blakes offer some very fine Scottish properties, many of which have featured on the organisation's books for years.

We've heard from two readers who like the look of a superbly located property at Glenelg, which is easily accessible to the short ferry crossing to the Isle of Skye. **Sleeping 4**, *Rams Cottage* is a recent conversion that combines comfort a*nd* character, and is well situated for memorable walking – plus the chance of seeing otters. Ref 14464.

A reader who stayed at *Four Winds*, overlooking the Firth of Forth ('fabulous views from every room, including the loo!') recommends it highly.

We've long known and liked the Ormsary Lodges (Refs SH8201-8203). Not featured.

Four Winds: you could spend a week or longer just gazing out of the window.

Sleeping 4, it is a traditional end-terrace fisherman's cottage renovated to 21st century standards. Ref B5743.

We've stayed in one of the well situated *Armadale Castle Cottages*, on Skye (overlooking the ferry point for Mallaig and the mainland). They **sleep 4 or 6**, and have **'Visit Britain' Four Stars**. Ref B5793/B5791.

Most usefully there are three very comfortable (**Four Stars**) apartments superbly located in Oban, a vital jumping off point for the Hebridean islands and some ferry trips that are a delight in themselves. **Sleeping 2, 4 and 6**, these *Esplanade Court Apartments* overlook Oban Bay: such a lot going on! Refs B5888, B5890, B5892.

More rural are the *Dalhousie Estates Holiday Cottages*, three detached estate cottages nestling in the scenic and unspoilt Glenesk area. One of the cottages is spectacularly located in a remote part of Glen Mark: *Glenmark Cottage* (Ref SM16) is a 'back to basics' property dating from 1870 – no electricity, but there is gas and an open fire.

Further details are available from Blakes, Stoney Bank Road, Earby, Barnoldswick BB94 0AA. To book: 0870 192 1022. Brochures: 0870 241 7970.

Live search and book: www.blakes-cottages06.co.uk

Port Charlotte, Islay
Lorgba Holiday Cottages

The location is extraordinary, effectively right on one of the best sandy beaches on the island. The three original holiday units are neat and compact, and all three living-rooms have French windows opening right on to the beach. One **sleeps 2**, the other two **sleep up to 4**, and in those two cases, cleverly arranged kitchenettes are part of the living area. The other two properties, *Carraig*

Lorgba Cottages stand within a few yards of Islay's finest and safest beach.

North and *Carraig South,* are much larger, very well designed and **sleep up to 6**. Being on slightly higher ground, they have superb views. All the cottages have central heating and the two newer ones even have peat fires too: glorious! Among the many charms of Islay are other splendid beaches, and access to Jura from the attractive Port Askaig ferry point. It is a delightful island, varied and full of interest. It also produces some of the finest malt whiskies in the world (several distilleries arrange tours).

'Visit Scotland' **Four Stars** (Carraig), **Three Stars** (Lorgba). TV. Dogs welcome. Cost: about £115 to £395. Further details from Mr and Mrs Roy, Lorgba Holiday Cottages, Isle of Islay, Argyll, Scotland. Telephone/fax 01496 850208.

Machrie, near Port Ellen/Bowmore   map 4/215
Machrie Hotel Lodges

Islay is one of our all-time favourite Hebridean islands, and the *Machrie Lodges* are superbly positioned near the Machrie Golf Course and the Machrie Hotel. The hotel has a reputation for providing the best food on Islay: a huge bonus for self caterers, and there's an ongoing programme of improvements to its lodges. We visited two of three that have been

You don't have to be a golfer...

upgraded – though they are all acceptable for a holiday base. We found these two delightful: closest of the group of fifteen to the golf links, and with superb views of Laggan Bay (though every property has panoramic views). We admired a spacious triple aspect sitting room/diner/kitchen, cosy bedrooms – two twins, one en suite – an excellent sense of colour co-ordination: we liked the deep-cushioned cane sofa and armchairs in dark green and tartan, the big reading lamps, the plain walls. **Sleep up to 6** (with sofa bed). TV. Dogs welcome in the 'standard' lodges. Linen/towels included. Cost: £180 to £750. Details: the Machrie Hotel, Port Ellen, Isle of Islay, Argyll PA42 7AN. Telephone 01496 302310. Fax 302404.

www.machrie.com   email: machrie@machrie.com

Carradale, Kintyre
Torrisdale Castle Cottages and Apartments

We love the way Kintyre has many of the advantages of an island (and much of the character of the Hebrides) plus the bonus of ease of access. In a sheltered, heavily wooded part of this quite exceptional, secret corner of Scotland, Torrisdale Castle is well down towards the Mull of Kintyre: it overlooks the Isle of Arran from its fine vantage point on Kintyre.

On the ground floor of the magnificent though not overpowering Torrisdale Castle itself, are the flats. We have visited and revisited them all, and always found a very high standard of finish. High ceilings, large rooms, comfortable sofas, well equipped kitchens or kitchenettes, and just enough individual little details (like secret alcoves that actually form part of the turrets) to add a touch of character and individuality to each one. The flats **sleep between 4 and 6**, with lots of space for an extra bed, and are **"Visit Britain' Three Stars**.

The cottages are on a leafy and exceptionally quiet estate, and are all well away from each other. They are not show-houses, but are 'practical' and notably inexpensive. *South Lodge*, which **sleeps 2**, is on the 'B' road that runs the length of the peninsula, but it is mainly used by local and holiday traffic. It has the advantage of overlooking a pretty and sandy bay which is, of course, readily available to all guests here. We particularly liked *Lephinbeag Cottage*, at the end of its own rough drive, overhung with tall trees and with a babbling burn rippling beside it. It is quite small (two bedrooms, **sleeping 4**) but one of those places that, with a peat or log fire burning, after a day tramping through the hills, has lots of charm.

Lephincorrach Farmhouse, with its spacious kitchen and dining room, **sleeps 10** in five bedrooms. *Garden Cottage*, **sleeping 4** in two bedrooms – a downstairs double and, intriguingly, an attic room reached by ladder – is beautifully, peacefully situated among trees. *Glen House* is a converted croft house, **sleeping 7** in three bedrooms.

Televisions. Dogs are welcome. Cost: about £150 to £490. Further details are available from Mr and Mrs Macalister Hall, Torrisdale Castle, Carradale, Kintyre, Argyll PA28 6QT. Telephone/fax 01583 431233.

www.torrisdalecastle.com
email: machall@torrisdalecastle.com

Spacious Lephincorrach Farmhouse sleeps 10 in five bedrooms.

The castle, looking out to sea, contains several impressively roomy apartments.

Cumbria and the Lake District

We're as content in a tucked-away Lakeland cottage in an icy February as during a hot August (though we insist on a log fire or a glass-fronted woodburner!) So don't take it for granted that the cottage that has a waiting list in high summer is available in winter: the Lake District is popular all year round. Especially among those idyllic places that are perched above or right beside famous lakes such as Windermere, Coniston, Derwentwater and Ullswater. After a recent visit, we know how they get those so-perfect photographs of looking glass lakes reflecting a cloudless blue sky and the awe-inspiring hills! Seen from above, unforgettable. But we are fond of less well known lakes such as Thirlmere, Bassenthwaite and Esthwaite, and of holiday cottages on the fringe of the Lakes-proper, such as the sleepy Eden Valley, still one of 'England's best-kept-secrets', or around the southernmost point of the region near the important focal point of Kendal. For there is something special about striking off into the empty hills on one of those windswept, bright and showery days of early spring when clouds scudding across the ever-changing sky are reflected in the waters of a lake, or walking through the grounds of one of the region's great country houses when winter closes in. As for Christmas or the New Year holiday, any group bigger than a couple will have to secure their cottage many months in advance.

Kirkland, near Penrith   map 8/220
Kirkland Hall Cottages

One of our most enjoyable cottage revisits of 2005 was to this delightfully situated group of cottages: one of our long-term favourites in all of Cumbria. On a bright, chilly early autumn day open fires and log burners were warming the cottages, and we envied the mainly regular visitors their cosy hideaways. We strolled round the gardens, which are great

Beck is a perennial favourite, and very cosy for just two people...

fun for energetic youngsters – and admired the rural views. At the foot of the Pennines, in an Area of Outstanding Natural Beauty, you're well placed both for visiting the 'The Lakes' and the Northumberland-Durham border country. The four cottages have hand-built farmhouse kitchens with dishwashers. Woodburners back up the central heating, fuel included. *The Haybarn* (**sleeps 6/7**) has a huge sit-in fireplace, a conservatory, two bathrooms and a minstrels' gallery. *Beck Cottage* is single-storeyed, in its own grounds. **Sleeps 2**. *Stables Cottage* has a really welcoming interior and a south facing patio. **Sleeps 4**. *Shearers Cottage* (**sleeps 4**) has its own private garden. One dog by arrangement in Shearers. **'Visit Britain' Four Stars**. Cost: from £195 to £650; short breaks in low season. Details: Lesley and Ian Howes, Kirkland Hall, Kirkland, Penrith, Cumbria CA10 1RN. Telephone/fax 01768 88295.

www.kirkland-hall-cottages.co.uk
email: kirklandhallcottages@hotmail.com

Bewcastle, near Brampton
Bank End Farm Cottages

Situated just three miles from where
you pass almost imperceptibly via
country lanes over the border into
Scotland, Bank End Farm is an
exceptionally quiet place, well away
from main roads. But it's actually
not hard to locate. Deep in glorious,
rolling, comparatively little-known
countryside are two cottages. There
is *Barn Cottage* and *Old Farm
Cottage* (the latter has a coal fire),

*There's always a warm and friendly
welcome from the resident owners...*

overlooking a pretty, flower-filled garden overlooking the River Black
Lyne. **Sleeping 2 and 6** respectively, both cottages are comfortable and
warm. A good range of imaginative and inexpensive home-cooked dishes
is prepared by the extremely kind and hospitable Mrs Liddle. Each cottage has a microwave, a dishwasher and electric blankets.

Well behaved dogs are welcome. Central heating. Televisions and video
players. Cost: about £210 to £380, including bedlinen and all fuel. Details
from Mr and Mrs Liddle, Bank End Farm, Roadhead, near Carlisle,
Cumbria CA6 6NU. Telephone/fax 016977 48644.

email: bankendfarm@tiscali.co.uk

Bailey, near Newcastleton   map 8/222
Bailey Mill Inn

In a quiet but attractive corner of
Cumbria only just inside the English
border (you can pop into Scotland for
a picnic!) we've featured these courtyard apartments for many years. We
know all five courtyard cottages in
the converted 18th century grain mill
in an arrangement of single and two-
storeyed buildings, one of them, *The
Folly*, **sleeping up to 8**. A bargain for
larger groups. Most **sleep 2 to 6**. A

*An ongoing programme of upgrading in
this popular group of properties...*

ground floor apartment called *The Store* houses the original archway, dated
1767. There's a jacuzzi, a sauna, a toning table, and a meals service in the
licensed bar. Dogs welcome. Baby sitting. TVs; microwaves. Looking in
on the Copelands' handsome horses, riding (and learning to ride) is very
much a part of Bailey Mill, and full-day stable management courses are
available 10am to 4pm (£25 per day), also full board riding holidays.
'Visit Britain' Two and Three Stars. Cost: about £178 to £598. Short
breaks – out of season – from £108 per cottage for two nights. Further
details from Pamela Copeland, Bailey Mill, Newcastleton, Roxburghshire
TD9 0TR. Telephone 016977 48617.

www.holidaycottagescumbria.co.uk email: pam@baileymill.fsnet.co.uk

123

Ambleside and Central Lakeland
Cottage Life and Heart of the Lakes*

It's 20 years since we first featured this important agency. It handles some real gems, several of which we have stayed in. Of course, we only have room to mention a handful of the 330 or so on the organisation's books.

Most of the 'Cottage Life/Heart of the Lakes' cottages are open all year round: winter has a big following, when people tend to ask for open fires – about half the agency's properties have them.

Some properties are in quite famous places, and they don't come much more famous than Far Sawrey, one-time home of Beatrix Potter. There, *Rowan Cottage*, **sleeping 5**, has lots going for it, such as a multi-fuel stove, views of fields and trees from the back and a pub a short walk away.

Lion and *Lamb* cottages, for example, are two charming properties that

Big family party? Consider Hart Head Barn, sleeping up to ten and superbly located in famous Rydal...

Lion and Lamb cottages are in the heart of Grasmere: you will be the envy of the people who throng to the village...

date back to the 18th century and are in the heart of Grasmere village, probably one of the Lake District's half dozen most sought-after holiday bases. Now carefully renovated and comfortably furnished, both cottages make an excellent holiday base. Both **sleep 6**.

Hart Head Barn was converted from an old Lakeland stone barn and as you might imagine now offers very substantial accommodation. With wonderful views, in a peaceful location, this outstanding property is situated in the hamlet of Rydal, between Grasmere and Ambleside. **Sleeps 10**.

A ten minute drive from Keswick, in the village of Mungrisdale, *Elind Cottage* is part of a Grade II listed barn, with a wealth of beams and evidence of a flair for interior design. It is full of character, and makes a very comfortable holiday home. **Sleeps 4**.

Just a couple of minutes' walk from the centre of Ambleside is *Wren Cottage*. Newly renovated and upgraded, while retaining many authentic features, this **sleeps 2** and will appeal to couples looking for a village (or perhaps small town) 'pied-à-terre'.

The properties range from **'Visit Britain' Two to Five Stars**, and all include free leisure club membership. Further details of all these and of course many more are available from 'Heart of the Lakes'/'Cottage Life', Fisherbeck Mill, Old Lake Road, Ambleside, Cumbria LA22 0DH. Telephone 015394 32321. Fax 33251.

www.heartofthelakes.co.uk   email: info@heartofthelakes.co.uk

Talkin, near Brampton
Long Byres

It's a rare cottage set-up where they say 'Do bring your children and dogs!' Better yet, owner Harriet Sykes (who runs the place and lives adjacent) says 'the more boisterous the better, and as many of each as you like.' She goes on to say, 'the cottages are child- and dog-proof. We are what we are, we know our market and we don't overcharge.' The formula seems to work: there are many repeat visitors. As well as enjoying forays to such famous places as Windermere, Keswick and Ullswater, guests tend to be people who appreciate this 'serenely wild' corner of the Cumbria/Northumberland border country.

We revisited one recent early autumn, and found that the character of the seven former farm buildings still comes over. The cottages look over the farm towards the fells. There is a small shop with essentials, and a speciality of home-made jams, marmalades and chutneys. Also, a tempting daily menu of freshly cooked, inexpensive dishes prepared by Harriet Sykes. All the houses are double-glazed and have central heating and fridges. They are, except for size (**sleeping from 2 to 5**), very similar, with spacious first-floor sitting rooms, and interiors are being upgraded year by year.

With their easy access to the Lakes, the Roman Wall country and the Scottish border, these are unpretentious and inexpensive, and have always brought a good response from our readers...

Interiors are unfussy and practical, and we've checked out the ongoing programme of upgrading...

All the cottages enjoy splendid views. A charming beck ripples along within 50 yards of the property. Talkin Tarn, as pretty as several of the Lakes-proper, is within walking distance; Talkin village, which is half a mile away, offers the choice of two excellent pubs. Brampton, three miles away, is the nearest town. It has a railway station, and the Sykes are happy to meet people from the train.

Dogs are welcome, and children will enjoy the pets' corner, the dogs, the cats, the horses and the newly acquired alpacas. Cost: about £160 to £385, including electricity, hot water, heating, linen and towels. Details from Harriet Sykes at Long Byres, Talkin Head, near Brampton, Cumbria CA8 1LT. Telephone 016977 3435.

www.talkinhead.co.uk
email: harriet@talkinhead.co.uk

Kirkoswald, near Penrith
Howscales

Half hidden away, very quiet and peaceful, Cumbria's Eden Valley is a 'best-kept secret' that also offers easy access to The Lakes. These five properties make a fine introduction to this corner of Cumbria. Extensive, beautifully kept gardens (runners up in the 'Cumbria In Bloom', self catering section, in 2004 and 2005) surround the property, with quiet sit-

Very comfortable, very well situated for touring: a super Eden Valley base...

ting-out places for guests to relax in and enjoy the marvellous open views of the surrounding countryside. The cottages are most lovingly cared-for, grouped appealingly round a cobbled courtyard. We've stayed here, in one of the three two-storeyed properties that have their open plan sitting room/dining-room and kitchen areas on the first floor to make the most of the splendid views. The other two are single-storeyed, one of them (*Hazelrigg*) a former milking parlour that is suitable for wheelchair-bound guests. This **sleeps 2** in a zip-link double. Our favourite is roomy *Inglewood* (**sleeping 4**), stylish and inviting, with superb views. TVs. No smoking. Dogs possible. Details from Liz Webster, Kirkoswald, Penrith, Cumbria CA10 1JG. Telephone 01768 898666. Fax 898710.

www.howscales.co.uk   email: liz@howscales.co.uk

Watermillock, near Ullswater
Land Ends   map 8/236

As you approach these cottages along little-used country lanes, you feel 'a hundred miles from anywhere', but in fact you're just a mile or so from Lake Ullswater. The four log cabins are in 25 peaceful acres of gardens and natural woodland, with streams and exceptional birdlife, on the slopes of Little Mell Fell. Opposite the cabins is "guests' own" lake, with

Bed and breakfast is also available here.

ducks and moorhens and areas of mown grass with seating for walking or relaxing. (Look out for red squirrels, tawny owls and woodpeckers.) Dogs are 'very welcome', and can get plenty of exercise. There is a second lake further down the grounds, and an 18-acre field for strolling in. You are surrounded by dramatic scenery, many attractions and superb hillwalking. The nearest village (Pooley Bridge) is three miles away, but there is a pub serving good food just a mile down the road.

Sleep 2 to 5. TVs. **'Visit Britain' Three Stars**. Linen is included, but not towels. Cost: about £260 to £540. Open all year. Details/brochures from Land Ends, Watermillock, Cumbria CA11 0NB. Telephone 017684 86438.

www.landends.co.uk   email: infolandends@btinternet.com

Windermere, Ambleside and beyond
Lakelovers*

We admire the staff of this agency who seem to know every stick and stone of the properties on their 'patch'. They certainly seem to have some of the most desirable Lake District cottages on their books.

We know a good proportion of them, and have stayed in several. Most recently in *Fell Cottage*, at Troutbeck, a semi-detached but still private house with impressive views (and a ten minute walk from *fabulous* views). **Sleeps up to 4**. Also *Rigges Wood*, virtually on the shores of Esthwaite Water, with partial views of that, and just two minutes' drive from the fascinating and historic village of Hawkshead. It's a warm and comfortable family house, **sleeping 6** in a double and two twins, with a most efficient coal-effect gas fire, a pleasant family dining room, lots of irresistible books and a good-sized back garden.

Also a few minutes' walk from Hawkshead and Esthwaite Water, *Roger Ground House* is a Grade II listed delight. **Sleeping up to 14** – one bedroom has a six foot wide bed – with, among so much else, two fine oak

Roger Ground is an exceptional property, combining history and modern comforts.

Valentine Cottage (not featured) makes a rather special and romantic retreat.

staircases, mullioned windows, stone-flagged floors, comfortable furnishings and decor, this property really is 'something special'.

On the shores of Lake Windermere, *Beech Howe*, **sleeping 6**, is very sought after. On a steep bank, separated from Windermere only by lush tree-filled gardens, with no less than 200 yards of private lake frontage, there are views of England's biggest lake from virtually every window. The smallish sitting room is especially charming and cosy and this, at one end of the extremely comfortable, carefully colour co-ordinated cottage has a double aspect, so it is always light, bright and inviting.

Among so many outstanding properties we like (and have stayed in) is *Curdle Dub*, at Coniston, a listed building in a pretty row within walking distance of the village and the lake. There is an open fire. **Sleeps 4**.

For a copy of an outstandingly well written and seductive brochure contact Lakelovers, Belmont House, Lake Road, Bowness-on-Windermere LA23 3BJ. Telephone 015394 88855. Fax 88857. Brochures: 88858.

www.lakelovers.co.uk
email: bookings@lakelovers.co.uk

Loweswater, near Cockermouth
Loweswater Cottages at Scale Hill

With nothing but whole-hearted praise from our readers, and never any kind of complaint, these most appealing properties have featured in our guide since the very first edition. That's *twenty-four years!*

Michael Thompson once owned and ran one of the best known hotels in the region, but some years ago this was transformed into highly regarded self catering cottages, now looked after by daughter Heather. (With echoes of their original incarnation as part of the hotel, some are serviced daily, which is a great rarity in self catering terms.) All of the cottages are very comfortable, attractively lit, and altogether welcoming. Each one has memorable views from the windows which, considering the location, is a huge bonus.

Sheila's, at the far end of the building, is open plan, with a triple aspect sitting room and French windows on to a private garden. When we last called, a cheerful fire was burning in the grate. **Sleeps 4** in two bedrooms, each with private bathroom. *Barty's,* in the middle of the original inn, and with access from the cobbled courtyard, has the great advantage of a sitting room across the whole of the building and is thus – something we like a lot – 'double aspect'. It **sleeps 2** in a four poster.

Opposite the former hotel is the converted Coach House, which contains four cottages. Low key in decor, and tasteful, they are kept up to a high standard of decoration with good quality wallpaper and carpets common to all. They are *Lanthwaite, Shell* (recently enlarged, and now with a four poster*) Brackenthwaite* and *Howe*. A detailed colour brochure provides a good impression of all the properties.

Dogs are welcome. There are televisions and central heating throughout. Cots, highchairs and all heating, lighting and linen are included in the

Scale Hill (arrowed): how is this for a cottage location? It is quite outstanding even compared with other parts of the Lake District, and our readers have come to love it.

rates. Cost: approximately £255 to £730 per cottage, depending – as always – on which cottage you choose and when you go.

For further details and a copy of that exceptional loose-leaf brochure, contact Heather Thompson, Scale Hill, Loweswater, near Cockermouth, Cumbria CA13 9UX. Telephone 01900 85232. Fax 85321.

www.loweswaterholidaycottages.co.uk
email: thompson@scalehillloweswater.co.uk

Elterwater, near Ambleside
Meadowbank/Garden Cottage

We always approve of cottages used occasionally by the owners themselves, and this outstanding property is one. In the heart of a sought-after village, with a good pub close, it's of permanent-home standard, with a stylish, spacious, uncluttered interior (we loved the red carpeting and the tartan covers in the main sitting room: see **Colour section A, Page 4**), an impressive, traditional pine kitchen, a medium sized, well tended

This must be one of the finest holiday houses in the Lakes: grab it when you can!

and enclosed garden that gives on to open fields. (We also admired the view from the main bedroom.) **Sleeps 8/10.** Within the garden, but unobtrusively, *The Garden Cottage*, **sleeping just 2** in a double, can be taken separately, or is an excellent addition to Meadowbank for a large family party. Three TVs/videos/Sky film/sports channels.

Bed-linen included. Pets not allowed. Cost: (Cottage) £230 to £350, (House) £570 to £1550. See the website for full details of price, availability and special offers.

www.langdalecottages.co.uk
email: lockemeadowbank@aol.com

Graythwaite, near Lake Windermere
Graythwaite Farm   map 8/244

Of course we love to potter on and around Lake Windermere. We love it even more since those headache-inducing waterskiers have been given the heave-ho. It's the western side we go for most, notably the rural, well wooded hinterland. Considering there are ten units available at Graythwaite Farm, which lies within four acres of woodland, they

In one of our favourite corners of the Lake District, these are half hidden away.

are, amazingly, hidden away from the country road that snakes from Newby Bridge to Hawkshead. Most of the skilful and harmonious conversions have an open fire or a woodburner, and they **sleep from a cosy 2 to a convivial 10**. It's a pleasant mile-long walk to the shores of Windermere, and there's a two-and-a-half-acre stocked trout pool, as well as access to Graythwaite's exceptional gardens, which are open to the public. Refs (of a sample three of the ten properties, respectively *Greenhowes Cottage, Bibby Lot* and *Eel House*) are LMX, LMY and LMR.

Details from English Country Cottages, Stoney Bank Road, Earby, Barnoldswick BB94 0AA. For bookings, telephone 0870 192 1028. You can also 'dial a brochure': 0870 192 0391. **www.ecc2006.co.uk**

Applethwaite, near Keswick
Croftside/Croft Corner/Upper House/Lower House at Croft House Holidays

Only just over a mile from Keswick are five properties, all in peaceful, rural settings, with stunning views to Skiddaw, Borrowdale and the north-western fells. In Croft House, three properties are dovetailed in a hand-some Victorian country house. *Croftside* is a large part of the main house, **sleeping 4/5**, while *Croft Corner* is a ground-floor apartment

Croft House: an exceptional location and super views, a mile or so from Keswick.

sleeping 2. A Croftside visitor said: 'After 25 years of Lakeland holidays this is the best accommodation we've stayed in.' Said another, of Croft Corner, 'Thanks for the little touches that made us feel so much at home'. A colleague stayed in *Lower House*, **sleeping 4**. She described great views, and 'everything light and open plan'. A visitor to *Upper House*, **sleeping 6,** said: 'Wonderfully equipped, fantastic view'. At *Croft Head Farm*, **sleeping 8**, a visitor highlighted 'the serene and picturesque location'. **'Visit Britain' Four Stars**. TVs/videos/DVDs. 'Sorry, no pets'. Linen, towels, heating, electricity, cot/high chair included. Open all year. Cost: £260 to £895. Short breaks from £156. Details: Mrs J L Boniface, Croft House, Applethwaite, Keswick, Cumbria CA12 4PN. Telephone: 017687 73693.

www.crofthouselakes.co.uk   email: holidays@crofthouselakes.co.uk

Ravenglass and Cockermouth

We happen to think the Cumbrian coast is one of the north west's best-kept-secrets, and one of our all-time favourite places is Ravenglass. Just a mile and a half from there, near Waberthwaite, in a high-lying situation with panoramic views of the Irish Sea and, if you're lucky, sunset over the Isle of Man, a detached barn conversion **(map 5/253)** combines masses of character with 21st century comforts. **Sleeping 6**, it makes a good base for a short break, and is

A semi-detached part of this substantial house in Ravenglass (not featured) is an excellent holiday base for 8. Ref W8463.

near a pub. Ref W4359. Inland, near Cockermouth, a semi-detached con-verted chapel has great views of the Lakeland Fells and the rather unsung Solway Firth. Very comfortable, it **sleeps up to 12**. Ref W8072. **(map 5/256)**

For availability and bookings, contact Welcome Cottages, Spring Mill, Earby, Barnoldswick, Lancashire BB94 0AA. Telephone (brochures) 0870 192 0809, 0870 336 2825 (bookings). A number of properties in France are also available.

www.welcomecottages.com

Borrowdale, Keswick and around
Lakeland Cottage Holidays*

The geographical coverage of this long established agency of 60 or so properties is very precise: everything is within a ten mile radius of Keswick, and that appeals greatly to readers.

The majority of properties are managed (bookings, cleaning, spring cleaning and maintenance) by the agency, and those that aren't have owners close by to maintain standards. The brochure is full of practical advice and, interestingly, understated cottage descriptions – the superlatives are saved for the landscape! If you want more illustrations, see the agency's website for galleries of digital photos, or take their 360 degree 'virtual tours' of selected properties.

During a recent autumn visit to the Lakes we picked out a good handful of properties we'd not seen before: big houses with fine views, stone cottages, white-walled cottages, farmhouses and town-house terraces.

Serious walkers would love *Townhead Barn*, **sleeping 6/8**. Situated in the quiet village of Threlkeld, it is off the beaten tourist track yet, amazingly,

Candlemas (not featured) is a newer property sleeping 4. Just ten minutes from Keswick centre, it has memorable views...

High Ground, below Catbells, is a rarity. Sleeping 8, it was built in 1910 by an Austrian Christmas card manufacturer!

less than five miles from Keswick. Six miles from Keswick, *Fell Cottage* is of one of several quietly and spectacularly situated cottages. With fabulous walking from the front door and 360 degrees of eye-popping scenery, it **sleeps 6** and has an open fire. It has **Three 'Visit Britain' Stars**.

In the tiny hamlet of Seatoller, in the Borrowdale Valley (most of the surrounding countryside is National Trust owned), is a former quarryman's cottage called *Bell Crags*, where we really liked the open fire in the sitting room and the patio by the stream plunging down from Honister Pass, with views across to the magnificent old High Stile oakwood. **Sleeps 5/6**. The agency has several properties in Keswick itself, and we were impressed by *Underne*, a comfortable, surprisingly spacious terraced cottage in a peaceful corner of this important centre. **Sleeps 4/5**.

Further details and a copy of an informative brochure are available from Lakeland Cottage Holidays, Melbecks, Bassenthwaite, near Keswick, CA12 4QX. Telephone 017687 76065. Fax: 76869.

www.lakelandcottages.co.uk
info@lakelandcottages.co.uk

Elterwater, near Ambleside
Wheelwrights Lake District Holiday Cottages

We've heard from a good number of readers who first discovered the delights of the Lake District after booking a cottage through Wheelwrights Lake District Holiday Cottages.

The company, which has been letting cottages in the heart of Lakeland for nearly 30 years, making it one of the first in its field in the whole country, handles 76 properties, and because it is one of the smaller letting agencies, the staff are familiar with every property and can advise on the best match for clients' particular requirements.

Wheelwrights' properties are set amongst some of the most stunning scenery in the Lake District – which is saying something! Many are in the Langdale Valleys (Great and Little), which are dominated by the magnificent Langdale Pikes. Others are in the picturesque villages of Grasmere, Hawkshead, Outgate, Coniston and Ambleside. They lie within a ten mile radius of Elterwater, where Wheelwrights' office is based, and all provide ideal points from which to explore the whole of the fabulous Lake District National Park.

The range of properties is wide. Some are converted barns or farmhouses, others are Lakeland-stone cottages and village houses, and there are some modern houses and apartments. They are all equipped to a very high standard with **'Visit Britain'** gradings from **Three** to **Five** stars. The smallest properties **sleep 2** and the largest **sleeps 15**. Most accept pets.

Prices per week range from £285 (low season) to £2000 (peak season). All the properties can be seen on the website – **www.wheelwrights.com** – on which you may also check the layout of each cottage by clicking on the floorplans button. (Not to scale.)

Contact the Wheelwrights office for any further information you may require about any of the cottages found on their website or to request a colour brochure:

Wheelwrights Lake District Holiday Cottages, Elterwater, Ambleside, Cumbria LA22 9HS.

Telephone 015394 37635.

Most Wheelwrights properties allow almost immediate access to some of the most romantic landscapes in the country.

The majority of the cottages and houses on offer are places of character. We know several, and will see more during 2006.

Bassenthwaite
Bassenthwaite Lakeside Lodges

Access to Bassenthwaite, one of Lakeland's most beautiful but least known lakes, is famously quite difficult, but these fine lodges border its shores, with easy and immediate access to the water.

Tucked away down a leafy lane among mature trees, and run with great professionalism, this community of about 60 log cabins/lodges, fifteen of them for holiday let, have been much praised by readers for more than ten years. Standards are high.

We especially admire the most recent properties, **sleeping up to 6,** in a private location on the edge of the development, with the most impressive lake views of all, but were very pleased to spend time in one of our long time favourites, *Overwater* (right by the lake) – and also to see *Broadwater*. This is especially geared to 'wedding day' and honeymoon couples, and we were very impressed by the walk-in closet that's big enough to take a wedding dress in all its glory.

While obviously not for those who want to be lonely as a cloud, this remains the sort of location where visiting children – and adults – will enjoy making new friends, though they can be private too. We noted, once again, the care taken in choosing top-notch kitchen and bathroom ranges, likewise comfy sofas more usually associated with up-market traditional holiday houses.

As well as generous balconies with gas barbecues and outdoor furniture, the lodges have picture windows, TVs and videos. There is a free video,

Right by the shore of one of Cumbria's least known but pleasantest lakes.

Interiors are sumptuous, and we were not surprised by all the repeat bookings.

books and games library. Nearby you can hire mountain bikes, play tennis and golf, and go horse-riding. Keswick is just ten minutes' drive.

Dogs are permitted only in the category of the smaller Parkland, Lakeview and Woodland Lodges. Linen and towels are, as you would expect here, included.

Cost: about £360 to £1010, depending on which property and when. Short breaks are available. Details available from Bassenthwaite Lakeside Lodges, Scarness, Bassenthwaite, near Keswick, Cumbria CA12 4QZ. Telephone 017687 76641. Fax 76919.

www.bll.ac
email: enquiries@bll.ac

Sebergham, near Caldbeck
Monkhouse Hill Cottages

In this guide for over twenty years, with a huge following among readers, these lovingly cared-for cottages are well located in the quieter, more northerly part of 'the Lakes'. Keswick (via lovely Mungrisdale), Bassenthwaite Lake, Cockermouth, the coast, the Eden Valley and the Northumberland border are all within a pleasant drive. Set back from a not especially busy B-road, they are easy to find but completely rural.

After regular upgrading, the cottages are among the best properties in Cumbria – *indicated by the fact they won the Silver Award in Excellence in England 2002*. They form a most attractive, exceptionally neat, clean and tidy enclave round a former farmyard, with impressive panoramic views, and they are run with understandable pride and great professionalism by the resident owners, who have three young children and are therefore tuned in to the needs of families on holiday.

We were keen to see the latest addition, which is *Great Calva*. Most usefully **sleeping 12 'plus 2'** in seven bedrooms, it has the always-desirable feature of an upstairs sitting room, a sauna and spa, and a **'Visit Britain'** grading of **Five Stars**. We met an extended family staying, coming to the end of their holiday and not wanting to leave.

Also recently on the scene, also with **Five Stars**, is *Cloven Stone*, designed for two couples. This too has an upstairs sitting room, which we loved, to make the most of the views, and two downstairs doubles – one of which can be reorganised as a twin. There are seven other cottages, each with its own particular endearing features. There are three which **sleep 2**, two **sleeping 4**, one **sleeping 6**, and one **sleeping 8**. Most will take at least one cot.

An award winning, absolutely pristine, neat and tidy arrangement of cottages.   *...with comfortable interiors, a food ordering service and children's playground.*

Cost: about £330 to £2125 (inc electricity, linen and towels). Also available is an on-line ordering service for, for example, three-course suppers, celebratory buffets, home cooked freezer meals, grocery hampers, freshly baked bread, papers, wine and beer, and more. Dogs are welcome in most cottages. Free use of hotel leisure club with indoor pool. TV/video/DVD, CD/radio. There's a laundry room, a games room, a children's playground.

Colour brochure from Jennifer Collard, Monkhouse Hill, Sebergham, near Caldbeck CA5 7HW. Telephone/fax 016974 76254.

www.monkhousehill.co.uk   email: cottages@monkhousehill.co.uk

Buttermere
Bowderbeck

This is a classic of its kind, and it's not hard to see why it's so sought-after. For the character of this picture-book cottage has been preserved: it has even doubled up as 'Dove Cottage' in a film about Wordsworth. But it now incorporates 21st century comforts, with for

Lake District cottages don't come much more authentic or well located than this.

example a timber extension at the end of the whitewashed-stone 17th century cottage of a kind Wordsworth would not have known; he'd have appreciated its view of Buttermere, which for many visitors is the most romantic and beautiful lake of all. The lake shore is only half a mile away, and children will love the little beck that runs alongside the cottage. (This makes Bowderbeck unsuitable for children under five.) Specifically, there are rugs on slate floors and a handsome (and original) stone staircase up to a roomy first floor, where there is a spacious main bedroom, a roomy twin, a single, a separate wc, shower and bathroom, plus WC. **Sleeps 7 'plus 1'**. Not suitable for pets. No smoking. Payphone. Linen supplied, not towels. Cost: about £400 to £625. No TV reception. Details from Michael and Anne Bell, New House, Colby, Appleby-in-Westmorland, Cumbria CA16 6BD. Telephone 017683 53548.

www.bowderbeck.co.uk   email: info@bowderbeck.co.uk

Burton-in-Kendal, near Kendal   map 8/268
4 Green Cross Cottages

The cosy 'traditional' cottage, well supplied with 21st century comforts without the loss of its character, is a rarity. More so when it's loved and occasionally used by its owners. This one fits the bill! Dating from 1637, with old beams, it's an ideal base for the Lakes, South Cumbria and the Yorkshire Dales. In a short terrace of cottages, with the rear on the main street, it has a charming living room

Comfortable and welcoming (and rather good value), in a village setting. We revisited in 2005...

with a dining alcove and limestone fireplace. We admired the 'cottagey' interior with its matching fabrics and the well equipped kitchen. There's a wide, easy staircase to the first floor, two bedrooms and a bathroom with large airing/drying cupboard. Parking for one car, courtyard garden; payphone, TV/video. The village is a charming 'mix,' with period houses, two shops, and pubs with restaurants. **Sleeps 4**. Cost: £160 to £350, including gas central heating. Short breaks from just £100. No smoking, pets possible by arrangement. Linen included. Maps, videos, books and games. We'd give it **Four Stars**! Details from Mrs Frances Roberts, 32 Sevenoaks Avenue, Heaton Moor, Stockport, Cheshire SK4 4AW. Telephone 0161 432 3408. **email: ft.roberts@btinternet.com**

Windermere and Ullswater
Matson Ground Estate Cottages

Just a mile from Windermere and its lake, but in a peaceful situation, Helm Farm is a top-quality conversion of traditional farm buildings. The locations and the cottages themselves are memorable. **Sleeping 2 to 5** in four units, each enjoys privacy and has been designed to a high standard. *Helm Lune* **sleeps 5** in a double and a triple (three single beds, two of which can form a second double). The Habitat style (lots of pine) is set off by a high ceiling, beams in the spacious living room, and an open fire.

Helm Eden **sleeps 4** in a double and two full size bunks, *Kent* **sleeps 4** in a double, with **2** in children's bunks. *Helm Mint*, **sleeping 2**, is on the ground floor only, and has a cosy L-shaped living room/kitchen. It is the only one without a fireplace. (Helm Mint is available at a reduced rate if taken with Lune, Eden or Kent.) All include linen, towels, TV, video/CD player (also DVD in Lune), plus microwaves. Washer/driers in all except Mint. Lune includes a dishwasher. Outside payphone, barbecue, shared garden with furniture. Fuel for open fires and night storage heating is included. Cost: £125 to £575; short breaks available. Not suitable for dogs. Footpath walks from the door. **'Visit Britain' Three Stars**.

We drove towards the lovely countryside around Ullswater and, in the beautiful Grisedale Valley, close to Helvellyn and many other mountains, found the spacious, modernised 17th century farmhouse called *Elm How* and the smaller, quaintly beamed *Cruck Barn* – adjoining properties **sleeping 10 and 2** respectively. There's a degree of remoteness, among stunning mountain scenery, in these 'away from it all' places. No TV reception due to the hills, but video and CD players are available, and a DVD in Cruck Barn.

Linen/towels provided. Dishwasher in Elm How. Microwaves, washer/driers. Open fire (fuel provided) in Elm How. Electric storage heating

We're especially fond of Elm How, which is in a really appealing location...

Cruck Barn: history, original features and mod cons rolled into one...

included. Barbecues. Not suitable for dogs. **'Visit Britain' Three/Four Stars**. Popular *Eagle Cottage* perches above Glenridding village and **sleeps 4**, with views all round, including the lake. Steep approach track. TV, video and CD player. Linen, dishwasher, microwave, open fire, storage heating. Cost: £225 to £1150. Not suitable for pets. **'Visit Britain' Three Stars**.

Colour brochure from Matson Ground Estate Company, Estate Office, Matson Ground, Windermere, Cumbria LA23 2NH. Telephone 015394 45756. Fax 47892.

www.matsonground.co.uk   email: info@matsonground.co.uk

Patton, near Kendal
Field End Barns/Shaw End Mansion

We have enjoyed a stay here, dropping down full of anticipation from a little used country road to the farmstead and its nest of barn conversions: as private as you want them to be, but fairly neighbourly too. (On our travels we had met a group of young professionals – readers of this guide – from North Yorkshire who had taken over the biggest property here for a weekend at a very advantageous price, and had 'a great time'.)

Just three miles north of Kendal, in this secluded, quiet rural setting, *Field End* has the River Mint running nearby. There are good views of the Howgill Fells, and some very popular lakes, including Grasmere and Windermere, are only about half an hour's drive. The five fine barn conversions are well away from any traffic noise and offer spacious accommodation for **between 2 and 10**. They enjoy full oil-fired central heating *plus* open fires in local-stone hearths, spacious kitchen/dining rooms and sitting rooms. We were not surprised that they have a Country Landowners' Association Farm Building Award Commendation.

Up on the hill, only about half a mile away, we also visited (for the first

Award-winning barn conversions in a peaceful, rural but not remote location.

Shaw End Mansion: a degree of grandeur, with great views from each apartment.

time) a most impressive, major restoration of a Georgian mansion called *Shaw End*, with its original facade intact. So it has a lot of history but the advantages of being what is effectively a new building.

There are four high ceilinged apartments, all accessed via the impressive main entrance, two on the ground floor, two – reached via a fine, sweeping pine staircase – on the first floor, all with superb interiors, including large sitting rooms with open fires, and exquisite views of the River Mint, in which children love to play. As with the Field End properties, Shaw End guests have the run of the 200 acre estate. Three apartments **sleep 4**, one **sleeps 6**.

Trout and salmon fishing (one rod) is available on the Mint. TV, washing machine, telephone, microwave, linen included, towels available for a small extra charge. Dogs welcome by arrangement. Cost: about £220 to £480. Details from Mr and Mrs E D Robinson, 1 Field End, Patton, near Kendal, Cumbria LA8 9DU. Telephone 01539 824220, fax 824464.

www.fieldendholidays.co.uk
email: robinson@fieldendholidays.co.uk

Crosby Garrett, near Kirkby Stephen
Mossgill Loft/Mossgill Chapel

In striking distance of the Lake District, on the eastern edge of Cumbria, these lovingly cared for properties are among our absolute favourites in the north of England.

Crosby Garrett is a delightful, well spaced out, blissfully quiet village in the Upper Eden Valley, distinguished by a viaduct on the Settle to Carlisle railway, with the fells only a few yards beyond.

It's excellent for walking both long and short distances, being only two miles from the Coast to Coast route and near the Pennine Way. The Cumbria Cycleway is just a mile away, and the Smardale Nature Reserve is half an hour's walk. The market town of Kirkby Stephen has pubs, restaurants and antique shops. A nine hole golf course is nearby.

A Victorian Baptist chapel conversion has created two attractive self-contained holiday lets, retaining many original features and furnished to a high standard. There is central heating throughout the building, log fires, off road parking and private sitting out areas. Fuel, electricity and linen are all included. A cot and high chair are available. Dogs welcome by arrangement.

Mossgill Chapel, which we visited for the first time in 2004, has a large tiled kitchen with an oil-fired Rayburn, electric hob, microwave and fridge/freezer. A warm utility room houses a washing machine and tumble dryer and provides plenty of space for drying walking clothes. An upstairs sitting room has an open fire, beams, comfortable furniture and TV/DVD. There are two bedrooms, one twin with en-suite bathroom and one downstairs double with a bathroom next door, including a shower.

Fitting harmoniously into the village scene.   *Lovingly planned and cared-for interiors.*

Stained glass windows are an attractive feature on the staircase. All is light and bright, with a stylish sense of colour and design. Cost: from about £290 to £375. Short breaks at a bargain £65 per night. **Sleeps 4 plus cot**.

Mossgill Loft is approached by a short flight of stone steps. There is a large living/kitchen area, a double bedroom and bathroom. There are lattice windows, beams, an open fire and rugs on wooden floors. Plus an electric cooker, microwave, washing machine, fridge and TV/DVD. The two properties can be taken together – the makings of a memorable family holiday. The owners' tennis court is available on request. Cost: from £185 to £250 per week. Short breaks at £50 per night. **Sleeps 2**.

Furtrher details from Clare Hallam, Mossgill House, Crosby Garrett, Kirkby Stephen, Cumbria CA17 4PW. Telephone 017683 71149. **email: clarehallamuk@yahoo.co.uk**

Wales

The survival of the language, the terrain and the vast supply of 'tangible' history means Wales is packed with interest and visitor-appeal. It feels bigger than many first time visitors expect – perhaps because it still has some pretty tortuous roads. Every few miles, every turn in the road seems to promise new things to see, more history to reach out and touch. Almost as soon as you're over the border (say via Ross on Wye, or Ludlow) the magic, the sense of the past and the scenic beauty envelop one.

A good number of readers have taken to the Pembrokeshire Coast and, for example, the Llyn Peninsula, in the north. In Pembrokeshire, Tenby is much-loved, while people who discover resorts such as Broad Haven and Newport tend to rave about them. There are lofty peaks and magnificent beaches, and although the most dramatic scenery is around Snowdonia, almost every corner of the Principality is holiday country. There are the rolling, lightly wooded English-Welsh borders, the brown moors of the Brecon Beacons National Park, our own favourite coastline around Barmouth, the rather proud, rather self contained town of Dolgellau and nearby Portmeirion, the architectural fantasy that's like a cross between Portofino and Munchkin-land. (We don't quite buy the 'Italianate' tag – we've never seen anywhere like it in Italy!) There are castles to storm, ponies to trek with, salmon and trout to catch, steam trains to travel on.

Or consider the scenic British Rail line that runs from Shrewsbury across to Welshpool, goes over the Mawddach estuary and then via Barmouth up to Harlech Castle and beyond. And there's the Isle of Anglesey: one of our favourite towns in the whole of Britain is Beaumaris, just over the Menai Straits, and the hinterland is as Welsh as anywhere we know.

St David's map 5/276
Beth Ruach

These are among the best we've located in the west of Wales. *Beth Ruach* is on a grand scale, up a private drive, spacious (and pleasantly cool on the hot day of our visit) with a particularly comfortable sitting room. It has a skilful layout of bedrooms and **sleeps (yes!) up to 16 people**. This also has sea and country views from upstairs: but, of course,

Beth Ruach is a very stylish, comfortable and spacious family house...

you would want to explore this fabulous part of Wales, not just look at it! Linen and towels included. TVs. Payphone. Cost: about £395 to £2195. Not yet seen by us (to be remedied in 2006) are *Hendre Loan*, in a fine, high situation in the St David's conservation area (**sleeping 6**) and *Whitesands* (**sleeping 12**), a colonial-style bungalow with fabulous sea views.

Details, with an excellent brochure, available from Thelma Hardman, 'High View', Catherine Street, St David's, Pembrokeshire SA62 6RJ. Telephone 01437 720616.

www.stnbc.co.uk   email: enquiries@stnbc.co.uk

Saundersfoot, near Tenby
Blackmoor Farm Holiday Cottages

Just two miles from the glorious Pembrokeshire coast, and only a short drive from Saundersfoot's glorious sands and much loved Tenby, these excellent cottages have been much appreciated by our readers for over twenty years. Though not 'remote', they are nicely tucked away via winding country lanes. Better yet: Blackmoor Farm is surrounded by its own 36 acres of pastureland, accessible only by a private drive.

Families with children have always praised these cottages: indeed, as we arrived on our last visit, young children were playing happily among the trees near these beautifully cared for cottages. They also appeal to people who appreciate purpose-built accommodation in an attractive courtyard location. Resident owners Len and Eve Cornthwaite try to ensure that families enjoy a warm, friendly atmosphere. Blackmoor Farm has cattle grazing peacefully, and the old stables in the spacious gravelled farmyard contain a resident donkey called Dusty: children can enjoy rides on Dusty outdoors most days. (Be warned: more than one adventurous child has asked if next time the family can book one of the well appointed, discreetly situated mobile homes!)

There are just three cottages, south facing, side by side in a courtyard setting. Accommodation is two-tiered. Downstairs there are two bedrooms (each with full size twin beds, which can convert to bunk beds) and a well fitted out bathroom with bath *and* shower. Upstairs there is a large open-plan room containing the kitchen/dining section and comfortable living area leading on to a small patio balcony. A sofa bed allows the cottage to **sleep a maximum of 6**. The single-storeyed *Stable Cottage*, a converted farm building, **sleeps 2,** and has an appealing triple aspect living room. The decor and furniture are modern, comfortable, simple but attractive. Each cottage is well equipped, heated by storage heaters and, with double glazing and good insulation, cosy in the early and late seasons.

Cost: about £268 to £496 (less than this for Stable Cottage). TVs. Linen is provided but not towels. Laundry facilities. Games room. Not suitable for dogs and other pets. More details from Len and Eve Cornthwaite, Blackmoor Farm, Amroth Road, Ludchurch, near Saundersfoot, Pembrokeshire SA67 8JH. Telephone/fax 01834 831242.

www.infozone.com.hk/blackmoorfarm
email: ltecornth@aol.com

South-facing balconies, each with a table and two chairs for alfresco meals.

Stable Cottage – just right for 2, and a modestly-priced introduction to Wales.

140

Walwyn's Castle, near Little Haven
Rosemoor

Tucked away in the Pembrokeshire Coast National Park, well away from any main roads, the quiet and attractively situated Rosemoor cottages have featured in this guide since it first appeared in 1983.

The sandy beaches of Little Haven and Broad Haven, which has a handy supermarket, are within three miles' drive and Haverfordwest, the old county town, is about six miles away. And Walwyn's Castle? It's the remains of a Norman castle superimposed on an Iron Age fort.

The cottages, all annually graded by **'Visit Britain'**, were created from the red sandstone outbuildings of the large Victorian house in which the Dutch owners live. Each cottage is described in detail, complete with floor-plans, in Rosemoor's attractive and informative brochure, illustrated by neat pen-and-ink drawings. The estate extends for 34 acres, of which 20 have been officially designated as a nature reserve. Walking trails lead through woodland and around the picturesque five-acre lake. For naturalists and bird-watchers, it's all a delight.

Each time we've visited, most recently last autumn, we've been impressed by their variety as well as their very high standards. Six are grouped round a large three-sided open courtyard which has a central lawn; at the back they look on to wooded countryside. These include the spacious combination, with internal connection, of *Peace* (**sleeping 5**) and *Apple* (**sleeping 6**). Apple has three bedrooms and two bathrooms, one of which is en-suite to a ground floor bedroom, professionally designed for disabled use. *The Coach House*, nearby (**sleeps 6**), is capped by a small belfry and has a patio on to a walled garden, while *Holly Tree* (**sleeps 3**) has a view of the lake.

Most of the cottages have dark slate floors topped by attractive rugs, with underfloor heating. We also admired the polished dark grey Welsh slate

The three-bedroomed Coach House is distinctively capped by a small belfry. It is of course just one of Rosemoor's several 'characterful' properties here in rural West Wales. It is handy for beaches and lovely countryside, but not remote.

working surfaces in the fitted kitchens and liked the smart modern bathrooms tiled in black and white. Cost: about £150 to £1420. Dogs welcome. Home-cooked meals available. Linen supplied. Laundry facilities. Four cottages have woodburners. Games room and playground. Brochure from John M and Jacqui Janssen, Rosemoor, Walwyn's Castle, Haverfordwest, Pembrokeshire SA62 3ED. Telephone 01437 781326. Fax 781080.

www.rosemoor.co.uk   email: rosemoor@walwynscastle.com

Llanfallteg, near Whitland
Gwarmacwydd Farm Cottages

Many years in this guide, many encouraging reader responses: at the centre of a working farm that children will love (lambs, calves, rabbits to meet, and ancient woodlands to explore) this is a particularly quiet and spacious arrangement of cottages. The focal point here is the owners' handsome Georgian home. Adjacent to the main house are *The Coach House* (**sleeps 4/6**) and *Butler's Cottage* (**sleeps 2/3**), which

A reliably warm welcome at this very quiet, spacious and comfortable set-up.

can be linked to make one bigger property. Across grassy open ground, but still part of the original farm, stand *The Old Barn* and *Tower Cottage*, **sleeping 6** and **2/3** respectively, and also combinable. Our favourite has always been the roomy, stylish Coach House, with a triple-aspect sitting room/diner and central heating. **'Visit Britain' Four Stars**. No smoking. TV. Well behaved dogs by arrangement. Linen (not towels) and heating included. Cost: £125 to £450. Details and brochure from Angela Colledge, Gwarmacwydd Farm, Llanfallteg, Whitland, Carmarthenshire. Telephone 01437 563260; fax 563839.

www.a-farm-holiday.org email: info@a-farm-holiday.org

Newgale, near St David's map 5/284
Bryn-y-Mor

What a location! Watched by grazing cows, we drove along the side of a couple of fields to reach this 1930s bungalow. It stands alone in a quarter of an acre of grassed ground, high on the cliff-top above Newgale Sands, seven miles from St David's. From it a gate leads straight on to the Pembrokeshire Coast Path along the cliffs or down to the sandy beach. The

Idyllically situated on cliffs overlooking St Brides Bay and sandy beaches.

cottage is simply furnished (though fully heated) and has four bedrooms (**sleeping 9**). These are all off the sitting-room, which also leads on to a long covered-in verandah facing the sea. Depending on the weather, this can be a wonderful sun-trap or a great spot for simply enjoying the view across St Brides Bay. There's a good stock of jigsaws and books but no TV, though an aerial is available for anyone who brings their own. Personally we much preferred watching the waves and birdlife! Dogs welcome. Linen and towels not included. Cost: about £300 to £525. Details from Simon and Susie Arbuthnott, Belgate House, Shobdon, Leominster, Herefordshire HR6 9NJ. Telephone 01568 708038. Fax 708106.

email: buthers@zoom.co.uk

Coastal Wales
Quality Cottages Cerbid*

In an idyllic, quiet backwater of deeply rural Pembrokeshire and, better yet, down a sleepy lane, Leonard Rees's Cerbid Cottages *have featured in this guide every year since it first appeared in 1983*. We revisited them a couple of summers ago, and rediscovered their distinctive charms.

The high standards here tend to be reflected by the quality of Leonard Rees's agency properties, ninety per cent of which are within five miles of the sea – a huge selling point.

For example, just a few minutes from Newgale beach, which consists of over a mile of golden sands, is *The Red Hen House*. A superb barn conversion with sweet-smelling honeysuckle over the door, it is idyllically set in a secret valley conservation area complete with a private south-facing garden and a nearby trout lake. The feature stone fireplace makes it a good bet for the shoulder season.

If you want a dramatic coastal location, you will be impressed, as we were, by *Craig Yr Awel*, on Whitesands Bay, just a few yards above the beach. We could enjoy a week here just watching the ever-changing sea

The Cerbid cottages effectively form a hamlet of their own – utterly peaceful, each cottage with a high degree of privacy, everything beautifully cared-for.

The Red Hen House is an admirable barn conversion, and is marvellously well situated. It has 'honeysuckle round the door', and an open fireplace...

below. During a most enjoyable visit we noticed lots of books to read, comfortable leather armchairs. There's an open fire which is an absolute delight when the sea mist comes down or autumn nights close in, and a glazed patio with, as you would imagine, spectacular views. **Sleeps 10**. Dogs are welcome here.

In the beautiful lush and wooded Gwaun Valley between Fishguard and Newport, *Pontfaen* is a most impressive Victorian country house which **sleeps 11**.

A handsome full colour brochure, which also contains details of the Cerbid properties, can be obtained from Leonard Rees, Cerbid (GHCG), Solva, Pembrokeshire. Telephone 01348 837871. Freephone 0800 169 2256.

www.qualitycottages.co.uk

email: info@qualitycottages.co.uk

Boncath
Fron Fawr

Though we have featured them since 1985, we recently revisited to check out these three established cottages (deceptively spacious and as clean as the proverbial whistle), and a new property. This **sleeps 8** and is double glazed and centrally heated, with a large wood-beamed lounge and a wood-burning stove. All the cottages

A short drive from good beaches that are one of West Wales's 'best-kept secrets'.

are equipped, as one of our readers put it, with 'virtually everything': TV, hairdryer, microwave, dishwasher and enough kitchen equipment to keep any cook happy. Fron Fawr is a short drive from some delightful seaside places (good beaches, views and never any crowds). You will find a rolling lawn with swings where children can play, and enticing paths into woodlands inhabited by badgers, rabbits and a resident pair of buzzards.

Cost: approximately £210 to £1200 per week. Linen, towels, gas, electricity, and wood are provided. The cottages have three or four bedrooms, and **sleep between 5 and 8**. Details and brochures from Jackie Tayler, Fron Fawr, Boncath, Pembrokeshire SA37 0HS. Telephone 01239 841285. Fax 841545.

www.fronfawr.co.uk email: ghcg.cottages@fronfawr.co.uk

In these frantic times, remoter cottages often appeal most...

Penrallt, near Boncath
Clydey Country Cottages

Admirable signing along a succession of country lanes led us to this 18th-century farm and its nine cottages, all beautifully converted from original outbuildings. Dewi and Jacqui Davies took over the 20-acre estate in 2003, giving up high-powered jobs in the City of London, because they wanted to enjoy bringing up their young family in a much more pleasant environment, particularly as Dewi comes from Wales. They have certainly found a lovely spot, on high ground deep in the Pembrokeshire countryside and boasting glorious views. As they say, it's 'a haven of outstanding natural beauty, peace and tranquillity'.

Already they've installed a good-sized swimming pool with sheltered sun terrace and also a sauna. The swimming pool will be indoor from Easter 2006, and there will also be the additions of gym and games room to complement the existing outdoor hot tub.

The decor and furnishings of the cottages (**sleeping 2 to 6**) have been chosen to complement the age and style of the buildings. They retain their wooden beams and stone inglenooks and now feature farmhouse-style kitchens and fireplaces with multi-fuel stoves. Most have four-posters and dishwashers. All have DVD players, some have satellite TV.

A nature trail leads down into woods and, when we called, a group of children of mixed ages were happily occupied in the playground area which includes a Wendyhouse, rope swing and sandpit. There are two resident ponies, two sheep and four chickens. Old farm implements and

This is indeed 'a haven of outstanding natural beauty, peace and tranquillity'...

...in twenty acres of grounds, with a heated swimming pool, and much more.

wheels are on display around the buildings, adding to the rural atmosphere, together with benches for enjoying the country air and views. The nearest shop is a couple of miles away and there's a bright orange (yes, really!) pub and micro-brewery, the Nag's Head, which guests told us is child-friendly and highly rated for its food.

Welcome pack provided of tea, coffee and milk, together with fresh flowers and basket of logs. Shared laundry room. Highchairs and cots available. Portable barbecues. Sorry, no pets. Cost: approximately £300 to £900. Details from Dewi and Jacqui Davies, Clydey Country Cottages, Penrallt, Lancych, Boncath, Pembrokeshire SA37 0LW. Telephone 01239 698619; fax 698417.

www.clydeycottages.co.uk   email: info@clydeycottages.co.uk

Newport, Pembrokeshire
Carreg Coetan

We especially remember this modern cottage (we have stayed with small children) for its lush backdrop of wooded hills and the fine, safe, child-friendly beaches close by. Named after the ancient group of massive stones just across the road (marked on the Ordnance Survey map), it is ideally situated for walking, bird-watching or just relaxing.

A comfy base in a very attractive part of West Wales, with lots to see and do.

On our most recent visit last autumn we met people who had been been several times, as it made the perfect antidote to their stressful jobs in Cardiff. Partly creeper-covered and neatly fenced, the cottage is well-equipped and comfortable with a bright welcoming interior. We especially like the cosy sitting room/diner and big picture window on to the patio which faces the garden and hillside beyond. The shops and pubs of Newport are within easy walking distance. **Sleeps 4** in a double and a twin. Car-port and space for two other cars. Linen included, but not towels. Pets welcome by arrangement. Cost: about £191 to £442. Details from Mr and Mrs Carey, Waunwhiod, Newport, Pembrokeshire SA42 0QG. Telephone 01239 820822.

www.scarey.clara.net   email: susan.carey@btinternet.com

Nannerth Fawr, Pembrokeshire   map 8/291
Showman's Trailer

Amid hilly countryside in deepest mid-Wales, though not far from the English border, we came across a most unusual and intriguing holiday property. In the grounds of a farmhouse that is the focal point of holiday cottages featured on the opposite page, we much admired this carefully restored vehicle of the 1930s. It is the kind of thing you see at a historic-vehicle fair, but will rarely get

We thought this would make a very romantic spot for honeymooners...

the chance to stay in. It **sleeps 2** in a small double, with the added possibility of a sofa bed for one extra person (made up from upholstered benches in the living area). There is a small woodburning stove, a TV and a kitchenette. There is a WC and shower adjacent, even a small verandah, garden furniture and, usefully, an adjacent barn suitable for barbecues. Linen included. Tent space available. Also – there's a games room, a play area and friendly animals five minutes away on the farm.

Cost: £120 to £160.

Details from **frank@cottageguide.demon.co.uk**

Wales

Blakes Country Cottages*

Among the Welsh properties on Blakes's books several readers of this guide have singled out for praise is handsome *Ceilwart Cottage*, at Llanaber, near Barmouth. With impressive views over Cardigan Bay, it is full of character, with, for example, stone-flagged floors, beamed ceilings and – delightfully – a stream with waterfalls that passes through the terraced garden.

Ceilwart **sleeps up to 6**, not big enough for some: thousands of cottage-fanciers devote time to locating properties big enough to sleep large groups. So any owners who can accommodate more than, say, ten people find their properties much in demand. Ref WN73.

A reader in Northumberland, for example, joined a family party that took over both the properties on Aberkin Farm, at Llanystumdwy, near Criccieth. *Aberkin Farmhouse* **sleeps 8**, and is WTB **Four Stars**, and is nicely complemented by single-storeyed *Dwyfach* and *Dwyfor*, both **sleeping 4**. Refs WN30, B5884 and B5885.

Colleagues have previously booked one of the agency's biggest properties for a reunion. This is *Park Hall*, in two and half acres just 500 yards from a sand and shingle beach (rather a well-kept local secret) near Llwyndafydd, in Cardiganshire. It **sleeps up to 18 adults and 2 children**, and has a licence to perform marriages. Ref B4932.

Ceilwart, at Llanaber, is a property of great character. It has an Aga!

Park Hall is a long-standing favourite wth readers. It sleeps up to 20 people!

Just a stroll from the pseudo-Mediterranean village of Portmeirion, and with sea and mountain views, *Plas Penrhyn* is well placed for exploring the Snowdonia National Park and has the Ffestiniog Railway and excellent sandy beaches nearby. Once owned by Bertrand Russell and used by the novelist Elizabeth Gaskell for her honeymoon, it is very much a family house, **sleeping 8/9**. TVs. Sorry, no pets. Ref WN74.

On a smaller scale, *Porth Bach* is right at the heart of the ancient town of Conwy (and even has the castle as a backdrop). **Sleeping 4**, it makes an excellent touring base. Ref 17985.

Further details from Blakes Country Cottages, Spring Mill, Earby, Lancashire BB94 0AA.

For a brochure call: 0870 241 7970; to book call: 0870 192 1022.

To look and book: **www.blakes-cottages06.co.uk**

Rhyd-Yr-Eirin, near Harlech

For more than twenty years we've had a special fondness for this cottage. We love its character and its unforgettable location. When we say it's isolated, we mean *isolated*! It's full of atmosphere. You are 900-feet up, sheltered by hills to the north and east, in an oak-beamed, three-bed-roomed, 17th century farmhouse with an unusual stone staircase, original sitting-room window, antique

Splendid isolation, lots of atmosphere.

furniture and a wide-ranging Welsh-holiday library. There is an open fire in the inglenook (coal/wood provided) and each room has a storage or wall heater. The all-electric kitchen, bathroom and shower-room are up to a very high standard. Harlech and the glorious, sandy beaches are only fifteen minutes away by car, allowing for gate-opening! There's a concealed TV, radio-cassette player, telephone, double-oven cooker, microwave, fridge-freezer, dishwasher, washing machine, spin-dryer.

Sleeps up to 7. Cost: £150 to £550 (discounts for two-week bookings). Well-trained dogs welcome. Details with map and plans of the house and garden (including the bog-garden) from Mr Chris Ledger, 7 Chelmer Road, London E9 6AY. Telephone 020 8985 1853.

www.rhydyreirin.com email: info@rhydyreirin.com

Llanbedr, near Harlech
Nantcol   map 5/313

Another extraordinary location. From this 14th century stone built Welsh longhouse, five miles from Llanbedr village up a narrow valley road, you can walk straight up into the hills. It is perfection for walkers, bird watchers and lovers of the countryside: a spectacular location, spectacular views. In other words – it's one in a hundred! You can explore Snowdonia, relax on sandy beaches or play

What should we show – the house itself or the fabulous view? We revisited in 2004 – a pleasure, not just a duty...

golf at Royal St David's, Harlech, a championship course. As we walked in, it was a joy to see real log fires burning at both ends of the living room. This oak beamed cottage is filled with many interesting pieces of old Welsh furniture. The spacious farmhouse kitchen was just as welcoming, with a large oak table and, yes, an oil-fired Rayburn stove. Another bonus: no TV! **Sleeps 7** plus cot. Linen not provided. Open all year. Short breaks possible. Pets by arrangement (small charge). Cost: from about £400. Details from Stephanie and John Grant, Bollingham House, Eardisley, Herefordshire HR5 3LE. Telephone 01544 327326. Fax 327880.

www.north-wales-accommodation.co.uk
email: grant@bollinghamhouse.com

Pwllheli
Gwynfryn Farm Holidays

Family-orientated in a popular location.

Alwyn and Sharon Ellis who own this 100-acre organic dairy farm on the Lleyn Peninsula in North Wales certainly cater for all ages. With pigs and chickens to feed, cows to watch being milked, two trampolines, an adventure playground and a good-sized indoor pool, its twelve stone cottages make an ideal base for families. Named after lakes in Snowdonia, they have been smartly converted from old farm buildings and **sleep from 2 to 8**. The newest, *Glaslyn* and *Crafnant*, are both graded **Five Stars** and have tiled floors, leather furniture and two bathrooms. B&B is available in the farmhouse. Pwllheli and the sea are just a mile away, part of a 50-mile stretch of 'heritage' coast noted for its sandy bays and rocky headlands. When we visited the farm, a small boy from Manchester on his third holiday there told us he liked the cows most of all and also going on the famous narrow-gauge railways of Wales. Cost: £210 to £950. Wood-burning stoves, dogs welcome, home-cooked meals available. Details from Gwynfryn Farm, Pwllheli, Gwynedd LL53 5UF. Telephone 01758 612536.

www.northwales-countryholidays.com
email: frank@gwynfryn.freeserve.co.uk

Portmeirion, near Porthmadog   map 5/315
Portmeirion Cottages   Colour section A, Page 5

There's something 'other-worldly' about it.

In 2005 we stayed (one night: all too brief) in this enchanting hillside village created by the distinguished architect Sir Clough Williams-Ellis. Begun in the 1920s, its higgledy-piggledy pastel-coloured buildings make staying there a real experience. We strolled on the lovely sandy beach at the foot of the village and bought some of its famous pottery. **Sleeping from 2 to 8**, there are fourteen cottages, each one a picturesque gem (some have small gardens). The cottages are cosy, 'lived-in', deceptively spacious. We spotted antiques, good beds, well-equipped kitchens and often superb views from upper windows. Newspapers, bread and milk are available from a shop and guests have free use of the Portmeirion Hotel's heated pool by the sea from May to September. You can also eat there – in style – or in the hotel by the village entrance. Cost from £529 to £1224; three/four night winter breaks from £276 to £518. Satellite TV, heating, towels and linen. Details from Portmeirion Cottages, Portmeirion, near Porthmadog, Gwynedd LL48 6ET. Telephone 01766 770000.

www.portmeirion-village.com   email: hotel@portmeirion-village.com

St Dogmaels, near Cardigan
Trenewydd Farm Cottages

A dependably warm welcome awaits visitors to Trenewydd Farm Cottages, which are to be found in a beautiful rural location near the North Pembrokeshire coast, just three miles from the historic market town of Cardigan.

One of our readers spoke of 'the obvious hard work' on the part of the owner, of her 'time, hospitality and genuine care'. Others described 'a lovely holiday, made all the more enjoyable by the gracious hospitality and lovely cottages'. A family from Maidenhead, in Berkshire, wrote: 'Apart from the beautiful countryside, lovely beaches and the many attractions in the area, we also feel very relaxed here due to the pleasant surroundings and the excellent hospitality.'

Said a young couple from Highgate, in North London, who first stayed at Trenewydd while attending a big family wedding in Cardigan: 'What started off as just a convenient place to stay became somewhere to go back to for a proper holiday. We have been back three times.'

The fully equipped and exceptionally well maintained cottages are within landscaped gardens with an outdoor heated pool (available between May and September), a barbecue, children's play areas and farmyard pets. Siani and Sam, the two donkeys, love a carrot and a nose rub. In spring there are orphan lambs to bottle feed, which both children *and* adults love.

The award-winning Poppit Sands is only two and a half miles away, with other beaches and coves within easy reach. The surrounding area provides

A heated pool fits nicely into the carefully landscaped gardens of these well-cared-for, owner-run cottages.

We've much enjoyed a short stay here ourelves.

rich coastal, mountain and inland walking, bird-watching, sea and river fishing, golfing, horse-riding, boat trips etc. There are many conveniently located historic sites, gardens, craft specialists and opportunities to sample local Welsh produce.

The cottages **sleep from 2 to 9**, with two cottages opening into one large one and therefore **sleeping up to 13**.

Costs are from £190 in the low season (two bedrooms, **sleeping 4**) to £875 in high summer (four bedrooms, **sleeping 9**).

Open all year. Short breaks available. For availability, check the Trenewydd website: **www.cottages-wales.com**

Or telephone 01239 612370 and speak to Cheryl.

Aberdovey
Aberdovey Hillside Village

On a sunny south-facing hillside overlooking the Dovey estuary in the Snowdonia National Park, this 'village' of 20 smart pebble-dash cottages and apartments, most **sleeping 4**, was designed and developed in the 1960s and '70s by John Madin, the noted Birmingham architect who built the BBC's Pebble Mill.

He built the first, *Eastward*, for his own family holidays and gradually added more along landscaped terraces. Now his family has grown to include nine grandchildren, but they still come to stay every year.

Each time we walk around the 'village' (most recently last autumn) we are impressed by the way the accommodation has been fitted so neatly into the hillside, surrounded by gardens and linked by terraces and paths.

All the properties make the most of the wonderful estuary view with a terrace or balcony big enough for eating *al fresco*. Several have a split-level design, such as Eastward and *Westward*. **Sleeping 8**, these both have four bedrooms (one ensuite) on the lower level, with spacious pine-clad sitting room and dining areas upstairs with tall picture windows and high ceilings. Guests can enjoy the view from the comfort of high quality leather suites or on the long balconies, with their garden tables and chairs.

Featured by us for over 20 years, with a strong following among our readers...

...the fabulous views are just part of the appeal of this remarkable place.

Dolphin and *Porpoise*, both **sleeping 6**, have magnificent panoramic views and an unusual sleeping balcony within a double-height livingroom. Accessed by a bulkhead ladder, the balconies are furnished with twin beds. Porpoise is suitable for people with restricted mobility, as it has no steps.

From the 'village', a narrow street twists down into the small seaside town of Aberdovey, which has a good sandy beach, tennis courts, bowling green and a links golf course. It's also on the Machynlleth-Pwllheli coastal railway line, one of the most scenic in Britain.

Outdoor playground, games room with table tennis and pool, and toddlers' playroom. Laundry. Dogs welcome. Cost from £185 to £835, including electricity, heating, bedlinen and complimentary membership of Machynlleth leisure centre (seven miles away). Short breaks available. Details/brochures from Aberdovey Hillside Village, Aberdovey, Gwynedd LL35 0ND. Telephone 01654 767522. Fax 767069.

www.hillsidevillage.co.uk   email: info@hillsidevillage.co.uk

151

Criccieth
Rhos Country Cottages

Full of comfort and style and well situated amid peaceful farmland just over four miles from Criccieth, these are handy for the Snowdonia National Park and also the coast. Rhos-Wen is a well equipped single storey bungalow-type cottage in the same grounds as Rhos Ddu. It **sleeps**

Hendre Farmhouse is a beauty – masses of space, lots of character and comfort...

6 in three bedrooms, one of them with a romantic four poster. There are two bathrooms, one with an excellent sauna. Rhos Ddu is light, airy and well equipped. The comfortable sitting room has an open fire. Upstairs there are two bedrooms, **sleeping 5**, and a bathroom with jacuzzi. Cost: about £200 to £700. The two properties have spacious lawned gardens. Half a mile away is Betws-Bach, a large farmhouse from about 1675, **sleeping 6**, and Grade ll listed. We admired ancient beams, a huge fireplace, a snooker table. Finally, Hendre Farmhouse is a beauty, quietly and privately situated at the end of a single farm track. It **sleeps 6 'plus 2'**.

Cost: £350 to £1000. Small dogs welcome. Every cottage is **WTB Five Stars**. Details from Mrs A Jones, Rhandir, Boduan, Pwllheli, Gwynedd LL53 8UA. Telephone/fax: 01758 720047 or mobile 0776 986 4642.

www.rhos-cottages.co.uk   email: cottages@rhos.freeserve.co.uk

Cottages on a farm are usually sure-fire winners with children.

Llanrug, near Llanberis
Bryn Bras Castle

The summit of Snowdon is only six miles away, the sea just four. Bryn Bras is a fabulous base from which to explore most of North Wales and the Isle of Anglesey. (There are pubs and restaurants easily accessible.) The Grade II* Listed mainly Regency-period castle lies in 32 acres of gardens and woods. It even has 'its own mountain', with panoramic views, and often features in guides to Britain's outstanding houses and castles.

All the spacious apartments are of a superior standard, beautifully appointed with antiques and bygones, each with a distinctive, gracious character of its own (most are geared to discriminating couples). Specifically, *Gerddi* (wonderful garden views and a rather elegant bedroom and Art Deco bathroom), The *North Tower* (a large circular tower bedroom with a Victorian carved bed), *Tan-y-Twr* (a charming short staircase from a comfortable living room to a romantic bedroom) and *Flag Tower* all **sleep 2**. The latter is our particular favourite: a circular 23-foot diameter lounge, kitchen and dining room on the first floor by way of a wide circular staircase. The room has ornate panelling and Romanesque pillars, adorned with delicately carved woodwork (even the doors are curved!). The large, romantic circular bedroom has an elegantly draped half-tester double bed. *Simdda Fawr* (a huge chimney

A rare chance to stay in an unusual Regency-period Romanesque-style castle.

Guests have the full run of the gardens, which are also remarkable.

in polished slate, with stained glass windows on either side), *Muriau* (in the oldest, Georgian, part of the castle, with a pretty courtyard and fig tree) and *West Wing* (small, cosy, rather private rooms, with antique furniture and views of Anglesey) all **sleep 4**.

Bryn Bras Apartments include dishwasher and microwave, and very many other items provided include hairdryers, toiletries, towels and welcome baskets with breakfast cereals etc. Hot water, central heating and electricity are free to all apartments (which have **Five Wales Tourist Board Stars**). There are 'special complimentaries' for Romantic Breaks.

Dogs are not allowed, nor, regrettably, to preserve the tranquillity of Bryn Bras, are children. Duvets, bedlinen and electric blankets are supplied with beds made up. Flexible start and departure days, as preferred, for any stay, at any time of the year. Short breaks all year round. Cost: £450 to £850; short breaks for 2 people for two nights from £195.

Details, brochures from Mrs Gray-Parry, Bryn Bras Castle, Llanrug, near Caernarfon, North Wales LL55 4RE. Telephone/fax 01286 870210.

www.brynbrascastle.co.uk   email: holidays@brynbrascastle.co.uk

North and Mid Wales
Snowdonia Tourist Services*

The locations are absolutely 'spot on': all the properties on the books of Snowdonia Tourist Services are in the Snowdonia National Park, or on the Llyn Peninsula, or the Isle of Anglesey, or the North Wales Coast. This well established holiday letting agency has about 145 properties, from traditional country cottages, farmhouses and bungalows to town houses and holiday chalets. All are graded by the Wales Tourist Board.

We did a cottage-guide revisit during the autumn of 2003, and saw several properties. These included *The Coach House* and *Granary* at Llangristiolus, on the Isle of Anglesey. Both are listed buildings, ideal for families. In eight acres of woodland and attractive gardens, just three miles from a sandy beach, The Coach House **sleeps 5**, the Granary **sleeps 4**. Pets welcome. At *Fox's Lair*, a large conservatory is an excellent vantage point for panoramic views of the sea, Caernarfon Castle and the Menai Straits. There's an open-style kitchen/dining area and sitting room with a large open (feature) fireplace. A pretty garden leads to woodland. One pet is welcome. **Sleeps 6.**

Among our long-term favourites is *Bryn Heulog*, a detached villa with uninterrupted views of the spectacular estuary and the mountains. Open

Amid eight acres of woodland and gardens, The Granary is on Anglesey.

Bryn Heulog has an open fire, and spectacular estuary and mountain views.

fire. **Sleeps up to 8**. No pets. Central heating throughout. *The Captain's Beach House*, in a private location on Aberdesach beach, is surrounded by dramatic sea and mountain scenery. **Sleeps 6**. One dog welcome.

And driving down towards the harbour at Porthmadog we came across one of a number of townhouses (*South Snowdon Wharf*), overlooking the estuary, with panoramic views of the Snowdonia Mountains. In some cases the sitting room is on the first floor to take advantage of the views.

Short breaks are available in many properties, and most are available all year round. Details and brochures can be obtained from Snowdonia Tourist Services, High Street, Porthmadog, Gwynedd. Telephone 01766 513829. Fax 513837.

You can visit the easy-to-use website for virtual tours of cottage rooms, see photos of most rooms and check availability:

www.snowdoniatourist.com

email: all@sts-holidays.com

Tal-y-Bont, near Conwy
Pant Farm

We like turning away from the main road and going along a private, gated track to get to this fine property. The main part of the farmhouse dates back to the 16th century, but restoration includes just about every 21st century creature comfort. It has a good-sized 'farmhouse' kitchen/ breakfast room with a dishwasher, a microwave and pine furniture. There's a utility room with washing

In ten acres of pastureland, this property has long been one of our readers' favourites in North Wales.

machine, a dining room with massive inglenook fireplace and a sitting room featuring inglenook, bread oven and TV/video, sympathetically extended with French windows to the garden. Upstairs there's an elegant master bedroom (king sized bed), a twin-bedded room with washbasin and a third bedroom with two single beds. The bathroom has a bidet, and a second bathroom comprises shower, toilet and washbasin. (There's also a downstairs loo/washroom.) The house has double glazing, gas fired programmed central heating during winter lets, a woodburner. Not suitable for dogs. **Sleeps 6**. Cost: £225 to £450. Available all year. Linen not provided. Details: Roger Jones, Roger's Retreats, The Old Granary, Tremadog, Gwynedd LL49 9RH. Telephone 01766 513555 or 01758 760216.

Tal-y-Bont, near Conwy
Robyn's Nest   map 5/331

Across the drive from Pant Farm, though self contained, *Robyn's Nest* shares a remarkable situation in ten acres of land, overlooking the River Conwy and positioned perfectly for the coast (ten miles) and the heart of Snowdonia (Betws-y-Coed's just six miles). Although it can be used to augment the Pant Farm accommodation for larger groups by 2/4, it can be rented separately. The house

It's just across the drive from Pant Farm, and enjoys the same remarkable location.

offers split level accommodation with a king sized bed in the main (ensuite) bedroom and a dining area and big sitting room on the first floor, overlooking the valley. Better yet, there is a woodburning stove, as well as programmed central heating available at an extra charge. The ground floor contains a modern fitted kitchen, separate bathroom and toilet and a twin bedroom. There's an old stable door out on to a private paved patio area.

TV/video. **Sleeps 4**. Not suitable for dogs. Cost: £450. Available main season/bank holiday weeks only. Linen not provided. Details: Roger Jones, Roger's Retreats, The Old Granary, Tremadog, Gwynedd LL49 9RH. Telephone 01766 513555 or 01758 760216.

Uwchmynydd, near Aberdaron
Talcen Foel

It would be hard to find a more away-from-it-all spot than this old Welsh farmstead cottage. It is in the hamlet of Uwchmynydd, below the summit of Mount Anelog, at the western tip of the Lleyn Peninsula. After a scenic drive along seventeen miles of country lanes from Pwllheli, we eventually found it up a gated track which climbed around a hillside bordered by heather and gorse before ending along the edge of a field.

In ten acres of pasture, it's a fine comfortable cottage (**sleeping 2 to 4**) with wonderful sea and mountain views. On a clear day the Irish coast and Wicklow Hills beyond are clearly visible and also the mid-Wales coast. Inside, the interior has been sympathetically rebuilt and modernised while retaining its original character. To make the most of the views, the spacious lounge – originally a cowshed – has windows on three sides, but is kept cosy in cooler weather by a woodburner in an attractive fireplace. Up a couple of steps you reach the kitchen-dining room which has a flag-stone floor and large inglenook with an oil-fired range. The fully-fitted galley kitchen area includes a microwave and washing machine. Both bedrooms, a double and a twin, are at the front and the double offers sea views from the comfort of its bed. Above the kitchen-dining room, an open 'crog loft den' on a balcony reached by a wooden ladder provides huge fun for children to hide away and play in.

When we called there, two Hertfordshire teachers were enjoying a mid-

A super new addition to the 'cottage guide' family, with fabulous views...

It is comfortable but not 'prissy', combining modern needs and history.

morning coffee on the patio. 'We've been coming regularly ever since it was converted in 2001', they told us. 'It's just what we need as a complete break from our classrooms'.

The cottage is on the Pilgrims' Way coastal path, two miles from the seaside village of Aberdaron (shops, pub and beach) and one from the excellent seafood restaurant at Penbryn Bach, mid-way between Sanctuary Cottage and Penbryn Bach Cottage (see opposite page).

Available July/August, first week of September, Christmas and New Year. Ideal for honeymooners, 'stressed out' couples, walkers and birdwatchers. 'Sorry, no pets'. TV, video. Linen not provided. Friday to Friday bookings. Cost: from about £450 inclusive of electric and storage heaters (winter) with reductions on fortnightly bookings.

Details: Roger Jones, Roger's Retreats, The Old Granary, Tremadog, Gwynedd LL49 9RH. Telephone 01766 513555 or 01758 760216.

Uwchmynydd, near Aberdaron
Penbryn Bach Cottage

Over the years, readers have been very complimentary about the properties featured on this and the two previous pages). Within four acres of pasture, this first is a 200-year-old one-time farmhouse with its own small garden. Adjacent is a small, seasonal licensed restaurant known for its seafood (quiet and self contained). Peacefully sited above Aberdaron Bay, en route for Wales's

Good views, an open fire, peace and quiet. Having a restaurant next door is a bonus, not a disadvantage.

'end of the world', this is a cosy retreat with vast, tranquil rural views. The house has a glazed entrance porch, an old ship's door entry to a hallway, a small comfortable lounge with beamed ceiling and an open fire, as well as French windows leading on to a sun porch, a ground floor double bedroom, a snug dining room, a well fitted kitchen and bathroom. A narrow, steep stairway leads to two 'crogloft' bedrooms, a double and a single. *Not suitable for young children and less agile adults, but ideal for two couples.* Available all year. **Sleeps 4 to 5**. TV. Not suitable for dogs. Linen not provided. Cost: £195 to £395. Details from Roger Jones, Roger's Retreats, The Old Granary, Tremadog, Gwynedd LL49 9RH. Telephone 01766 513555 or 01758 760216.

Aberdaron   map 5/328
Sanctuary Cottage (Bryn Du Farm)

Tucked away along narrow lanes on the Llyn Peninsula, this has sandy beaches within a mile and a half and a network of footpaths leading to the sea. The large lounge has an inglenook fireplace with multi-fuel stove, an old dresser with Willow Pattern plates, TV/video and dining table. Open stairs lead to the first floor, with one double bedroom, one twin bedded room and a third bedroom with bunk beds. All the rooms are

A sanctuary indeed, warm and stylish.

small and cottagey, with rural views. The bathroom has an electric shower over the bath. There's a well-modernised kitchen/diner with cooker and microwave. A utility room off the kitchen houses the fridge/freezer, washing machine/dryer, and dishwasher. Fronting the length of the cottage is a large conservatory with cane furniture and dining table and chairs – well recommended by guests! Windows are double-glazed. **Sleeps 6**. Cost: £195 to £450. Available all year. Not suitable for dogs. Linen not provided. Details from Roger Jones, Roger's Retreats, The Old Granary, Tremadog, Gwynedd LL49 9RH. Telephone 01766 513555 or 01758 760216.

Pentre Cwrt and Maesycrugiau

Here are two cottages of real character, both of them in most attractive
locations, and both recommended by
readers of the guide. The former
(Ref W4588 in the Welcome
Cottages brochure) is a former
woollen mill in three acres that
stands beside a trout stream, and
retains lots of original features, as
well as a woodburner. The sitting
room/dining area is on the first floor,
to take advantage of the views, and
there is even a pool table. It **sleeps**

*This especially cosy cottage is at
Maesycrugiau, near Carmarthen.*

up to 7. The latter (Ref W8409) is also in a fine situation in the valley of
the River Teifi. It too – the wing of a larger property – has a woodburning
stove and **sleeps 6**. There is a four poster bedroom and an attic bedroom
that our own children would have loved. One is just five miles from the
Brechfa Forest, where there are mountain bike trails, and a pub/restaurant
is only a mile away.

For availability and bookings, contact Welcome Cottages, Spring Mill,
Earby, Barnoldswick, Lancashire BB94 0AA. Telephone (brochures) 0870
192 0809; 0870 336 2285 (bookings). Properties in France available too.

www.welcomecottages.com

Llangennith, Gower Peninsula map 5/345
Longcroft Cottage/Tankey Lake Livery

At least two readers picked up on
our reference to these cottages in last
year's guide. In walking distance of
one of the many sandy beaches on
the Gower Peninsula, with sea and
mountain views, *Longcroft* is a 200
year old detached cottage with its
own large enclosed patio garden.
Sleeps 4 in a double and a twin;
shower room/WC. There are lots of
beams, and a slate floor in the modern, well equipped kitchen. Ref

*Comfortable cottages, with good walking
from the door and beaches nearby...*

OMH. And at *Tankey Lake Livery*, Llangennith, nestling in 31 acres of the
owner's small working farm, are two single-storeyed cottages called
Bluebell and *Buttercup*, conversions from a 16th century barn. One **sleeps
2**, the other **sleeps 4**, and both are suitable for wheelchair access. Refs
JYW/JAM. Outdoor pursuits include surfing, windsurfing, canoeing,
pony trekking, bird-watching, fishing, golf, hang-gliding and caving.

Further details available from English Country Cottages, Stoney Bank
Road, Earby, Barnoldswick BB94 0AA. Booking line 0870 192 1028;
'dial-a-brochure' 0870 192 0391.

www.ecc2006.co.uk

Brecon Beacons and around
Brecon Beacons Holiday Cottages*

This much admired agency is run by the energetic Liz Daniel, who recently won the accolade of 'Best Small Business in Wales', and has figured in the finals of 'Welshwoman of the Year'. It is a remarkable organisation, with over 270 cottages and farmhouses in and around the Brecon Beacons National Park.

Liz's properties range from a tiny cottage such as *Blaentrothy*, providing a very high level of comfort **for 2** people in a lovely setting, to spacious, rambling farmhouses **sleeping – yes! – up to 50** that are ideal for families and reunions.

We have visited and revisited over the years, and most recently we saw two of the larger properties. Firstly, the remotely-situated (but by no means bleakly lonely) *Crofftau*, whose long, beautifully-furnished sitting-room/dining room upstairs has a steep beamed ceiling, wood burning stove and spectacular mountain views on both sides. It is hard to believe that it was once a barn. **Sleeps 8**. Cost: £820. We don't have enough space to do justice to it but, for example, we were much impressed by the panoramic views, the space, the antiques, the pictures, the huge first floor living room and its rare and extraordinary 1950s Wurlitzer juke-box.

Dovecote Cottage, with a hard tennis court and three miles of fishing on the River Usk, is in a most beautiful location, with views of the Listed

Crofftau is one our favourite houses in the whole of Wales. Not least because there's a Wurlitzer juke-box!

Duffryn Beusych is a cosy charmer, and the owner will prepare a meal for guests on arrival 'at cost'.

octagonal 18th century dovecote and ancient stone bridge over the river. The impressive sitting room has heavy oak beams, having once been the old laundry, a large wood-burning stove in an inglenook fireplace and comfortable sofas and chairs. **Sleeps 8**. Cost £690.

Neat and pretty *Duffryn Beusych* is beautifully situated, with memorable views of The Sugar Loaf and the Black Mountains. Better yet (as far as we are concerned!) the approach to it is via a steepish farm drive and over two fords. It **sleeps 3/4**, and has a woodburning stove.

Details from Elizabeth Daniel, Brecon Beacons Holiday Cottages and Farm Houses, Brynoyre, Talybont-on-Usk, Brecon, Powys LD3 7YS. Telephone 01874 676446. Fax 676416.

www.breconcottages.com   email: enquiries@breconcottages.com

Sennybridge, near Brecon
Cnewr Estate

The Cnewr Estate is a great place from which to enjoy The Brecon Beacons National Park to the full. You can choose between a big 1890 farmhouse and a shepherd's cottage, both of them on the 12,000-acre estate (owned and farmed by the same family since 1856), and all much praised by readers over the years.

We sometimes happen on houses or cottages that fit perfectly into their surroundings and give immediate access to much treasured corners of the country: we would include these.

The whole area is ideal for walking, and you could spend a day on the mountains without leaving the estate. There is fly-fishing on the estate's Cray Reservoir, *one of only four in Wales with wild trout*, as well as the hill streams.

Cnewr Farmhouse, which **sleeps 12** in five twins and one double, has a long dining table big enough to seat everyone comfortably in the huge well-equipped kitchen. The main sitting room has unspoilt views down the valley and there is also a TV-lounge/children's room, two bathrooms and shower room. The owner's private dining room is available by arrangement for special occasions. There's lots of warmth and a good number of 'country antiques'.

The other property is beside the Sennybridge to Ystradgynlais road but the windows facing it are double-glazed, though there is little traffic. *Fan Cottage* overlooks Cray Reservoir, having been built as a shepherd's cottage to replace a house lost when the reservoir was built. It has one double and two twin bedrooms, bathroom, sitting room, dining room and large kitchen. It **sleeps 5/6**.

Each property has an open fire (logs provided free), payphone and TV. Well-behaved dogs welcome. Linen and towels provided. Cost, including heating and electricity, from about £185 to about £600. Short-breaks are available at less busy times of the year.

Detailed brochures are available from the Cnewr Estate Ltd, Sennybridge, Brecon, Powys LD3 8SP. Telephone 01874 636207. Fax 638061.

www.cnewrestate.co.uk
email: cottages@cnewrestate.co.uk

Cnewr Farmhouse can accommodate twelve people. It's a comfortable, rambling place of great character...

Fan Cottage, where we have stayed briefly, overlooks peaceful Cray Reservoir, amid fine scenery...

Abergwesyn
Trallwm Forest Cottages

Located most unusually at the heart of a working forest, in a deeply rural part of mid Wales, this is a clutch of cottages converted from former farm buildings. All are WTB **Four Stars**. *Siskin*, a detached stone cottage, is **for a couple** (non-smokers). *Nant-Garreg* is full of character, has oak beams, an inglenook fireplace and **sleeps 4**. Two cottages, *Kestrel* and

Peace, perfect peace, deep in the forest. There are mountain bike trails and a Mountain Bike Centre: details on www.coedtrallwm.co.uk

Red Kite, are two-bedroomed and very comfortable. *Trallwm Farmhouse* **sleeps 7**, has a large lounge/diner and a blend of rustic and modern, with one of the three bedrooms downstairs. *Magpie* is a cosy cottage for a non smoking couple. *Trawsgyrch,* a large, traditional Welsh stone farmhouse overlooking hayfields, is well equipped for the **9/10 it sleeps**. Cost: from about £237, fully inclusive, for 2 people. One well-behaved dog is welcome by arrangement (in Nant-Garreg, Siskin and Trawsgyrch). TVs throughout and phone in Nant-Garreg, Siskin and Trawsgyrch only, plus payphone for general use. Details from George and Christine Johnson, Trallwm Forest Lodge, Abergwesyn, Llanwrtyd Wells, Powys LD5 4TS. Telephone/fax 01591 610229.

www.forestcottages.co.uk email: trallwm@aol.com

Golden Grove (Towyn Valley)   map 5/338
Ro Fawr Farm

The three cottages here, close to Dryslwyn, are quite superbly situated: not only are you within an 'SSSI' (a Site of Special Scientific Interest) with for example buzzards, red kite, badgers and deer to be seen, but close to three ancient castles, and only five miles from the National Botanic Garden of Wales. *Y Llaethdy* (The Dairy) is an interesting single storey building that was once cow

Cosy cottages in a rather 'underplayed' part of South Wales, full of rural charm and interest...

stalls. It **sleeps 2** in twin beds that link to make a big double. There's an open fire. Two storeyed *Y Bwthyn* (The Cottage) dates back to 1802, and it too has an open fire. **Sleeps 4** in a double and a twin. Without a Welsh name, but appealing nonetheless, the *Victorian Barn* is a fine first-floor conversion, also **sleeping 4** (in two twins that, as with The Dairy, can be moved together to make extra-large doubles).

Details from Ro Fawr Farm, Golden Grove, Dryslwyn, Carmarthenshire SA32 8RP. Telephone 01558 668505.

www.rofawrfarm.com
email: ann@rofawrfarm.com

The West Country

The West Country has so much going for it – the proximity of the sea, the wild moors, the two national parks, the great stately homes. (And it *is* a fact that the climate is generally a few degrees warmer than elsewhere in Britain.) We remember from childhood (and later) holidays marvellous sunsets, luscious crabs, clotted cream and Cornish pasties, coastal footpaths, ancient castles. On the eastern side of the River Tamar from Cornwall is Devon, with dramatic tors and moorlands fringed by charming villages. Notably, and uniquely in England, it has two separate (unlinked) coasts – a north and south. On the borders of Devon and Somerset, Exmoor is pony trekking and walking country, where wild ponies and deer roam freely. Exmoor has a stretch of coast it can almost call its own, and some spectacular views. In Somerset, Cheddar Gorge and Wookey Hole are memorable. Over the border in Dorset, it is easy to find country houses off the tourist beat and holiday resorts full of history and charm (Lyme Regis is a delight.) And the best of Wiltshire is the essence of rural England, unchanged for hundreds of years. It is dotted with ancient pubs, and half its holiday cottages seem to be thatched!

Botelet, near Herodsfoot
Manor Cottage   map 6/348

With its origins mentioned in the Domesday Book, oak beams, flagstone floors and open fireplaces, this 17th century listed longhouse is – not surprisingly – a real favourite among cottage guide readers. The dining room doors open on to a private walled garden created from earlier ruins, and the kitchen features a covered floodlit well (a first for us!).

A spacious traditional farmhouse, suitable for family groups and couples.

Coupled with this is a flair for design for which Richard Tamblyn has been featured in Elle Decoration. The cottage has been furnished to a standard that makes guests instantly feel at ease: they often choose to stay twice a year. Brass beds are made up with antique linen, the fire is lit and the table laid; with 300 acres, with a neolithic hill-fort, fields, lanes and a woodland walk, there is plenty to explore. The Tamblyn family have been on the farm since 1860 and the present generation live in the Georgian farmhouse across the cobbled courtyard.

Sleeps 5 in three bedrooms (double, twin, single); one bathroom, one shower room. Linen is supplied. Dishwasher, fridge/freezer, washing machine, dryer, microwave, TV, video, CD/tuner. Woodburning stove. Babysitting. Dogs by arrangement. Cost: £270 to £970. Please note that a further cottage (*Cowslip*, not yet seen by us) is available. Further details from Julie Tamblyn, Botelet, Herodsfoot, Liskeard, Cornwall PL14 4RD. Telephone/fax 01503 220225; fax 220909.

www.botelet.co.uk
email: stay@botelet.co.uk

Treworgey Manor, Liskeard
Coach House Cottages

One of our inspectors has commented that Treworgey Manor and its holi-day cottages have 'the happy knack of maintaining a high degree of com-fort without losing the character of the place'. It was one of our readers who first brought the manor, in the same family for over 500 years before coming under the stewardship of Jeremy and Jane Hall, to our attention. She said 'It's a fabulous conversion, beautifully and imaginatively done.'

Even the large heated outdoor pool looks no more out of place than the ancient clock tower, the symbol of this architecturally pleasing group of 16th century courtyard cottages. An all-weather tennis court, games room and boules pit complete the outdoor attractions.

Discovering this beautifully cared for Cornish oasis of comfort and style on a warm summer afternoon raised our morale considerably!

You could even hold a small dance in *The Coach House* which, **sleeping 8**, has a half size snooker table in the sitting room. There is one double bedroom with en suite bathroom, a further double bedroom, one twin-bedded room, a bunk-bedded one, a bathroom and a separate shower room, making it ideal for two families, or for those bringing grandparents. *Paddock View* and *Deer Park* both **sleep 6**, but vary in the distribution of bedrooms and also in decor, each being delightfully distinctive, with good use made of original beams, paintings, ornaments and objects of interest from the old manor buildings.

Middle Barn **sleeps 4** in a double bedroom and a twin, and has an upstairs bathroom. Pets are accepted in this property. Dogs will certainly appreci-ate the walks, the Manor being tucked into 100 acres of pasture and woodland. Children will also have fun exploring the nooks and crannies around the courtyard, not least the mysterious priest's hole.

With a roaring log fire for company there is every temptation to stay put in your own little world. Which is where short breaks, weekend parties – renting all four cottages – come into their own. Each garden has a table and chairs, plus barbecue.

Electricity and calor gas are included, and also an initial basket of logs (each property has a open log fire); linen is supplied, except beach towels; there is a laundry room, payphone and TVs with DVD players. Cost: about £160 (three night short break) to £1180. Details are available from Jeremy or Jane Hall, Coach House Cottages, Treworgey Manor, Liskeard, Cornwall PL14 6RN. Telephone 01579 347755. Fax 345441.

www.treworgey.co.uk email: info@treworgey.co.uk

Duloe, near Looe
Trefanny Hill

Readers once told us they booked a cottage here with the aim of making it their touring base for a week. 'But', they said, 'we never left "the village", as we came to know it. It is such a retreat from everyday cares, so peaceful and nostalgic.'

Visitor loyalty is certainly high: during the last thirty-plus years the Slaughter family have never been without people who have stayed here before, and on some occasions they have been full of regular visitors.

It's hard to believe that over 40 years ago, when the Slaughter family first discovered Trefanny Hill, it was a desolate ruin. Nestling above a tributary of the West Looe River, this ancient farming settlement was at one time a thriving, medieval smugglers' hamlet which in the last century was granted its own school, smithy and chapel. Even today, Trefanny Hill

There is a village atmosphere at Trefanny Hill. The cottages are well spread out and enjoy a feeling of independence.

Each cottage has its own individual character. They range in size from those for 6 to mini cottages just for couples.

retains a village atmosphere. The cottages are lovely, their stone or white -painted walls draped with ivy, roses and other climbers and looking just like everybody's idea of what a country cottage should be. Each has bags of character, and reveals the Slaughters' amazing eye for detail. There are seventeen cottages in all—well spread out, each with its own garden.

There are five different sizes of cottage, appropriate to the size of your family, ranging from a cosy cottage just for **2** (either with an antique brass double bed or four poster, or king-size/twin beds) to a three-bedroom for **6** (7 with a cot). Among the little extras you will find are plenty of books (including a set of coffee table items on wild flowers, trees, birds). There are video recorders, hairdryers, electric blankets, hot water bottles, alarm clocks. The kitchens are fully equipped with filter coffee makers, spice jars, wine coolers, microwaves, dishwashers and extras galore. All the cottages for 3 or more also have a washing machine/tumble dryer installed, while the smaller ones without this have access to washing machines and dryers in a traditional Cornish building nearby.

Each garden has chairs, a table, a parasol and a good barbecue so you can enjoy fine weather to the full. Standing in 75 acres, Trefanny Hill is surrounded by rolling greenery and commands a wide panorama over the Looe Valley. Among the permanent residents are the ducks on their pond, the chickens, doves, cats, Jacob's sheep and shire horses. The wild flowers in springtime are particularly magical. There are no half-hidden eyesores that detract from the peaceful atmosphere. The interiors of the cottages are like private homes. The furniture is good, old and varied. Each cottage is different; some have Laura Ashley and Sanderson wallpaper and fabrics, most have oak beams up to 400 years old, and log fires.

Perhaps the most memorable part of our most recent visit was strolling downhill past the heated outdoor pool that is accessible to all Trefanny's guests – it is amazingly scenically situated, and always warm – and then through fields towards a wooded stream where we discovered *Tregarrick Millhouse*, another of those substantial family houses that make these journeys so worthwhile. We do not have the space to convey all its delights, but noted most appealing reds and greens in the decor and, outside, large grounds with a stream and a mill pond. **Sleeps 6**.

A tea and coffee tray greets every arriving guest, and all linen – crispy white, generous in size – is provided. Shared amenities include that beautiful heated swimming pool, a children's play area, a grass lawn with bad-

Most unusually, cottage guests at Trefanny Hill have their own cosy little inn, which is much enjoyed for drinks, snacks and full meals.

In this attractive setting, people staying at Trefanny Hill have ready access to one of the most impressively situated outdoor pools in Cornwall!

minton net, a golf net for driving practice and more. There is an attractive lake with wildlife, a full size tennis court, and an enchanting bluebell wood.

The tiny inn within the hamlet is also a popular feature, where you can relax in a cosy, informal atmosphere for drinks or candlelit dinners. Dishes are cooked to order using fresh local produce (freshly caught local fish and organic steaks being the specialities of the house), or alternatively you can eat in the privacy of your own cottage by choosing from the full and varied menu offered by a home cooked meals service.

More fishing (lake, river and sea), windsurfing, including hire and instruction, riding, golf, sailing and many more activities are all available in the area. Each cottage has an information folder and relevant Ordnance Survey maps. We wish this was universal!

A typical comment culled from the visitors' books in the cottages reads 'For a long time we have looked for a holiday that offers top class hotel accommodation with the freedom of self-catering – at last we have found it'. Said one Lancashire visitor, 'it's the most honest brochure I have seen in many years'. And a Surrey couple have been to stay – yes! – 41 times!

Cost: about £150 to £1945. Children and well behaved pets are welcome. Details from John and Suzanne Slaughter, Trefanny Hill, Duloe, near Liskeard, Cornwall PL14 4QF. Telephone 01503 220622.

www.trefanny.co.uk enq@trefanny.co.uk

Duloe, near Looe
Treworgey Cottages

For all its usefulness, the **'Visit Britain'** grading scheme doesn't accord cottages special credit for being in idyllic locations. So in our book (literally) these are **Five Star**-plus, with all the comfort and style that implies *and* a memorable situation.

High above the River Looe, with spectacular south-facing views over patchwork fields and the river itself, they are outstanding. Better yet, owners Lynda and Bevis Wright have landscaped the prettiest of individual private gardens for each cottage, with masses of flowers.

Each cottage exudes good taste and is individually styled, mostly with family antique furniture, original paintings, wool carpets, oriental rugs, plenty of lamps and books. Bedrooms have exceptionally attractive four posters or beautiful brass beds with really comfortable mattresses, antiques, lace and fresh flowers.

Add to this a delivered candlelit dinner (from Treworgey's mouthwatering menu) by your roaring log fire, a good video from the Wrights' comprehensive library and you'll think you have died and gone to heaven! (Don't worry about the washing up – the dishwasher will do it!)

There is plenty to do here too (the Eden Project, for example, is only half an hour away), and the landscaped outdoor pool is stunning. Readers are full of praise about that: 'really warm...open and steaming as late as October, when the weather allows'... There is excellent riding available on site, an all-weather tennis court, indoor and outdoor playground with wendy house and more, and a delightful collection of animals: the goats

Unusually for this sort of set-up, every property has its own cottagey garden...

Such a lot of style and attention to detail has gone into every one of the interiors...

and Bramble the pony spend most of their time befriending guests.

Short breaks are welcome out of season. With log fires and ample central heating, Treworgey is very popular in winter and for Christmas and New Year. (By the way Treworgey is easy to get to by train – there's even a tiny toy station down the lane at Sandplace.)

Cost: from about £275 per week to £2071, according to cottage size and season. **Sleep from 2 'plus baby' to 8**. Children are welcome. Telephone 01503 262730. Fax 263757.

www.cornishdreamcottages.co.uk

email: treworgey@enterprise.net

Looe Valley
Badham Farm Holiday Cottages

There are not many 'deeply rural' properties you can still reach by train. But this is one, via Causeland Halt on the scenic Looe Valley Line – a most charming feature that Jan and Pauline Scroczynski plan to make more of as they continue to upgrade these popular cottages. Newly built is the ground floor two bedroom timber frame *Oak Cottage*, with block and render facing, **sleeping 4,** and *Ash Cottage*, similarly built, accessible to the disabled, and **sleeping 5**. Likewise the three bed-room *Larch Cottage,* **Five Star** rated and **sleeping 6**. Again wheelchair friendly, it's in two acres of landscaped garden, close to a pine forest.

Both 'deeply rural' and near the sea – a powerful combination in holiday houses.

All neatly complement the other six cottages, **sleeping between 2 and 10** in the *Farmhouse*. Bonuses include an animal and bird paddock, a coarse fishing lake and tennis court, along with a convivial bar and a large games room.

Dogs at £20 a week. Cost from about £200 to £1000 including heating; also short breaks. Contact Jan and Pauline Scroczynski, Badham Farm Holidays, St Keyne, Liskeard, Cornwall PL14 4RW. Telephone/fax 01579 343572. **www.badhamfarm.co.uk email: badhamfarm@yahoo.co.uk**

Coverack, near Helston
Trevarrow Cottage map 6/360

The quaint Cornish fishing village of Coverack, very well located on a south easterly corner of the Lizard peninsula, is the kind of place that photographers drool over. And this idyllic looking cottage looks as good as any you might see on chocolate box lids or jigsaws. Also, Trevarrow would surely win the prettiest-cottage-in-the-village award on account of its pastel-pink walls and thatched roof. Better yet, it was once a smugglers' hideaway. Though it has been properly modernised, it still has its original shipwreck beams and inglenook fireplace. It has an excellent and well-equipped kitchen with, microwave, washing machine/tumble dryer. Short breaks at an advantageous price are available off peak. Electricity is included, as is

Trevarrow is one of the prettiest houses in one of Cornwall's most sought-after coastal villages.

linen (though not towels). Friday to Friday bookings. No smoking. **Sleeps 6**. Cost: about £395 to £825. Further details from Amanda Wiseman, Shenstone Court, Court Drive, Shenstone, Lichfield, Staffordshire WS14 0JQ. Telephone 07980 370373 or fax 01543 481272.

email: wisemanaj@googlemail.com

Pelynt, near Looe
Tremaine Green

Effectively making up a hamlet in its own right, the cottages at Tremaine Green convey a charming sense of belonging, and there are usually opportunities for children to make new friends.

In this group of traditional craftsmen's cottages, the whole family will appreciate the games room with table-tennis, pool, darts and other games. They'll also appreciate the lovingly kept, award-winning gardens. Good beaches and restaurants are a short drive away, as is 'quintessential' Polperro. Also, there's a hard tennis court, putting green, swing-ball, pigmy goats, rabbits, miniature ponies etc to feed. Hamlet, the owners' blue Great Dane, completes the picture.

Every building is named after its original use, such as *Blacksmith's*, *Carpenter's* and *Miller's*, and each is decorated inside with interesting pictures and artefacts, particularly antique tools. Leather hobnail boots and saddlery are interesting reminders of *Ploughman's* history, while *Cobbler's* boasts authentic relics from a shoemaker's.

There are eleven cottages altogether (**sleeping 2 to 6**), each with its own

We love the fact that Tremaine Green's cottages are private and self-contained...

...but are at the same time part of a tucked away hamlet, 'part of a whole'.

individual charm. Most have exposed stonework to add to their character and many have an antique four-poster or half-tester bed at least in the main bedroom. Cots and occasional single beds are available in most cottages. The kitchens in cottages **sleeping 4** or more have dishwashers and fridge-freezers. We liked the comfortable settee/deep armchairs in Ploughman's and the inglenook fireplace with the original cloam (bread) oven, also *Dairymaid's* antique half-tester bed, the pretty fabrics and the open fire. *Tinner's*, which has a bunk bedroom and shower downstairs, plus two doubles upstairs, is popular with families, as children sleeping in the bunks can feel independent.

The double glazing and the oil-fired central heating make all this cosy in winter. (Four cottages have real fires as well.) Videos and DVDs are available for rent, and Penny Spreckley has written a leaflet on local dog-walks. Tickets for the Eden Project (14 miles) are for sale to avoid queuing at the ticket office. Dogs and other pets welcome. Linen provided. TVs, videos and DVDs. Cost: about £165 to £885. An excellent brochure is available from Justin and Penny Spreckley, Tremaine Green Country Cottages, Pelynt, near Looe, Cornwall PL13 2LT. Telephone 01503 220333; fax 220633.

www.tremainegreen.co.uk   email: stay@tremainegreen.co.uk

Praa Sands
Sea Meads Holiday Homes

The location is impressive: a mile-long sandy beach, facing due south into the broad sweep of Mounts Bay, a nine-hole golf centre, riding stables within easy reach. And of course there's the charm of the properties themselves.

But the greatest draw, especially for families, is that glorious beach which is only a five minute walk; you can not only see and hear the waves, you can almost touch them!

On our last revisit we were delighted to rediscover the properties on a private road almost hidden from the little cluster of buildings above the beach. Sea Meads is a group of five detached houses, each with its own private garden facing the sea, spacious lounges with large sliding patio windows through which to enjoy those views, dining areas with serving hatch from modern kitchens equipped with dishwashers, fridge-freezers, cookers with extractor hoods, microwaves, washing machines, clothes driers, bathrooms with heated towel rails and wall heaters – everything to permanent-home standards.

*Solmer, Sunwave, Sea Horse*s and *Sunraker* are all similar. On the ground floor there is a twin-bedded room with en-suite bathroom and toilet, and a small room with double bunk beds. Upstairs are two large bedrooms (one double, one twin) – each has a small balcony with magnificent sea views, and a second bathroom with shower unit. The ambience is one of brightness and light, with comfortable furniture and charming domestic touches. There is plenty of space, a private garage to each house, room in the garden for ball games, all-in-all a recipe for the most exacting family who just want to laze about or go in for strenuous activity. **Sleep up to 8**.

This is a typical bedroom-balcony view!   *Semi-tropical gardens, superb interiors.*

The fifth house, *Four Winds*, **sleeping 5**, is lower lying and separate from the others. We loved the big, comfortable sitting room and the linked sun lounge on to the sea side; we also liked the different-level dining area and the ensuite bedroom with impressive sea views.

Cost: approximately £255 to £1045, depending on which property and when you go. TVs/videos. Dogs are welcome. Linen is included, towels available on request. There is a games room, with table tennis, pool and darts. Details from Best Leisure, Old House Farm, Fulmer Road, Fulmer, Buckinghamshire SL3 6HU. Telephone 01753 664336. Fax 663740.

www.bestleisure.co.uk

St Austell
Bosinver Cottages/Lodges

We were not surprised that 'Bosinver', as we've known it for over twenty years, won the accolade of 'Self Catering Establishment of the Year' in the Cornwall Tourism Awards for 2005.

For we have watched with admiration as Pat and David Smith have completely rebuilt most of their nineteen cottages. Among appreciative comments in Bosinver's attractive 'brochure', we noted this one: 'It doesn't matter how many times we visit, every time we arrive we're greeted by something completely new! Where do you lot get so much energy?'

During our most recent visit we were completely bowled over by *Coliza*, a lovely thatched two-storey cottage (**sleeping 4** plus cot). It looks and feels really old, with oak beams inside and an inglenook fireplace, yet had only been completed a few months earlier.

By contrast, *Buddleia* and *Hydrangea* (both **sleeping 4**) are neat modern bungalows with two ensuite bedrooms each, cream/pine decor, granite fireplace with gas 'woodburner', flagstone fitted kitchen and sunny conservatory. They overlook a meadow where horses graze.

The cottages are scattered among trees, gardens and meadows around the 30-acre estate, just three miles from the sea and a five-minute stroll from Polgooth's village shop and pub. Pat furnishes each one individually, visiting antique shops and sales and is always on the lookout for local materials and traditional crafts. Bosinver has received a Green Tourism Award for safeguarding the environment, but also provides plenty to do. One family told us they had problems getting their children away from the

A 'Green Tourism' Award and more (see above) from the Cornwall Tourist Board.   ...and plaudits from us for a massive upgrading during recent years.

adventure playground with its trampoline, slides, playhouse, rope bridge and climb-on tractor. There's also a heated outdoor pool (April to September), sauna, tennis court, coarse fishing and games room with table-tennis, pool, darts and table football. Bikes can be hired.

Cots and highchairs available. Dogs by arrangement. No smoking. Some properties Friday-Friday, some Saturday-Saturday. Short breaks (minimum three nights). Cost: from about £127 to £848. (Farmhouse, a 400-year old thatched longhouse **sleeping 11**, £216 to £848). Details from Mrs Pat Smith, Bosinver Farm, St Austell, Cornwall PL26 7DT. Telephone/fax 01726 72128.

www.bosinver.co.uk   email: reception@bosinver.co.uk

Fowey
Fowey Harbour Cottages*

Deliberately specialising in properties around Fowey Harbour, on the south Cornish coast, this long-established agency is run with style. Cottages include *Harbour Cottage*, with direct frontage to the harbour in Fowey (two bedrooms, **sleeping 6**: **'Visit Britain' Three Stars**), *The Penthouse*, in the centre of Fowey, a four-storey town house with parking space

Harbour Cottage is right on the waterfront: you can literally step from the garden into your boat...

and a roof-top terrace from which there is a 360° outlook over the harbour (three bedrooms, **sleeping 6**: **'Visit Britain' Four Stars**), *17a St Fimbarrus Road*, Fowey, an apartment in a tall Victorian terrace house with windows overlooking the whole of the harbour (two bedrooms, **sleeping 4**: **'Visit Britain' Three Stars**) and a selection of stone-built cottages in the village of Polruan on the other side of the harbour, including *Chy Vounder*, a compact cottage with harbour views from the bedrooms (two bedrooms – one with bunks – **sleeping 4**: **'Visit Britain' Two Stars**). Most **sleep 4 to 6**. Dogs welcome most, all have TV. Linen for hire. Cost from £125 to £1000. Short breaks at certain times. Details from David Hill, 3 Fore Street, Fowey, Cornwall PL23 1AH. Telephone 01726 832211. Fax 832901.

www.foweyharbourcottages.co.uk   email: hillandson@talk21.com

Fowey
Tides Reach   map 6/366

Following earlier reader reports, we visited this grand five-storeyed property, with its splendid Fowey Estuary and river views, last autumn. Quietly located, it is close enough to the town centre (walking distance) to combine the spectacular vista from huge windows with the benefits of shopping in

Properties with memorable views always get our readers' vote. They'll go for this!

Fowey, which is full of quaint streets and literary history. With Whitehouse Beach just two minutes away, you could hardly be nearer the sea; the Eden Project is about 20 minutes' drive, the Lost Gardens of Heligan about 35. Or you could simply gaze across the water for memorable views of boats bobbing in the tree fringed estuary. Specifically, this renovated property, ideal for families, **sleeps 4** in two bedrooms, one with a king-sized bed and an ensuite shower room, the other with two three-foot singles that can be linked to form a six-foot double. Nearby, you'll find good sandy beaches (one just two minutes from the house), golf, sailing and fishing. TV/video/DVD player/CD player. Not suitable for dogs. Cost: £320 to £650, including gas central heating. Linen and towels provided. Details from Mrs C S Parnell, 50 Esplanade, Fowey, Cornwall PL23 1HZ. Tel 01726 832150.

email: tidesreach@tesco.net

Polperro
Holiday Cottages Polperro*

Tucked away among Polperro's narrow, winding, traffic-free lanes (it's one of Cornwall's most picturesque fishing villages – perhaps the most picturesque) – we found *Kirk House*, a cleverly-converted 19th-century chapel. Providing **Five Star** accommodation for **up to 10 people**, it's one of the jewels in the fifty (and rising) properties offered by Holiday Cottages Polperro, whose office occupies the building's ground floor.

Boat trips, stunning cliff walks, access to the beach and a natural rock swimming pool are all nearby, and the Eden Project is only 30 minutes' drive away.

The house's centrepiece is a vast open-plan loft-style living/dining area, which has the original chapel roof timbers exposed, a woodburning stove

Island Cottage and Island House are parts of a particularly striking building.

Kirk House (facing) is a Five Star beauty, notable even in Polperro terms.

(logs provided) and stripped pine floors. There are five bedrooms: a king-size, a double, two twin and one with full-size bunk beds. Outside, a secluded courtyard garden with barbecue is a real sun-trap, but has a patio heater for cool weather. Tea/coffee, red and white wine, flowers and a limited-edition copy of a local print greet guests on arrival.

While in Polperro, we also looked round four other Holiday Cottages' properties, all within a stone's throw of each other. *Island Cottage* (**sleeping 2 to 4**) is part of a five-storey 16th-century building, one of the oldest in the village, which occupies a sunny position by the sea and is stylishly decorated and furnished in cream throughout. *Island House* (**sleeping 5**), which occupies the upper floors of the same building, is of a similar high standard, with beautiful views across the harbour and out to sea.

Just across the harbour, *PierInn House* (*sic*), **sleeping 6**, and, under it, *PierInn Studio*, **sleeping 2**, are also beside the water. Indeed, the Studio's balcony juts out over it. Without losing their original character, both properties have recently been modernised and furnished to a very high standard, including leather sofas, stripped-pine floors and fitted kitchens.

Details are available from Holiday Cottages Polperro, Talland Street, Polperro, Cornwall PL13 2RE. Telephone 01503 272320. The company has also recently opened offices in Looe and Mevagissey.

www.holidaycottagespolperro.co.uk

email: enquiries@holidaycottagespolperro.co.uk

Polperro
Marigold and Penny

Long-term readers' favourites, these two fishermen's terraced cottages are tucked away down one of the narrow streets of this picturesque fishing village. Each has a small, square, low-ceilinged room on each of the three floors – a kitchen/dining-area at the bottom, sitting room with TV on the first floor and a bedroom at the top

Cosy, unpretentious, very reasonably priced for such a famous location...

with a four poster bed. They have been comfortably adapted **for 2 to 4** people each. *Penny* is one terrace back from the harbour in 'The Warren' at the most desirable end of Polperro, and close to the smuggling museum. *Marigold* is a couple of streets back, but still has a view of the busy little harbour. At Penny you'll be tempted to spend time in the bedroom, as it has a harbour view. At Marigold, where the rooms are slightly bigger, steep steps outside the back door lead up to a sloping garden and seat to enjoy the view over the village rooftops. Cost: about £175 to £385. Fully equipped. Heating *and parking* included. Linen provided but not towels. Details and photos from Martin Friend, The Maltings, Malting Green Road, Layer de la Haye, Essex CO2 0JJ. Telephone/fax 01206 734555.

email:martinfriend6018@aol.com and/or **teresa@tesco.com**

Portscatho map 6/355
Pollaughan Cottages

From the welcoming cream tea to a carefully selected basket of toys for children: with such nice personal touches, it's not surprising that these imaginatively planned properties were the West Country winners in the 2004 England for Excellence South West and Cornish Tourism award

Among so many other good things, a new hard tennis court is a major attraction.

scheme. 'It's wonderful here, and I trust it won't be our last visit,' one wheelchair guest in *Owl Cottage,* **sleeping 2,** told us when we visited last year. Like *Willow Barn,* which **sleeps 6,** it is geared for accessibility, though as with *Farm House,* a Victorian charmer, **sleeping 5,** with antique pine furniture, and *Swallows Barn,* **sleeping 2,** the main thrust is in providing a home from home (Valerie Penny even offers freshly prepared meals from a huge menu). Add farmhouse tours for the kids, an all weather tennis court and a highly praised 'pick your own veggie' patch and you have the measure of this unique hideaway in 22 acres of prime Roseland countryside. Unsuitable for dogs. Linen and towels included. Short breaks. Cost: about £300 to £1030. Valerie Penny, Pollaughan Cottages, Portscatho, Truro, Cornwall TR2 5EH. Telephone 01872 580150.

www.pollaughan.co.uk   email: info@pollaughan.co.uk

The Roseland Peninsula
Roseland Holiday Cottages*

Based in Portscatho, this medium-sized agency is notable for its variety. There are 66 cottages, dotted around the idyllic semi-tropical Roseland Peninsula whose southerly point is postcard-pretty St Mawes. Most are by, or very near, the sea. All are described in detail in its stylish brochure – a real armchair 'voyage of discovery'. On our most

Martha's Cottage is thatched, Grade II listed, and near a super family beach!

recent visit we noted two that were totally different: *Martha's Cottage* (**sleeping 4**), an old Grade II listed thatched house at Treworthal, four minutes' drive from Pendower Beach, and *3 Tregarth Cottages* (**sleeping 6**), one of three smart new terrace houses on the hillside above St Mawes, five minutes' walk away. Its lounge (upstairs) opens on to a balcony with lovely sea and river views. At Gerrans, the old village chapel near the harbour has been divided into two imaginatively designed houses: *Sunday House East* (**sleeping 8/10**) and *Sunday House West* (**sleeping 6**).

Details/brochure from Roseland Holiday Cottages, Crab Apple Cottage, Portscatho, Truro, Cornwall TR2 5ET. Telephone/fax: 01872 580480.

www.roselandholidaycottages.co.uk
email: enquiries@roselandholidaycottages.co.uk

Portscatho, near Truro
Pettigrew Cottage

Quite simply, being in one of the most sought-after coastal villages in Cornwall, this is much in demand. It is just the sort of seaside hideaway artists and writers dream of – yet it equally well suits a small family. Rich in history, tucked away only 150 yards from the harbour, it was once the home of sailmaker Edward Peters, great-great-grandfather of the present owner, Hilary Thompson,

A lucky find in sought-after Portscatho (cottage on the right, with side entrance).

who has written a book about him. It still feels like a family home, which is much of its charm: the kitchen/diner is equipped with electric cooker, microwave and more. **Sleeps 4**, in a first floor front double bedroom, with sea view, and a back twin bedroom with a view over the small back garden with a cobbled yard and barbecue area. The living-room has an open fireplace made of local stone, handy for early or late holidays to which this cosy property is suited. Linen on request; cot on request; TV. Car parking (one vehicle). Dogs by request. Cost: from £200 to £400. Details from Hilary and Philip Thompson, Chenoweth, 1 The Quay, Portscatho, Truro, Cornwall TR2 5HF. Telephone 01872 580573.

email: philnhil@tiscali.co.uk

Helford River and Falmouth
Cornish Holiday Cottages*

This agency is one of the best of its size that we know, in Cornwall or elsewhere. There are just 40 or so genuinely 'hand-picked' properties, and we know for a fact that owners (we've heard from them) compete to get on the organisation's books.

Tregullow, in Maenporth, is a modern bungalow **sleeping 4**. It occupies a wonderful clifftop position overlooking Falmouth Bay. The sumptuously comfortable L-shaped lounge, with French windows and an open fireplace of Cornish slate, makes the most of the view. An archway leads from the neat dining room with pine dresser into the kitchen, fitted with oak cupboards, electric oven, hob, microwave and dishwasher.

In a leafy residential area is *Helford Point*, a property of high quality **sleeping up to 8**. It is a four-bedroomed bungalow in a large garden, with stunning views of the mouth of the Helford River and Falmouth Bay.

Closer to Falmouth – in fact, just two minutes' walk from the High Street – *6 Jane's Court*, **sleeping 4/6**, is in Packet Quays, with views from the two bedroomed apartments over Falmouth Harbour. Built in 1985, it is part of an architect's award winning complex. So expect high standards.

Helford Point has fabulous views out to sea, and lies in an Area of Outstanding Natural Beauty. It sleeps 8.

Though close to Falmouth town centre, 6 Jane's Court is quiet. It too has amazing views.

Different in character is *Sail Loft* (**sleeps 5** plus cot), part of the group of holiday cottages at Calamansac, in the wooded western headland of Port Navas Creek overlooking the Helford River. Designed to maximise the views of the river, the first floor living accommodation is entered via a bridge and balcony from private car parking.

We also loved the *Rose Cottages*, in the so-picturesque waterside village of Durgan. They are three charming old fishermen's cottages – modernised but retaining all the original features – just a stone's throw from the beach. Each **sleeps 4**.

Cost: from about £160 to £1575. Dogs and young children welcome. Further details available from Emily Boriosi, Cornish Holiday Cottages, Killibrae, Maenporth, Falmouth, Cornwall TR11 5HP. Telephone/fax 01326 250339.

www.cornishholidaycottages.net
email: Info@cornishholidaycottages.net

Cornwall – countywide
Forgotten Houses

It would take many weeks to visit all of what the brochure calls 'these unusual holiday homes' (largely in Cornwall) – a modest way of saying that they all benefit hugely from their location, architecture or history. Which as Stephen Tyrrell, the brains, and occasional renovator behind this extraordinary concept, forthrightly states in his brochure (full of historic and architectural details) means most are listed, and many have been carefully modernised. This also means that some, by necessity, 'do not meet the modern standards of use or convenience'.

Nor will he budge from this formula, telling us during a visit last summer that his strict criteria meant turning down some properties rather than create a suburban version of the countryside. Instead, most properties – about 35 in all – are built of stone, with walls two feet thick under slate roofs. Nearly all have fireplaces or stoves with wood supplied as part of the rent – as well as television and washing machines, books and games.

The approach is perhaps best summed up by the most famous house, *Mellinzeath*, close to the Helford River. Thought to have been rebuilt after a fire in 1665, it **sleeps 4/5**, with a Land Rover ride for guests and their luggage to the house – a 600 metre walk from your car! 'Return to the roots and get back to basics,' urges one guest. 'A beautifully restored cottage, and a fireplace that takes six-foot logs has been burning continuously for six and a half days.'

Although most have two, three or four bedrooms, there are also a few larger properties – such as *Manorbier Castle*, Pembrokeshire, **sleeping 12** plus cot. Fascinating, but with walls and towers you should keep a careful eye on the children.

Last year we took a fresh look at *Lower Bosvarren*, one of six houses in the hamlet of Bosvarren, up a tree lined drive just ten minutes' drive from Falmouth. A listed Elizabethan farmhouse, redecorated in 2002 and 2004 and fun for families, it retains original features, including the roof of small 'scantle' slates and two granite bread ovens. It **sleeps 8** in four double bedrooms, plus cot, and is oil fired centrally heated.

Previously we saw *Bosbenna,* a spacious house with three big bedrooms and a 'Heidi' attic up a ladder. *Badgers* (Helston), **sleeps 4/6,** and likewise has a gallery loft with two beds reached by ladder for two adventurous children. 'Having been to Cornwall many times we can honestly say Badgers is the loveliest cottage we have stayed in,' wrote one guest.

Bosvathick Lodge, near Falmouth, **sleeping 4,** though the smallest of all the properties, has its own little drive, lawn and large garden. Like most others it accepts dogs, and, again like so many others, it seems, is close to a prize-winning pub.

Send for a copy of a functional, not glossy but intriguing, very detailed brochure, which includes floor plans, from Forgotten Houses, Bosvathick, Constantine, Falmouth, Cornwall TR11 5RD. Telephone 01326 340153. Fax 340426.

email: Info@Forgottenhouses.co.uk

Or see the well regarded website: www.forgottenhouses.co.uk

South West Cornwall
St Aubyn Estates

We have much enjoyed our travels to the four separate and highly desirable coastal locations in the south and 'the far west' of Cornwall where James and Mary St Aubyn offer really high quality holiday properties in stunning coastal locations.

One of them is near the historic town of Marazion (near Penzance) and six are near the dream-holiday picture-postcard village of Porthgwarra.

At *Venton Farmhouse*, Marazion, for example, we love the space, the quiet, the upgrading to an extremely high standard with no loss of character. Among many good things is the view across the water to St Michael's Mount, the spacious walled garden (unusual for a seaside location) and a private path to the rocky beach below. We admired excellent local pictures, six foot double beds in several instances, a superb dining table, a top notch kitchen, stylish and understated colours. With **Five 'Visit Britain' Stars** (no surprise), it **sleeps 10**, and is not overpriced from £665 to £1945.

Within a few minutes' drive of Land's End, via narrow high hedged lanes towards the sea at Porthgwarra, we located picturesque *Corner Cottage* and *Cove Cottage*. Literally yards from the cove, each was occupied by people delighted by their find. In Cove we admired a well planned combined kitchen/dining room/sitting room, and an unusual basement with a glassed-over stream below. **Sleeps 4** in a double (ensuite) and a twin. In

Venton Farmhouse is a superb property, overlooking St Michael's Mount...

We looked at two fine properties in picture-postcard Porthgwarra Cove...

Corner we liked the double brass bedstead, the expensive pine floor. **Sleeps 2**. Each has central heating.

Also at Porthgwarra, *Higher Roskestal* is a fabulous conversion of a detached farmhouse with stunning sea views. It **sleeps 6** in three bedrooms, all ensuite (**'Visit Britain' Five Stars**). *Three Chimneys* is a complete renovation of two hill-top cottages, **sleeping 8,** and is the latest addition to the portfolio. More remote is *Faraway Cottage* at Nanjizal, **sleeping 4**. Also at Nanjizal, *Bosistow Farmhouse* **sleeps 7**.

Details and brochure from Clare Sandry, St Aubyn Estates, Manor Office, Marazion, Cornwall TR17 0EF. Telephone: 01736 710507. Fax 719930.

www.staubynestates.co.uk

email: godolphin@manor-office.co.uk

St Martin, near Helston
Mudgeon Vean Farm Holiday Cottages

Owner Sarah Trewhella puts it neatly in her informative leaflet: 'Come and share the tranquillity of our small farm near the Helford River'. Two cottages, *Swallow* and *Swift,* are identical, **sleeping 2 to 4, plus cot/zed-bed**. Nicely converted from the former dairy, they have a cosy open-plan sitting room/dining room/ kitchen around an open fire. The third, *Badger*, **sleeping 2/6 plus cot**, is attached to the farmhouse. The

There's an outdoor play area, a table tennis room, and a private woodland walk.

small arable/orchard farm has inspiring valley views and produces apple juice and cider. The farm, with **Three Stars** from Southwest Tourism, is bordered by a beautiful National Trust walk to the Helford River, and the coves of the Lizard and the beaches of North Cornwall are in easy driving distance. Cost: about £120 to £400. Dogs by arrangement (£10 pw). Linen included. Details from Mr and Mrs J Trewhella, Mudgeon Vean, St Martin, near Helston, Cornwall TR12 6DB. Telephone 01326 231341.

www.cornwall-online.co.uk/mudgeon-vean/ctb.htm
email: mudgeonvean@aol.com.

St Tudy, near Wadebridge
Chapel Cottages   map 6/385

Many years in this guide, so many excellent reader reports. Original stable front doors, beamed ceilings, polished slate floors, window seats and (in three) large granite fireplaces with cloam ovens amount to 'masses of character'! *Chapel Cottages,* which we revisited recently , are a group of four listed stone-built cottages on the edge of the quiet village of St Tudy (a shop and an inn are a short walk

Several years with us, a visitor-friendly base from which to explore Cornwall.

away). Each cottage has a character of its own, with good bedrooms – one with a double and a single bed, the other with twin beds – and everything on hand. The pine kitchens are attractive, with individual washing machines. In easy reach are Bodmin Moor, the Eden Project, the Camel Trail to Padstow, and the beaches of Trebarwith, Polzeath and Daymer Bay.

Cost: about £150 to £410 per week. TV. Linen, cots and high chairs are included. Private parking. Not suitable for pets. Details from Clifford and Margaret Pestell, 'Hockadays', Tregenna, near Blisland, Cornwall PL30 4QJ. Telephone/fax 01208 850146.

www.hockadays.co.uk   email: chapelcottages@aol.com

Port Gaverne, near Wadebridge
Gullrock

The little seaside village of Port Gaverne, nicely off the beaten track, is a charmer, and these cottages, just two minutes' stroll from a sandy beach, are rich in local history.

Half-hidden away nicely down a narrow lane lies a convivial arrangement of cottages on three sides of a grassy courtyard with flower borders. The building was originally constructed about 200 years ago to cure and store the fish catches landed in the cove, and was used for this until the turn of the century.

The cottages are sensibly priced (particularly good value outside the main season), 'unpretentious and practical' units in what can sometimes be an expensive corner of the West Country. We particularly liked the bigger, *Seaways*, which **sleeps 6** in three double or twin rooms, with a spacious sitting room and a pleasant outlook on to the courtyard at the front and trees at the rear. The charming and cosy flat called *Creekside*, looking in part over the courtyard, is cleverly arranged to **sleep 6** in four bedrooms.

Each unit has a dishwasher, microwave, fridge-freezer, TV and video, CD/radio cassette and full central heating. An outbuilding houses washing/drying machines, a payphone and an assortment of garden furniture. The grounds include not only the courtyard, but an outer garden with barbecue and picnic area, and there is a parking space for each cottage. The

Even by coastal Cornish standards, this is an exquisite little place.

And the cottages themselves are in a pretty and rather historic courtyard.

beach, just 75 yards from Gullrock, is very sheltered, providing safe bathing and fascinating rock pools. The coastal path crosses the head of the beach, leading over the westward headland to the village of Port Isaac, and east along wild and remote clifflands to Trebarwith.

Visitors' pets are welcome, and Gullrock's resident pets are all friendly. Sample prices, which include electricity and heating, are: £160 February, £390 May, £720 August. Discounts are available to parties of three people or fewer from April to October, except in the summer school holidays.

Full details from Malcolm Lee, Gullrock, Port Gaverne, Port Isaac, Cornwall PL29 3SQ. Telephone 01208 880106.

www.goodcottageguide.com/self_catering_accommodation/gullrock.html
email: gullrock@ukonline.co.uk

Crackington Haven
The Old School Cottages

Tucked into the hillside immediately below the beautiful Norman church of St Genny's in the tiny hamlet of Churchtown is the Old School. Closed as a school in the 1960s, the sturdy stone building has been cleverly converted into holiday cottages. It makes an ideal base for holidaymakers of all ages as this part of the North Cornish coast, an Area of Outstanding Natural Beauty owned by the National Trust, offers unrivalled swimming, surfing and walking.

The building has superb sea views and is a short walk from Crackington Haven beach, across the headland and down the coast path to the beach. Just behind the beach are a pub and two cafes. One of the cafes, The Cabin, barbecues meat from its own farm in the evenings. In the other direction, the path leads to secluded beaches offering perfect solitude.

On our most recent visit, last autumn, we were pleased to see round *The School House*, originally the head teacher's house. It became available last year, joining *Lanes*, *Francis* and *Bloomers* (all named after former head-teachers) which we've featured in this guide for 22 years.

All are equipped to a high standard, with slate flagged or varnished wooden floors strewn with rugs, central heating, open fireplace or cast-iron stove for burning coal or logs, TV, electric stove, dishwasher, microwave, picnic tables, patios and individual gardens.

The School House (**sleeping 6/7**) has a large sitting room, kitchen/diner, double (with sea view) and twin bedrooms on the first floor and a twin with extra futon on the second floor (also sea view).

Lanes (**sleeping 4**) is at the front of the building, south facing, so the sun streams into its kitchen/diner and large sitting room all day long. There is a bathroom downstairs with one double bedroom and one twin upstairs.

Bloomers and Francis (both **sleeping 5**) enjoy superb sea views from all rooms, with accommodation on three floors. They have a large living/dining room each with picture windows and door on to a terrace, a spacious double bedroom and bathroom on the first floor and twin and single rooms on the second floor.

Cost about £250 to £693, including linen. Laundry room with payphone. Dogs welcome except in The School House. Details from Martin Smith, 1 Lower Kelly, Calstock, Cornwall PL18 9RX. Telephone 01840 230771.

www.stgennys.co.uk   email: oldschool@stgennys.co.uk

Even for Cornwall, these cottages are superbly located. But happily...

...the quality of the accommodation more than matches the geographical situation.

Crackington Haven
Mineshop Cottages

It's really something when you holiday here to have some of the most dramatic coastal scenery in Cornwall just a short stroll down the lane. And as you go from one tiny, hidden lane into another (shortly after you turn west off the A39 Camelford-Bude road and come, finally, to leafy Mineshop) you feel a million miles from the workaday world.

On our last summer revisit, Mineshop's wandering ducks were being fed by guests sitting contentedly on the verandah of *The Old Shippon* in the cool of the evening. They (the guests, not the ducks, although the latter may have tried to accompany them!) planned to walk down the green and tranquil footpath to the beach at Crackington Haven (excellent pub and coffee shop). In one of the lodges, in the same green and sunny location, a couple were brewing up and simply enjoying the view of the garden.

Mineshop has a strong following among people who like getting 'away from it all' without feeling isolated: the owners of the Mineshop cottages live in the centre of what is effectively a private hamlet. More than half of each year's visitors have been before, and one family has been 30 times!

Effectively under the same ownership, but elsewhere in this dramatically striking corner of North Cornwall, is a quite excellent cottage, beautifully located high on a headland, and very private. This, *Cancleave*, has dramatic views of the famous bay. There are comfortable sofas and lots of pine. Outside, there is a big lawn adjacent to the coastal footpath. **Sleeps 8** in four bedrooms.

The delightful Crackington Haven beach is just a short walk from the cottages...

...one of which is the spacious and private Old Shippon.

Cost: approximately £150 to £768 per week, according, as usual, to size and season. Short breaks from £100. Bedlinen is supplied in all the cottages. (Cots provided.) TVs, laundry room. Obedient dogs are allowed.

For futher details please contact Mr and Mrs Tippett, Ref: GH, Mineshop, Crackington Haven, Bude, Cornwall EX23 0NR. Telephone 01840 230338.

www.mineshop.co.uk
email: info@mineshop.co.uk

Blisland
Hockadays Cottages

This quiet gem of a retreat, in deeply rural North Cornwall, is approached delightfully via leafy lanes. For people who want to slow their pace of life, yet still be within fifteen minutes' drive of the spectacular coast, about 25 minutes from the Eden Project, plus the nearby Camel Trail

Such a lot of care and attention goes into these 'two-plus-baby' cottages...

to Padstow, it's a winner. Both charming cottages, *Demelza* and *Rowella*, are looked after by caring and conscientious owners. Each is within a converted 17th century barn that feels very private, and each is a wonderful hideaway **for 2** plus a baby. Among the details are white painted walls setting off oak beams, wall lamps, some original features such as wooden lintels, small paned windows, and cottage doors. Each has a living room, a separate well equipped kitchen, double bedroom and bathroom. One is an 'upside down' house, with the bedroom downstairs. There is a big garden, parking, and excellent views. The nearby Blisland Inn is a 'Campaign for Real Ale' award winner. TV. Linen is included. Regrettably, they are not suitable for pets. Cost: about £140 to £310. Details from Margaret Pestell, 'Hockadays', Tregenna, near Blisland, Cornwall PL30 4QJ. Telephone/fax 01208 850146.

www.hockadays.co.uk   email: tregennacottages@aol.com

St Issey, near Padstow   map 6/405
Trevorrick Farm Cottages

On-site owners Melanie and Mike Benwell have created the caring atmosphere so evident in our visit last year. Ducks to feed, a well equipped outdoor play area, a games room and a heated pool all appeal greatly to families and couples. The six barn conversions, refurbished in recent years, are in an Area of Outstanding Natural Beauty, close to beaches and

Easy access to some of North Cornwall's many sandy beaches is a bonus here...

the Eden Project. *Lily Pad Cottage* (a four-poster and a log burner), and the popular *Old Round House* are cosy hideaways **sleeping 2**. Single-storeyed *Serendipity* (**sleeps 2 to 5**) is suitable for people with limited mobility. *Owl's Roost* (with log burner) and *Curlew Cottage* are two storeyed; *Badger's Way* (single storeyed) is the largest of all, with a log fire and a garden. These **sleep 4 or 5**. TV plus video and DVD. **Three to Four Stars**. Cost: £225 to £895. Out of season short breaks. Dogs welcome in some cottages, linen included; baby-sitting and B & B available.

Details from Melanie and Mike Benwell, Trevorrick Farm Cottages, St Issey, Wadebridge, Cornwall PL27 7QH. Telephone/fax 01841 540574.

www.trevorrick.co.uk   email: info@trevorrick.co.uk

The West Country
Classic Cottages*

This absolutely outstanding family-run organisation was founded in 1977 by Tony and Clare Tregoning. Based in Helston, and affectionately known as 'Classic' by most of its clients and many people in the travel business, it has featured in this guide *without a break for 24 years*.

Classic accepts fewer than half the properties that are offered, and even then invariably insist on various improvements being made. So it's not surprising that the organisation is known for its uncompromisingly high standards. Altogether, Classic has nearly 600 properties to choose from, so everyone can be sure of finding somewhere to suit their needs.

Most properties are in Cornwall but there's a good selection in Devon and a handful in both Dorset and Somerset. Each one is illustrated with at

Thatched and 'beamy', The Hermitage is one of several cottages in Crantock, 'across the estuary' from Newquay.

Forge Cottage is another: most attractive from the outside, its interior is light and bright, and there's a wood-burner.

least two colour photos in Classic's detailed and attractive £350-plus page brochure.

'Classic Cottages is ferociously proud of the West Country,' it says. 'We scour every cliff, cove and cranny for just the right properties with just the right owners. The climate helps, as do the views.'

Guests are always welcomed with fresh flowers and a tea tray. Then, once they have settled in, a comprehensive 'Minimum Inventory' ensures that they have everything on the premises that they could possibly need 'to bake a cake or cook a roast'.

Our most recent visit was in the October half-term week of 2004, when we met several families delighted with their accommodation. Some were staying in the quiet village of Crantock, where Classic has seven properties, just across the estuary from Newquay. It's a popular place for people who want the thrill of Atlantic surf on a sandy beach but find Newquay itself rather too 'lively' for their liking. It has the advantage of a post office/store, antique and crafts shops, and a good pub. The properties include *Forge Cottage*, a Grade II listed stone building (**sleeping 4**), a short walk from the beach, *The Hermitage*, a thatched white cottage (**sleeping 4**), and *Rosemaddon Cottage* (**sleeping 6**), whose large sitting-room is bordered on two sides by a minstrels' gallery.

On the other side of Newquay, *Anneth Lowen* (**sleeping 4**) is a beautifully appointed little detached house in the hamlet of Bosoughan. It has its own enclosed terraced garden, a cosy kitchen/breakfast-room with a Rayburn and microwave, and a spacious sitting/dining-room with gorgeous fabrics and a wood-burner. One of the two pretty bedrooms overlooks the garden (which has a small pond) while the other has views of open country.

We also went to one of Classic's recent additions, *Upton Farm*. This conversion of two redundant barns is one of the most stylish and sumptuously comfortable we've ever seen. It commands a breathtaking position on high ground, 500 feet above sea level, a mile from the sea (the coastal path is ten minutes' walk away) near Trebarwith Strand. *Upton Mill* (**sleeping 8**) has a spacious open plan living-room with open rafters and

Upton Farm is a recent conversion of two redundant barns. Near the coastal footpath and just a mile from the sea...

...it is one of the most stylish and sumptuously comfortable we've seen. This is the roomy interior of Upton Mill.

kitchen and dining areas. A galleried hallway leads downstairs to four bedrooms, all ensuite. *Hyde Barn* (**sleeping 6**), which also has its levels reversed, has a sunny courtyard and raised garden; one of its three bedrooms is ensuite. The owners also offer B&B of a similarly high standard in the adjoining farmhouse where they live.

In complete contrast, we saw *Lowen Cottage*, a snug end of terrace cottage (**sleeping 3**) in a narrow street leading down to Boscastle harbour. It has Cornish slate floors, a multi-burner stove, and a small Shaker-style kitchen overlooking the garden. There are two upstairs bedrooms, one with an attractive brass bed. This is an idyllic retreat, perfectly situated a

Trewane Cottage has great charm, with a very fine and spacious drawing room.

And Trewane Mill is both spacious and cosy. A bonus is its enclosed garden.

few minutes up the road from the village centre, but unfortunately it is not suitable for children from one to twelve, or for pets.

Seventeenth-century *Trewane Cottage* (**sleeping 6**) near Padstow, close to the wide sandy beaches of Rock and Polzeath, with spectacular walking and cycling all around, is packed full of comfort and character. Also available is *Trewane Mill* (**sleeping 6**). This former flour mill (the spring-

Man o'War has long been one of our favourites in 'sea buffeted' Cadgwith.

Anneth Lowen is a beautifully appointed detached cottage sleeping four people.

fed millpool is still there) is notable for its large country kitchen with an Aga and for its own enclosed garden.

Another we've long liked is *Man o'War* (**sleeping 8**) in the sea-buffeted village of Cadgwith near the end of The Lizard peninsula. It is the archetypal seaside cottage, full of character but also exuding loving care. The sitting-room enjoys romantic views of the waves and of fishing boats tucked in for the night. Approached by a short, steep drive, it has its own parking space a short walk away. The ivy-clad cottage is Grade II listed and has been furnished with every comfort.

Visitors to Corfe Castle tend to gaze admiringly at Brook Cottage...

...and that is without even getting to see the especially charming interior...

Among Classic's locations outside Cornwall, one of the most distinctive is the village of Corfe Castle in Dorset. At the entrance to the village, *Brook Cottage* is a picture-book, semi-detached Grade II listed building, **sleeping 6**. Its sitting/dining-room is especially appealing, with heated Purbeck stone floors, a wood-burner effect gas stove, exposed beams and a substantial pine dining table. Delightfully, a stretch of the famous Swanage Steam Railway, perfect for exploring this historical area, overlooks the cottage's enclosed garden.

For further information and a copy of the impressive and extremely readable Classic Cottages brochure, contact Classic Cottages, Leslie House, Lady Street, Helston, Cornwall TR13 8NA. Telephone 01326 555 555. Fax 555 544.

www.classic.co.uk   email: enquiries@classic.co.uk

classic cottages

Padstow
Harbour View

Here's another of those fabulously well situated properties we've located on our travels. At the heart of one of Cornwall's favourite small resorts, this attractive three-storeyed Grade II listed building on the quayside enables one to observe everything that's going on! It was built as the Harbour Master's office 400 years ago, when sailing boats brought cargoes from around the world. Now yachts and fishing boats keep the harbour busy, and during the summer the quay is one of the liveliest spots in North Cornwall.

A favourite among Good Holiday Cottage Guide readers for many years...sensibly priced accommodation in one of Cornwall's most sought-after holiday destinations.

The building incorporates four apartments: S*tepper* and *Gulland,* on the first floor, and *Pentire*, occupying the whole of the second, have superb views over the harbour, so we were not surprised to learn that painters like to settle down with a brush in their sitting-room window-seats. Stepper and Pentire have two bedrooms, Gulland has one. *Daymer*, at the back, has one bedroom and is suited to people wanting a base at a reasonable price.

All are **'Visit Britain' Three Stars**. Washing machine and tumbler dryers; there is a dishwasher in Pentire and Stepper. TVs. Linen included. Car parking; dogs extra. Cost: about £160 to £650 per week. Further details from Mrs Tereen Oliver, telephone/fax 0707 120 2105.

---

*The editors of *The Good Holiday Cottage Guide* welcome calls from readers needing more information about properties than we can easily give in these pages. Perhaps when the location is more important than the cottage itself – say for a wedding or a reunion – or when a big group of friends or colleagues wants to take over a whole complex. (A number of owners welcome extended families but will actually refuse non-family groups.) There are no charges for this, no fancy premium rate calls...just phone **01438 869489**.

*Owners and even agents are welcome to contact us for advice about marketing their properties. Though most of them are skilful at this, a fresh look from an independent observer can be useful. There is of course no charge for this: phone **01438 869489**.

Tintagel
Tregeath

This traditional farmworker's cottage has proved popular with readers ever since we first published in 1983. We revisited last year, and confirmed that in its way it's a real charmer. Quietly situated on a little-used country road, it is 'unpretentious', with a degree of character. There's a small rear patio, ideal for lazing in the summer sun, listening

Not far from Tintagel, this does not claim to be a show-house, but we like it, and have always had good reader reports.

to very little except the sound of sheep from adjoining farmland.. About a mile from Tintagel, and one and a half from the surfing beach at Trebarwith Strand, this is no showhouse, more a sensible family home with a very convenient galley-kitchen, a combined sitting/dining room and stairs up to two bedrooms (note that one has a 4'6" wide bed; the other a 4' wide bed). There's a good-sized single room that's adjacent to the sitting room, a washing machine and separate tumble dryer, and a pleasant enclosed and safe garden. **Sleeps up to 5** plus cot. **'Visit Britain' Three Stars.**

Cost: £110 to £410. TV/video in each bedroom. Payphone. Single dogs welcome. Further details from Mrs E M Broad, 'Davina', Trevillett, Tintagel, Cornwall PL34 0HL. Telephone/fax 01840 770217.

Stratton/Pyworthy, near Bude
Lovers Retreat/Hopworthy Farm   map 6/399/400

As far as we're concerned, any comfortable, quiet, warm and well run property near Bude is immediately 'in the frame': it's one of our favourite places in the whole of the West Country. In Stratton, a mile and a half from the resort, three-storeyed 200-year old *Lovers Retreat* has a five foot wide 'sleigh' bed and a woodburning stove. **Sleeps 3, Four Stars,** Ref 17925. In a more rural situation, you can even bring your own

Lovers Retreat, sleeping three, is handy for Bude, and in a historic village...

horses to Hopworthy Farm, a short drive from Bude and in striking distance of Dartmoor. Graded with an admirable **Five Stars** from 'Visit Britain' it offers stabling, livery and the use of an indoor school. Impressively, and in line with much current demand, *Hopworthy Farmhouse* **sleeps up to 18** – Ref 18016.

Details from Blakes Country Cottages, Spring Mill, Earby, Barnoldswick BB94 0AA. To book: 0870 192 1022. Brochures: 0870 241 7970.

Live search and book: www.blakes-cottages06.co.uk

Cornwall – countywide
Cornish Traditional Cottages*

This was the first holiday cottage letting agency in Cornwall, which developed after the original Cornish Traditional Cottages directors bought and renovated a derelict cottage in Padstow for family use. What began as a hobby developed into a business, and by the early 1970s others wanted them to let their cottages.

Since its beginnings the agency has prided itself on its personal service. You can speak to 'a real person' (not a machine) between 9 am and 9 pm seven days a week. Then there is the 'smiles' system of rating properties – generated entirely by customers from the grading the company asks them to give a cottage's fittings, furnishings and equipment.

We certainly smiled last autumn when we came across two cosy charmers in a cobbled street close to the National Trust harbour of Boscastle. Here

Carveth is yet another of the agency's properties that enjoys a superb location.

Bridge Cottage, sleeping 6, is in the highly sought-after village of Boscastle.

the agency offers two character cottages, each sporting three smiles. *Bridge Cottage* (**sleeps 6**), though completely renovated, retains its period charm, with a view overlooking the river leading to the harbour mouth from the king size double bedroom, one of three upstairs.

Likewise, *Millstream Cottage* offers a double fronted cottage whose front door opens on to a small sitting room with beamed ceilings, windows to the lane and looking to the headland at the harbour mouth. **Sleeps 4**.

Superbly well located, at the head of a tidal creek on the River Fowey (from the comfort of your cottage you can watch the ebb and flow of the tide, probably putting the cottage into the 'we hardly left the place for a week' category so beloved of cottage guide readers) *Pont Quay Cottage* **sleeps 4/6** – including a double-bunk room suitable for children.

It's just a mile by car and car/pedestrian ferry to Fowey or – even more appealingly – half a mile by boat on the Pont Pill creek. (Guests can make arrangements to bring their own boats.)

Also enjoying watery views – in this case across St Ives Bay towards Godrevy Lighthouse – and just fifteen minutes' walk from a sheltered, sandy beach, *Bosledra* is a newly renovated bungalow most usefully **sleeping up to 8**. Among other good things it has a five foot bed in the main bedroom and an open fire. Charmingly, you can get into St Ives via one of the most scenic railways in the country: there's a local station nearby.

On the approach road to Mousehole (remember to pronounce it 'Mousel'), *Carveth*, **sleeping 4**, is the upper part of a detached house with good sea views from a double and twin bedroom and, even more notably, with views of the splendid St Michael's Mount – from a bright and sunny sitting room with five big windows. Opposite the cottage there's a footpath to a stony beach and a rockpool and – a first for us – a children's seawater bathing pool, exposed at high tide.

Garden enthusiasts will love the cottages at Tregrehan, which has a famous collection of camellias, rhododendrons and conifers. The walls of the estate's old grain mill enclose a secret garden at the entrance to *The Coach House*, which has a bunk room and a king size bedroom, both with an additional single bed. *Sprys Cottage* is tucked away from the main courtyard and **sleeps 2** in a double room. *Gamekeepers Cottage* is the end cottage in the old carriage house and **sleeps 4** in a king size double and a twin room. There is a spacious walled garden, entered through a glazed

Deeply rural Fentondale sleeps 4, and dates in part from the 17th century...

Pentire Cottage, on Pentire Farm, has an open fire and memorable views...

door from the rear twin bedroom. The cottages here are graded 'two-smiles'. The Eden Project and Carlyon Bay's golf course are less than ten minutes' drive away.

At the end of a rough track – but enjoying spectacular views over the Camel Estuary – is Pentire Farm, with one-smile properties. These include the *Farm Wing* (**sleeps 6 to 8**), with four bedrooms, one with substantial bunk beds, and *Pentire Cottage* (**sleeps 4 to 6**) with a working open fire. Beamed farm-style kitchen. One bunk room downstairs, a double and a room with two pine singles upstairs.

More deeply rural in location, lying opposite farm buildings, is *Fentondale Cottage*, a three-smile renovated and extended detached cottage of 17th century origin. More beams, slate floors and the occasional changes of levels. **Sleeping 4,** it stands alone in the farming hamlet of Fentondale, about five minutes' drive from St Breward, which has a post office/stores, a church and a pub with a small restaurant.

Pets are welcome in about a third of the agency's properties.

For further details and an excellent brochure, with a clear and attractive illustration of each property, contact Cornish Traditional Cottages, Blisland, Bodmin, Cornwall PL30 4HS. Telephone 01208 821666, fax 821766.

www.corncott.com

email: info@corncott.com

Croyde and beyond
Marsdens Cottage Holidays*

Marsdens is something of a North Devon institution, with a reputation for absolute integrity and properties of a very high standard. In the 23 years in which we have featured this agency in our guide we have never had anything but the most wholehearted praise.

Among much else, readers appreciate the fact that all the properties are inspected annually, and that the staff all have an intimate knowledge of North Devon.

All the properties have 'Visit Britain' star gradings, up to Five, and the agency itself is the largest in the West Country that has a policy of having all its properties inspected. Dishwashers, microwaves, pools (even in some properties that are close to beaches) are commonplace. Around half the 250 or so on Mardens's books are in and around Croyde, a small charming village of thatch, with dunes between it and Croyde Bay's wide sandy beach. The rest are scattered across the area from the small sandy resort of Instow around the coastline to Exmoor.

Camelia Cottage lies at the foot of famously steep Porlock Hill...

This beauty in pretty Croyde, called Sweets Cottage, is 300 years old...

New to the portfolio in 2005 was *Camelia Cottage*, a charming, stone-built property at the foot of famous Porlock Hill, **sleeping 4.** Among so many good things going for it, it has easy access to Exmoor and National Trust-owned villages. (Porlock Meadow is a particular delight for bird watchers – there's a huge variety of birds – as well as red deer, foxes, badgers, bats and butterflies.)

In a wonderful position at Saunton is a detached bungalow, *Sandhills*, which has recently undergone a major refurbishment. Breathtaking views over the burrows, and the first Biosphere reserve in the United Kingdom, give this property a unique appeal. There is even footpath access to the beach a few hundred yards away and with a large, gently sloping lawned garden this is an excellent family proposition.

Walnut Tree Cottage, at Blakewell, is only two miles from Barnstaple and is within walking distance of a well stocked trout farm – fish suppers could take on a new meaning. The property has been completely renovated with a contemporary feel with excellent kitchen and bathroom and two bedrooms. An extensive brick paved patio enjoys a sunny aspect and an ornamental pond and fountain provides a relaxing environment in which to while away your holiday time.

Sandhills is not only memorably well situated, but has fabulous views to boot.

Walnut Tree is two miles from Barnstaple – and well placed for fish suppers!

The Mill House (**sleeps 10**), a 16th century listed mill house, stands right on the water's edge of Lee Bay. With antique furnishings, it is also modern, the kitchen having an electric double oven, hob, microwave, fridge/freezer, dishwasher, washing machine and pine table. The original milling room is still there, plus an inglenook fireplace, bread ovens, a boathouse and the sound of crashing waves. *Sweets Cottage* is one of the thatched cottages in the village of Croyde – perhaps the best known. The 300-year-old property has featured on picture postcards, and has a wonderful inglenook fireplace and beams. It also has a large enclosed rear garden with summerhouse and barbecue, with fine views over the village and has **accommodation for 10.**

Mortehoe is a small village on the National Trust coastline and is home to the delightful *Rosemary Cottage*, **sleeping 5**, enjoying extensive coastal and sea views. The master bedroom enjoys an en-suite bathroom and a door to a south facing decked patio with wonderful views, ideal for sunbathing and al fresco meals. The newly installed fully equipped kitchen adjoins a pretty dining room with adjoining lounge.

Also, *Vention Garden Cottage* at Putsborough is in a wonderful situation with spectacular views across Woolacombe's golden sands. The property has a Mediterranean touch, with white painted wooden floors, rugs and palm trees. The heated outdoor pool in Grecian style completes the perfect location with steps leading directly to the sandy beach. **Sleeping 8,** the property is in high demand with its three-quarter acre gardens ensuring privacy.

Details and an outstanding brochure from Marsdens, 2 The Square, Braunton, Devon EX33 2JB. Telephone 01271 813777, fax 813664. Full online availability and booking on the website:

www.marsdens.co.uk email: holidays@marsdens.co.uk

Rosemary Cottage is a stylish place in a particularly attractive part of the North Devon coast...

Vention Garden Cottage has a 'Mediterranean feel', with a Grecian-style outdoor pool and palm trees...

191

Cornwall and beyond
Farm and Cottage Holidays*

This family run agency has been operating since 1979. We first came to know it when a reader praised *Old Holcombe Water Farm*, at Clatworthy, five miles inland from Watchet, in North Somerset. It has three delightfully converted barns (**sleeping 2 to 4**) across lawns, and an orchard across from the 17th century farmhouse. Children delight in helping with jobs from collecting eggs to milking, as well as enjoying the farm's own clot-

Near Boscastle, in North Cornwall, this lovely house (not featured) sleeps 8.

ted cream and occasionally ice cream! And a regular reader has her eye on *Destiny Cottage*, near Port Isacc, in North Cornwall. On a working farm, **sleeping up to 5**, it is of a very high standard and offers excellent walking. But these are just samples of over 550 properties in Cornwall, Devon and Somerset, offering a wide choice of rural and coastal properties, sleeping from 2 to 20. Details/brochures, with details of a wide range of interesting properties, from Farm and Cottage Holidays, Victoria House, 12 Fore Street, Northam, Bideford, Devon EX39 1AW. Telephone 01237 479698 for brochures or 479146 for bookings.

www.farmcott.co.uk for up to date availability and on-line booking.

Scorrier, near Truro
The Butler's Cottage   map 6/362

This is very much our readers' kind of place – stylish, sensibly priced, quiet and very comfortable. They also approve of the thoroughbred horses that graze in the park that fronts the elegant main house. Butler's is a comfortable, spacious, recently renovated wing of 'the big house'. We admired the terraced garden at first floor level, the super and well equipped flagstoned kitchen, the antiques, the excellent paintings and prints, the first floor sitting room with beautifully chosen sunflower yellow sofa and armchairs, the long bath in the excellent bathroom. All is stylish and elegant, but not

This is one of our personal favourites in Cornwall – quiet, comfortable, stylish.

uncomfortably so: you can put your feet up here and unwind. All in all, this is a gem: the only thing lacking is the butler to wait on you. With an open fire in the sitting room, central heating, books and board games, we thought this would make a good base in the autumn, winter or spring.

Sleeps 4. TV/video; payphone. Pets are possible by arrangement. Linen and towels are included. Breakfast pack. Cost: about £250 to £360. Weekend breaks. Details from Richard and Caroline Williams, Scorrier House, Scorrier, Redruth, Cornwall TR16 5AU. Telephone 01209 820264. Fax 820677. **email: rwill10442@aol.com**

*ladwins Farm, Suffolk. Impressive rural
ews, a notable pool and sauna. Page 32.

*Peartree Cottage, Norfolk. A memorable
coastal location, a stylish cottage. Page 42.*

*ere Lodge, Norfolk. In delightful gardens, with the bonus of an impressive leisure centre,
ese are well recommended. It's an uncrowded, accessible part of Norfolk. Pages 45/47.*

*ld Farm Cottages, Norfolk. A real tour
e force, near the Broads. Page 48.*

*Clippesby Cottages, Norfolk. Happily, both
rural and not far from the sea. Page 51.*

*orfolk Holiday Homes. Just one of many
aside gems on their books. Page 52/53.*

*Townend Cottage, North Yorkshire. A cottage
we know well; the Moors are close. Page 66.*

Farsyde Mews Cottages, North Yorkshire. These have so much going for them, such as horses to ride and easy access to one of the most sought-after stretches of the Yorkshire coast. Page 72.

Fold Farm Cottages, North Yorkshire. It's the genuine article: a real 'village idyll'. Page 73.

Dalegarth/The Ghyll, North Yorkshire. Cottage excellence deep in the Dales. Pages 74/75

Peak Cottages, Derbyshire. A much-loved part of England, reliable cottages. Page 80.

Cressbrook Cottages, Derbyshire. No need go to Switzerland: you'll find it here! Page

Bee Cottage, Northumberland. 'Traditional' or modern, with Holy Island views. Page 94.

Blairquhan, Ayrshire. Properties of great character, long-term favourites. Page 98.

Outstanding even in 'cottage guide' terms, Large Holiday Houses in Scotland...

...includes for example Auchinroath House (left) and Achinduich (above) Page 104.

Loch Cottage, Perthshire. Many years in this guide, a Scottish classic Page 100.

3 Dalfaber Park, Inverness-shire. Modern and well situated for touring. Page 103.

Culligran Cottages, Inverness-shire. A classic Highland location, good fishing. Page 106.

Torrisdale, Kintyre. Go down the beautiful peninsula: it's a world away. Page 121.

Glen Coe Cottages, Argyll. One of the most amazing of all cottage locations Page 110.

Bank End Farm, Cumbria. You're still inside England, but only just! Page 123.

Attadale, Wester Ross. Even in terms of the Highlands, this is a fabulous place...

... with (normally) unlimited access to the estate. Just imagine the invigorating walk

...the wildlife you'll see and a memorable escape from 'the real world'. Page 109.

Long Byres, Cumbria. Twenty-three years with us: a 'serenely wild' spot. Page 125.

Meadowbank, Cumbria. This is definitely one of our Lake District 'top ten'. Page 129.

Monkhouse Hill, Cumbria. One of our sta for 23 years: so much 'TLC'. Page 134.

Clydey, West Wales. Readers have loved these cosy, welcoming cottages. Page 145.

Rosemoor, West Wales. 'Family-orientated near good beaches, deeply rural. Page 14

Portmeirion, Gwynedd. A fantasy-world by the sea, cottages a delight. Page 149.

Aberdovey Hillside Village, Ceredigion. Fabulous views, properties ideal for families. Page 151.

Pant Farm, North Wales. Featured in this guide for over 20 years, these outstanding cottages have the big advantage of woodburning stoves <u>and</u> central heating. Page 155.

Brecon Beacons Holiday Cottages, Mid Wales. A most attractive region and a superb portfolio of properties characterise one of the best cottage agencies in Britain. Page 159.

Trallwm Forest Cottages, Mid Wales. Quiet, not pricey, 'deeply rural'. Page 161.

Treworgey Coach House, Cornwall. Comfort and style, lots to do, a hundred acres. Page 163.

Trefanny Hill, Cornwall. Private, well spaced out, lots of individual character. The place is like a hamlet in its own right, and even has its own country inn, serving excellent food. Pages 164-165.

Bosinver, Cornwall. Both very rural and handy for the sea. Energetic, most welcoming owners who have turned these properties into some of the best in Cornwall. Page 170.

Sea Meads, Cornwall. Strikingly close to the sea, lots of modern comfort. Page 169.

Gullrock, Cornwall. A little-known sandy beach just a short stroll away. Page 179.

Mudgeon Vean, Cornwall Very much geared to families, very informal. Page 178.

Mineshop, Cornwall. Twenty-three years in this guide, an amazing location. Page 181.

Classic Cottages, Cornwall. In twenty-four years we have never, once, had a whisper of a complaint about this outstanding West Country agency's properties. Page 183-185.

Tregeath, Cornwall. Unpretentious but comfy, much liked by readers. Page 187.

Braddon Cottages, Devon. A reliably peace escape from everyday hassle. Page 206.

Marsdens Holidays, North Devon. An exceptional agency, with 'no duds'. Widely admired specialists in a very appealing, less overrun part of the West Country. Pages 190-191.

Mill Field, North Devon. One of our all-time personal favourites. The views are great, and the comfortable house is occasionally used and much enjoyed by the owners. Page 202.

Colour section A, Page 7

Wheel Farm, North Devon. A pool that families love, a tennis court, award-winning gardens, and a good range of very well cared for cottages – near the sea but very rural too. Page 209.

Wooder Manor, Devon. You can hardly get closer to the heart of secret, ancient Dartmoor than in o▮ of these fine properties. Your dog (by arrangement) will love it here. Page 207.

Compton Pool, Devon. Close to the sea but completely rural. In new ownership, these well converte▮ and most attractive cottages are predictably popular among families with small children. Page 212.

Horry Mill, Devon. A much-liked 'traditional' cottage, a fine wooded location. Page 201.

Fursdon, Devon. Ever fancied life in an oh-s▮ English country house? Try this! Page 216.

Countisbury/Coombebrook
Wellhouse and Pump Cottage

Most usefully **sleeping 8** (and, by
the way, recommended by readers),
Kipscombe Farm (Ref HTU) is a
spacious self contained wing of a
fine 17th century farmhouse. There's
a woodburning stove in an inglenook in a big, beamed sitting room.
Guests have access to 640 acres of
National Trust farmland, and the
'twin' coastal villages of Lynton and
Lynmouth are under three miles
away. Also recommended are two

*Wellhouse is a picture pretty charmer –
quiet and reasonably priced.*

small 'but perfectly formed' cottages near Abbotsham, specifically in a
small, sheltered valley next to the owners' home. Each **sleeping 2**,
Wellhouse (Ref FVV) and *Pump Cottage* (Ref FVU) are picture-pretty –
see above! We love the fact that you can pick up the National Trust
Coastal Path at the end of a half mile walk via lanes and meadows. Note
too that Bideford is only a little more than two miles away.

Further details from English Country Cottages, Stoney Bank Road, Earby,
Barnoldswick BB94 0AA. For bookings telephone 0870 192 1028. You
can also 'dial-a-brochure': 0870 192 0391.
www.ecc2006.co.uk

Hollocombe, near Chulmleigh   map 7/445
Horry Mill Cottage

This cottage quickly caught the
attention and imagination of readers
of this guide who appreciate a
remote rural scene as notable today
as it is in a faded photo on the wall
of the cob-style cottage. **Sleeps 4** in
a double room and a twin. The fully
equipped bathroom has a free-standing electric shower. We admired the
huge inglenook fireplace and bread
oven in the sitting room, also the

*Absolute peace and quiet: a delight...
See also Colour section A, Page 8.*

small south facing sun parlour with grapevine. There is a well equipped
kitchen and dining room seating six and high chair. An open fire, with
logs provided free, complements oil fired central heating. The Hodgsons
will collect local dishes ordered in Crediton, or elsewhere. Pophams
restaurant, with a national reputation, is close by. Linen and towels provided. TV, video and stereo/CD player. One dog by arrangement. Non
smokers preferred. Cost: from £260 to £525. Details from Sonia and
Simon Hodgson, Horry Mill, Hollocombe, Chulmleigh, Devon EX18
7QH. Telephone 01769 520266.

www.horrymill.com   email: sonia@horrymill.com

Lee Bay, near Croyde
Mill Field Cottage

This is one of our own long-term favourites in the guide. We've seen it in all weathers, and it's a delight. The location is stunning: one of the most beautiful parts of the North Devon coast, overlooking Lee Bay, surrounded by National Trust land. The cottage stands in its own garden and fields and there is a fabulous

A charming base with spectacular views, used from time to time by the owners...

view over the bay. It has been upgraded over the years to a high standard. We like the large sitting/dining room, with its many books, leading into the sun room in which one could spend a fortnight watching the tides in the bay. Local features and pleasures include excellent surfing at Woolacombe, Croyde and Saunton, golf courses, horse riding, sea trips from Ilfracombe to Lundy and for anglers and naturalists, plus walking on coastal paths and beaches. It's recommended for spring or autumn breaks.

TV, payphone. **Sleeps 7** in three single rooms and two doubles plus cot. There are two bathrooms, a garage and parking space. Well behaved dogs by arrangement. Cost: £390 to £825. Further details from Michael or Sally Wilkins, 10 Coalecroft Road, Putney, London SW15 8LP. Telephone 020-8788 6438.

email: mw@celticmarine.co.uk

Langtree, near Great Torrington
Stowford Lodge Holiday Cottages   map 7/412

Well away from any traffic, accessed via narrow, high banked lanes typical of this part of Devon, these four properties have proved very popular with readers. They **sleep 6, 4, 4** and **4**, and have been converted from farm buildings with style and skill. *Warren* and *Halcyon* are suitable for wheelchairs. A special feature is the indoor heated swimming pool: lovely warm water, curtained windows; wall pictures/hangings, underwater light-

We admired exposed beams, good beds, pretty covers, books and games.

ing. A mile away, amid farmland, are *1 and 2 South Hill Cottages*, refurbished, semi-detached, spacious cottages **sleeping 4**. We like these immensely. They are secluded and enjoy good views and privacy, off-road parking, shared garden, private patio, and open log fire. TV. Dogs welcome (small charge). Linen provided. **'Visit Britain' Three Stars**. Cost: £220 to £570. Details and brochure from Sally Milsom, Stowford Lodge, Langtree, Torrington, North Devon EX38 8NU. Telephone 01805 601540, fax 601487.

www.stowfordlodge.co.uk   email: stowford@dial.pipex.com

Bridgerule, near Bude
Glebe House Cottages

High-lying Glebe House is a lovely late-Georgian stone house in five acres of formal gardens and woodland, commanding beautiful uninterrupted views. But it's not 'in the back of beyond', being on the edge of the pleasant village of Bridgerule.

All of the seven spacious, warm and comfortable cottages have exposed beams and mellow stone walls, and are '**Visit Britain' Four Stars**. They **sleep from 2 to 6**. We admired the carefully chosen fabrics, comfortable chairs and sofas, old farm implements and saddlery items on the walls.

Very well situated for exploring both North Cornwall and North Devon...

...these are cottages we have known and liked for well over twenty years.

The Old Stables and *The Mews* are similar in layout, with large living rooms on the ground floor. The Mews has a canopied bed and a spa bath while Old Stables has a king-size bed and a double whirlpool bath. *Little Barn*, *Granary* and *Coach House* have their living rooms upstairs with fine exposed roof timbers. At ground level each master bedroom has an ensuite shower room as well as the main bathrooms.

Granary and Little Barn have 'minstrels' galleries' to provide additional sleeping accommodation. These two can be linked to take larger family groups. *Gamekeepers* and *Poachers* provide accommodation to an extremely high standard while maintaining their old world charm, with exposed beams and other period features. Both cottages have four-posters in the main bedrooms and double whirlpool baths.

All are welcome, including honeymooners, 'senior citizens', and families with young children. Cots, highchairs and baby listeners are free, and there is a children's play area and games room. Central heating, electricity and bed-linen are all included. TV. Cost: from about £260 to £895. Pets are not allowed.

Details and a brochure are available from James and Margaret Varley, Glebe House, Bridgerule, Holsworthy, Devon EX22 7EW. Telephone 01288 381272.

www.glebehousecottages.co.uk
email: ghcg@glebehousecottages.co.uk

Combe Martin, near Ilfracombe
Wheel Farm Country Cottages

Effectively a little hamlet, very well placed for traditional family seaside holidays though comfortably just-inland, this has long been one of the most popular groups of cottages we feature. During one recent revisit we met readers (a young couple with a small baby) staying in one of the cottages and asked what they liked most about Wheel Farm. They said: 'It's private, but we don't feel cut off. It's in the country but near the sea, and we love the gardens.'

Nestling in a sheltered valley close to the picturesque village of Combe

Stable and Linhay: everything is 'just so', and the North Devon location is a delight.

Every cottage has a beautifully planned and reliably comfortable interior.

Martin, near beautiful, wide, sandy beaches such as Woolacombe's (fifteen minutes' drive) and Croyde (twenty minutes), and overlooking Exmoor National Park, Wheel Farm provides an ideal holiday setting for all the family. The eleven acres of grounds have award-winning gardens, patios, millponds (fenced), grassland and wooded copse walks.

Converted from an old water mill (the wheel still remains) and barns, the cottages have exposed stone walls and beams, rustic charm, and yet provide all modern amenities. All have full gas central heating, microwaves, TVs, videos and dishwashers (except those just for 2).

Four of the cottages have four-poster beds; six have wood-burning stoves. They are furnished to a high standard with Victorian farmhouse antique and pine furniture, deep upholstered suites, good quality fitted carpets and drapes. They range from cosy units designed **for 2** to bigger ones that spaciously **accommodate 6**, plus cots. Facilities include an impressive heated indoor swimming pool, sauna, mini fitness room, LTA standard tennis court, children's playground – all free of charge.

Linen and mid week maid service are included, towels available for hire. Laundry room with token-operated washers and dryers. Groceries can be provided for arrival and hand baked pies, pastries and cakes are available. Arrangements can be made for baby sitting, tennis tuition, taxis, riding, golf, cycling. **'Visit Britain' Four Stars**. 'Regret no pets.' TVs. Cost: about £250 to £1150; short breaks low season only. **Closed end of October 2006 to mid-March 2007**. Brochure from Mr and Mrs J G Robertson, Wheel Farm Country Cottages, Berry Down 16, Combe Martin, North Devon EX34 0NT. Telephone 01271 882100. Fax 883120.

www.wheelfarmcottages.co.uk email: holidays@wheelfarmcottages.co.uk

Brendon, near Lynmouth
Rockford Lodge

This cottage is one of our all-time favourites, particularly for its location: it's a special pleasure to leave our car in the main part of the hamlet of Rockford (just a pub and a handful of cottages) and walk a few yards over a footbridge across the tumbling River East Lyn to see Rockford Lodge again and, sometimes, to meet the contented people staying in it.

One of the *The Good Holiday Cottage Guide* inspectors, who has compiled a 'top ten' of his favourite cottages, includes Rockford Lodge in it. He – like us – enjoys places that ramble a bit, and have something of a farmhousey character. Tucked away in a secret, wooded valley on the edge of mysterious Exmoor, Rockford has a big kitchen with a cosy Aga, fitted carpets, lots of books, paintings and a very big upstairs bathroom. The river that rushes past the garden fence does not do so loudly enough to keep one awake! The footpaths in the beautiful woods outside the conservatory-like 'river room' beckon one for walks. Described over the years by readers as 'a genuine home from home' ... 'wonderfully well equipped' ... 'the setting is marvellous', the cottage is used quite frequently by the owners themselves. **Sleeps 6** plus cot.

Dogs are welcome but not cats. TV. Cost: about £400 to £675. Further details available from Mrs E M Adnitt, 82 The Row, Lane End, High Wycombe, Buckinghamshire HP14 3JU. Telephone 01494 882609.

email: ema.rockford@sagainternet.co.uk

Many years in this guide, Rockford Lodge has a most unusual situation ...

... whereby you park your car and then cross a river via a footbridge. Delightful!

Please note: we cannot vouch for every property on an agency's books, but only those we have seen. Most agents have at least a handful of modest properties that appeal to a specific market (for example, fishermen, walkers and stalkers), or sometimes properties at the extreme edge of the region they deal with that are not typical of what they offer. But in principle the agencies we feature are reliable and conscientious...

Ashwater, near Holsworthy
Braddon Cottages and Forest

Close to the Devon/Cornwall border, most appealingly at the end of a long drive, we have long admired these six properties, all separate and detached, with lawns and gardens to boot. They are surrounded by hundreds of acres of meadow and woodland that is part of the owners' imaginative broadleaf planting scheme. All have woodburners and fine views over the well stocked three-acre fishing lake. Fishing is free, reserved for residents.

Country lovers should note – here you're away from any noisy roads.

The Linhaye and *Lake House* are large, purpose-built houses **sleeping 12 plus 2**, each convertible into two self-contained, sound-proofed apartments. Microwave, dishwasher, washing machine, dryer, gas central heating, double glazing, barbecues. There's an all-weather summer house near the lake, an all-weather tennis court and a games room with a full size snooker table. TV/videos, payphones. Linen/towels provided. Well behaved dogs welcome. Open all year. **'Visit Britain' Three Stars**. Cost: £140 to £1250, bargain breaks from £80 2ppn. Details from George and Anne Ridge, Braddon, Ashwater, Beaworthy, Devon EX21 5EP. Telephone 01409 211350.

www.braddoncottages.co.uk email: holidays@braddoncottages.co.uk

Nr Brendon/Nr Bude   map 7/429/426

We like the way many North Devon properties offer the chance to explore much of the best of North Cornwall as well as certain parts of Somerset and Exmoor. A fine 300 year old farmhouse *on* Exmoor (Ref W3271) has a great deal going for it: a magnificent 30-foot long farmhouse style kitchen with dining area, beams and – yes – *two* woodburners. This handsome property, with a pub serving food just two miles away, **sleeps up to 8**. In the appealingly named village of Welcombe, a mile

This striking house at Welcombe is exceptionally well situated in terms of things to see and do...

from Welcombe Bay and well placed for some of the most spectacular places along the North Devon and the North Cornwall coast, an eye-catching house (Ref 40147, **sleeping 7/8**) has the makings of a memorable family holiday. This too has a woodburning stove.

Welcome Holidays, Spring Mill, Earby, Barnoldswick, BB94 0AA. Telephone (brochures) 0870 192 0809; (bookings) 0870 336 2825.

www.welcomecottages.com

Widecombe-in-the-Moor
Wooder Manor

Here is a neat grouping of properties converted from an old coach-house and stables. And with the Bell family's Dartmoor home close by (it's a working farm amid 170 acres of woodland, moor and granite tors), guests, as we rediscovered last year, are guaranteed a personal welcome. Widecombe-in-the-Moor is a mere half mile away. (See Colour section

Dartmoor is magical, and these properties, open all year, are at its heart.

B, Page 2 for the view from Wooder Manor.) *Wooder House* itself **sleeps 12** in five bedrooms; its ambiance comfortable and relaxing. Two cottages **sleep 6**, the others **sleep 4.** Ideal for walking, fishing, canoeing, cycling or riding. Central heating and a laundry room; bed linen by arrangement; microwaves, TV, metered electricity. Cots and highchairs free; log fires in *Honeybags* and Wooder House. **'Visit Britain' Three/Four Stars**. Dogs by arrangement. Cost: from £180 to £460, £240 to £520 or £600 to £1020 **sleeping 4, 6 or 12** respectively. Ample parking. Details from Angela Bell, Wooder Manor, Widecombe-in-the-Moor, Newton Abbot, Devon TQ13 7TR. Telephone/fax 01364 621391.

www.woodermanor.com

Higher Clovelly/Hartland Point
Lundy View/Blegberry Farm   map 7/438

We love cottages with good views, and here are two that as well as having lots of other good things going for them have a notable outlook both over countryside and coast. With memorable views of Bideford Bay and Lundy Island, *Lundy View* (Ref 17431) is one of a number of properties within a converted Grade II listed barn. Unusually, the main bedroom has its own spiral staircase leading to a 'viewing room'. **Sleeps 6**. In an Area of Outstanding Natural

The Blegberry Farm Cottages are superbly well situated, and very comfortable too...

Beauty, the two *Blegberry Farm* properties on the owners' Grade II listed farm are full of character, retain a number of original features – such as beams and stone walls – and are very close to secluded sand and shingle beaches with coves and rockpools. They **sleep 11 'plus 1'** and **6**. Refs 17440 and 17441.

Details from Country Holidays, Spring Mill, Earby, Lancashire BB94 0AA. For brochures: 0870 607 8514; for bookings: 0870 192 1040.

To 'look and book': 2006www.country-holidays.co.uk

Devon: coast and country
Toad Hall Cottages*

With never anything but praise from readers, we have featured this agency for sixteen years. Perhaps people like it so much because it specialises in coastal, rural and waterside cottages that include romantic retreats, seaside villas and picture-postcard hideaways, all in sought-after locations throughout Devon, Exmoor and now Cornwall.

A visit to Thurlestone, South Devon last September confirmed this impression. Dotted along the main village street are archetypal thatched or character cottages with flower-strewn gardens. Among them, *Bay Tree Cottage*, dating back to the 17th century, has an abundance of exposed beams and a secluded garden. **Sleeping 6**, it is close to the village pub and shop.

The beach is a fifteen minute walk away. The completely renovated and cosy *Nook*, **sleeping 5** plus cot, is attached on one side. Add *Jubilee Cottage*, a honey coloured property, **sleeping 6**, *Just-a-Cottage*, a tiny cottage built in 1683, **sleeping 4**, and the elegant top of the range *Stable Cottage*, **sleeping 6/8**, and you have the measure of the place.

There's also *Higher Furlong*, a spacious detached family house, **sleeping 10**, on the exclusive Yarmer Estate with sweeping views of the bay. Along with *Warren House*, **sleeping 9**, with superb gardens, and *Thorpe Arnold*, **sleeping 8**, adjacent to the 9th green on the Thurlestone Golf Course, it illustrates the wide scope the agency offers.

This was also evident at *Pound Cottage*, Simonsbath on Exmoor, so called because it was once a sheep pound. **Sleeping 6**, plus cot, the single-storeyed property fronts the road that leads across Exmoor. Previously we have praised *Cliff Cottage* at Dittisham, in The Dart Valley, **sleeping 6**. Also *Alice Cottage*, at Start Bay, South Devon. Once owned by Christopher Robin, the son of AA Milne, the author of Winnie The Pooh, it is peaceful, private and comfortable, with many personal touches. **Sleeps 6** plus cot.

Every cottage on the agency's books is known to at least one member of the Toad Hall staff. About half the properties accept dogs and many have open fires. Details and a comprehensive brochure are available from Toad Hall Cottages, Elliott House, Church Street, Kingsbridge, South Devon TQ7 1BY. Telephone 01548 853089. Fax 853086.

www.toadhallcottages.com
email: thc@toadhallcottages.com

Cliff Cottage: you are close enough to the water to choose a crab for your tea...

Alice Cottage, in a tiny hamlet, was the home of the real-life Christopher Robin...

Salcombe, near Kingsbridge
Salcombe Holiday Homes*

Closely associated with sailing and fishing, this delightful South Hams resort also enjoys a 'local' climate that's especially pleasant even by West Country standards. Agents Tim and Ginny Windibank delight in promoting local properties which match their own expectations: that means exacting standards, with members of staff *visiting each property prior to every arrival*. (There are 150-plus properties, including many cosy cottages and flats for **2/4** people.)

In the summer of 2005 we visited a number of properties we hadn't seen before. For example, *The Wood*, with panoramic views, is a truly mind-blowing family owned mansion, with not only a superb outlook over South Sands but, **sleeping up to 15**, highly suited to that special once-in-a-lifetime family occasion or reunion. Polished oak and carpeted floors in the vast drawing/sitting-room, seven bedrooms and servants' quarters **sleeping a further 3** characterise this stylishly furnished property in landscaped, terraced gardens. (See also **www.thewood-devonuk.com**)

Close by, *Mount Sylvan*, **sleeping 6**, has an intriguing spiral staircase to the first floor, where two bedrooms command South Sands views. Though unsuited to youngsters under eight, this well furnished property is ideal for a family with older children seeking personal space.

Within a few minutes' walk of the town centre and waterfront, *Devon Villas* is an imposing restored semi-detached Victorian family house **sleeping 12.** The cellar area alone will delight children: just right, with a sizeable garden, for two families to share.

The Boathouse, **sleeping 4/6**, enjoys the tang of the sea and an award-winning architectural flair: stripped pine, almost minimalist, rather snazzy. There are for example curved doors, a spiral staircase and a ceiling panel which can be raised to provide extra light.

For a colour brochure contact Salcombe Holiday Homes, Orchard Court, Island Street, Salcombe, Devon TQ8 8QE. Telephone: 01548 843485.

www.salcombe.com email: shh@salcombe.com

See also the sister agency: Dartmouth Holiday Homes, 1a, Lower Street, Dartmouth, Devon TQ6 9AJ. Telephone 01803 833082.

www.dartmouthuk.com email:dhh@dartmouthuk.com

The Wood, sleeping 15, is one of the most remarkable properties within an exceptional portfolio.

Mount Sylvan is a super house, sleeping six, well suited to families seeking a bit of 'personal space'.

Holbeton, near Plymouth
Carswell Farm Cottages

Carswell, an organic dairy farm, occupies 800 acres by the sea on a quiet stretch of South Devon coast. Two off-the-beaten-track cottages on the farm have been converted for holidays. In *Shepherd's Cottage* (**sleeping 6**) we really liked the flagstones in the kitchen section and a beechwood floor in the lounge area (with a wood-burning stove). Upstairs a double bedroom with washbasin overlooks the

Corner Cottage is 'not just a pretty face': it most usefully sleeps eight people...

small garden and fields beyond. It shares the bathroom with twin and bunk bedrooms; also shower-room downstairs. *Corner Cottage* (**sleeping 8**) has a ground floor bedroom for 3, plus two doubles and a single upstairs. The Sayers family like to involve guests in farm life and children love to visit the milking parlour. For walkers, the South West Coast Path which runs by the farm leads to 'secret' sandy coves. Electric cooker, microwave, dishwasher, washing machine, TV/video. Central heating and logs provided. Table tennis. Cost from £200 to £875. (Dogs welcome, but downstairs only.) Details from Zoe Sayers or Peggy Honey, Carswell, Holbeton, Plymouth PL8 1HH. Telephone 01752 830492/830282; fax 830565.

www.carswellcottages.com email: enquiries@carswellcottages.com

---

Membury, near Axminster   map 7/442
Cider Room Cottage

This sort of cottage is, sadly, increasingly rare. 'Traditional', with much of its original character intact, it lies deep in the rolling Devon/Somerset border country, next to the family-in-residence but with plenty of privacy – we like it very much. The location is rural and peaceful, but not isolated, and the cottage is neat and attractive: it will suit people who prefer an individual cottage to being

Very reasonably priced indeed, but certainly worth its Four Stars grading, this cottage is cosy and traditional...

part of a complex. The views of green, hilly farmland are delightful, and there are ducks, dogs, cats and pet Vietnamese pot-bellied pig to delight small children. Candlelit meals can be enjoyed in the owners' home. The cottage has a spacious, comfortable stone-flagged and carpeted sitting room, two pretty bedrooms, lots of beams, rustic stone walls (there is a shower-room, not bath). We spotted lots of books and fresh flowers.

TV. **'Visit Britain' Four Stars**. Dogs by arrangement. Cost: £165 to £285. Details from Pat and David Steele, Hasland Farm, Membury, Axminster, Devon EX13 7JF. Telephone 01404 881558. Fax 881834.

email: ciderroomcottage@rscontracting.co.uk

Beacon, near Honiton
Red Doors Cottages

Deeply rural, but just three miles from busy Honiton, these have easy access to the Blackdown Hills. Fitting harmoniously into their surroundings are a Grade II* listed Red Doors farmhouse and a group of exceptional cottages. There are **sleeping from 2 to 8 plus cot**, with an indoor, well heated

Kitchen of Orchard Cottage: but every one of the super cottages has character.

swimming pool, a games barn, a 'secret garden', a play area, a croquet lawn and more. All but one cottage has a woodburner. We looked into several at random and thought them so full of style, character and comfort. (We especially liked *Swallows Loft*, an ultra-modern *tour de force*.) A typical comment about Red Doors comes from Donna Preston, of Bristol: 'Our cottage and its surroundings were beautiful, the best we've ever found. We'll be back for a return visit soon. A huge thanks to Karen and Chris for making Red Doors such a wonderful and relaxing place.' Short breaks. TVs/videos/CD players. Central heating, linen, towels, logs and a welcome hamper are all included. Dogs by arrangement. Cost: about £395 to £1450. Details/brochures from Chris Shrubb, Red Doors, Beacon, Honiton, Exeter EX14 4TX. Telephone/fax 01404 890067.

www.reddoors.co.uk   email: chris@reddoors.co.uk

Dartmouth
The Boat House   map 7/444

Even by the standards of English Country Cottages (and indeed *The Good Holiday Cottage Guide!*) this is absolutely outstanding. Built over the site of the original boat-house on a bend in the River Dart, with views both upriver to the town and its Naval College, and down to the

Even in 'ECC' terms, this is a quite extraordinary property...

open sea, it is fashioned after a liner, with its 'cabins' fully panelled in light sycamore. All the living accommodation is on the first floor, with access down two flights of steps. The living room has a huge bay window overhanging the river to take advantage of the views. There is an open fire and a door to a balcony with external steps down to the garden. The dining room is panelled; the spacious kitchen has stripped pine floors and maple units. There are three double rooms (six foot beds, one zip-linked), and a room with full-size bunk beds. There are two bathrooms. Spiral stairs lead down to a large games room (with table tennis) and a door to the garden. Ref HHG. Further details from English Country Cottages, Stoney Bank Road, Earby, Barnoldswick BB94 0AA. For bookings telephone 0870 192 1028. You can also 'dial-a-brochure': 0870 192 0391.

www.ecc2006.co.uk

Compton Pool, near Torquay
Compton Pool Farm Cottages

Featured in this guide for almost 20 years, these cottages are in a location that readers (especially families) have raved about: only ten minutes' drive from the centre of Torquay, but entirely rural, with easy access to Torbay, and Dartmoor only a short drive away.

From the spring of 2006, however, the properties will become even more sought-after. For in the hands of new owners (who have previously run successful self catering in the same area) serious upgrading has put them on an entirely different plane.

There are far too many good things for us to detail here, but, for example, indications of the exceptional quality of these cottages are in the marble floors to kitchen/dining areas, the well appointed bathrooms and shower rooms with power showers, the hand crafted contemporary furniture produced in the UK.

There are expensive king size beds in all double bedrooms and full size singles in twin rooms (no bunks), the best quality soft furnishings, with

Absolutely top-notch accommodation in the care of new, on-site owners that matches the variety of all the things there are for the whole family to 'see and do'.

all bedding and towels included, flat screen digital TVs, DVD players and Bose HiFi systems (plus extra TVs in all double bedrooms).

There are eight cottages, namely *Ambrook* (**sleeping 8**), *Arch* (**4**), *Bidwell* (**6**), *Bow* (**2**), *Crazy Well* (**6**), *Kester* (**4**), *Redlake* (**4**) and *Wray* (**4**).

Significantly, the numbers of people the cottages originally slept have been reduced, with guests' comfort in mind.

There is plenty for guests to do in the area, with wildlife parks, a rare breeds farm, a butterfly farm, steam railways, learning to sail. There is a super indoor swimming pool to enjoy, and a tennis court on site.

As regular readers will expect, Compton Pool is high on our agenda for an extended visit in the early spring of 2006!

Details from Compton Pool Farm, Compton, Devon TQ13 1TA. Telephone 01803 872241. Fax 874012.

www.comptonpool.co.uk

email: info@comptonpool.co.uk

Okehampton
Fourwinds

We were impressed as we swept into the spacious driveway of this handsome 1860s property (now three substantial holiday homes), and even more impressed by how sumptuous, warm and well insulated they are. There really is 'no expense spared' in the conversion, and it's not sur-

Sumptuously comfortable, well-cared-for.

prising they've acquired a huge following in a short time. This has been helped along by the superior pets' corner, where children love to meet tame pigmy goats and chickens (all have their own names), ducks, a goose and two ponies. There are safe and enclosed gardens. (You won't get lost here, as the A30 dual carriageway runs close. But it's out of sight: the view from the cottages' front windows is of rolling hills that beckon walkers.) Two-storeyed *Tor View* **sleeps 4 'plus 2'**, *Brokan,* a first floor apartment, **sleeps 8 'plus 2'**, and *Orkney,* a ground floor apartment, **sleeps 4**. Note: the latter two can be opened up to make one large property for **up to 14**. TVs/videos. Linen/towels included. Baby sitting. Welcome pack, laundry facilities. **'Visit Britain' Four Stars**. Cost: about £250 to £625. Details from Sue Collins, Fourwinds, Tavistock Road, Okehampton, Devon EX20 4LX. Telephone/fax 01837 55785.

www.eclipse.co.uk/fourwinds email: four.winds@eclipse.co.uk

Modbury, Ivybridge
Oldaport Farm Cottages

We like cottages 'miles from any-where', especially if there's a quiet beach a mile and a half away. So do many others, as last year's visit to this property, tucked away in the South Hams, confirmed. One couple have been back ten years running. Cathy Evans runs the four cottages and the

You could be 'miles from anywhere', but Salcombe and Kingsbridge are handy....

70-acre farm (**map 7/435**) overlooking the beautiful Erme estuary. Much thought and care has gone into the conversions. Three cottages, **sleeping 2/4, 6** and **6**, were created from the old stone cowshed and dairy. The fourth, *Orchard* – single storeyed and **just for 2** – overlooks the paddock where miniature Shetland ponies graze beside chickens and ducks. Latch doors, pine furniture and comfortable furnishings convey the right mood, and there are games and books. The farm is famous for its championship Lleyn sheep. The South Coastal footpath is nearby, as is Dartmoor. **'Visit Britain' Four Stars**. Laundry room, payphone. TV. Bedlinen included. Cost: £210 to £610. Dogs welcome low/mid season. Short breaks, low season. Details from Miss C M Evans, Oldaport Farm Cottages, Modbury, Ivybridge, Devon PL21 0TG. Telephone 01548 830842. Fax 830998.

www.oldaport.com email: cathy@oldaport.com

Dartmouth
Dartmouth Holiday Homes*

With the sun sparkling on the sea, packed pleasure boats puttering up the river, and cream and brown trains transporting people on the restored Dart Valley Railway, this chic, beautifully cared for resort is rather special. Better yet, it lies in a delightful corner of Devon.

There are a good number of holiday homes in the town (some self-contained houses, many apartments), the best of which are looked after by the highly professional and welcoming Ginny and Tim Windibank and their staff. Ginny and Tim also own the successful Salcombe Holiday Homes (see Page 209). They recently took over the business from the respected Tessa Angles on her retirement after twenty five years.

We looked at a cross section of what they have available, all of them with the sort of view that could keep one sitting quietly in a bay window or on a balcony – just gazing at the river and the town – for hours on end.

We visited *The Chart House*, which, **sleeping 8**, is a remarkable detatched property standing in a commanding position with amazing panoramic views of the river and out to sea. Well furnished and with high ceilings, it is memorable for the huge sun room running down the sides of the house with access to the paved deck accessible from the good sized sitting room, and the substantial sheltered garden.

Sleeping 10, *36 Clarence Street* is a spacious period townhouse close to the heart of the town. It has recently been refurbished to a very high standard, with fabulous views from the feature attic sitting room. From the kitchen is an atrium with glazed roof, terracotta floors and comfortable seating. The property also benefits from garage parking and a pretty terraced, part lawned garden at the rear with views to the harbour.

Properties in 'Above Town' nearly all benefit from views over the river and towards Kingswear. *61 Above Town* is no exception: **sleeping 4**, the property has light, well equipped accommodation. The balcony, off the sitting room, is a great place to watch the boats sail across the harbour.

With coastal and country walks, nearby beaches, sailing, fishing, great shopping and super restaurants Dartmouth is a great place all year round.

Details and brochures from Dartmouth Holiday Homes, 1a Lower Street, Dartmouth, Devon TQ6 9AJ. Telephone 01803 833082. Fax 835224. **www.dartmouthuk.com email dhh@dartmouthuk.com**

A good number of the properties are high above Dartmouth...

...and those that aren't mostly have easy access to this extraordinary town.

Rattery, near Totnes
Knowle Farm

Readers have described these properties as 'a paradise for pet-loving young-sters'. Former enthusiastic self-caterers Lynn and Richard Micklewright have put into practice everything they learned during their own holidays. Open your cottage door, and a collection of chickens, ducks, pigs, rabbits and donkeys will parade before you. Delightful! Then there are the outdoor play areas, and one of the best indoor playrooms for under fives we have seen, including a ballpool, slide and toys. There's a genuine attempt to answer children's needs without neglecting adults. This is reflected in the cottages, converted from stone and slate barns with wood burning stoves.

Moncks Green **sleeps 6** plus cot, with a double, twin and bunk rooms down-stairs, plus bathroom/wc with shower. Upstairs is a large living-room with high ceiling and exposed trusses, commanding impressive views, also a din-ing-room and shower-room/toilet. *Applecross*, **sleeping 4** plus cot, has dou-ble and bunk rooms downstairs with bathroom/toilet with shower. Again

In 44 acres, the farm has an exceptional playroom and a whole host of pets...

...as well as swimming for all the family in a most inviting indoor pool.

there are good views from the upstairs living/dining room. *Clematis*, **sleep-ing 2** plus child or cot, is a cosy single-storey cottage with a wood panelled ceiling in the living/dining room area, full of character like the others. *Woodbine* (**sleeping 8** plus cots) is suited to two families. Downstairs it has a galleried living/dining area with high ceiling, exposed beams and trusses, a double bedroom with en-suite facilities, and a twin room. The first floor gallery sports a gorgeous sitting area, a double and bunk room, plus bath-room/wc with shower. *Post Box*, a 16th century thatched cottage in a nearby village **sleeps 4** plus cot. Very pretty with old beams and a stone fireplace, this has double and twin rooms upstairs, kitchen, living/dining area, bath-room/toilet with shower downstairs, and its own private garden.

The farm, in 44 acres, also offers a 34 by 17 foot heated indoor pool, tennis court, and indoor table tennis and pool table. Dartmoor is about five minutes away, the coast about half an hour. Not suitable for pets; electricity and heating by meter; duvets (with linen) supplied. TV. Highchairs, cots and stair gates. Cost: from about £230 to £1450.

Details from Lynn and Richard Micklewright, Knowle Farm, Rattery, near Totnes, Devon TQ10 9JY. Telephone/fax 01364 73914.

www.knowle-farm.co.uk

email: holiday@knowle-farm.co.uk

Fursdon, near Exeter
Fursdon

The 700-acre estate in the Exe Valley in rural mid-Devon has been the home of the Fursdon family *since 1259*. The present generation, David and Catriona, let out two apartments on the first floor of the handsome manor house whose origins date from the 13th century. *Garden Wing* (**sleeping 3**), opening on to the walled rear garden, has a large double bedroom, a small single and a cosy sitting-room with open fire (logs supplied) and enough books to keep the most avid reader happy for months.

(Our most recent visit was memorable for the sight of doves peeping in the kitchen window of the *Garden Wing* apartment!)

Park Wing (**sleeping 6**), which enjoys magnificent views over the land-scaped parkland at the front of the house, has a large en-suite double bedroom. Two further (twin) bedrooms are at the back and share a shower room. The spacious lounge, again with masses of books, and the large kitchen both enjoy the front view too. Catriona, who masterminds the decor, chooses furnishings and colours that suit the age of the rooms. Both apartments have good-sized kitchens with dining-tables and are equipped with gas-cooker, dishwasher, fridge-freezer and microwave.

We were not at all surprised to learn that one family has been coming here regularly for seventeen years and another has visited several times from Alaska. Guests can make use of the extensive gardens and woodland. Young visitors particularly enjoy getting to know the three friendly ponies

Not just another holiday booking, but a chance to savour a fine country house...

...in which the advantages of good-quality kitchens are not forgotten.

and Catriona's flock of black Welsh Mountain sheep, while tennis players will be delighted by the well-maintained grass court (bring your own racquets). Swings and slides for children. Table-tennis in a barn. Fishing is available on a private stretch of the Exe, two miles away.

TV, DVD, CD player. Washing machine and dryer in courtyard. Linen and logs provided. Cot and highchair available. Bookings Friday-Friday. Cost: about £300 to £700 per week. Short breaks available. Not suitable for dogs. Details from Catriona Fursdon, Fursdon, Cadbury, Exeter EX5 5JS. Telephone 01392 860860. Fax 860126.

www.fursdon.co.uk.

email: holidays@fursdon.co.uk

216

The West Country
Helpful Holidays*

A remarkable organisation by any standards, but happily still very much a family concern, 'Helpful' is known throughout the travel and leisure industry for its uncompromisingly high standards. Their 25th anniversary in 2006/2007 coincides with that of *The Good Holiday Cottage Guide* itself, so we have every reason to congratulate them!

We've been pleased to know and feature the agency for over twenty years without a break, and from an outspoken and very 'involved' cottage-guide readership have never heard anything other than praise.

The Bowaters believe in saying what properties are really like – warts and all – and have an exceptional variety, from boat houses and 'beach houses' to historic country houses and picture-book thatched cottages.

Their properties are spread all over the West Country, from Land's End to Somerset and Dorset – seaside and inland. And a glance at their unconventional brochure, detailing approximately 530 cottages, underlines their 'truth will out' philosophy.

We visited three fairly representative properties quite recently, and the bond between the agency and the owners to 'bring out the best' was instantly recognisable.

'Helpful' were, for instance, closely involved in the design of *Great Cleave* (**sleeping 8**), formerly a threshing barn and one of a group of three located down a long lane, with wonderful Dartmoor views, close to Drewsteignton. The 'upside-down' look, with the upstairs living/dining room rising high to the apex, with fine beams and tresses, works a treat. *Old Orchard*, **sleeping 4**, got our stamp of approval for its freshness and rural charm, as did *Little Cleave,* fractionally smaller but also **sleeping 4**. All share eight acres of pastureland, a fenced pond with ducks and chickens (complimentary free range eggs usually available).

A mile and a quarter from Sampford Courtenay, one of the prettiest of the mid-Devon villages (with the last half mile a simple farm track) the sudden appearance of Hathertom farmhouse – amid 210 wooded acres, with panoramic views of Dartmoor – lends an almost oasis-like air to two delightful properties. First *The Cottage*, a large 'upside down' detached property, has lots of beams in a lofty open-plan living area, with french windows on to a huge terrace ideal for sun lovers or barbecues. And the views are stunning! **Sleeps 6**, with three en-suite bedrooms downstairs.

This impressive property (Ref L51) sleeps up to 18. It is in Devon's 'South Hams'.

This remarkably situated place is at Port Isaac, in Cornwall. Sleeps 15. Ref P16.

Within the pre-Norman detached *Farmhouse* there's an 'ox-roasting' inglenook fireplace, and antique furniture sits easily alongside 21st century needs. An ancient drover's track passes close by: it was the medieval main road through mid-Devon. **Sleeps 8** in four bedrooms reached by a neatly crafted staircase. A shared heated indoor swimming pool is available.

Five miles from Cullompton, Halsbeer Farm incorporates four thatched cottages, three adapted for wheelchair user, that happily retain the distinctive flagstones and original timbers. *Cider* and *Swallow* both **sleep 6,** while *Haybarn*, which we looked over, has a sturdy Elizabethan style four poster and a galleried landing. **Sleeps 7.** The fourth property, *Apple*, is the farmer's fine thatched farmhouse. **Sleeps 3.** A huge barn, converted into a conservatory, can seat gatherings of up to 25; an indoor swimming pool is complemented by a children's play area.

Another delightful journey of discovery led us to *Lower Elsford*, near Lustleigh. It is a classic rural Devonshire enclave, four skilful barn conversions adjacent to the owners' house in 35 acres of garden and farmland, from which at certain points it is possible to see the sea.

Among many good things, we admired deep sofas, woodburners, high ceilings, good quality rugs and table lamps, and many charming personal details. A well heated indoor swimming pool in a converted piggery (we loved the piggy murals!) even has an open fire: a first for us! There are lots of animals for children to make friends with. **Sleep 2 to 5.**

Beyond the River Tamar that separates Cornwall from Devon, and in a tucked away corner that many travellers scurrying westwards miss, we found *Clift House*, an absolute delight. It is beautifully situated on one of

Many Helpful properties are 'amazing'. This beauty is at East Portlemouth, in the 'South Hams'. Ref L213. Sleeps ten.

Close to the western edge of Dartmoor, at Lydford, this fine house sleeps up to six people in comfort. Ref A51.

the creeks that feed into Plymouth Sound. Partly 13th century, with a wing added shortly after the Civil War, it has masses of character, and **sleeps up to 11**.

Helpful is increasingly strong on large houses for large parties. These include a brilliantly converted barn (with an impressive tally of ten bedrooms and ten bathrooms) which has superb views of the River Dart, and a former hotel superbly situated in St Agnes on Cornwall's north coast of sandy surfing beaches.

Extraordinary *Sandridge Barton*, **sleeping 12**, which 'Helpful' describe as 'sensational', is a fabulous Georgian mansion in a secluded location overlooking the Dart Estuary, with a mosaic-lined indoor swimming pool any middle-ranking Roman emperor would have been proud of.

Other supremely well sited, very high quality sea-view houses, **sleeping 10 or more people**, are near Prawle Point, Salcombe, in southernmost Devon, and Port Isaac, in Cornwall.

On Dartmoor is *Brimpts Barn*, near Dartmeet, **sleeping 32**. On offer there are activities that include horse-riding, canoeing, rock climbing, mountain biking, orienteering, abseiling, caving and rough or clay pigeon shooting. Houses with their own indoor swimming pools include one in fascinating Boscastle, Cornwall (busy in summer, moody and magnificent in autumn and winter), another a Grade II listed thatched former farmhouse in Chideock, south-west Dorset.

In Somerset, they have cottages, farmhouses and a superb country house on Exmoor and on the slopes of the Quantock Hills. These include a Grade II listed miller's house in the county's lush farming centre, and a converted cider barn from which you can walk to the tops of the Mendips.

There is a detached late-Victorian gem of a house in Bath-stone just a mile and a half from the centre of Bath itself, and in Dorset there are notable cottages in valleys beneath the downs.

Naturally they have many cottages in and around Chagford, their very popular little home town on Dartmoor's edge, and in its neighbour, Drewsteignton, a village above the dramatic River Teign valley, near amazing Castle Drogo. Here there are four classic thatched cottages. All of these have the considerable attraction of open fires or woodburners.

Euan and Su Bowater are owners themselves. Slumbering under a traditional thatched roof in the Teign Valley below Castle Drogo is their picture-postcard Gibhouse, in peaceful gardens by a stream, with superb views of rolling hills.

Weekly prices range from about £144 to £7200. Dogs are welcome in many properties. Details are available from Helpful Holidays, Chagford, Devon TQ13 8AW. Telephone 01647 433593. Fax 433694. Or have a look at their website:

www.helpfulholidays.com

email: help@helpfulholidays.com

Gibhouse is an idyllically located cottage near Castle Drogo, above. Note: it gets booked up early! Ref A14.

Just inland from Torbay, this house (at Stoke Gabriel) sleeps twelve. Ref C618.

And, inside the National Park, at Mary Tavy, this charmer (Ref A132) sleeps 5.

Upottery, near Honiton
Otter Falls

You'd hardly believe you're just three hours from London in this exceptionally peaceful spot. Amid 130 acres, on the edge of the Blackdown Hills – something of a 'best kept secret', and much under-rated – there are cottages converted from what were originally farm buildings (including one-time barns) and Finnish lodges overlooking fishing lakes. All the accommodation

Peaceful but not isolated. Unusually, you can choose a cottage or a Finnish 'lodge'.

has either a log fire or a woodburning stove – which always gets our vote, and which, added to the cosy, comfortable, nicely lit interiors, make these properties a good choice for an autumn or winter break. Some have four poster beds.

For details of these and other Devon properties (and other holiday accommodation throughout England, Scotland and Wales) contact The Cottage Collection, 17-23 Ber Street, Norwich NR1 3EU. Telephone 01603 724809.

www.the-cottage-collection.co.uk

email: bookings@the-cottage-collection.co.uk

The Isle of Wight
Freshwater   map 7/483/484

Good quality properties on the ever-popular island are quite hard to come by, partly because strict planning regulations mean that there is a severe shortage of self catering accommodation. 'Welcome', however, have a good number of worth-while places. Among these is an excellent detached house on the edge of Freshwater village, close to a sandy beach and most usefully **sleeping 9/10**. Very much a family house, it used to be a vicarage. Ref

Very much a family house, this former vicarage at Freshwater sleeps up to ten.

W8158. Also, close to the beach at Freshwater Bay, *No 3 Old Coastguard Cottages* (Ref W8342) is a pretty terraced Victorian cottage **sleeping up to 5**. It's located in a quiet lane with a lawned garden, and, delightfully, you can walk from the gate just the short distance to the beach.

For availability and bookings contact Welcome Cottages, Spring Mill, Earby, Barnoldswick, Lancashire BB94 0AA. Telephone (brochures) 0870 192 0809, (bookings) 0870 336 2825.

www.welcome2006.co.uk

Beer
Jean Bartlett Cottage Holidays*

A highly regarded fixture in this guide for many years, concentrating very astutely on a specific and very popular area, this medium-sized agency has been described in glowing terms by many readers, *with never a complaint.*

'Jean Bartlett' handles properties from Honiton to the coast of East Devon and West Dorset: some grand, some modest and inexpensive. We have visited about a dozen, most in sight of the sea and one or two right on it.

On our most recent visit we looked at *Hope* and *Creole* cottages, both former fishermen's houses with beautiful gardens, right in the centre of Beer village, at *Chapel Cottage*, a quietly situated thatched beauty just inland, and at *The Belvedere* and *The Look Out,* spacious and most appealing apartments, with sea views, also right at the heart of Beer.

Hope and Creole (**sleeping 5/6**) are furnished to permanent home standards and are much admired by passers-by. They have good sized sitting rooms with deep sofas and chairs, upholstered window seats and an original beamed fireplace. Both have modern kitchens, three bedrooms and a bathroom (Creole has an additional *ensuite* bathroom) plus the benefit of a private parking space.

For guests seeking absolute top-of-the-range accommodation, the agency offers several **'Visit Britain' Five Star**-rated properties. For example, there is *Steppes Barn* – a spacious barn conversion near the River Axe, which has plenty of space for guests who wish to take advantage of the location and bring a boat.

Picture-book villages such as Branscombe are a short drive, as are the resorts of Sidmouth and Lyme Regis. Near Branscombe, for example, *Rockenhayne Farmstead* has a delightful stone-built cottage and a stunningly well restored barn that retains its original 16th century oak beams. For people happy with more basic accommodation there is also a static caravan, commanding superb views of the wooded valley.

Costs range from about £160 to £2000. Dogs accepted in about half the properties by arrangement. Details/brochures from Jean Bartlett Holidays, Fore Street, Beer, Devon EX12 3JA. Telephone 01297 23221. Fax 23303.

www.jeanbartlett.com
email: holidays@jeanbartlett.com

Hope and Creole Cottages offer a rare chance to be based in the heart of Beer.

Chapel Cottage is 'a quietly situated thatched beauty just inland' ...

Corfe Castle
Scoles Manor

Even by our standards the location is remarkable: the view of Corfe Castle, framed between the Purbeck Hills, has been the inspiration of many a painter. Close to the castle, these three cottages have been imaginatively created within a long barn/ dairy. They have large windows, pine furniture, smart kitchens and such

Many years in this guide, and geared to family holidays: babysitting available.

features as exposed stone walls and oak beams. Owners Peter and Belinda Bell live in the adjoining manor house. The thirty-acre estate, enviably located at the end of a 600-yard farm track, is home to ducks, gamefowl and doves. And the Purbeck Way footpath to Corfe Castle or the sea passes by the property. There are sandy beaches at Studland and Swanage, a short drive, or you can walk to small coves. A cosy pub is just two fields away. All are ETC **Four Stars**. Single-storeyed *Dairy* has four double rooms and two bathrooms, *Great Barn* three double rooms (two bathrooms), *Little Barn* two bedrooms (one with bunk beds). Central heating, bedlinen, payphones, starter pack of groceries, babysitting. Open all year. Cost: £225 to £1030. Short breaks. Details from Peter and Belinda Bell, Scoles Manor, Kingston, Corfe Castle, Dorset BH20 5LG. Telephone 01929 480312. Fax 481237. **www.scoles.co.uk email: peter@scoles.co.uk**

Dunster, near Minehead
Duddings Holiday Cottages   map 7/462

Four miles inland from Minehead – though more about Exmoor's leafy glades and deer-haunted, bracken-covered hillsides – and about five minutes by car from pretty Dunster, these mostly look on to a convivial courtyard. We were probably most impressed with *West Wing*, **sleeping 10/12**, and the very cosy *Exford* and *The Annexe*. All twelve cottages have been converted from a variety

Handy for the coast and glorious Exmoor.

of old farm buildings, and we liked the combination of mod cons and the rusticity. There's a warm indoor pool, tennis, table tennis, a pool table, trout fishing and a nine hole putting green. All the cottages now have **Four 'Visit Britain' Stars. Sleep from 2 to 12**. TV. Dogs welcome. Linen but not towels included. Cost: about £190 to £1800. For details of these and other Dorset properties (and other holiday accommodation throughout England, Scotland and Wales) contact The Cottage Collection, 17-23 Ber Street, Norwich NR1 3EU. Telephone 01603 724809.

www.the-cottage-collection.co.uk
email: bookings@the-cottage-collection.co.uk

Coastal Dorset
Dorset Coastal Cottages*

It's a mark of this organisation's considerable style that it concentrates purely on traditional cottages: most date from the 17th, 18th or 19th century. To insist that they should also be within ten miles of England's important World Heritage 'Jurassic Coast', between Studland and Lyme Regis (most are within five), is an even greater challenge.

But it has paid off, which says a lot about the charm of this part of the country and the persistence of Charles and Jennie Smith in pursuing their idea of the perfect country cottage. Many are thatched, with open fires.

Our first visit was to Winfrith Newburgh, where the agency is based: we were very taken with *Milton Cottage*, a traditional thatched cottage, **sleeping 4**, with two-feet-thick walls and distinctive 'eyebrow' dormer windows. Similarly, *Jasmine Cottage* (**sleeps 4 plus cot**), is an 18th century mid-terrace cottage in the pretty village of Upwey, with easy access to ridge walks. Weymouth is three miles away.

This, along with *Bow Cottage*, Charmouth, a detached property **sleeping 4/6 plus cot** and close to a sandy beach (ideally placed for fossil hunting) are in accordance with the agency's character-cottage pledge.

There are around a hundred properties in the portfolio. Some can accommodate large groups, such as *The White House,* at Kimmeridge. This not only has direct access to the Coast Path and sea views, but with five bedrooms and five bathrooms, it **sleeps 10 plus cot.**

In the Bridport area, *Medway Farm*, Askerswell, tucked down a private road in a rural setting, has accommodation for **up to 10/12 people**. This is shared between two stone barn conversions, *Coombe Barn* (**sleeping 4 plus cot**) and *Haydon Barn* (**sleeping 6 plus cot**). Anglers take note: a sloping field leads to a well stocked trout and coarse fishing ponds.

Many cottages take pets, and most are available for short breaks. *All include linen and towels, as well as electricity, gas and oil.* Details from Dorset Coastal Cottages, The Manor House, Winfrith Newburgh, Dorchester, Dorset DT2 8JR. Telephone 01305 854454. Fax 854988.

Note that the agency's cottage-grading is reviewed annually against questionnaires returned by clients...

www.dorsetcoastalcottages.com
email: hols@dorsetcoastalcottages.com

Studland and the beach, with 'Property No 302' in the foreground.

Milton Cottage, Winfrith Newburgh, has two attractively beamy bedrooms.

South and West
Hideaways*

The widely admired family-run agency has some of the best cottages we know in the south and south west of England. Many are picture-book places 'suspended in time': a chance to catch the flavour of some of England's most unspoilt corners.

Based between Salisbury and Shaftesbury, Hideaways is strongly represented where Wiltshire blends lazily with Dorset and Hampshire; it also extends into Cornwall, Devon and Somerset, with a good selection of properties in the Heart of England, and more besides.

A rare instance of a quite excellent cottage in the Forest of Dean, where (in one of England's best-kept-secret places) really good self catering is thin on the ground, *The Old Pumphouse* is outstanding. **Sleeping up to 6,** it is approached by a woodland track and stands on its own in a clearing

With its handsome old beams, and accommodation all on the ground floor, Drovers Barn appeals to us a lot.

Used occasionally by the owners themselves (a good sign) Shedrick slumbers in deeply rural Dorset.

by a trout pond. A real 'hideaway' indeed! Another is tucked away in the New Forest. *The Lodge,* near Fordingbridge, is a sunny three-bedroom thatched cottage which shares the owners' three-acre landscaped woodland garden. With distant views over the Forest from its balcony and terrace, this is another 'hideaway'. **Sleeps 6/7.**

Dorset is true thatched cottage territory, and last autumn we visited *The Owl Box* in the hamlet of Throop, twelve miles from Dorchester. This cosy Grade II, ultra-romantic cottage lies deep in the countryside, where the sound of barn owls provides a suitably soothing accompaniment. Once a thatched brick and cob barn, lovingly converted to a cottage with a spacious, open living-room, original beams and timber cladding, this is heaven-sent for those who dream of the ultimate bolthole. **Sleeps 2.**

On a previous Wiltshire-Dorset visit we were impressed, among others, by *Shedrick,* a 17th-century thatched cottage situated on its own deep in the Dorset countryside near Chard, which lost none of its character (oak beams, low ceilings) when it was modernised. So it has a cosy atmosphere and the convenience of a large fitted kitchen. The three bedrooms (**sleeping 6**) are a double with ensuite shower room/wc, a double with a brass bed, and a twin. The garden has a secluded patio area and barbecue.

Kate's Cottage, Winterbourne Kingston (**sleeps 5**), is over 200 years old and lies along a track on the village edge. It is well placed for visiting some of the most spectacular stretches of coastline in England.

We have also admired *The Old Stable*, **sleeping 4**, a traditional thatched cottage in the meandering village of Rockbourne, on the northern edge of the New Forest. Romantic *Garden Loft* (**sleeping 2**), also in Rockbourne, is a cosy studio flat tucked away beyond a wrought iron gate and up a flight of steps. In a nearby village, *The Coach House*, standing opposite the former village rectory, incorporates a particularly impressive, heavily beamed and timbered bedroom with sloping ceilings. **Sleeps 2 'plus 2'.**

In Somerset, the long climb to Middle Burrow Farm, near Timberscombe, is rewarded by the initial sight of *Upper Barn* (**sleeps 4 plus cot**), a fascinating property, as much for its interior as its exterior. Converted from a former threshing barn, some 300 years old, it is unique in that an archway divides the ground floor where the bedrooms are located – one a twin, the other a double. Staircases from each lead to the first floor and a long beamed sitting-room, sensitively furnished. A bridleway leads to open moor a quarter of a mile away: Dunster is four miles away, the attractive village of Wootton Courtenay under a mile. Well behaved pets welcome.

The Old Stable, in pretty Rockbourne, in Hampshire, is one of our favourites. It has an open fire and several antiques.

The interior combines a strong sense of history with 21st century comforts. It is on the northern edge of the New Forest.

Sleeping 4/6 plus cot, *Drovers Barn*, at Shrewton, makes an ideal base for visiting Wiltshire's best known historic sites, including Stonehenge, Avebury and ever-enigmatic Silbury Hill. The accommodation is all at ground floor level, with oak beams, reclaimed pine floors and a particularly stylish interior decor. The property looks out on to a two-acre garden bordering the River Till.

In the South East, a cluster in West Sussex include the *Old School House*, Grade II listed, nestling twelve miles inland from Worthing in West Chiltington. (**Sleeps 2.**) Part of the house (originally the large Victorian schoolroom) incorporates a light, open-plan sitting/dining area. In Kent, *Little Barn* is rather special. **Sleeping 2 'plus cot'**, it is in the garden of the owner's 15th century farmhouse between Benenden and Cranbrook, in an Area of Outstanding Natural Beauty.

Details of these and other properties from Hideaways, Chapel House, Luke Street, Berwick St John, Shaftesbury, Dorset SP7 0HQ. Telephone 01747 828000, fax 829090.

www.hideaways.co.uk
email: enq@hideaways.co.uk

Lyme Regis, Charmouth and around
Lyme Bay Holidays*

The notable success of this agency – featured in our guide for ten years – surely lies in the fact that most of its properties are within ten miles of quiet, sandy, slightly old fashioned Charmouth, which we'd call one of Dorset's best kept secrets, and of the genteel seaside resort of Lyme Regis.

Some properties stick in our mind for their real character. One is *Pound House Wing* (**sleeps 4 'plus 1'**), close to Hawkchurch, rich in atmosphere and full of intriguing corners. This is a happy property, geared to the present day but furnished in sympathy with its history as the converted wing of a 14th century farmhouse. It even has its own priest-hole, discovered during renovation. There are exposed beams and flagstone floors.

The property, in twelve acres of grounds with bluebell woods, is a quarter of a mile from the road but accessible along a well maintained track suitable for most family cars. We liked it a lot when we visited last autumn, and it's only fifteen minutes from the coast at Lyme Regis.

We're keen on a picture-postcard thatched cottage tucked prettily away in a secret, miniature valley and called *Sunshine Cottage*, in which on a blustery day a couple were very cosily installed (it sleeps **just 2**). Dating back in part to the 16th century, this charming property has a third of an acre garden. We also liked a spacious detached family house called *Penderel*, **sleeping 7 'plus 1'** plus cot. We appreciated the big rooms, the open fire, the quietness – even though Charmouth's high street is only a matter of yards away. It has now been upgraded to **Four Stars**.

We also admired a row of pastel-coloured properties on Marine Parade, all distinctly different but enjoying unique sea front views. 'An outstanding location' said **'Visit Britain'** of one. Two of the most appealing are *Benwick Cottage*, pictured below, and *Library Cottage,* which features a south-facing terrace that has an unobstructed view of the exceptional bay.

Dogs are welcome in over a third of the 200 to 210 properties. For a copy of the brochure, with good colour line drawings and precise descriptions, write to David Matthews, Lyme Bay Holidays, Wessex House, Uplyme Road, Lyme Regis, Dorset DT7 3LP. Telephone 01297 443363, fax 445576. Freepost SWB20289, Lyme Regis, Dorset DT7 3BF. There's a very comprehensive website, with internal photographs and on-line availability and booking:

www.lymebayholidays.co.uk   email: email@lymebayholidays.co.uk

Pretty Benwick is likely to have been familiar to Jane Austen, who loved Lyme.

This pretty thatched cottage makes a cosy hideaway for two people...

Chew Magna, near Bristol
Chew Hill Farm Cottages

On a bright autumn day in 2005 we
revisited these exceptionally neat-
and-tidy, scrupulously clean, bright
and spacious cottages, situated on a
high lying farm from which (including certain rooms in the three holiday houses) there are impressive
views over the Mendip Hills and
sometimes quite memorable sunsets.
The properties have featured in this
guide *since its very beginning in*

*Twenty-four years in this guide, and
never the suggestion of a complaint...*

1983. Being close to the sweeping Mendips, visitors are well placed for
visiting Bath, Cheddar Gorge, Wookey Hole, and Bristol, with its theatres
and shops. In *Bailiff's House*, which **sleeps 6**, we admired the big kitchen
with its smart units, washing machine and microwave, the very large
triple aspect sitting room and separate dining room. There are private gardens. The pleasantly high-ceilinged *West Lodge* is Victorian and **sleeps 4**
in a double and two singles. *East Lodge* **sleeps 6** and has a 22 ft long sitting room. TVs. Linen provided, towels for hire. Dogs possible by
arrangement. Cost: £200 to £600. **'Visit Britain' Three Stars**. Details
from Mrs S Lyons, Chew Hill Farm, Chew Magna, Bristol, North
Somerset BS40 8QP. Telephone 01275 332496; mobile 07831 117186.

Poole   map 7/476
Fisherman's Quay

We sometimes think we could do
with a week or a fortnight here, just
gazing at the view! What a tonic!
With its wide and uninterrupted
views of Poole Harbour (said to be
the second largest natural harbour in
the world), from which car ferries
run to the Channel Islands and to
France, this three storeyed house is

*Take binoculars to make the most of the
extraordinary wide-ranging views...*

in a spectacular location. Looking down over the impressive Fisherman's
Harbour, two balconies offer an extraordinary vantage point from which
to watch every type of waterborne activity – not least, the skills of the
pilots guiding huge ships to their berths near Poole Quay – itself bustling
with smaller craft and pubs, restaurants, galleries, shops and museums.
There are two double rooms, one en-suite, and one twin, main bathroom
(both bathrooms have showers), a first floor sitting room with those
panoramic views, a well fitted kitchen, dining area, a ground-floor cloakroom, patio and barbecue. Not suitable for pets, infirm or very elderly
people, or very young children. Non smokers preferred. Parking space
and integral garage. Central heating is included. Cost: £350 to £700.
Further details are available from Dr D Halliday, 1 Grange Drive,
Horsforth, Leeds, West Yorkshire LS18 5EQ. Telephone 0113 2584947.

227

South and South East

Despite the ravages of trains and boats and planes we are constantly surprised at how much of rural Hampshire, Kent, Sussex and Surrey have gone into the 21st century so miraculously well preserved – though you do have to go 'the extra mile' to find real pin-drop silence. Really good (and quiet) properties are hard to come by, but we have located several. We also think of the smell of wood-smoke on autumn days, undulating hop fields, 'tile hung' cottages, sleepy red-roofed villages beneath wooded escarpments, manicured topiary gardens. Within easy reach of several of the cottages featured in this section are Winston Churchill's Chartwell, near Westerham, Knole House, at Sevenoaks, Sissinghurst Castle, the celebrated Pantiles, in Tunbridge Wells – perhaps the most elegant 'shopping precinct' in England – the historic Cinque Ports. It's scattered with castles of the toy-fort kind – Bodiam, Hastings, Arundel, Leeds, Hever – and great cathedrals such as Winchester, Chichester and Canterbury (we would certainly include Guildford's: 1930s plain-Jane from the outside, exquisite inside). It is also the most fruitful corner of Britain for antique-hunters, with a good sprinkling of old-fashioned tea shops, many in gabled old towns that have defied the depredations of developers. And we have noticed readers now include Paris in their 'interesting days out' list – for it's an easy matter to pick up a train at Ashford and have lunch in Montmartre instead of, say, Midhurst.

Milford-on-Sea
Windmill Cottage map 2/478

This neat, tidy, modern, Georgian-style red brick property has proved to be a perennial favourite among readers of this guide. Pleasantly in keeping with the rest of Milford-on-Sea, whose village green and 'character shops' maintain a sense of bygone and rather genteel charm, the house is a joy, with good quality carpets, and is pristinely clean and well cared for.

This is a modern, clean and tidy house with everything you could need to give you a virtually chore-free holiday...

The through sitting/dining room has a bow window to the front and French windows to the enclosed back garden. Every electric appliance is in the neat kitchen, including a washing machine, dishwasher, fridge-freezer, tumble drier and microwave. There are three bedrooms (one double, one twin, one a small single). **Sleeps up to 5**. There is a modern bathroom, and ample parking space plus a garage in a nearby block. The New Forest, Lymington and Bournemouth are all within easy reach. Village shops are a seven minute walk, and cliffs, together with a pebbly beach, are three minutes by car.

Cost: about £220 to £545. TV. Dogs are welcome at £9 each. All linen is included, as well as heat and lighting. Incoming telephone. **'Visit Britain' Three Stars**. Further details and brochure from Mrs S M Perham, Danescourt, Kivernell Road, Milford-on-Sea, Lymington, Hampshire SO41 0PQ. Telephone 01590 643516. Fax 641255.

Lymington
New Forest Cottages*

We've noticed from our correspondence over the years that a good number of readers were introduced to the charms of the New Forest courtesy of this organisation, which we have featured in the guide for over two decades.

From their office on a neat, cobbled slope leading down to Lymington's quayside, the staff handle around a hundred carefully vetted properties in and around the region.

On the Solent foreshore, with fabulous views across to the Isle of Wight, is *Sowley Gate House* (**sleeping 10**). This spacious holiday home stands in a large, sunny garden surrounded by open forest and farmland, with direct access to a private shingle beach.

The Bee Garden, in the village of Norley Wood, is – typically for this agency – full of character and charm.

Park Farm Cottage is another thatched gem, of which there are many on the agency's books.

Also in the forest is *Dell Cottage* (**sleeps 7**), tucked away along a lane, yet within five minutes' walk of a country pub and just a short drive from Lyndhurst.

Facing Lymington's Town Quay and the fishing boats, yachts and cabin-cruisers on the river is a stylish second floor flat in *Admiral's Court*. The large sitting room/diner has a picture window and a glazed enclosed balcony. **Sleeps 6**.

Between Lymington and Beaulieu, *Bee Garden* is a spacious thatched bungalow, **sleeping 6**, in the tiny village of Norley Wood: it has a pleasant open plan sitting/dining room and a spacious and well-screened garden. Ponies also graze immediately outside *Badgers Walk,* a cottage (**sleeping 5**) in the forest outside Burley. *Hawthorne Cottage,* on the outskirts of Brockenhurst, is a delightful Victorian cottage (**sleeping 3**) overlooking a sweep of open forest – perfect for a romantic week.

Details and a colour brochure can be obtained from New Forest Cottages, Ridgeway Rents, 4 Quay Hill, Lymington, Hampshire SO41 3AR. Telephone 01590 679655. Fax 670989.

www.newforestcottages.co.uk

Benenden, near Tenterden
Old Weavers' Cottages

Dating in part from the 16th century, but enjoying 21st-century 'cons'...

'Bring your passports' is our advice to visitors to these picturesque cottages that date from the early 1600s. The Channel Tunnel is only 25 minutes' drive away, so you could pop to France for a day or even just dinner. Several National Trust properties are handy too, as well as towns such as Tenterden, notable for its antique shops. Sandy beaches are also within easy reach. Attractively situated overlooking rolling pastureland, the cottages have been sympathetically modernised. Original features such as oak beams and thick stone walls (sound-proof and cosy) are enhanced by pine furniture and doors. Each has a corner kitchenette in the sitting/dining area and sliding glass doors opening on to a long south-facing terrace.

Two cottages (**sleeping 4,** Ref KC4901/KC4902) are two-storeyed, with double and twin bedrooms; the third (**sleeping 2,** Ref KC50) is a ground floor apartment with wheelchair access. There's a glass-covered swimming pool open in summer.

Details from Blakes Country Cottages, Earby, Barnoldswick, Lancashire BB94 0AA. Bookings: 0870 192 1022; brochures: 0870 241 7970.

www.blakes-cottages06.co.uk

'In brief'

Fordingbridge: Alderholt Mill   map 2/493

Part of this picturesque working mill dates back nearly 700 years. On the northern edge of the New Forest, it has been converted into two smart flats, *Miller's End* (**sleeping 2**) and the *Granary* (**4/5**). Miller's End, on the ground floor, has a double bedroom, while Granary Flat above it has a single plus a double in the eaves, plus a sofa-bed in the lounge. The mill race (stream) flows under the building from the garden from where we looked out over idyllic countryside. Cost £250 to £490. No children under 8 (because of the mill stream) or smokers. Pets by arrangement. Details from Sandra and Richard Harte, Alderholt Mill, Sandleheath Road, Alderholt, Fordingbridge, Hampshire SP6 1PU. Telephone 01425 653130. Fax 652868.

www.alderholtmill.co.uk
email: alderholt-mill@zetnet.co.uk

Chiddingly, near Hailsham
Pekes

Turn off a busy road, follow a quiet lane bordered by trees up to Pekes and (yes, really) you go back in time, especially in the case of the partly-Tudor manor house – renovated in 1550! – that is the focal point of the estate and a clutch of the most characterful holiday houses we know.

During a recent visit, accompanied by the owners (Mrs Morris is the grand-daughter of the man who bought the estate in 1908), we looked inside three of the five distinctively different properties in and around that fine Tudor house. They enjoy the jacuzzi, a sauna, and an indoor swimming pool. There is a tennis court and lawn badminton.

Mounts View has stunning views from the good sized sitting room, off which there is a dining alcove (very 1930s!). **Sleeps 6 plus 2.** The humblest property of all is the cosy, tile-hung *Gate Cottage*. Up the steep staircase are a double and a twin bedded room, with space for 2 on a bed-settee.

All the cottages have well equipped kitchens: washing machines, tumble dryers, mixers and dishwashers. *Tudor View* is close to the main house, has an open fire and a smart kitchen/diner. The twin bedroom leads into the double bedroom, with a door on to the patio and garden. **Sleeps 5 plus 2.**

We have always liked *The Oast House,* which has its own private 'state of the art' jacuzzi in a cabin in the grounds. Its porticoed entrance leads into a biggish hall and a large, circular dining room. The kitchen has a table big enough for the largest get-together; the sitting room has French windows on to the garden. The green-covered stairs and big landing lead to the master bedroom with an enormous four-poster bed. There is a second large circular family room with a double and two singles, a twin bedroom and a very small single. **Sleeps 7 plus 5.** *The Wing* is unusually shaped, with a smart kitchen and several inter-connecting rooms. **Sleeps 5.**

Cost: Oast House £1220 to £1586; Cottages and Wing £375 to £820. Mounts View £795 to £1060. Short breaks: Oast House £825 to £1045. Cottages and Wing £235 to £490. Mounts View £470 to £650. (Different prices apply to Christmas and New Year.) TVs. Children welcome, also dogs, especially in the three cottages. Central heating and open fires or open-front woodburners. Linen for hire. **'Visit Britain' Three/Four Stars.** Details from Eva Morris, 'Pekes', 124 Elm Park Mansions, Park Walk, London SW10 0AR. Telephone 020 7352 8088. Fax 020 7352 8125. Also 01825 872229, Saturday to Monday.

www.pekesmanor.com   email: pekes.afa@virgin.net

A fine Tudor manor house, with a non-Tudor swimming pool and tennis court.

We've always liked the Oast House, especially its large, circular family room.

231

Appledore
Ashby Farms Cottages

Rural Kent is a largely unsung corner of England that most outsiders never discover. But Ashby Farms Cottages offer the chance to get to grips with, for example, the Weald of Kent and – within striking distance – the hauntingly beautiful Romney Marsh.

Roughlands, outside Woodchurch, is a conventional detached bungalow, quite roomy and blissfully quiet, with pleasant open views and gardens back and front. Fully fitted modern kitchen and bathroom. There is a twin and double-bedded room, with a bed available for a 5th person.

Only a hundred yards away but completely hidden in woodland, the specially designed and pine built *Fishermen's Lodges* (**sleep 6**) reminded us of Scandinavia, even down to the setting, close to two isolated fishing lakes. The familiar A-shape encompasses a large double bed sleeping area reached by an open rung wooden ladder. On the main level are two twin bedrooms, bathroom and a modern well-fitted, galley-style kitchen. Sliding patio doors open on to a large wooden verandah. There are pinewood walls and furnishings, full carpeting, and the lounge/dining area benefits from the full height of the lodge.

Numbers 2, 3 and 4 Spring Cottages, in the adjacent small village of Kenardington, are within a terrace of brick-built dwellings (a shepherd lives in the other one). Each **sleeps 5** in three bedrooms reached by steepish stairs. They are simply furnished, but bright and attractive, have modern kitchens and bathrooms, fitted carpets and TVs. Fine rural views from the rear. Pretty front gardens.

On the road leading into Appledore is a semi-detached cottage called *65 The Street*, unpretentious but with a good-sized kitchen and a modern bathroom. Modestly furnished, **sleeping up to 5** in three bedrooms, it is well placed for those who like to be close to shops and pubs. There is a neat garden at the back, and attractive rural views.

Cost: about £120 (for a short break) to £450. Dogs welcome. Fishing permits are available at £40 per week for a family of 4 (also by the day), and rough shooting at £12.50 a day. Linen and towels for hire. Further details from Ashby Farms Ltd, Place Farm, Kenardington, Ashford, Kent TN26 2LZ. Telephone 01233 733332. Fax 733326.

www.ashbyfarms.com
email: info@ashbyfarms.com

Fishermen's Lodges: Scandinavian flair, close to two isolated fishing lakes. Easy-to-maintain interiors.

Spring Cottages: No frills, but clean, tidy, and bright.

elpful Holidays – Devon, Cornwall and beyond. This West Country specialist is virtually a ousehold name. They feature some real beauties, including houses right by the sea...

..and hidden-away properties where you'll hardly meet a soul during your stay. The agency s especially well known for the number of its big houses that will suit large groups...

..ut has its share of 'roses-round-the-door' thatched cottages, and places with historical ssociations, such as the two amazing places above. Pages 217-219.

artmouth Holiday Homes, Devon. Super iews from many properties. Page 214.

Jean Bartlett Holidays, South Devon. A well run local agency, lovely cottages. Page 221.

Rural Retreats, The Cotswolds and beyond. They are known and admired for their absolute reliability and comfort, and have a famous attention to detail. Pages 107 and 260/261.

The Swiss Chalet, Herefordshire. An impressive and unusual property: readers love it! Page 251.

Exhall, Warwickshire. A skilful use of space and very well placed for touring. Page 26

Pekes, East Sussex. 'Incomparable', say readers. Also 'unique...great fun!' Page 231.

Owlpen, Gloucestershire. An unforgettable place:'rural England stands still'. Page 25(

Stanton Court, Gloucestershire. Our favourite: idyllic cottages in an exquisite village. Page 258.

The Old Dairy, Gloucestershire. The cottag is a joy, the view a double-joy. Page 264.

English Country Cottages (main feature, Pages 272/273) also covers Scotland and Wales (there's a separate brochure for Scotland). The organisation is now virtually a household name...

Above and above right, there's an extraordinary collection of cottages and fine houses that seem to sum up the best of what's to be had, for example, in Cornwall and the Cotswolds...

Their Welsh programme is appreciated by the tourist board, and they've secured many 'traditional' cottages, as above. Also above, right: a charming North Yorkshire cottage.

over the British Isles, their range is huge, but they are known for their properties of racter, historic interest and comfort. These two are in Cornwall and Cumbria...

Vivat Trust, Shropshire. Some marvellous restorations, an inspiration to stay in. Page 26.

Heath Farm Cottages, Oxfordshire. Quite remarkable – a tour de force! Page 267.

'Village and Country', Co Clare. Stylish places in a sought-after location. Page 284.

Ballina, Co Mayo. Modern comfort, clean, tidy, inexpensive, great for touring. Page 281 .

...akes Cottages – main features on Pages 119, 147 and 276/277 – is one of the three or four ...st prominent agencies in the country. It has 'properties with facilities', many rural jewels...

...nd several places ideal for extended families, such as this (above left) in rural Somerset and ...ove right) near the sea in Wales. This one sleeps up to twenty!

...nong so many properties of character is this beauty near Barnard Castle, in much underrated ...unty Durham and (above right) this country property, again near the sea in Wales.

...rural Suffolk you can stay in the wing of a handsome country house, above, and, in Derbyshire's ...ak District, among so many possibilities, this charmer in the Hope Valley..

National Trust Cottages have come on in leaps and bounds during the past few years. As you might expect, virtually all their properties are full of character and rich in history...

By definition, properties tend to be in interesting locations. Those featured here are (top) in Norfolk and, above, Scotland and Northern Ireland. Main feature: Pages 24/25.

Bruern Cottages, Oxfordshire. In a little known but handsome village setting village setting, dominated by a great country mansion, these are like little palaces. Interiors are exquisite...

...with fine antiques, original paintings, expensive carpets and fabrics; gardens are in keeping, and there's a nice balance between keeping one's privacy and 'meeting new people'. Page 269.

Country Holidays (main feature on Pages 274/275) have a bigger selection of individual cottages than any other operator, so holidaymakers needing variety tend to be regulars.

They appreciate this fine mill in North Yorkshire, adjacent to a waterfall once sketched by J M W Turner, and this deeply rural property near Kendal, on the edge of 'the Lakes'.

Among people's dreams-come-true are such places as (above left) an unusual farmhouse in Derbyshire and, right, a beauty near Cheriton Bishop, in rural Devon.

There's this superbly well situated cottage in the West of Scotland, close to a sandy beach, and a delightful place in Naunton, near Bourton-on-the-Water, in the Cotswolds.

Colour section B, Page 7

With over 9,000 dream cottages…

ENGLAND · WALES · SCOTLAND · IRELAND · FRANCE

…where will you escape to next?

There has never been a wider choice of superb self-catering cottages for you to discover. Plan your escape now to some of the most beautiful properties situated in the most sought after locations.

All our cottages are regularly inspected and graded so you can always expect quality properties, with excellent facilities – a real home from home. From quaint, romantic hideaways in beautiful rural settings, to spectacular sea, lake and mountain locations, superbly appointed, many with pools, just waiting to welcome you.

Over 9,000 cottages @ one address
Visit www.cottages4you.co.uk where you can search through all of our properties, which will allow you to choose the one that is perfect for you. It's simple to use and many of our properties have a virtual tour, allowing you to discover your dream get-away before you leave home.

So visit www.cottages4you.co.uk now to discover your perfect holiday cottage

cottages4you

Goudhurst
Three Chimneys Farm

Parts of rural Kent are as neat and pretty as a picture, and during a recent summer it was a pleasure to veer off from charming Goudhurst and then along a little-used mile-long track to revisit a group of what are without a doubt among the best holiday cottages in the south east of England. It comes as no surprise to us that they are former winners of the much-prized Kent Tourism Award for Excellence. In glorious countryside (some super views from a couple of the cottages) this a real hideaway, though you don't feel isolated, and you are only about an hour from London. One can walk or cycle into the nearby forest, or stay on the farm, feed the ducks, perhaps play tennis or croquet.

These beautifully furnished cottages, very stylish and with a great sense of colour and design, are equipped to a high standard: all of them have automatic washer/driers, dishwashers, microwaves, fridge freezers, televisions with video or DVD player, mini-music centres (that is, CDs, tapes,

These superbly well situated cottages exude 'tender loving care' on the part of owner Marion Fuller. They make a fine base from which to explore what in our opinion is much-underrated rural Kent. We enjoyed getting away from busy roads during a recent autumn visit and basking in the peace and quiet of Three Chimneys.

radio), hairdriers, bathrooms with bath *and* shower, and more. There is electric heating (included May to October), plus woodburners. There are five properties, **sleeping from 2 to 7** (but keep an eye on the top-notch website for possible changes to the configuration of the cottages in 2006). There's much to see: Goudhurst is two miles away, and within ten miles are Sissinghurst, Scotney, Great Dixter and Batemans.

Dogs are welcome in one cottage (by arrangement with Marion). Linen and towels included, towels for hire. Cost: about £285 to £700. **'Visit Britain' Four Stars**. Details from Marion Fuller, Three Chimneys Farm, Goudhurst, Kent TN17 2RA. Telephone/fax 01580 212175.

www.threechimneysfarm.co.uk
email:Marionfuller@threechimneysfarm.co.uk

Readers sometimes ask 'How are owners/agents chosen to be in this guide?' Most come via reader recommendations, occasionally from regional tourist boards. Others contact us directly. Regular readers might spot cottages they have not seen for years: it could be that a cottage or group of cottages have been on a long let or have been marketed through an 'exclusive' agency, or that there has been a change of ownership....

Golden Green, near Tonbridge
Goldhill Mill Cottages

Featured in this guide for over 20 years, these have become great favourites with many readers. And on a more 'official' basis, they have been festooned with awards: they have won the South East England Tourism Self Catering Holiday of the Year Award *four times* and twice received the Silver Award in the England For Excellence Self Catering 'Oscars' from the English Tourism Council (now 'Visit Britain').

When you see *Figtree Cottage*, it's difficult to imagine the site was once pigsties, for this seemingly small property opens into a spacious high ceilinged, south facing, living-room with a large comfortable sofa that converts to a double bed, an open log burner and dining area. We liked the use of reclaimed bricks, tiles and oak beams. **Sleeps 2** plus child.

Figtree clicks in neatly with its big brothers. We have previously praised *Ciderpress Cottage,* converted from a pair of Tudor barns, **sleeping 4 plus an occasional 2** on a sleeping gallery, for its soft furnishings, good paintings and antiques, also its curtained gallery reached by apple ladder from the living-room. There is a top-notch kitchen, and a master bedroom equipped with en suite bathroom, as is the second bedroom.

Walnut Tree Cottage, likewise converted from the old cowshed in a group of buildings dating back to the Tudor period, rightly enjoys a reputation for its close carpeted comfort, linked with its colour coordinated duvets and curtains, and is congenially lit with wall lamps. Attractive water colours hang on pastel walls. There's a seriously comfortable three piece suite and a free-standing log fire in the living room, a wrought-iron spiral staircase to the upper floor (contained within the roof space, with exposed beams), and a 'last word' kitchen. **Sleeps 6** – each of the three (two five-foot doubles, one twin) bedrooms has an en suite bathroom. Immediately outside is the charming garden by the river, the mill stream, the swans.

All three stand within the 20-acre grounds surrounding Goldhill Mill, mentioned in the Domesday Book. And each carries the **'Visit Britain'** top **Five Stars** grading. Figtree is also rated Mobility Level 2 in the National Accessible Scheme for disabled people, Ciderpress Level 1.

Non smokers please. TV/video. Telephone. Linen/towels provided. Barbecue available. Floodlit tennis court. Cost: £240 to £775. Long-term winter lets possible. Details from Shirley and Vernon Cole, Goldhill Mill, Golden Green, Tonbridge, Kent TN11 0BA. Telephone 01732 851626; fax 851881.

www.goldhillmillcottages.com   email:vernon.cole@virgin.net

Walnut Tree is quiet and full of character.   *And all the interiors blend old and new.*

Eastwell Manor, near Ashford
Eastwell Mews

The nineteen individually styled cottages or courtyard apartments in the grounds of the sumptuous Four Star Eastwell Manor Hotel are quite exceptional. Readers have loved them, and it was a delight for us to revisit in the autumn of 2005.

The hotel, an ivy-clad Jacobean-style stone mansion with turrets, tall chimneys and arched leaded glass windows, lies in 62 acres of parkland and landscaped gardens surrounded by a working estate of 3000 acres.

Everyone staying in the cottages or apartments has use of all the hotel's extensive facilities as if they were a hotel guest. Indeed, the cottages and apartments are sometimes used to provide extra bedrooms when the main building is full, so they are equipped and furnished to the same standard.

With one, two or three bedrooms – each en-suite and with its own TV – they have been cleverly converted from the old Victorian stables. Each apartment or cottage has spacious accommodation with kitchen, dining and living areas. All of them are superbly furnished, with top-quality fabrics and linen. They are a short walk from the hotel and its convivial bars

With the fine hotel (and all its impressive facilities) as a focal point...

...these stylish and comfortable cottages really do offer 'the best of both worlds'.

and award-winning wood-panelled restaurant (AA 'Two Rosettes' and RAC 'Blue Ribbbon').

The hotel's Pavilion leisure complex is even closer. It has a brasserie restaurant, a cocktail bar, a 20-metre heated pool, a 'Dreams' beauty therapy salon and a spa that incorporates steam room, sauna, jacuzzi and hydrotherapy pool. Upstairs is a state-of-the-art gymnasium.

A further advantage is that the Eurostar station at Ashford is only a few minutes' drive away and the Eurotunnel terminal just 20 minutes' drive. So you're well-placed for a day-trip to France.

The cottages and apartments can be rented on a self-catering basis or hotel-bedroom basis. All have satellite TV, video, fax and ISDN. Well-behaved dogs welcome. Costs on a weekly basis from about £440 to £1100. Short breaks also available.

Details and brochure from Eastwell Manor, Eastwell Park, Boughton Lees, Ashford, Kent TN25 4HR. Telephone 01233 213000.

www.eastwellmanor.co.uk

email: enquiries@eastwellmanor.co.uk

Cotswolds, Heart of England, Welsh Borders, Home Counties

Time and again people express their astonishment that the Cotswolds have survived intact for so long. About a hunded miles from London, 25 from Birmingham, lies a Munchkinland of old walled gardens, honey-coloured villages snug within rolling green valleys, clear rivers and shallow trout streams, sturdy manor houses and fine churches. Roughly speaking, the Cotswolds stretch all the way from Gloucester and Herefordshire in the west to Bath in the south, and to Oxford in the east, passing close to the fertile Vale of Evesham on the way. Probably the most popular village of all is Bourton-on-the-Water. Less commercialised are the Slaughters (Upper and Lower), Moreton-in-Marsh, the straggly village of Blockley, imposing Broadway, Winchcombe. Our own favourite is probably Stanton – but not many people know it. There's Cirencester, with its Roman amphitheatre, and Stratford-upon-Avon is closer than you might think. To the west and the north is country known as the 'Heart of England'. You'll see ruined abbeys, castles, half timbered buildings, cider-apple orchards. To the east are the Chilterns, the upper reaches of the Thames, rural Hertfordshire and a range of undiscovered country that is 'so near but so far'.

Richards Castle, near Ludlow
The Barn   map 9/499

We've long considered this to be a very desirable and rather romantic hideaway, **sleeping up to 4**. With panoramic views, at the end of a leafy drive that leads uphill to the owners' house, *The Barn* is indeed a converted barn, timbered throughout, skilfully done. It is a little gem, with a charming sitting room, a 'deck' leading to an orchard and garden, two smallish but cosy bedrooms, which respectively have a double bed and *a four foot double plus a single sleeping platform*.

We thought this ideal for a couple wanting a little space. Modest outside, it is a real charmer (and roomy) inside...

A well equipped kitchen and dining area is incorporated within the living room. We were pleased to note a Clearview woodburning stove – effective and trouble-free (logs included), but with that lovely glow that 'makes' a room – thoughtful lighting, absolute peace and quiet. Organic vegetables and free-range eggs are often available. TV. Electricity, linen and towels included. Not suitable for dogs. Non smokers preferred. **'Visit Britain' Four Stars**. Cost: about £225 to £420. Details from Sue and Peter Plant, Ryecroft, Richards Castle, near Ludlow, Shropshire SY8 4EU. Telephone/fax 01584 831224.

www.ludlow.org.uk/ryecroft
email: ryecroftbarn@hotmail.com

Catbrook, near Tintern
Foxes Reach

In 2005 we revisited this gem of a stone cottage. Only about a mile and a half from romantically ruined Tintern Abbey, it has great walking and cycling from the doorstep and is well placed for good pubs, visiting the Forest of Dean, the frontier castles of Raglan and Chepstow, the Three Choirs and the Abergavenny Food festivals, as well as "Nelson's"

This is a real charmer – quiet but not isolated, and getting loads of 'TLC'...

Monmouth. We've long admired the immaculate cottagey interior, the quality carpeting and flagged floors, the lighting, well chosen pictures, the well stocked sheltered garden, the woodburner in the appealing sitting room, the wrought iron beds in all the light, bright bedrooms (two doubles and two singles: the cottage **sleeps 6**), and the two newly fitted bathrooms. Very well equipped kitchen, with dishwasher and open-plan dining. Satellite TV/DVD/video/CD/stereo. Internet access. One well behaved dog is welcome. **WTB Five Stars**, plus walkers', cyclists' and Gold Welcome Host awards. High quality linen/fluffy towels/heating included. Cost: £220 to £700. Spring and autumn luxury breaks a speciality. Details: Fiona Wilton, Ty Gwyn, Catbrook, near Chepstow, Monmouthshire. Tel 01600 860341.

www.foxesreach.com   email: fionawilton@btopenworld.com

Kemeys Commander, near Usk
Vanilla Cottage   map 9/514

This too is a joy – immaculate, romantic, rurally located above the River Usk, yet only three miles from 'floral' Usk itself. We also looked in in 2005. It's ideal for visiting the Brecon Beacons, Tintern, Abergavenny and Roman Caerleon. There's river-bank walking from the door, two golf courses adjoining, river fishing, excellent restaurants and pubs nearby. We

In both Foxes Reach and Vanilla Cottage 'book early to avoid disappointment.,,,

liked the modern and antique mix, the sparkling bathroom and kitchen with dishwasher and open plan dining, the flagged floors, the fragrant garden with sun trap terrace, the woodburner in the cosy sitting room. Both bedrooms have wrought iron beds with quality linens (a single, a king sized four poster). Stairs are quaintly steep and twisting; steep steps also outside: not suitable for the infirm or toddlers. Satellite TV/DVD/video/CD/stereo. Internet access. Dog welcome. Linens/robes/fluffy towels/heating included. Cost: £180 to £410. **WTB Five Stars-plus**. Walkers' award. Top three finalist in the WTB 'Best Places to Stay'. Short breaks a speciality. Details from Fiona Wilton, Ty Gwyn, Catbrook, near Chepstow, Monmouthshire. Tel 01600 860341.

www.foxesreach.com   email: fionawilton@btopenworld.com

Tintern, near Chepstow
Riverside Cottage

Watching the River Wye go by...

Technically just inside Wales – you can't see the join – this property stands (memorably) about as close to the River Wye as you could be without actually getting your feet wet. Detached, stone built, most attractive to look at (though the best view is from the far side of the river), the house is within easy walking distance, alongside the river, of Tintern Abbey. And there is much excellent and more serious walking beyond. With stone walls, exposed beams, rugs on a tiled floor, the house **sleeps 4** in a double and a twin; the L-shaped sitting room has an open fire. Ref ODA.

Note: there is a terrace adjacent to the river where after cottage-visiting on a busy summer Saturday in 2005 we were pleased to lean and put our minds into neutral. But – though there are railings – children should be watched. In fact, the property is 'unsuitable for small children'.

Details from from English Country Cottages, Stoney Bank Road, Earby, Barnoldswick BB94 0AA. For bookings telephone 0870 192 1028. You can also 'dial-a-brochure': 0870 192 0391.

www.ecc2006.co.uk

Wollerton/Lower Dinchope
The Pound/Lower Dinchope Big Barn map 9/497/498

The Pound is a classic of its kind, a period beauty wth Four Stars to its credit.

We love the way black and white half timbered cottages fit so comfortably into the mostly deep-green Shropshire landscape (they also match the black and white cattle!). As do many readers, including one who recommended *The Pound* at Wollerton, near Drayton. **'Visit Britain' Four Stars**, it's a lovely period piece, well over 300 years old. **Sleeping up to 6**, it is made even more appealing by a number of antiques. Ref 12221. On a bigger scale, *Lower Dinchope Big Barn* is a spacious, well equipped barn conversion which, usefully, can **sleep 15** in comfort and style. With oak beams and half timbered walls, twin stairs to each wing and plenty of space, it will suit larger groups. Only two miles from Craven Arms, it has large gardens, with meadow and woodland beyond. In addition to the main sitting room – it has a woodburner – there is a children's sitting room. Ref 12348.

Country Holidays, Spring Mill, Earby, Barnoldswick, Lancashire BB94 0AA. For bookings, telephone 0870 192 1040. Brochure line: 0870 607 8514. Live search and book: **www.2006country-holidays.co.uk**

Stanton Lacy, near Ludlow
Sutton Court Farm Cottages

Grouped congenially around a courtyard, these skilfully converted stone farm buildings have long been a favourite among 'cottage guide' readers. Although this is no longer a working farm, it is surrounded by farming activity. (The lambs in the paddock in springtime are a reliable source of entertainment.) The cottages enjoy peace and quiet in an idyllic situation close to the owners' timbered farmhouse and provide an exceptionally comfortable base for exploring the quiet Shropshire countryside and the historic market town of Ludlow only five miles away. Many varied attractions are within easy reach: ruined castles, black and white villages, gardens, farms, shops and markets.

The six cottages (*Barleycorn, Woodsage, Sweetbriar, Hazelnut, Holly* and *Honeysuckle*, **sleeping 4, 6, 4, 4, 2 and 2** respectively) are comfortably furnished, with wood burners in Barleycorn and Woodsage. Each bathroom has an overbath shower, and there are TVs, videos and CD music systems. There are fitted carpets, night storage heating and electric blankets for the winter months. Holly is all on the ground floor, and has additional features suitable for accompanied wheelchair users. Honeysuckle is a first floor apartment, **cosy for 2**, with chairs outside to enjoy the evening sunshine. They all enjoy **'Visit Britain's'** highly desirable **Four Stars** classification.

There is an information room, payphone, laundry facilities and a children's playroom. Horse riding, cycle hire, trout fishing and golf are nearby. Cream teas and home cooked evening meals may be provided given at least 24 hours' notice. Christmas and New Year are special here, with *real* Christmas trees, decorations and mince pies awaiting visitors, a remarkable number of whom return here time and time again.

This excellent place is comfortably within our and our readers' top twenty in the British Isles, and probably in the top five in the Heart of England/Welsh Border country...

The cottages are open all year round and also offer bed and breakfast and short breaks from two nights. Well behaved pets are welcome in some cottages, at an extra charge. Cot and highchair available. Cost: from £208 to £499 (linen, towels, electricity and logs included). Details from Jane and Alan Cronin, Sutton Court Farm, Little Sutton, Stanton Lacy, Ludlow, Shropshire SY8 2AJ. Telephone 01584 861305, fax 861441.

www.suttoncourtfarm.co.uk

email: suttoncourtfarm@hotmail.com

Cirencester
Cotswold Water Park: Lakeside Lodges

Over the years, while cottage visiting in Gloucestershire, we've spotted The Cotswold Water Park from a distance. Its 11,000 acres make a peaceful and attractive location for a tranquil holiday break in a rural setting with, among other good things, picnic and barbecue sites, a beach of Blue Flag standard, cycle tracks, windsurfing, sailing and much more.

A different slant on a Cotswold holiday.

Lakeside Lodges provide accommodation within the Park, **sleeping from 6 to 8**, though the configuration of beds varies. Some have two doubles and a twin room, others may have a double master bedroom and a children's room with bunk beds. Pets are welcome. All have an open plan living area cum dining area downstairs, opening on to a private sun deck. As well as the immediate charms of the place, the Cotswolds offer a mass of 'places to go and things to see'.

Details from The Cottage Collection, 17-23 Ber Street, Norwich NR1 3EU. Telephone 01603 724809.

www.the-cottage-collection.co.uk
email: bookings@the-cottage-collection.co.uk

Frampton-on-Severn, near Gloucester
The Orangery   map 9/506

This 18th century 'garden house', Grade II listed, is quite something. The best way to approach it is via the early-Georgian mansion that is Frampton Court and alongside a lily-strewn, carp-rich, ornamental canal. Guests in this fascinating property do have access to these gardens and grounds but also have their own side entrance, giving on to the delightful

A great rarity, full of character and charm.

and unspoilt estate-village, itself in a conservation area. The interior is fascinating and 'comfortable' rather than grand: you should not expect Versailles. We are impressed by the tiled fireplaces in the (south-facing) drawing room and dining room, by the antique furniture, by the spiral staircase, by the fabrics based on the 'Frampton Flora' painted by five sisters in the 1800s. Cost: about £500 to £750 per week. **Sleeps 8**. Long weekends possible. TV/video. Central heating. Well-behaved dogs welcome. Details from The Secretary, Frampton Court Estate Office, Frampton-on-Severn, Gloucestershire GL2 7LP. Telephone/fax 01452 740698.

www.framptoncourtestate.co.uk
email: clifford@framptoncourt.wanadoo.co.uk

Goodrich, near Ross-on-Wye
Mainoaks Farm

After an early lunch in Ross on Wye in the summer of 2005 we arranged a short-notice re-inspection of these superbly well situated cottages. 'Superbly well' means close to the shores of the River Wye, which is quite rare for a holiday house and much sought-after.

Turning off a B-road, we followed a farm lane and arrived at this quiet enclave of well converted stone built farm cottages. Each has its own character, ranging from 'bijou' to 'farmhousey and rambling'. Arriving by chance as a team of cleaners was busy preparing the cottages for incoming guests, we took time to look at all the cottages, noting for example the fine views from some windows, exposed beams, a nice spiral staircase.

They vary usefully in size – *Cider Mill*, for example, **sleeps up to 7**. We noted a number of appealing features: a woodburning stove in *Peregrine*, **sleeping 6**, which we also thought had 'a nice family atmosphere' and which was *converted* in 1659! It has a cruck beam in the bedrooms; Cider Mill's big, convivial dining table; the four poster bed in *Huntsham* (**sleeps 4**); the upstairs sitting room in *The Malthouse* (an 'upside-down' house, so designed as to make the most of the view).

The quality of the conversion work is exceptional with fine stone and brickwork and an impressive attention to architectural detail.

Ross-on-Wye and Monmouth are about ten minutes' drive, and Cheltenham Spa and the cathedral cities of Hereford, Worcester and Gloucester are easily accessible. The farm has a mile of frontage to the River Wye, and salmon and course fishing beats can be booked locally.

A marvellous and unusual location, and very sympathetic conversion work.

Rather 'rustic' and comfortable rooms that reflect the very stylish exteriors.

There are several golf courses, pony trekking, mountain bike tracks and inspiring waymarked Forestry Commission walks.

TVs, DVDs, radios/CD players and microwaves in each. Linen and towels included. Dogs by arrangement. Short breaks. available. '**Visit Britain' Three/Four Stars**. Open all year. Cost: about £230 to £790.

Details from Patricia Unwin, Hill House, Chase End, Bromesberrow, Ledbury, Herefordshire HR8 1SE. Telephone 01531 650448.

www.mainoaks.co.uk

email: info@mainoaks.co.uk

249

Owlpen, near Uley
Owlpen Manor Cottages

Readers often ask if and when we've stayed in the cottages we write about. We've stayed twice at Owlpen, which we have a special affection for, as it has featured in this guide since our tentative beginnings in 1983. We stayed most recently in the late summer of 2005, in light, spacious *Manor Farm*, at the very heart of the estate.

With its softly enfolding hills, its mellow buildings, its woods and pastures, Owlpen is an amazing survivor, a thousand miles from the rat-race, a small corner of England preserved at its most nostalgic and unspoiled.

The nine cottages, and fine Tudor manor house where owners Nicholas and Karin Mander live, complement the idyll. The cottages are scattered throughout the many-acred valley, along a lane here, up a track there, in sight of the main house, or tucked away in the woods. *Grist Mill* (**sleeps 8/9**) – we've stayed in it: a remarkable historic survivor – and *Woodwells* (**sleeps 6**), are favourites. But on a late summer day we also admired *Summerfield* (**sleeps 2**), *Marlings End* (**sleeps 5**), *The Court House* (**sleeps 4**), *Peter's Nest* (**sleeps 2**), *Tithe Barn* (**sleeps 2**), *Manor Farm* (**sleeps 4**) and *Over Court* (**sleeps 5**). The latter two can be let as one large family house **sleeping 9**, with an internal door from one to the other.

We can also recommend the cosy restaurant, where visitors to the manor house rub shoulders with cottage guests. In a converted old cider house,

The Grist Mill is a historic building skilfully adapted to modern use...

...but it's just one of several properties of great character in an amazing location.

this feels like a cross between a smart restaurant for an occasion and an upmarket pub. There's an excellent, sophisticated menu, and good wines.

The Manor House and three of the properties are officially 'listed' as buildings of architectural and historic interest, but their intrinsic charm is enhanced by contemporary comfort and cosiness, and an exceptional flair for decor, fabrics and furnishings. There are remote control TVs, videos, radio/alarms, antiques, telephones, hairdryers and food mixers (some have dishwashers, microwaves, freezers, washing machines, log fires and four-posters), and an on-site laundry service. All the cottages have **'Visit Britain' Four Stars**. They have central heating, and are set off by well chosen paintings, deep sofas, good quality fabrics and some king-size beds.

For a copy of the most attractive colour brochure, contact Nicholas and Karin Mander, Owlpen Manor, near Dursley, Gloucestershire GL11 5BZ. Telephone 01453 860261. Fax 860819.

www.owlpen.com   email: sales@owlpen.com

Canon Frome, near Ledbury
The Swiss Chalet

On a warm late summer day, needing to check the local map even though we had been here before, it was a pleasure to rediscover this (really!) unique property, recently repainted and 'freshened up'. By a weir on the River Frome, The Swiss Chalet is a most delightful and amusing holiday cottage. It has the makings of a romantic stay **for 2**. From a comfortable but naturally not large, double

This is one of the most romantic places we know: you can hide yourselves away!

bedroom, on the ground floor, you ascend a 'ship's ladder' to the first floor where you can hide yourselves from the world. From a balcony overlooking the water you will probably see kingfishers, and in late autumn see salmon jumping the weir. There are deep and comfortable sofa/chairs, a kitchenette with dining bar, lots of warmth, a high beamed ceiling: all this adds up to a remarkable holiday retreat.

TV. Dogs by arrangement. Cost: about £183 to £354. Linen provided. Further details from Julian and Lorna Rutherford, Mill Cottage, Canon Frome, Ledbury, Herefordshire HR8 2TD. Telephone 01531 670506 or 07881 405405.

email: julian.rutherford@virgin.net

Fairford/Chedworth
The Mill Cottages/Littlecote   map 9/519/529

The Mill Cottages, at Fairford, are two little gems within a handsome Grade II listed Mill House. Just a short walk from Fairford's peaceful market square, one is bordered by water on three sides and both have open fires. **Sleep 6 'plus 1' and 7 'plus 1'**. Refs NQL and NXE. Also, quite near the fabulous Chedworth Roman Villa (stunning mosaics) pretty, detached *Littlecote* makes a handsome small base for exploring the area. Or you could just stay put

Millstream Cottage (the two gables, above) is one of 'The Mill Cottages'.

and unwind in comfort. (The living room, for example, has an open fire and rugs on a flagstone floor.) **Sleeps 3 'plus 1'** in a zip-link twin and a single plus a second single bed. Ref NW6.

Details from from English Country Cottages, Stoney Bank Road, Earby, Barnoldswick BB94 0AA. For bookings telephone 0870 192 1028. You can also 'dial-a-brochure': 0870 192 0391.

www.ecc2006.co.uk

251

Docklow, near Leominster
Docklow Manor

The location is a delight: very quiet, though not isolated, amid peaceful countryside, and with views towards the Black Mountains and Brecon Beacons. Most recently, on a perfect late August morning, we turned off the Bromyard to Leominster road and then along a tree lined private drive to revisit one of the consistently best loved cottage enclaves we know: it has featured in this guide every year *since it was first published in 1983.*

Docklow is in easy reach of Ludlow, one of the handsomest towns in England. There are National Trust mansions and gardens nearby, and the cathedrals at Hereford and Worcester are easily accessible.

We met the fairly new owners for the first time. They, Jane and Brian Viner, have retained and refurbished three of the original seven cottages. We looked in all three, and met very contented guests – in one case, readers of *The Good Holiday Cottage Guide.*

Specifically, *Woodlands Cottage* has three double bedrooms and a well-equipped kitchen, with dishwasher, washing machine and tumble dryer. It has its own front garden, with a barbecue and glorious views. *Yewtree Cottage* has two double bedrooms, a comfortable kitchen/living-room, and a private back garden with access to a secluded orchard. *Manor Cottage* is a romantic hideaway, with a four-poster bed. Like neighbouring Yewtree, it overlooks an ancient stone cider press: a picture-postcard setting.

Staying at Docklow is like being part of a traditional English village.

Cottage interiors are comfortable, warm, quiet and have plenty of character.

Each cottage has a TV, video recorder, and books, videos and games. The more energetic can enjoy the manor house's five acres of formal gardens and woodland, or play table tennis and table football in the Victorian conservatory. Guests are encouraged to feed the free-range bantams, and play with Fergus, the golden retriever. (Note: well behaved dogs are welcome.) Children are welcome: the Viners have three, who deliver occasional treats to the cottages such as home-made ice-cream. The Viners also offer dinner either in their manor house, or, pre-prepared, supplied to the cottages.

Cost: from £175 for three nights in Manor Cottage in low-season to £550 for a week in Woodlands in peak season. **'Visit Britain' Three Stars**. Linen included.

Details from Docklow Manor, Docklow, Leominster, Herefordshire HR6 0RX. Telephone 01568 760668. Or you can book through the website:

www.docklow-manor.co.uk   email: enquiries@docklow-manor.co.uk

Calmsden, near Cirencester
The Tallet Holiday Cottages

It's really special: this lovely, light, spacious, beautifully situated property is one of our Cotswolds favourites. On the warm summer afternoon of our first visit it was a pleasure in itself to locate it at the end of a series of narrow country lanes that see almost no traffic.

It is a delight, and we would love to stay in it ourselves. Ideal for a group, this clever conversion by Nicholas and Vanessa Arbuthnott (he is an architect, she a fabric designer) **sleeps up to 12**.

To help you get your bearings, the family home is on one side of the inner courtyard that in itself contributes so much character to the house, the holiday property – actually a converted cow byre and barn – on the other. Also attached to the Arbuthnotts' own house is Vanessa Arbuthnott's studio: her designs are on the fabrics, ceramic tiles and much else around the

'Calmsden' is right: this is a peaceful, beautifully located place to unwind in...

...with stylish, spacious, well planned interiors. We rate this very highly.

house. Among many good things are a huge drawing room, with lots of lamps that in the evening help turn this splendid property into something even more welcoming and charming, and lovely paintings and prints. Most rooms are at least double aspect. Four bedrooms have singles that can be pushed together, meaning that as doubles and not singles they are six foot wide beds; one has a double bed. One large bedroom sleeps four (a pair of bunk beds, a pair of twins).

When we visited, children were sporting on the football pitch and the trampoline, their parents playing badminton and tennis. Definitely one of our 'top twenty', this is **'Visit Britain' Five Stars**. There is an outdoor swimming pool available by appointment, as is the tennis court.

A real bonus is that Kemble train station is just fifteen minutes' drive away, with direct links to London Paddington.

Linen and towels included. Pets welcome. Non-smokers only. Cost: about £890 to £1150. Details from Mr and Mrs Arbuthnott, The Tallet, Calmsden, near Cirencester, Gloucestershire GL7 5ET. Telephone/fax 01285 831437.

www. thetallet.demon.co.uk
email: vanessa@thetallet.demon.co.uk

Upton upon Severn
The Orangery at Little Boynes

A few minutes' drive along country lanes from quaint old Upton upon Severn, this detached cottage, converted from a former orangery, close to but independent of the owners' house, feels private. Pristinely clean and tidy, it was warm and cosy on a bright but chilly day. It has **Four Stars** from **'Visit Britain'**. Formerly an orangery, it has accommodation **for 4 'plus 2'** in two bedrooms (a double and a twin), a well-equipped kitchen, an open plan sitting/dining room with a log burner and a sofa bed, a separate bathroom/WC and a second WC. Guests share use of the indoor swimming pool (32°C, open all year round) the spa and jacuzzi, the games room and the gardens. Linen and fuel included. Digital TV, DVD, video, music system. Microwave and fridge/freezer. Shared laundry room with washing machine/dryer. Secure cycle stowage; drying facilities for cyclists and walkers. Cost: about £250 to £525. No pets, no smoking, no children under seven. Details: Chris and Sheila Martin, The Orangery at Little Boynes, Upper Hook Road, Upton-upon-Severn, Worcestershire WR8 0SB. Telephone/fax 01684 594788.

This was a lucky find last summer...

www.little-boynes.co.uk   info@little-boynes.co.uk

Sedgeberrow, near Evesham
Hall Farm   map 9/538

We know these properties well, and have stayed several times. The six cottages are exceptionally sympathetic barn conversions that benefit from their quiet village location (a shop/post office, a good pub) on the edge of the Cotswolds, a few minutes' drive from busy Evesham. Each retains a number of original features. The cottages are fully equipped to a high standard, and the rather cosy interiors (good beds!) include a number of antiques. Guests can relax in an acre of gardens, or use the owners' heated outdoor pool, only a five minute walk away. **Sleep 2 to 6.** Cost: about £215 to £680, including linen, towels, heating and electricity. TV, video, DVD in all cottages. Dishwasher in most. Pets not accepted.

Reliably comfortable, with easy access to the Cotswolds and Shakespeare country.

Details from Rebecca Barclay, Hall Farm Cottages, Sedgeberrow, Evesham, Worcestershire WR11 7UF. Telephone 01386 881243.

www.hallfarmcottages.net
email: enquiries@hallfarmcottages.net

Tewkesbury
Courtyard Cottages, Upper Court

Featured in our guide since 1983, this is very stylish indeed. Upper Court is a classic Georgian manor, with cottages run with energy and skill by owners Bill and Diana Herford. It is located along a quiet, leafy lane near the handsome church in Kemerton, a charming Cotswold village at the foot of Bredon Hill.

We called most recently to see *Watermill*, which **sleeps 10**. Separate from the other cottages, with a superb outlook over the lake, it is cosy and compact, with its own little garden and underfloor central heating and a huge inglenook fireplace. One bedroom is on the ground floor, with an ensuite shower. Also quite new, *The Garden Studio* **sleeps just 2**: on the ground floor, it is a wing of the main house, as is *Dovecote*, a super hideaway **for 2**, also with stunning views overlooking the lake.

The house's fifteen acres of garden and grounds (featured in the National Gardens Scheme) are idyllic, and embrace a watermill mentioned in the Domesday Survey. As the Herfords have an antique business, the cottages are full of antique furniture. Beds are made up for your arrival; there are plenty of towels, and you can order 'Cordon Bleu' home cooked meals to be brought to your door or waitress-served. Daily help and baby sitting are also available – if you book early.

Guests can enjoy the outdoor all-weather tennis court and table tennis, an outdoor pool in summer, or croquet. There's excellent riding, and clay pigeon shooting on the hill. A major attraction is the beautiful lake, a two acre wilderness that is home to wildfowl, swans, heron, ducks and geese. You can take the boat out, row around the two islands, have a picnic, barbecue or just enjoy the surroundings. This is an excellent spot for a special celebration or a house party: on three sides of the courtyard, in *Stable* (**sleeps 5**), *The Courtyard Cottage* (**sleeps 7/8**) and *The Coach House*

Cottages in the lee of the big house...   *...but private and self contained.*

(**sleeps 11**) one can comfortably sleep up to 24. (The Coach House can seat up to 24 in a 45-foot square sitting room/dining room.) The cottages range from **'Visit Britain' Four to Five Stars**. Linen, towels and heating (as hot as you like!) included. TVs/videos, CD/radio/cassette players. Cost: about £275 to £1540. Short breaks.

Details from Diana Herford, Upper Court, Kemerton, near Tewkesbury, Gloucestershire GL20 7HY. Telephone 01386 725351. Fax 725472.

www.uppercourt.co.uk
email: herfords@uppercourt.co.uk

255

The Cotswolds
Discover the Cotswolds*

This agency gets much of its strong following from its personalised, 'hands on' approach. With just 30 or so cottages on her books, owner Alison Lewis knows every-stick-and-stone, which our readers love.

There's a nice mixture of rural and village or small-town locations. For example, in a little jewel of a village called Condicote, *The Old Chapel* is a romantic hideaway **for 2 people**, plus a 'guest bed' for children over eight. There's a woodburning stove.

Another property we like is a superb, mellow Cotswold stone house in the village of Paxford, part of which is a holiday house. This is *Walnut Wing Cottage*, **sleeping 4**.

Among places we have yet to see but have had glowing reports of is *Swallow Barn* (**sleeping 6**). Peacefully situated in the hamlet of Duntisbourne Rouse, a fifteen minute drive from Cirencester, it's one of a pair on the owners' farm. Comfortably furnished to a very high standard – it's **'Visit Britain' Five Stars** – amid idyllic countryside, this makes a super retreat. Families will appreciate the bonus of a large grassed area away from the cottage and safely fenced off, especially designed for children's games.

One of our favourite Cotswold villages is Oddington (the two good pubs are a bonus!). There, 'Discover the Cotswolds' has *Rose Cottage*, a little gem quietly located on a back lane. **Sleeping 4**, and incorporating a number of original features, it has an open fire and 'a tiny but south-facing and secluded back garden'.

But lack of space prevents us from doing more than scratch the surface of this admirable organisation: the well organised, easy to use website will reveal all.

Walnut Wing Cottage (on the left) shares the historic character of this classic Cotswold stone beauty...

Home Farm Cottage is 'the real thing' – on a working farm, about 400 years old. Better yet, it's near Chipping Campden.

Details/brochure from 'Discover the Cotswolds', 2 School Cottages, Cider Mill Lane, Chipping Campden, Gloucestershire GL55 6HX. Telephone 01386 841441.

www.discoverthecotswolds.net
email: info@discoverthecotswolds.net

Poole Keynes, near Cirencester
Old Mill Farm

We've stayed several times, and love the quiet but not hard-to-find location...

After the comparative hustle and bustle of nearby Cirencester we enjoy detouring to these quietly situated converted barns – at the end of a series of meandering country lanes. On two sides of the not-very-busy farmyard are four cottages **sleeping from 2/3 to 7** (all have space for a cot). We really liked – and have stayed in – *Thames Cottage*: it literally backs on to the stream that is the infant River Thames. Stylish, comfortable, light and bright, it has some exposed stone walls, lots of pine. It has a double room downstairs, and the main (galleried) double has a five foot bed. Next door is *Granary*, the littlest, also with a five foot double and backing on to the stream: both cottages have a little balcony. We didn't see *Tuppenny Cottage* but met a family enjoying their stay in single-storeyed *Stable*, with french windows on to the yard and the biggest sitting room/diner. Dogs welcome. TVs. Linen, not towels included. Dishwashers in the larger cottages. Cost: £195 to £700. Details from Gordon and Catherine Hazell, Ermin House Farm, Syde, Cheltenham, Gloucestershire GL53 9PN. Telephone 01285 821255. Fax 821531.

www.oldmillcottages.co.uk   email: catherine@oldmillcottages.fsnet.co.uk

---

Poole Keynes, near Cirencester   map 9/523
Island Lodge

We've featured some amazing properties in this guide, and this is a winner...

This is an extraordinary place. Island Lodge is a traditional Finnish log house on a private, secluded 100-acre lake in the Cotswolds. It's a 'Site of Special Scientific Interest', mainly because of its over-wintering wildfowl, its nightingale colony and its *seventeen* species of dragonfly. Coarse fishing is available (excellent pike for example) and the property, which has a two mile perimeter path landscaped around it, comes with a four-man rowing boat. The path has superb lake views and is of course a vantage point from which to observe wildlife. Specifically, there is a covered verandah with memorable lake views, an open plan living room with woodburner, two large double bedrooms (single or double beds). There is a well fitted kitchen, a bathroom with shower *and* bath, electric central heating. Cost: about £465 to £800. Short breaks available at two thirds of the weekly price. Dogs welcome. **'Visit Britain' Four Stars**. Details from Log House Holidays, Poole Keynes, Cirencester, Gloucestershire GL7 6ED. Telephone 01285 770082. Fax 770053.

www.loghouseholidays.co.uk   email: relax@loghouseholidays.co.uk

Stanton, near Broadway
Stanton Court Cottages

Not only would we put these cottages among our top three or four in England, we would probably choose Stanton as our favourite Cotswold village. Which – as readers who know this corner of England will appreciate – is really saying something. Readers agree with us about the cottages: after 23 years in this guide, *we've never had anything but praise*. It must be due to the combination of picture-postcard looks and a rare (but not prissy) attention to guests' comfort and warmth.

We have actually stayed in three cottages – *Peach, Rosemary* and *(*three times*) Paddock –* though we know them all. Romantic Peach is a delightful hideaway **for 2**, with a galleried bedroom. One perfect summer evening, with our children sporting in the open air pool, we could hardly tear ourselves away from the exceptional gardens, but had an appointment in the excellent pub at the top of the hill – cosy in winter, with an open log fire and candlelight, a suntrap in summer, with amazing views, and excellent walking to Broadway and Snowshill.

The atmosphere at Stanton Court is perfect: friendly, but private when you want it to be, the picture-postcard golden stone village, hardly changed since it was first built in the 16th and 17th century, a fine backdrop. Stanton lies close to the wooded lip of the Cotswold escarpment, surrounded by some of the richest greenery in England.

The cottages are grouped around the courtyard of the village's principal house, which was built by Elizabeth I's chamberlain. Its garden, sheltered by ancient trees, notably some majestic yews, is mostly lawn, backing on the village churchyard. Since the house was built on such a grand scale, the parts of the original complex that have been transformed into self-contained units are mostly quite spacious.

We admire the way modern comfort has been combined with original features.   *This superb Elizabethan mansion is quite a focal point for the cottages.*

In brief, *Courtyard Cottage* is closest to the imposing entrance gates, **sleeps 4** in one double and one twin and has good views of the surrounding countryside, especially the imposing Malvern Hills. In little Peach, the bigger two-storeyed *Rosemary* and delightfully spacious, single-storeyed *Shenberrow* we came away with an impression, among other things, of big, comfortable beds, expensive and elegant tables and standard-lamps, deep sofas in subtle, modern colours. We admired so much of the detail and attention to comfort and remember especially Peach's unusual conservatory and its inviting open fireplace. The cottage is, incidentally, on three levels, with a galleried bedroom that has a romantic atmosphere. We were especially delighted by Rosemary, with its high pitched roof, its brass bedsteads in one of the twin rooms, more of those deep sofas and wing chairs. It **sleeps 6** in a double and two twins. Shenberrow, another fairly recent addition to the Stanton family, also has charm: it **sleeps 4**, has two bathrooms and is suitable for wheelchair-bound guests.

Paddock used to be the potting shed. The original stone walls and occasional outcrop of historic timbers are featured here, and, in fact, recur throughout most of the cottages at Stanton. It offers one-level accommodation, and so is suitable for the elderly or the handicapped. It **sleeps 2** in a twin or double (ie zip-link beds), and also has a double sofa bed in the (surprisingly spacious) sitting/dining room. As with all the cottages, it comes fully equipped with linen and towels and has full gas central heating, TV/DVD/ video, and a telephone. It can be combined with Peach Cottage to **sleep 4**.

Studio Cottage continues the chunky wooden beam theme. It too has quarry tiled floors and a large walk-in pantry that puts the cottage's interior into its true perspective. You'll find the dining room and large sitting room (with lovely views) equipped with a convertible settee. Parties of **up to 7** can be accommodated in *Garden*, actually a first floor flat, in three bedrooms (a double and two twins), two with their own hand basins, and there is an enormous lounge, along with a grandfather clock, antique pine furniture, and co-ordinated soft furnishings.

Another of our favourites, though we would happily stay in any one of the Stanton Court properties, is *The Granary*, characterised by a huge lounge, with a stone fireplace, and a bold craftsman-built modern wooden staircase, leading to the beamed roof gallery corridor, off which the three bedrooms lead. It is a house of enormous character.

The cottages manage to be impressive and intimate at the same time.

The village is a delight, and Stanton Court, at one end, is its pride and joy.

Stanton Court has its own tennis court and a heated outdoor pool. There is a centrally heated games room, a children's adventure playground, a laundry room and a new reception area. A range of inexpensive food is available in the cottages, and there is even an off-licence. **'Visit Britain' Four Stars**.

Cost: about £382 to £1126 per week, including heating and electricity. Well behaved dogs welcome – maximum two per cottage. Details from Stanton Court, Stanton, near Broadway, Worcestershire WR12 7NE. Telephone 01386 584527. Fax 584682.

www.stantoncourt.co.uk   email: sales@stantoncourt.co.uk

The Cotswolds and beyond
Rural Retreats*

There is, as they, say, 'something about Rural Retreats' properties', and over the years we have come to recognise the special style the company creates within the places it has in its portfolio.

The many readers who have discovered Rural Retreats through *The Good Holiday Cottage Guide* won't be surprised to know that they only accept about one in four of the properties offered.

Being based at Moreton-in-Marsh, Rural Retreats are particularly strong in the Cotswolds, but their selection of over 400 properties now extends all over England, Scotland and Wales, from Cornwall to the Scottish Highlands.

On arrival, you'll be greeted with a complimentary hamper sitting on the kitchen table, a bottle of wine chilling in the fridge, and often a log fire waiting to be lit. Many of the properties are several hundred years old, so you can expect to find plenty of character too. And there are invariably nice interior touches like handsome table-lamps, expensive curtains, good quality rugs, pretty bedspreads and complimentary toiletries.

Another bonus is that at any time of the year you can choose which days of the week you want to arrive and leave (minimum stay is often only two nights). TVs, bedlinen, towels, electricity, fire logs and cots/highchairs are all included in the price; the only item charged extra is calls from the payphone. Dinner delivery to the door is often available too, and at some properties you can even arrange for an expert cook to take over the kitchen and prepare dinner.

The fine brochure simplifies the task of choosing where to stay by having very clear maps and an index which lists the properties by size, by whether they have ground-floor bedrooms and by whether dogs are allowed. And an 'activity' index shows those suitable for guests who want a swimming pool, a hot tub, tennis, fishing or cycle hire.

The Pendeen Lighthouse properties are an experience, not just 'a place to stay'!

The Henhouse, near lovely Ludlow, Shropshire, is at least 400 years old.

Some of the most interesting properties, thanks to Rural Retreats' partnership with Trinity House, are former lighthouse-keepers' cottages. Three of them, all single-storey, are in a group of four at the foot of the famous Pendeen lighthouse, just six miles north of Lands End. Built in 1900, it was automated in 1994, but an attendant who lives in the fourth cottage conducts brief tours for the public four days a week, Easter to September.

And you must be prepared for the fog-horn to sound when necessary! *Vestal* and *Solebay* cottages both **sleep 4**, *Argus* **sleeps 3**. Ref CW-032/3/4.

Two lighthouse-keepers' cottages ideal for keen golfers are situated beside the Cromer lighthouse on the north Norfolk coast, adjacent to the 18-hole Royal Cromer course. *Valonia* **sleeps 6** and *The Link* **sleeps 2**. Ref NO-034 & 051.

There are in fact now twelve sites, from Yorkshire to Cornwall and the Channel Isles, that feature lighhouse keepers' cottages.

Among Rural Retreats' many lovely old properties in the Cotswolds, the aptly-named *Cotswold Cottage* at Tetbury is a period semi-detached stone building, **sleeping 5,** with TV in each of the three bedrooms. Its gardens are unusual in that the front one has a pond and small waterfall and the rear one has a hot tub (for year-round use). Ref CO-163.

In the Peak District, walkers appreciate *Memorial Cottage* at Eyam as an ideal location. **Sleeping 2** plus a child, it is a Grade II listed stone terraced house a few minutes' walk from the centre of the beautiful unspoilt village, high in the moors of the National Park. Ref DE-024. Nearby, in a restored 18th-century cotton mill on the River Derwent, a spacious ground floor apartment **sleeping 4/6** is available. Each room is south-facing and has lovely views. Ref DE-025.

Dating back to at least the early 17th century, *The Henhouse*, at Cleedownton, near Ludlow, looks nothing like its name. Sumptuously created from a former barn, cowshed and one-room cottage, it's a smart stone building alongside a Grade II listed farmhouse. **Sleeping 5**, it has three bedrooms (a double, a twin and a four-foot bed), a spacious sitting-room and kitchen/dining area. There's a large shared garden and magnificent views. Ref SH-008.

In Devon, *Westfield*, at Newton Ferrers (**sleeping 5**), is a charming detached 1927 house occupying a commanding position in half an acre of grounds above the estuary of the River Yealm. The sitting and dining rooms both have open coal fires as well as central heating, and there is a spacious full-length verandah, perfect for soaking up the sun. Ref DV-016.

Holcombe is near Hemyock, which has a pub, a post office, a shop and a 'chippie'.

Lochenkit is in a most desirable remote setting on the edge of the moors.

Further details from Rural Retreats, Draycott Business Centre, Moreton-in-Marsh, Gloucestershire GL56 9JY. Telephone 01386 701177.

www.ruralretreats.co.uk
email: info@ruralretreats.co.uk

Winchcombe
Sudeley Castle Country Cottages

We have now stayed in three of the cottages here (*Oliver Cromwell, Queen Mary* and *Queen's Cottage*). We always experience a strong sense of the history that permeates this fabulous castle and its surroundings, and marvel at the train of events that makes it possible to stay, if not in the castle itself, then close by.

Winchcombe too is one of our favourite small Cotswold towns. It's full of character and history, but the best thing of all is that it adjoins Sudeley Castle, much visited for its exquisite interior and its fabulous gardens. There's a further bonus, for the tranquil 1200 acre Sudeley estate embraces – just five minutes' pleasant stroll from the castle itself – a cluster of thirteen holiday properties finished to high standards, each with its own individual character.

Grouped around a central courtyard so neat, clean and tidy it always seems to us as if it is swept twice daily, there are Cottages and Mews Cottages, The King's Apartments and The Mill Court.

Oliver Cromwell, **sleeping 4**, which is one of the Mill Court properties, is a light, spacious, beamy two storeyed arrangement with a twin and a spacious double bedroom. We also remember the impressive *Lady Jane Grey*, **sleeping 5**, in a double, a twin and a single, with a sitting room that opens on to a small patio and a shared garden. We also found Queen's Cottage and *Emma Dent*, **sleeping 4 and 5** respectively, are interesting and comfortable (the latter being 'Visit Britain' **Four Stars**). Queen's Cottage is a clever and practical conversion of the estate's original engine house, with a charming (enclosed) first floor sleeping gallery.

A sympathetic conversion of old buildings into very comfortable cottages...

...and a rare chance to stay so close to such an impressive and historic place...

The two Mews Cottages are full of history, overlook the gardens and the river, and have open fires. Other property names are intriguing: *Anne Boleyn,* Queen Mary, *George III, Prince Rupert*. For Sudeley's famous associations run like a thread through the history of England.

Not suitable for pets. Cost: about £239 to £729. Further details from The Cottage Administrator, Sudeley Castle, Winchcombe, Gloucestershire GL54 5JD. Telephone 01242 602308. Fax 602959.

www.sudeleycastle.co.uk

email: cottages@sudeley.org.uk

Exhall, near Alcester
Glebe Farm

There's a skilful use of the available space in the conversion here of one-time barns that stand around three sides of a traditional farmyard. Of the ten properties, five are single storeyed cottages, *The Stable* is a sizeable, two storeyed, and chintzily comfortable house with lots of beams and lots of warmth (shower only, not bath). One of the cottages, *Mill Meer,* is suitable for people with limited mobility. Most recently

Neat and warm cottages well placed for Shakespeare Country and the Marches. There are two good pubs in the village, both serving food, and others just a short drive away...

available, within a handsome converted barn, are *Duck Pond* and *Goose*, deliberately made for flexibility. There are two apartments done to a very high standard in a separate, detached, one-time cartshed, called *The Granary* and *The Cart Hovel.*

One dog per cottage welcome. TV. All linen and towels, electricity and heating included. Cost: about £150 to £500 (but check this, as new owners took over these properties just as we were going to press).

Details from 01438 869489. **email: frank@cottageguide.demon.co.uk**

Buckland, near Broadway   map 9/534
Hillside Cottage/The Bothy

Yes, OK, we love Stanton most. But nearby Buckland comes close. At the end of the picture-postcard village street (it's a no-through-road) you continue uphill to locate three comfortable, private, self contained properties. Two are 'upside down' (first floor sitting rooms, from which you look down on the outer reaches of this leafy, honey-coloured village), the new one – *The Nook* (**sleeps 2**) – is on the ground floor. All are adjacent to but have separate entrances from the owners' home. We like the

Comfortable and warm, not frilly. Regular readers will be pleased to know that a third property has been added. It sleeps 2, and can be linked with Hillside.

beamed ceilings, the open fires, the comparative roominess, the comfy sofas. One of *Bothy's* bedrooms has a four-poster, and Bothy and *Hillside Cottage* both **sleep 4**. There is a good sized indoor heated pool available all day, and a garden with barbecue. A bonus for walkers: the Cotswold Way is yards from the cottages. TV with teletext. Linen/towels included. **'Visit Britain' Four Stars** in two: grading awaited for The Nook. Dogs welcome. Cost: about £280 to £560. Details from Bob Edmondson, Burhill, Buckland, Worcestershire WR12 7LY. Telephone 01386 853426. Mobile 07811 353344. **www.burhill.co.uk   email: bob.e@tesco.net**

263

Cleeve Hill, near Winchcombe
The Old Dairy

We've thought about listing cottages that have exceptional views but we know it's a bit subjective, and that some owners with a bit of scrubland outside the kitchen window would say 'Include me too!'. But this really is amazing. Whenever we call in to see this outstandingly well-cared-for and characterful cottage we also build in time to enjoy the view. For not only is this property a delightful *tour de force* done to a superb stan-

One of our personal Cotswolds favourites, and an amazing view to boot...

dard (not surprisingly, **'Visit Britain' Four Stars**), it also has a quite amazing 180-degree panorama over the Severn Vale to the Black Mountains. After taking a narrow track off the Winchcombe/Cheltenham road, one snakes past the owners' house, then climbs higher. We love the huge sitting room, its woodburning stove and oak floor, the vaulted ceiling and the gallery at one end. Downstairs, from that main room you go through to a stylish kitchen. A good-sized bathroom leads to a pristine double bedroom (ensuite). Upstairs are two twin rooms, and another bathroom. The house is light and bright and heated partly by solar panels.

Sleeps up to 8 (including the use of a futon). TV/video/DVD/CD. Linen/towels included. Not suitable for pets. Cost: about £350 to £1100. Details: Rickie and Jennie Gauld, Slades Farm, Bushcombe Lane, Cleeve Hill, Cheltenham, Gloucestershire GL52 3PN. Telephone and fax 01242 676003. Mobile 07860 598323 and 07764 613284.

www.cotswoldcottages.btinternet.co.uk
or www.btinternet.com/~cotswoldcottages
email: rickieg@btinternet.com

The editors of *The Good Holiday Cottage Guide* welcome personal calls and emails from readers about properties in the British Isles or abroad, and about things to see and do in the area that is of interest. Every property featured in this guide has been seen by at least one inspector, sometimes two or three of them, but there may be specific questions readers want to ask that are not covered in individual write-ups or round-up agency features. We are always very pleased to link people up with properties that may suit them, and there is no charge...

Telephone 01438 869489.

email: frank@cottageguide.demon.co.uk

The Cotswolds
Manor Cottages and Cotswold Retreats*

Owners and agents based in the Cotswolds tend to be very protective of the place. Typically, this medium sized agency (established fifteen years ago) deals almost exclusively with properties that offer the true 'Cotswolds experience' – places of real character and, sometimes, historical associations, as well as picture-postcard locations.

Most recently we visited a couple of the agency's houses in the village of Lower Quinton, between Stratford-upon-Avon and Broadway. *Elmhurst* (**sleeping 9**) and *Gable Cottage* (**sleeping 7**) are real charmers, though different in character. The latter is a plushly comfortable jewel, a real no-expense-spared *tour de force*, in which the powerful (and very recent) combination of a specialist builder and an interior designer is a delight to see. Elmhurst is more farmhousey in character. We like the big 'family' kitchen, the spacious bedrooms in most cases, the country antiques, the unfussy comfort.

Rose Terrace, Evenlode. Not featured here but known by us – delightful!

Kellams, in picture-postcard Lower Slaughter, sleeps 4.

At Tarlton, near Cirencester, *Old Farm* is a clean-cut **Five Star** beauty **sleeping 6 'plus 1'**. Dating from the 17th century, it is full of charm and character, with light, spacious rooms featuring beams and inglenook fireplaces. The 'dream kitchen' overlooks a sheltered patio that in turn looks on to a large secluded garden and the countryside beyond. There is plenty of scope for good walking directly from the house.

At Lower Slaughter, *Kellams* is full of antiques and faces on to the pretty, bubbling river. It **sleeps 4**, with two bathrooms. And *Applegate*, at Todenham, near Moreton-in-Marsh, is an attractive place that is attached to the home of the charming and welcoming owners. **Sleeps 2**.

Most sleep **from 2 to 4/6**, with a sprinkling of cottages that will take **7/9**, and three or four will **sleep 8/9**. Because of the location of the Cotswolds and the now established demand from London weekenders, among others, short breaks are often available at a sensible price.

Dogs and other pets are welcome in about half the properties. Brochure/details from Chris Grimes, Manor Cottages and Cotswold Retreats, Priory Mews, 33A Priory Lane, Burford OX18 4SG. Telephone 01993 824252. Fax 824443.

www.manorcottages.co.uk
email: chris.grimes@cottagesetc.com

Cottage in the Country*
(Incorporating Cottage Holidays)

This long established agency has as its main patch the Cotswolds, Oxfordshire and the Thames Valley, with a nod to Herefordshire, Shropshire, Buckinghamshire and Hertfordshire. It has always appealed to overseas visitors as well as holidaymakers from within the UK. Oxford, Stratford-upon-Avon, Ledbury and Windsor are among the places that attract. There are also houses within the Thames Valley, there are properties easily accessible by train from central London. The ones we know tend to be in the Cotswolds or Worcestershire or Herefordshire, where there are some real beauties.

They have a great choice, including three stunning cottages near Hereford, a real little jewel in pretty Swinbrook called *The Coach House* and (new for 2006) a lovely property a few miles from Henley-on-Thames with a huge sitting room with beams and a vaulted ceiling.

With **'Visit Britain'** gradings of **Two to Five**, and properties that are all known by the staff, this organisation comes highly recommended.

Details from Cottage in the Country, Tukes Cottage, 66 West Street, Chipping Norton, Oxfordshire OX7 5ER. Telephone: 0870 0275930. Fax: 0870 0275934.

www.cottageinthecountry.co.uk
email: ghc@cottageinthecountry.co.uk

Bevere, nr Worcester/Yarpole, nr Leominster

The first of these is very handsome indeed, a grand Georgian house with a classic sweeping gravelled drive, and views towards Worcester cathedral. There are three fine reception rooms, six spacious bedrooms and most appealing gardens, with for example many trees and shrubs. In true country house party style there is an all-weather tennis court **(map 9/515)**. **Sleeps up to 10.** Ref W40640. Neatly sleeping half that number of people, a picture-perfect black and

'Our sort of place': this fine Georgian house is in striking distance of Worcester.

white cottage at Yarpole (the style is variously known as 'magpie' or even 'licorice allsorts'!) is a good base **(map 9/502)** from which to explore the gloriously accessible Malvern Hills, the Welsh border country, 'Shakespeare Country' and the Cotswolds. It is for example only ten miles from much sought-after Ludlow. **Sleeps 5**.

For availability and bookings, contact Welcome Cottages, Spring Mill, Earby, Barnoldswick, Lancashire BB94 0AA. Telephone (brochures) 0870 192 0809, 0870 336 2825 (bookings).

www.welcomecottages.com

Swerford, near Chipping Norton
Heath Farm Cottages

These are almost 'in a class of their own'. We revisited two seasons ago, and, having inspected the latest property to become available, came away even more full of admiration. For this is a superlatively comfortable and thoughtfully equipped group of five cottages, which make an excellent base from which to explore the whole of the unspoilt Cotswolds, the glories of Oxfordshire and, further afield, Shakespeare Country.

There's a pretty, flower-filled courtyard with a mature water garden, 70 acres of meadows and woodland readily accessible, extraordinary views of large tracts of rural Oxfordshire from the courtyard and some windows of the five golden ironstone cottages, and exceptional interiors.

David Barbour, who with his wife Nena has created such a haven of comfort at Heath Farm, is a master craftsman with his own joinery business. For example, all the interior doors and the windows, the kitchen units and much of the furniture is hand-made *on site*: a joy to see. (In one of the larger properties, attached to the Barbours' own house, we admired handsome hand-made high backed dining chairs in elm from the farm itself.)

Beechnut and *Hazelnut* **sleep 2**, but both also have sofabeds. They are compact, comfortable and private, with rugs, expensive small sofas, cosy lamps, a skilful use of space. Across the courtyard are *Chestnut*, **sleeping 2** (but it also has a sofabed), and *Walnut,* **sleeping 4**. They are exceptional by any standards, with lots of space, a six foot double bed in the latter, rugs on slate floors. Walnut is a little palace, with a big sitting room, ceiling to floor windows, fabulous views (it's on two floors), a magnificent dining table, exposed stone walls, handsome beams, a superb bathroom/perhaps the most impressive shower-room we've ever seen! The most recently available cottage is *Cobnut*, **sleeping 4** in two ensuite twins/doubles (that is, zip-link beds). Among so many good things, there are extraordinary views from the master bedroom and a top of the range power shower.

All have open fires for which logs are provided. Cobnut is **'Visit Britain' Five Stars**, the others are **Four Stars**: we'd have thought **Five** throughout. Electricity, central heating, linen and towels included. Non smokers only. 'Sorry, no pets.' Cost: £276 to £658 (Christmas/New Year cost extra). Credit cards accepted. Details/brochure from David and Nena Barbour, Heath Farm, Swerford, near Chipping Norton, Oxfordshire OX7 4BN. Telephone 01608 683270/683204. Fax 683222.

www.heathfarm.com   email: barbours@heathfarm.com

Award-winning properties, effectively all 'Visit Britain' Five Stars...

...are outstanding, among much else, for the craftsmanship of the interiors.

267

Churchill, near Chipping Norton
The Little Cottage

Fitting harmoniously into one of the 'Oxfordshire Cotswolds' villages (a good pub/restaurant), this cosy and inexpensive cottage has a wood-burner, oak beams, a neat sitting room enhanced by good quality, co-ordinated furnishings, adjacent to a well planned kitchen that leads to a pretty garden. There's lots of pine, a separate dining room, a metal, not plastic, bath in a good-sized bath-

Neat and comfortable, and very reasonably priced for a popular location.

room and a charming twin/double bedroom. Picturesque, quiet, little-known Churchill, on the eastern edge of the Cotswolds, has a fine church, a village green and a quantity of traditional, honey-coloured stone cottages, of which The Little Cottage (in the middle of a terrace of three and on a not very busy B-road) is one. **'Visit Britain' Four Stars**. Non smoking. Small TV/video. Laundry available (washer/drier). Not suitable for dogs. Central heating over which guests have control. Linen/towels included. Cost: £215 to £305 **for 2** plus cot. Short breaks off-season: three nights for £160. Details from David and Jacky Sheppard, Gables Cottage, Junction Road, Churchill, Oxfordshire OX7 6NW. Telephone 01608 658674.

www.littlecottage.co.uk

East Hagbourne
The Oast House, Manor Farm   map 9/548

On the edge of the village of East Hagbourne, below the Berkshire Downs and half way between the 12th century church and the farm-house where owner Robin Harries lives, *The Oast House* is quietly situated. It is more spacious than its Virginia creeper-covered appearance suggests, and has five bedrooms. (The one on the ground floor can be used for alternative sleeping arrange-ments.) The master bedroom has a

Very much a family house, with a tennis court by arrangement.

five foot bed. The living room has a Victorian style gas fired stove as an appealing back-up to the central heating. On the ground floor there is also a separate dining room, a modern kitchen which includes a dishwasher, and a utility room with washing machine and drier, a shower and a third loo. **Sleeps 6/8**. TV/video plus satellite TV. Not suitable for dogs. This excellent house is **'Visit Britain' Four Stars**. Further details are available from Robin Harries, Manor Farm, East Hagbourne, Oxfordshire. Telephone/fax 01235 815005.

email: manorfarm.easthag@virgin.net

Bruern, near Chipping Norton
Bruern Cottages

The handsome village of Bruern, all manicured grass and tidy verges, is memorable for us: we will always recall the silent, misty autumn morning on which we first saw it. Perfect! It's no surprise that so many people return to stay in one of the eight cottages prettily arranged on three sides of a courtyard at the heart of this very 'English' place, with others tucked quietly away nearby.

It's also no surprise that Bruern Cottages won the then ETB's much respected Self Catering Award in the England for Excellence scheme in 1998 and again in 2003: having seen literally thousands of cottage interiors on our travels during the last twenty years, we rate these as exceptional.

Each is like a mini-stately home, with open fires, particularly attractive, soft and subtle lighting, deep sofas, fine paintings and prints, many antiques, good quality rugs and carpets, five-foot four-poster beds in sev-

This is the sort of place that gives self-catering in Britain a good name...

Standards are very high indeed, but there is nothing stuffy or formal here...

eral cases, show-house kitchens, the sort of bathrooms you would find in discreet, expensive Mayfair hotels. The whole place seems to reflect the care with which it is run, and there are lots of those little touches that mean so much, such as well chosen books and games, frozen (but home-cooked) dishes, maid service and baby sitting, and a welcome hamper.

We looked at most of the cottages (all but one named after famous race-courses) while they were being prepared for new guests. Each has its own character, as well as its own particular fans, and they **sleep from 2 to 8**.

The main communal gardens are lovely, and each cottage also has at least its own private terrace, while several have their own enclosed garden. All have TVs, DVD/video players and hi-fis. Linen and towels are included, and there is a choice of blankets or duvets. Direct dial phones. Games room. Children's play area. Shared use (at specific times) of a heated outdoor swimming pool and hard tennis court. **'Visit Britain' Five Stars**. Not suitable for pets. Changeover day is either Friday or Monday.

Cost: about £526 (for the smallest cottage out of season) to £4686 (for the biggest in high season). Their website is spectacular, and well worth a visit for its own sake. Telephone 01993 830415. Fax 831750. Mobile 07802 182092.

www.bruern.co.uk   email: enquiries@bruern.co.uk

'To do or not to do'

Some advice for self caterers...

Don't turn up with more people than you have actually booked for: this seems to annoy owners/agents more than orgies, murder and dogs being sick. And don't strip a car engine on the deep-pile carpet in the sitting room. (Somebody did, near Bristol: see Paragraph 1, opposite page).

Don't take white rabbits to your cottage when they say 'No pets', even if you are a conjuror. Somebody did in the Peak District, and he was! And even if they do take pets, don't turn up with three Alsatians when you have had enough trouble persuading a cottage-owner to accept a Pekinese.

Don't be ashamed to have a good lie-in when you fancy it. It is something one can never really do in an hotel. And do find something more interesting to put in the visitors' book than 'We had a lovely time'. Do try the owner's home-cooking (often pre-frozen meals) if available, and especially when you first arrive after a long journey.

Don't arrive before 3pm unless you want to embarrass the cleaner, or, even worse, surprise the dowager duchess who owns the cottages on her hands and knees in the kitchen.

Do take a few favourite ornaments and, especially, books; these work wonders if you don't easily feel at home in strange houses. A pair of favourite bookends is a handy thing to pack.

Do feel free to move the furniture around (though most owners actually hate this), but do replace it as you found it. But do own up to breakages. Unreported objects missing or broken can be infuriating.

Do take hot water bottles, and maybe even a portable heater. Remember the old adage, 'my house is cosy, yours is warm-*enough*, his is freezing'.

Don't forget that a lot of excellent rural properties are still accessible by rail and that most owners will meet you at a convenient station.

Do check that 'suitable for the disabled' means just that, and not simply that you will find a couple of wide doors and a low sink. Does the property conform to Royal Association for Disability standards?

Do note that Value Added Tax is included in all the prices we quote.

Don't bottle up complaints and problems. Tell owners or agents about your worries on the evening of your arrival, if possible.

'Do this...don't do that'

Some well-meant suggestions for owners and agents:

Do take a deposit against damage and dirt. We wish everyone featured in this guide would do so, but few do. Inconsiderate tenants will thus be reminded of their responsibilities. (We've never heard of potential customers saying 'We won't go there because they want a deposit'...)

Do decide whether pets are welcome or otherwise. There are owners who'll accept cats but not dogs, and vice versa, and a number who'll accept everything except caged birds. Leaving the question of pets open to negotiation can mean trying to run with the hare and hunt with the hounds. Owners and holidaymakers end up on edge, wondering if that cute Border terrier ('Honest, we'll only bring one small dog') will have more impact on the furniture than a pair of elderly Dobermans (-men?).

Do give detailed how-to-get-there instructions. Internet cartographic print-outs are useful, and a bit of local information is a bonus ('Turn left *before* The Eunuch and Mermaid, not after'...'There's a hand made sign by the old oak tree'...)

Do include a folder with information about local pubs, restaurants and shops. Not just menus from smart places and glossy brochures from commercial attractions, but 'the nitty gritty': which fish and chips shops serve fresh, not frozen fish, which pubs have rude landlords, where there's an old fashioned ironmonger's that will sell you six odd nails when you don't want that plastic pack of 100...

Don't say 'Short walk to sandy beach', if that beach is really quicksand, and the nearest one to play ball games on is a fifteen minute drive.

Do by all means clean cottages to within an inch of their lives, but do leave salt cellars and pepper pots with their contents intact. It's something few tenants think to bring, and their absence has ruined many a fish supper! Leaving dried herbs and spices, vinegar etc is better still.

Do let it be known in your brochure/fact sheet if any single beds are only 2 feet 6 ins wide or any 'double' beds are only four feet wide. And (it will improve bookings) consider buying five feet wide beds and even zip link singles that make six foot wide beds: they are hugely popular.

Do give guests control over the heating (and charge them accordingly). When a gale-force wind is blowing the sleet around, it is no consolation to be told when you enquire why the central heating does not appear to be working: 'Good Heavens, this is *June*!'

English Country Cottages*

As far as we are concerned English Country Cottages' annual brochure is completely compelling. Also, our reader responses from the USA and Canada show a greater awareness of 'ECC', as it is popularly known, than any other agency. It features cottages in both England and Wales, with locations that among much else take in picturesque villages and lonely clifftops. Big or small, smart or quaint, each property is described in the hefty 580-page brochure, which is helpfully grouped into ten colour-coded regional sections. Each of these starts with an introduction to the area and details of an interesting local event to help entice the potential holiday tenant.

For people looking for a large property, the brochure has a useful index of those accommodating ten or more people. Properties with swimming pools are also listed, separated into private and shared ones. So no one

'How will we find you?' asked visiting friends. They won't need a map! Ref CNN. Lighthouse Cottage is in Norfolk.

In a beautifully situated Dorset village, the mainly 18th century Old Post Office is Grade II listed. Refs DJY and DJZ.

should have any difficulty in finding their own special 'treasure', whether for a full holiday or short break.

In south Devon we've stayed at *Tuckenhay Mill*, near Totnes, which lies in a tranquil wooded setting beside Bow Creek, five miles from the sea at Dartmouth. Its buildings have been tastefully converted into 21 cottages and apartments (**sleeping from 2 to 10**), many with their own garden or patio. Everyone in them has access to two exotic indoor pools ('Roman' and 'Waterfall'), sauna, steam room, jacuzzi, snooker and badminton. Outdoors there's a third pool and also tennis and croquet. Ref FCK-HFU. *Danes Court*, a former country vicarage at Ravensbarrow, in Cumbria, has been cleverly divided into three delightful cottages, all **sleeping 4**. Within a large enclosed garden, they have woodland and fell walks straight from the door in this Area of Outstanding National Beauty. Lake Windermere is four miles away and Kendal eight. The nearby Grizedale Forest is ideal for walking or cycling, and has nature trails linking the numerous stone and wood sculptures scattered amongst its trees. Ref LQT-LSV.

When visiting North Wales we get a sense of being well away from the hustle and bustle of city life. It's a feeling that becomes even stronger if we cross the Menai Bridge on to Anglesey. One of English Country Cottages' twenty or so properties on the island is *West Lawn*, a spacious detached bungalow (**sleeping 7**), which has its own secure garden and direct access to Rhosneigr's vast sands. The beach, a popular venue for windsurfers, has safe swimming as well as canoeing and sand-yachting. Riding, golf and sailing are available nearby too, as well as Anglesey's castles, museums and nature reserves. Ref JAC.

One couple we know personally has such faith in English Country Cottages that they don't even bother to read the property descriptions. Instead they simply take it in turn to shut their eyes, open the brochure at random and put their finger on one. The first time either of them lands on one for just two people, they book it. 'We've ended up in all sorts of lovely places, and we've never been disappointed,' they say.

Their most recent stay was at *Apple Loft*, one of five cottages (**sleeping between 2 and 8**) at Woodend Farm, just outside Tewkesbury, in Gloucestershire. Imaginatively converted from listed barns, they enjoy the shared use of a heated outdoor swimming pool from mid-May to mid-September. There's also a banqueting barn on the farm where up to 22

Tuckenhay Mill, in South Devon, offers 21 properties to choose from. This is the shared outdoor pool. Ref FUB.

High House, at Dunster, Somerset, sleeps up to ten in great style and comfort. The main bedroom is amazing. Ref EKA.

people can dine together. This makes an ideal venue for celebrations and family get-togethers as a full catering service is available. Ref NPM.

Greenwood Grange Cottages, at Higher Bockhampton, in Dorset, are in the heart of the countryside where Thomas Hardy set his tales, just two miles from Dorchester (his 'Casterbridge'). Many of the 17 cottages have been converted from barns which his father built in 1849. **Sleeping 2 to 8**, furnished to four-star standard, they are in four acres of peaceful grounds with two all-weather tennis courts, badminton and croquet lawns and a children's play area. Indoor facilities include a 32ft x 18ft heated Roman-style pool, sauna, solarium, fitness room and games room. Ref DGY-DUC.

Most ECC properties are of course in the countryside or by the sea, but they have a few city ones too, including a handful in London. One is *Hazlitt Mews*, a cosy first-floor apartment **sleeping 2/4** in a gated mews in West Kensington. Converted from part of a former stable block, it's in easy walking distance of the stylish shops in Kensington High Street. Ref PZP. In Bath, *Eastwood Lodge* is a lovely detached 18th-century cottage with views over the city. Formerly a gardener's lodge, it **sleeps 3**. Ref EOF. And in York, *The Penthouse* at Westgate (**sleeping 4**) is a spacious duplex apartment with superb views of the Minster and river. Ref IJB.

Details from English Country Cottages, Stoney Bank, Earby, Barnoldswick BB94 0AA. Brochures: 0870 192 0391, bookings 0870 192 1066.

www.ecc2006.co.uk

Country Holidays*

'Quaint cottages, contemporary barn conversions, properties with pools, city centre pieds-à-terre: you'll find them all in this beautiful country of ours' say Country Holidays. And who are we to argue with that?

We have checked out a good number of their 4000-plus properties, spread across England, Scotland and Wales, and stayed in a few. Invariably we have found them tidy, clean and, essentially, good value.

Many are available for short breaks, costing from only £15 per person per night. A bonus for those who can get away during the week is that four midweek nights cost the same as three weekend nights.

Each property is inspected annually and graded to 'Visit Britain' standards and criteria. So making your choice is easy, from the 1-star 'Acceptable overall level of quality; adequate provision of furniture, fur-

Grade II listed Luntley Court, sleeping up to 15, is one of the finest houses in Herefordshire. Ref 13708.

Mainly 17th century Hillcrest is ideally located in the Lake District, with an especially fine drawing room. Ref 15734.

nishings and fittings' up to five stars for 'Exceptional overall level of quality; high levels of decor, fixtures and fittings, together with an excellent range of accessories and many personal touches'.

In addition some properties have a Gold Award. Totally separate from the Star gradings, these are awarded solely because holidaymakers have rated a particular property as 'excellent overall' in carefully monitored customer-satisfaction surveys.

Another very useful aspect of the Country Holidays operation is its Holiday Homefinder telephone service. Tell the adviser who answers what sort of property you want and they will make suggestions and check availability there and then.

If you fancy the idea of staying in a Five Star/Gold Award property, *Trelawn*, at Hayle, near St Ives in Cornwall could be just what you want. It's a spacious detached house **sleeping 13**, so is ideal for families or large parties wanting to holiday together. The long sandy beach of Hayle Towans, good for surfing or sandcastles, is within a mile and a shop and pub are only five minutes' walk away. Ref 15639.

Another large property is *Luntley Court* at Dilwyn, near Hereford, which **sleeps 15**. Dating from 1674, this Grade II half-timbered mansion is one of the county's most beautiful buildings, noted for its oak panelling, original oak staircases and large galleried dining-hall. The rural ten-acre estate is bordered by a small stream. 3 stars. Ref 13708.

Country Holidays also have a good choice for those at the other end of the scale who simply want a quiet retreat for two, or to escape alone – like a friend of ours who regularly seeks a little hideaway to work on her TV scripts. Her favourite is *North End Barn* (3 stars), a timber-clad converted barn (*sleeping 2*) accessed by a 300-yard track at Stelling Minnis, seven miles south of Canterbury and the Channel Tunnel. It has a double bedroom and a small enclosed garden, and is within easy reach of London, being only ten minutes from the M20. Ref 15645.

For families with lively children, *Whitmuir Hall*, near Selkirk in the Scottish Borders is ideal. (We have stayed) Originally an Edwardian manor house, its buildings have been converted into twenty comfortable cottages and apartments **sleeping 2 to 6**. The 32-acre grounds include an indoor heated pool, sauna, games room and graded mountain bike tracks. Ref 5308/15, 14034, 15785/7, 60814, SW30/1/2/7/8 & 40, SW 3701.

Oakfield is an exceptional Georgian property in the southern part of the Cotswolds. Sleeps up to 16. Ref 17421.

Werngochlyn Farm has an indoor pool, and there's even stabling for visiting horses. Sleeps from 2 to 6. Ref 6252/5.

In Scotland, *Nuide House* at Kingussie is a substantial stone house **sleeping 10/11** in an elevated position in the heart of the Cairngorms National Park. Surrounded by extensive lawns and looking on to glorious countryside, it makes an excellent base for all sorts of activities. Ref 19138.

Chickens, pigs, sheep, goats, geese, ducks and horses help keep visitors entertained on the ten-acre *Werngochlyn Farm* at Llantilio Pertholey, near Abergavenny, in south Wales. Riding is available too (with instruction if desired) and also stabling for those who want to bring their own horse – and there's an indoor swimming pool. Accommodation is in four interesting barn conversions, all 2-star, **sleeping from 2 to 6**. Ref 6252/5.

In North Wales, a three-quarter-mile private drive from the Conwy-Rowen road leads to three tastefully furnished 5-star/Gold Award cottages, created in 2002 from the ballroom attached to Coed Mawr Hall. They share a landscaped garden, but each has its own patio with extensive mountain views. Two **sleep 6** and one **sleeps 4**. Ref 16150/1/2.

Details from Country Holidays, Spring Mill, Earby, Barnoldswick, Lancashire BB94 0AA. Country Holidays, Spring Mill, Earby, Barnoldswick, Lancashire BB94 0AA. For bookings, telephone 0870 192 1040. Brochure line: 0870 607 8514.

For a Holiday Adviser, telephone 0870 192 1040. To look and book:

www.2006country-holidays.co.uk

Blakes Country Cottages*

With over 4000 properties on their books, Blakes are a major-player on the self-catering scene. Their 2006 brochure divides England, Scotland and Wales into 20 regions, and indexing is designed for example to make it easy for anyone looking for a large property, a property with a swimming pool or even city-based accommodation: it's sometimes forgotten that a cottage holiday doesn't have to be in the countryside.

In addition, each of the twenty sections starts with tips for days out, information about the area's cuisine and a useful 'If you only do one thing' suggestion, all provided by local property owners or Blakes' own regional managers. And the brochure also shows whether a property is available for short breaks and – if so – for how many nights and at what times of the year. These can cost from as little as *£15 per person per night.*

In the heart of 'Wordsworth Country', handsome Loughrigg (Ref B5983) sleeps 8.

One of the sumptuous bedrooms in Yeldersley Hall. Ref B4240/1/2.

Header bars against each property highlight important features such as those that accept pets and those which can be checked out in more detail by a 'virtual tour' on the Blakes website.

As before, every property has been quality assessed using the Visit Britain criteria. Five stars mean 'exceptional' while, at the other end of the scale, 1-star cottages suit those, perhaps on a tighter budget, who are happy with somewhere simpler but still want to be assured of cleanliness and comfort. Some properties have also been given a Gold Award because previous holidaymakers rated them as 'excellent overall'.

One of the 5-star category that we know well is a beautiful first-floor apartment (**sleeping 4**) in *Yeldersley Hall*. This splendidly restored Georgian country house stands in twelve acres of landscaped gardens and paddocks at Ashbourne in the Peak District. Stepping into the apartment, reached by a spiral staircase from the courtyard, you immediately feel absorbed into the grand country-house lifestyle. The rooms are exquisitely furnished, spacious and overlook the gardens. One bedroom, with a Victorian half-tester bed, is en-suite; the other has coronet-draped antique twin beds. In addition two smaller apartments, both **sleeping 2** and graded 4-star, are available in a former stable block – one on the ground floor, one upstairs. Ref B4240/1/2.

Among the properties given a Gold Award is *The Bakery* in the pretty and quintessentially English village of Clanfield, in the Cotswolds. Close to the village pond and lovingly restored, it thoroughly deserves its 4-star grading and makes a delightfully romantic hideaway (**sleeping 2**). One couple we know decided to maintain the building's original role by baking their own bread while staying there. 'We could almost sense the old bakers cheering us on,' they told us afterwards. 'The loaves tasted really special.' For days out, Oxford, Cheltenham, Stratford-upon-Avon and Blenheim Palace are all within an easy drive, or more energetic guests can set off along the Oxfordshire cycleway. Ref 17396.

Heyhoe, at Walcott, in Norfolk also has a Gold Award. This 2-star detached timber holiday bungalow (**sleeping 4**) stands at the top of the sea wall just above the sandy beach. Eighteen miles from Norwich, it is also well placed for visits to the Poppy Line Steam Railway at Sheringham and to Cromer, famous for its crabs. Ref AB38.

Further north, anyone who enjoys dreaming of trains but doesn't want their sleep disturbed by them would enjoy *The Station House* at Brompton by Sawdon, about six miles inland from Scarborough. The pic-

The Station House is a long-time favourite with readers of this guide. Ref NM1401 ff.

Meadow View is near the heart of ancient Hawkshead, Cumbria. Ref B5935.

turesque building, part of the former Scarborough-Pickering line, still has its original platform, now a neat terrace with picnic tables above the lawn and garden. Inside are five south-facing apartments, all 3-star (**sleeping from 2 to 3/5**). Ref NM1401/4, NM15, 14426 and 17265.

In Cornwall, on the unspoilt Lizard peninsula, five apartments and a cottage are available at *Coverack Headland*, a handsome Edwardian building on Chynalls Point that was formerly a hotel. In large gardens and grounds with wonderful sea views, with its own sandy beach and tennis court, it's an idyllic place to stay. A path leads down to the old fishing village of Coverack and the location is ideal for walkers, bird-watching and seeing rare wild flowers. Mullion's 18-hole golf course is nine miles away. **Sleeping 2 or 4**, the accommodation is graded 3-star, apart from a 4-star apartment that sleeps 6. Ref CT68, B5020/1, B5894, 90137 and B6265.

Part of a watermill, *Mill of Auldallan* is a beautiful 4-star cottage (**sleeping 4 to 6**) beside a stream and waterfall in an acre of grounds at Kirriemuir, in Scotland. Fifteen miles north of Dundee, it lies amid the beautiful Angus Glens, a haven for walking, golf, fishing and birdwatching. Other pleasures available while one is staying there range from satellite TV to a natural spring water supply. Ref 17521.

Details from Blakes, Spring Mill, Earby, Lancashire BB94 0AA. To book, telephone 0870 192 1022.

www.blakes-cottages06.co.uk

Welcome Cottages*

Over the years a noticeable number of our readers have found all sorts of good reasons for booking with this agency. Pet owners do particularly well as pets go free (most properties accept them). Furthermore guests taking a dog between October 1st and April 1st get £25 off the cost of their holiday.

Fuel, power and bedlinen are usually included in the price and, except during school holidays and half-term, couples get 20% off at many properties from October to May (even if they areaccompanied by a small child up to the age of 5).

We know Welcome turn down around two-thirds of the cottages offered to them. Yet their properties, which are spread all over England, Scotland, Wales and Ireland, plus a handful in France, remain notably affordable.

Conventional, perhaps, but comfy, and handy for the Peak District. Ref W40593.

We're fond of the Isle of Arran, and this roomy house is a useful base. Ref W8162.

Welcome also have the advantage of having their own clear and simple colour-coded grading system. This ranges from Comfortable ('everything you'll need for an enjoyable break' via Good Quality ('relaxed and pleasurable ambience') up to Lovely ('more like a home than holiday accommodation') and – at the top – Beautiful ('furniture, furnishings and decor chosen with the express purpose of creating a beautiful holiday home').

In the 'Beautiful' category is a superb barn conversion at Somersal Herbert, in the Peak District, which **sleeps 14/18**. Each of the seven bedrooms is en-suite, and one has wheelchair access. It's on a 150-acre farm and shares a floodlit all-weather tennis court and stabling with four other large properties (**sleeping from 11 to 20**). These are a farmhouse and three barn conversions – two graded 'Lovely' and two 'Good quality'. Catering can be provided if required. The Alton Towers theme park is just seven miles away. Ref W40521.

Also graded 'Beautiful' is a 16th-century Grade II listed farmhouse **sleeping 8** at Cwm Main, near Bala, in north Wales. It's on a 100-acre farm where pheasants and ducks are reared. Lovingly restored, the building's original character is now combined with modern facilities throughout. There's a wealth of huge beams and oak wall panels, two inglenook fireplaces and an impressive wooden spiral staircase. All four bedrooms have uninterrupted views and one is en-suite, with a four-poster. Chester, Llangollen and Snowdonia are all within easy reach, and the beautiful Bala Lake (watersports, leisure centre and steam railway) is eight miles away. Ref W2399.

Guests staying in a spacious 1950s bungalow (**sleeping 6**) in the hills above St Austell in Cornwall are spoilt for choice as to how to spend their time on holiday – swim in its pool, relax in its colourful two-acre garden, go on the beach, play golf at Carlyon Bay, or visit the tall ships harbour of Charlestown, the Eden Centre, Lanhydrock House or the enchanting Lost Gardens of Heligan. All are within three miles of the property, which is rated 'Good quality'. Ref W8022.

A considerable number of thatched properties are on Welcome's books, including a charming old cottage with a pretty garden in the village of Ludham, thirteen miles from Norwich and seven from the sea. The wildlife and windmills of the Norfolk Broads can be explored in day cruises from nearby Potter Heigham and Wroxham. Other attractions in the area range from bird and seal colonies to stately homes and steam railways. Graded 'Good Quality', the property **sleeps 2**. Ref W3645.

What a location! Right by Bamburgh Castle, in Northumberland. Ref W40467.

This spacious barn conversion is superbly situated in the Lake District. Ref W8760.

Eight miles north of Banbury, an open-plan studio apartment **sleeping 2** is available in the beautiful conservation village of Wormleighton. Graded 'Good quality', it's on the first floor of a modern building, above a games room. Quiet and secluded, the property has stunning views of the surrounding countryside beyond the Oxford Canal, a mile away. Ref W8300.

An artist friend of ours reckons that north-west Scotland is unbeatable for seascapes and mountains to paint, but its attraction for us is the scope for bird-watching and walking. At Laide, near Gairloch, a 'Beautiful' property (**sleeping 6**) is only yards from the shore and a small sandy beach. Built in the 1700s but lovingly renovated, it has original wood panelling in several rooms, a four-poster style box bed and even its own sauna. Ref W143.

One of our most memorable holiday experiences ever was waking up in the Ring of Kerry in south-west Ireland. We had arrived after dark the previous evening. When we looked out of the bedroom window, the scenery was breathtaking. A modern bungalow (**sleeping 5**) near the village of Glenbeigh makes a good base for enjoying the area, as well as having beautiful mountain views. Graded 'Good quality', it is close to Caragh Lake, noted for its fishing, boating and hill walking, and only four miles from sandy beaches. Ref W31129.

For availability and bookings, contact Welcome Cottages, Spring Mill, Earby, Barnoldswick, Lancashire BB94 0AA. Telephone (brochures) 0870 192 0809; 0870 336 2825 (bookings).

www.welcomecottages.com

Ireland

It's probably Ireland's age-old charms that make this one of the most appealing destinations in Europe, though its booming economy, the hassle-free adoption of the euro, the easy airline links and a young and forward-looking population make it much more than a twee museum piece. We remember strolling through Killarney after dark, listening to traditional music being played in what seemed like every other pub, the sun setting over the bleakly beautiful coast of Connemara, and finding 'b and b' en route between cottage visits in a faded but still grand Georgian mansion. We think of the deep green of the countryside bordering the coast of North Antrim, of the mystical quality of the early-morning light over Lake Killarney, and of the wild blue mountains of Connemara. We are not fishermen, but remember seeing anglers' eyes light up over a candlelit dinner in romantic Delphi Lodge, among the hills on the Galway-Connemara border, when describing their day's battles with salmon. We hear from readers who enjoy 'two-centre' Irish holidays. One family, regular users of the book but first-time visitors to Ireland, stayed first in a thatched cottage at Kinvara, nicely poised for explorations of Galway and the Connemara National Park, and then had a week within the Ring of Kerry.

Note: when telephoning Ireland you should dial your own international prefix (eg 00) then 353 followed by the area code (eg 51, not 051), then the number. Within Ireland, however, you should prefix the area code with '0', eg 051. Note also: a small number of contact phone numbers in this section are UK ones.

Waterford Co Waterford: map 10/588
Woodstown House Country Estate

This is very stylish indeed, either attached to or within a short stroll across lawns from a fine country house in 35 acres of wooded parkland. (The latter properties are part of a sympathetically converted arrangement on three sides of a paved stable courtyard.)

We have stayed in *Number One, Dower House*, attached to the main house, and much appreciated the spacious sitting room off which there is a well appointed kitchen, a smart bathroom and a twin bedroom. A second, double, bedroom, with antique furniture, is down a corridor. There are elegant paintings, a big open fire (all the properties here have open fires *and* central heating, a patio, deep armchairs and sofas, and most have ensuite bedrooms). One house is 'wheelchair friendly'.

An attractive feature is the double hard-core tennis court contained within the confines of the original walled vegetable garden. This stands close to the *Courtyard Cottages*, which are neat and appointed in four-star hotel style with colour co-ordinated fabrics. All are two storeyed with not large but comfortable bedrooms, and all have direct dial phones, TV, open fires, microwave, dishwasher, washing-machine/dryer, and more.

Details available from Woodstown House Holiday Cottages, Woodstown, Co Waterford. Telephone 353 51 382611.

www.accommodation.ie/waterford/self-catering.htm

Killarney, Muckross
Killarney Lakeland Cottages

Killarney is the most popular tourist destination in Ireland, and usually buzzes with life. Brian O'Shea's landscaped, well-spaced, villagey arrangement of white-painted traditional-style cottages is in a quiet parkland setting seemingly miles from the town centre (though actually quite close). In two separate groups, each is surrounded by trees, a well planned distance from its neighbours. Every one has a peat

Traditional-style cottages in a very sought-after location...

fire. The number each property sleeps varies **from 4 to 7**. There is access to two hard tennis courts, a good games room, bikes, and in each cottage TV with multi-channel reception and direct dial telephone. Not suitable for dogs. Cost: about €200 to €1000. Details/colour leaflet from Brian O'Shea, Killarney Lakeland Cottages, Muckross, Killarney, Co Kerry. Telephone (outside Ireland) – your international code plus 353 64-31538, fax 353 64 34113.

www.killarney.cottages.com
email:info@killarneycottages.com

Ballina   map 10/563   Colour section B, Page 4
'The Holiday House'

Used occasionally by the Suffolk-based owners, this neat, modern, semi-detached house, just 45 minutes from Knock airport, makes a *notably inexpensive* base from which to explore much of the glorious west of Ireland. A town property but quietly situated on a little-used road that runs alongside the River Moy, it **sleeps 5** in a double, a twin and a single. It is well carpeted through-

It's a pleasant fifteen minute walk into lively Ballina alongside the River Moy.

out, and as well as central heating there are *two* open fires – a great bonus for those so-enjoyable spring and autumn breaks. There is easy access to the river and walks along it (a fifteen minute walk to the town centre) and it's just eight miles from the fabulous sandy beach at Enniscrone. Fishermen will love this: among much else there's salmon fishing on the Moy from February to September. Cable TV, small 'music centre'; large storage shed for housing fishing gear. Not suitable for pets, and there are no special facilities for babies or small children. *Costs are very reasonable*. Details from Mr and Mrs Burke, 57 Head Lane, Great Cornard, Suffolk CO10 0JS. Telephone 01787 311626.

email: m.burke@amserve.com

The South of Ireland
Country Cottages in Ireland*

The Irish Country Cottages brochure is one of the two or three most spectacular we know – and we see some beauties! Rich in colour, it cleverly conveys the essence of what makes this beautiful and historic country so popular among travellers.

About 250 elite properties are featured, divided into five regional sections. A lyrical description at the start of each section helps you decide which would suit you best, whether for a holiday or short break.

Many are in the westerly counties that are so memorable for their spectacular cliffs, springy turf carpeted by wild flowers, technicolour sunsets and vast golden sands. Less well-known regions are featured too, from the rocky headlands of Donegal and the hills of Wicklow to the fabulous beaches of the south.

For a large group the *Old Monastery,* at Cahersiveen, in Co Kerry, **sleeps 16**. Built in 1840 as a merchant's house, it was used by the Christian Brothers for over 100 years. Now fully renovated, but retaining old wood floors and stained-glass windows, it provides spacious and comfortable accommodation. Ancient castles, prehistoric burial grounds, standing

The Old Stone Barn, four miles from famous Skibbereen, combines traditional features with 'mod cons'. Ref YAA0.

Park Hotel Cottage, at Kenmare, has spectacular views and is adjacent to Kenmare's golf course. Ref ZIR.

stones and medieval crosses all wait to be explored nearby. It's also a good area for walking, cycling, climbing, watersports, riding, tennis, golf and every sort of angling from wild salmon to shark fishing. Ref ZO3.

There are striking sea views from *Strand Cottage* at Caherdaniel, also in Co Kerry, where floor-to-ceiling windows help guests enjoy them to the full. **Sleeping 6**, it is just five minutes' walk from a sandy beach. The beamed living room has an open fire. Ref YYN.

In Co Cork, several properties are available around Kinsale, which has some of the best seafood restaurants in Europe. A short drive west of it, *Harbour Court* (**sleeping 4**) is part of an attractive row of neat individual houses near Courtmacsherry. It is on one of the prettiest parts of the coast and has lovely sea views from its small garden. Ref YSB.

Details from English Country Cottages, Stoney Bank, Earby, Barnoldswick BB94 0AA. Brochures: 0870 241 7925; bookings 0870 192 1044.

www.icc2006.co.uk

Connemara
Connemara Coastal Cottages*

Knowing how fond we are of Ireland, an American reader wrote to us to say how useful this guide had been in finding properties there of character, and described the locations she had loved most. We quickly realised that in most cases she meant Connemara: 'romantic sunsets over the water, endless beaches, marvellous seafood'. During our most recent Irish visit we spent time with a small, personally run agency we'd heard excellent reports of, and saw a good handful of the properties on their books. For example, two extremely comfortable cottages, pride and joy of the owners, overlooking the water at Cleggan village, and a thickly carpeted cottage (called *Doon House*) attached to the charming owners' house: rural views but, of course, not far from the sea, and a light, bright cottage conversion almost surrounded by water, with fabulous sea and mountain views, called *Ross Point*.

Among the properties we've had very good reader reports of is a modern bungalow in the centre of Cleggan, overlooking Cleggan Bay. **Sleeping 5**, it's just a short walk to the pub, a restaurant and shops. Don't miss a trip on the twice-daily ferry to Inishbofin. Ref 099.

Pets welcome in most. Details of these and other beauties in an excellent loose-leaf brochure from Julia Awcock, Connemara Coastal Cottages, Cloon, Cleggan, Co Galway. Telephone 353 95 44307.

www.cc-cottages.com email: cccottages@eircom.net

'Some like it modern'. And most will appreciate the panoramic views.

The light, bright main bedroom (double aspect) is an attractive feature.

'In brief'

Grayling, at New Quay, on the coast of Co Clare, is one of our west coast favourites. **Sleeping 7**, the neat, tidy, detached white bungalow is a charmer – one of our best finds on a recent visit to the west of Ireland. Though it's very much a holiday home (**map 10/585**), it's of permanent-home standard. It is just five minutes' walk from a safe and little-used beach. Prices are very reasonable.

Details from Noel and Susan Callaghan, Ballytarsna House, Kilshanny, Co Clare. Telephone 353 65 7071055. Fax 7071717.

Bantry
Whiddy Holiday Homes

On board a small passenger ferry you cross beautiful Bantry Bay, fringed by green hills, to Whiddy Island. Ten minutes on the water, a world away. Depending on which of the three most appealing cottages is yours (usefully, their owners live on the island in summer), you might be driven a couple of miles along a bumpy track, past a freshwater lake

An outstanding quartet of spacious and comfortable cottages, with Shannon airport just an hour away.

with a rowing boat freely available to cottage guests, past hedges of scarlet fuchsia that are a summer trademark of the west of Ireland. All three are utterly quiet, all with sea views 'to die for'. Rowing on the lake, exploring every nook and cranny of the island by bike or on foot, climbing to the eerily beautiful, deserted Napoleonic fort, would fill a happy week or, in good weather, a fortnight of serious unwinding. Fishing and sailing can be arranged without difficulty. Linen and towels included. TV. Dogs welcome.

Booking details available from Greta Steenssens, Roddam 83-2880, Bornem, Belgium. Telephone: 00 32 3 889 61 11. Fax: 00 32 3 889 41 71.

email: walco.pottery@skynet.be

Ballyvaughan
Village and Country Holiday Homes

Colour section B, Page 4

map 10/573

At the heart of the 'character' village of Ballyvaughan, surrounded by the limestone hills of the Burren and on the shores of Galway Bay, these are some of the best self catering properties we know in Ireland. The enclave of well appointed cottages (each with its own garden, quiet and private) is located in a courtyard. The owners also have two apartments, bright, deceptively spacious, within a few yards of the courtyard cottages. All properties have quality fabrics

A rather pleasant decision for visitors to make: in the village or by the sea? Both sets of properties are quite outstanding.

and furnishings, easy-on-the-eye colours, well equipped kitchens. The country houses **sleep 6**, the village properties **4 or 6** (there are two styles, plus the new apartments). TV. Linen. Cost: about €50 to €550. Details from George Quinn, Frances Street, Kilrush, Co Clare. Telephone (outside Ireland) – your international code plus 353 65 90 51977. Fax 65 90 52370.

www.ballyvaughan-cottages.com
email: sales@ballyvaughan-cottages.com

Delphi, North Connemara
Boathouse Cottages/Wren's Cottage

We've stayed here twice, and would recommend it wholeheartedly as a place to unwind in beautiful surroundings. We love it, and would rate it among our favourite half dozen places in this guide.

Delphi is in a beautiful mountain setting, reminiscent of a idealised classical 18th century landscape: great looming hills, misty valleys, rushing rivers, dark woods.

Serious fishermen probably know Delphi, and walkers should consider it. It is a wildlife paradise, known for wild flowers, otters, peregrine falcons, pine martens and badgers. You will find it where western Mayo nudges into Connemara, a few miles north of Leenane.

Almost adjacent to elegant Delphi Lodge, the original four cottages (Boathouses) are very cosy, quite unpretentious, with deep chairs and sofas, lots of antique pine, big open fires (making them a most appealing choice for an autumn or winter break), traditional stone floors with rugs downstairs and carpets upstairs. These four are most attractively bordered by shrubs and old stone walls; two **sleep 4** in two twins, the other two **just 2** in a double bed.

During our most recent visit we saw a newly restored cottage, Wren's. On the approach road to Delphi Lodge, overlooking the lough in the Delphi Valley, it has a greater degree of privacy, and has been furnished and equipped to a very high standard. It **sleeps 6** in three bedrooms.

Boathouse Cottages are full of character and charm. We have met people in residence, and they have all loved their cottage and its romantic location.

Wren's Cottage, newly renovated, is the pride and joy of the Delphi ownership. Idyllically, it overlooks the lough, and is bound to attract a following of its own.

Linen and towels are included. All cottages have telephone. Wrens has Sky TV, Boathouses have DVD players. Not suitable for very young children or dogs. Cost: about £500 to £1200. Details: Delphi Lodge, Leenane, Co Galway (postal district). Telephone 353 95 42222. Fax 42296.

Note: Excellent bed and breakfast accommodation is available in Delphi Lodge, and cottage guests may sometimes have candlelit dinners here, usually on a communal basis: such a bonus for lone travellers or people from overseas wanting to make new friends.

www.delphilodge.ie
email: stay@delphilodge.ie

285

Ireland Directory*

Without wanting to be too sentimental about it, visiting Ireland can be an uplifting experience: we like it more and more each time we go. And all the irresistibly beautiful counties that regularly draw visitors and, increasingly, self-caterers are well represented in this exceptional selection of around 500 cottages. Each one is graded 'Beautiful', 'Lovely', 'Good Quality' or 'Comfortable'.

For exploring the south, or to go fishing or horse-riding, a comfy cottage near the village of Conna, 25 miles north-east of Cork, makes an excellent base. It's close to the River Blackwater, known for its trout and salmon. Graded 'Lovely' it **sleeps 6** and has the advantage of wonderful views of Conna Castle and Bride Valley. Ref W5048.

On the west coast, the impressive coastline of the Ring of Kerry makes it one of the loveliest drives we know. A tastefully furnished bungalow (graded 'Lovely' and **sleeping 4**) is well placed for exploring it, just three miles from the lively village of Glenbeigh. In a peaceful scenic valley, soothed by the sounds of a nearby mountain stream, it is close to some of Ireland's highest mountains, yet there is a sandy beach only four miles away. Golf, horse-riding and fishing are available nearby. Ref W31130.

A former farmhouse, refurbished to **sleep 5**, also in the 'Lovely' category, on a mature one-acre site in the countryside near the village of Woodford, is well placed for those who want an active outdoor holiday. Golf, riding and pitch and putt are within easy reach; a nearby oak forest nature reserve and the Sliabh Aughty mountains provide scope for walkers; and the Shannon (six miles away) and Lough Derg cater for those who enjoy river pursuits like boating, water sports and fishing. Ref W31233..

A rare example of a spacious new house near lovely Dingle, Co Kerry. Ref W5653.

Older, but modernised, sleeping 6, this is quietly situated in Galway. Ref W31154.

Down in Ireland's south-east corner, its sunniest part, a detached modern family-friendly house in the coastal village of Duncannon enjoys sea views from the sitting room and front garden. A golden sandy beach, harbour and historic fort help keep everyone entertained and local attractions include the Hook Lighthouse and Tintern Abbey. Graded 'Good Quality', it **sleeps 5**. Ref W6796.

For availability and bookings, contact Welcome Cottages, Spring Mill, Earby, Barnoldswick, Lancashire BB94 0AA. Telephone (brochures) 0870 192 0940, 0870 336 2825 (bookings).

www.irelanddirectory.co.uk

Bansha
Lismacue Coach House

In a superb location for touring (the Glen of Aherlow, Tipperary, historic Rock of Cashel, and beautiful Cahir beyond it, Killarney, the Dingle Peninsula, Co Clare and more besides), here is a skilfully converted two storeyed coach house conversion attached to the owners' grand listed Georgian mansion, where very up-market 'bed and breakfast' is avail-able. **Sleeping up to 7** in one double, two twins and a single, it has the

You'll be in the annexe, but comfortably so: you'll not be 'a poor relation'...

advantage of a wood-burning stove and even a sauna. The single bedroom, conveniently for older or less able people, is on the ground floor. There is a covered garage.

Among comments from people who have stayed. Adam and Lucille Pauley, of Cambridge, Massachusetts, write 'a wonderful week in peaceful and scenic surroundings', and Joelle Wyser-Pratte, Palm Beach, Florida, says 'We are already looking forward to returning'. And William Koyle of Orangeville, Ontario, said 'To look out on the Galtee Mountains from Lismacue has to be one of the best views in Ireland'.

Not suitable for dogs. Linen and towels included. Details from Kate Nicholson, Lismacue House, Bansha, Co Tipperary. Telephone (62) 54106.

www.lismacue.com

Reports of the-death-of-the-brochure are greatly exaggerated. For all the convenience of the internet, nothing quite beats a good quality glossy brochure to leaf through in the comfort of your armchair...

Dunmore East
Harbour Village

We've had many encouraging reports about The Harbour Village, an 'excellent' development of four types of property (one type of house, with four bedrooms, **sleeps 8**, a second type of house, with three bedrooms, **sleeps 6/7**, the lodges **sleep 5/6**, the cottages **5**) on a five acre wooded site, in the heart of the quiet and attractive village of Dunmore East, with its thatched cottages, its harbour and its beach.

A Mr Bidston, of South Wirral, said 'it is a gorgeous area – one of the prettiest parts of Ireland'. The reception service is good and properties are furnished to a high standard and well equipped with, for example, washing machine/tumble dryer, microwave, dishwasher in lodges and houses. Master bedrooms have en-suite bathrooms. Cots and highchairs available on request. Gas fired central heating; also open peat/log fires.

Satellite TV. Bedlinen is included; towels can be rented. Most credit cards accepted. Dogs welcome by prior arrangement only. There are three championship golf courses within fifteen minutes' drive.

Details and a brochure from The Harbour Village, Dunmore East, Co Waterford, Ireland. Telephone (51) 383373; fax (51) 383696.

www.waterford-dunmore.com

In a very attractive part of Ireland, easy to get to, these substantial properties stand in five wooded acres...

Each property – there are four different types – has a character of its own. But all are of a consistently high standard...

The larger agencies featured in this section carry advice about travelling to your holiday cottage in Ireland, and can usually make bookings for you and offer advantageous ferry rates. There are nine ferry routes from England and Wales, with that from Swansea to Cork being the best known for cutting out a lot of the driving for people based in the southern half of England.

Our favourite way to travel to Ireland is to fly and then hire a car. Flights can be cheap (even if Ryanair, the obvious choice for most people, seem to be turning discomfort into a fine art) and car hire is very competitive...

Pastures new...

Readers of *The Good Holiday Cottage Guide* who stay in self catering properties abroad as well as in the UK were among the first to encourage us to widen our horizons, as did the noticeable number of UK cottage owners who *also* have properties to let in France, Italy, Spain and beyond. For the moment we've confined ourselves to France, Italy and Spain, with a nod to Scandinavia, Cyprus and, in Germany, Bavaria. We'd be pleased to get more reader reports and recommendations of self catering properties in those and other countries...

One of our best recent discoveries were self-catering cottages on the Baltic islands of Bornholm (Denmark) Goland and Öland (Sweden) Åland (Finland) and Saaremaa (Estonia), which provide the same high standard of accommodation as those on the Scandinavian mainland.

The islands are memorable for their delightful scenery and fine bathing beaches. Except for Öland, which is connected to the Swedish mainland by a four and a half mile bridge across the sea, a holiday on the islands involves a ferry trip through one or more of the beautiful Baltic archipelagoes – a delight in itself...

More details from Scandinavian Holidays, 8 Boreham Holt, Elstree, Hertfordshire WD63QF. Telephone + 44 (0) 20 8953 8874.

email: info@scandinavianholidays.freeserve.co.uk

Denmark

Island of Fyn
Hindemae Mill

On the picturesque island of Fyn, this converted 200 year old mill, with an attached miller's cottage, provides comfortable and centrally heated accommodation for **up to 12 people** in six bedrooms, with three bathrooms. This year sees a super *It's a lovely introduction to Denmark...* new dining room/kitchen, washing machine and dryer. There is a cosy sitting-room off the dining/kitchen and a huge octagonal family room with squishy sofas and open fire. This room covers the entire ground floor area of the old mill. There's a games room. satellite TV, video games and small office with internet access. There is large garden surrounded by beechwoods, with lovely country walks. Two adult bikes are provided. Fyn has many sandy beaches, the nearest about five miles away. Access: via Copenhagen (90 minutes by motorway and road bridge) and Esbjerg (ferry from Harwich) also 90 minutes via motorway. By air from Stansted to Esbjerg. Cost: about £600-£1600 per week. Contact Victoria Sutherland: telephone 01855 811207. Fax 811338.

email victoria@torrenglencoe.com

Vence (Alpes Maritimes)
Villa Paradise

Recently constructed Villa Paradis (**sleeping 8**) has all the advantages of new fittings, uncluttered space and yet still with charm and character from the unusual furnishings, some from Morocco and many of them hand-cast pieces of unique wrought-iron. The bathrooms and showers are all tiled with hand-made tiles, and the wardrobe doors are North African hardwood, specially imported.

The house is on the outskirts of Vence, where there is a medieval walled 'cité', and, close by, other perched medieval villages such as St Paul de Vence and Tourrettes sur Loup. Sightseeing in the area reveals spectacular views along the Gorge du Loup. Within easy access to Nice, Cannes and the whole of the Côte d'Azur, the villa provides comfortable living, peaceful surroundings, unrestricted views and good accessibility.

Largely open plan on the main living area, there is a spacious salon with full width patio windows opening on to the pool terrace. French satellite TV, CD and DVD. New kitchen with maplewood and stainless steel fitments. On the same level are two bedrooms, one twin with shower room/WC en suite and a master double with views to the swimming pool. The first floor has two further bedrooms.

email: azuruk@boltblue.com

Vence/Grasse (Alpes Maritimes)
Villa La Salamandre

This villa (**sleeping 5 to 6**) is situated just outside Vence and ten minutes from St. Paul de Vence, with its famous restaurants, *jeu-de-boules* court and art galleries. It has a splendid view over the hills towards the mountains. The villa lies in a calm residential area and has its own private grounds with automatic gates and large private pool. The garden is immaculately maintained, and has a most beautiful rose garden.

The villa itself is on two levels. The main entrance door gives access to a hall with access via French doors to the living room on one side and the hall to the bedrooms on the other side. The living room has a sitting area with comfortable sofas and chairs around an open fire place with a TV with satellite and music system. On the other side is a large wooden dining table that seats six people with access to the covered veranda and garden. The kitchen is exceptionally well equipped.

On the same floor there are two bedrooms, each with a double bed. They share a bathroom There is also a study that can be made in another bedroom with single bed. On the upper floor there is another bedroom with a large comfortable single bed and nice views over the garden.

email: azuruk@boltblue.com

Hérault
Magalas

A fast, easy drive from Montpellier airport (80 km, much of it via motorway) brought us early on an October evening to the – for us! – unexpectedly ancient and absolutely charming hilltop village of Magalas. The origin of the name in the old local dialect is said to mean 'a pile of old stones'. But don't let that put you off: it's a delight, full of narrow, spiralling alleyways with sudden views of distant wooded hills and vineyards. It's especially deserted, silent and full of atmosphere after dark, with cats in the shadows and, if you're lucky, shafts of moon-light illuminating the half-hidden courtyards of 500-year old houses.

We knew our villa was in a small, new, residential development, but had assumed it was some way out of Magalas. In fact, it's just a very pleas-ant five minute walk from the house up towards the market square, close to which there are restaurants, bars, small shops, two bakers and a pâtisserie.

Though it's essentially 'practical' and designed for easy living and maintenance, it has certain very appealing features. For example, we

Easy, uncomplicated modern living on the edge of a fascinating ancient village...

...with a really inviting sitting room that at any time is 'so nice to come home to'.

liked the good sized sunken sitting room, more than adequate for the eight people the house sleeps. The October weather was very mild, but we eyed the (safely enclosed) fireplace with satisfaction, remembering the pleasures of other houses in rural France and the scent and instant heat from stores of olive wood: get it when you can. We also liked the first floor twin room (extra privacy, and an ensuite shower to boot), a bath and shower in the main bathroom boules court at the rear, the swimming pool, by all accounts a serious sun-trap in summer. There's a spacious paved terrace with an awning. There's good touring from Magalas to, for example, the coast at Sète and Mèze, to the attractive town of Pezenas and the lower reaches of the Massif Central.

Cost: approximately £180 to £950. Further details from Tim and Jo Gray, Kembroke Hall, Bucklesham, near Ipswich, Suffolk IP10 0BU. Telephone 01394 448309.

email: tdgray@msn.com

Nérac
Moncaut

We stayed here recently, and were delighted by it. It's a 'Maison de Maître', which sits well back from a moderately busy road and is in fact hardly disturbed by traffic. It's a real family house, which is used from time to time by the owners themselves. and therefore functions properly! There's plenty of heating,

A fine, spacious, comfortable house of character, with an excellent pool and very well tended gardens.

instant hot water (two actual baths), a well equipped kitchen, a big out-door pool – with shade – kept in tip-top condition by the efficient care-taker. He also looks after the six acres of grounds, within which there are separate sitting-out areas: we loved our *al fresco* meals on the shaded paved terrace outside the kitchen. The main, first floor bedrooms are spacious, even elegant. And the hall and the staircase are a joy. **Sleeps 10**. Ref DL22.

Though the surrounding scenery is not dramatic, it's pleasant, and we were deeply impressed by the virtually traffic-free minor roads. The country town of Nérac, fifteen minutes away by car, is a charmer, with lots of cafes and restaurants, plus boat trips and a preserved-railway jaunt. Details from Dominique's Villas: see Page 301.

Dinan (Brittany)
Moulin de Lorgeril

A reader from Suffolk who joined a family party staying in this 'really comfortable, really romantic' con-verted mill thinks 'cottage guide' readers will love it. The surround-ings are peaceful – mainly wood-land, fields and lakes. The main part of the house has a large sitting room cum diner with a stone fireplace and french windows, two bedrooms, a

Loads of character, and easily accessible from the UK while still 'very French'...

well equipped kitchen and separate stairs from the kitchen to that boon in wet weather – a games room. But the real attraction is the tower. On three levels, it has a sitting room with woodburner and french windows and stairs that lead to a double bedroom. From that there are further stairs to a fourth double bedroom with a sunken bath.

Cost: about £600 to £800. Details from Mrs P Lintern:

Telephone/fax 01749 342760.

Dordogne
Souillac Country Club

Readers quickly caught on to this much-admired enclave of properties, which we have featured for the last two years. Nestling in the hilly forests of the picturesque Dordogne valley, near the river/town of Souillac, this young-family-orientated club is a favourite all-year-round holiday destination for British and French alike. We know it well, and have found the staff, both English and French, most welcoming, with good suggestions of what to do and see in the region.

The scenery in this part of France is breathtaking, with deep gorges and castles perched on cliff-tops. It's most impressive in October, when mists rise up from the deep river valleys and the trees take on a multitude of colours. This is the land of foie gras and truffles, of honey and umpteen varieties of bread and mushrooms: British first-time visitors to the weekly market in nearby Sarlat are amazed by the local produce.

The detached houses (all privately owned and managed by the club when the individual owners are not in residence) have views of the eighteen-hole golf course and surrounding countryside. They are all spacious and fully equipped, with large patios, where in peaceful surroundings we enjoyed watching the sunset over a glass of wine.

The houses are in small well separated hamlets, with private swimming pools, and residents can also use the many central amenities, including two swimming pools, tennis, boules, golf, and in July and August the children can join in the fun at the Kids' Club. The excellent restaurant provides a welcome change from cooking at home, and the bar is a friendly meeting place after a game of golf or tennis. The whole region

The detached houses have views of the golf course and the surrounding country.

In a peaceful situation, 'they are all spacious and fully equipped'...

is a popular holiday destination. Apart from that beautiful scenery, medieval market towns and the numerous restaurants for which Périgord is famous, there's extra-good walking and horse-riding.

More information is available on 00 33 (0) 565 27 5600.

www.souillaccountryclub.com
email:rentals@souillac-countryclub.com

France — countrywide
Large Holiday Houses in France*

From the people behind the hugely successful *Large Holiday Houses in Scotland* (see Page 104), this is a really impressive collection of chateaux, villas and farmhouses. It's something larger groups should definitely check out. The range of accommodation increases by the month, and so far there are around 40 properties of differing sizes, with a good geographical spread.

The *Chateau de la Garinie* is a good example of the sort of place on offer. This 14th-century chateau in a six-acre estate in the beautiful Aveyron region has fairy-tale turrets and towers and, inside, the stone spiral staircases, glittering chandeliers and sumptuous antique furnishings. A large private pool sets off an enchanting property. **Sleeps 10**.

Chateau Cazenac: if it looks good from the outside, you should see the interior!

Chateau de la Garinie: it's also amazing, but typical of what's on offer...

Just as (almost literally) fabulous, *Chateau de Bruneval*, in the Dordogne, is one of the prettiest in the region, which is saying something. The family home of a specialist restorer of historic and classical buildings, it is completely private and secure, and is especially memorable when floodlit at night. **Sleeps 10** in great style.

Similarly, while the pointed towers and ivy-clad stonework of *Chateau Cazenac* are undeniably magnificent, it is the expertly realised interiors that will really take your breath away. The plush bedrooms with fantastic canopied beds, beautiful antiques and original textiles have to be seen to be believed. Also worth a mention is the warm and inviting kitchen, with its huge old fireplace. **Sleeps 15**.

For more of this, plus some simpler properties, visit the website:

www.LHHFrance.com

email: LHH@LHHFrance.com

Telephone 01381 610496

[All properties are inspected by, and carry the seal of approval of, Large Holiday Houses Ltd, but are booked direct with the owners.]

France – countrywide
The France Directory*

A couple from Suffolk, who for several years have holidayed in English cottages we feature in this guide, have twice followed up France Directory properties we have featured. They enjoyed breaks in Brittany and the Loire. Namely, in a detached cottage **sleeping up to 8**, close to the medieval Breton town of Dinan (Ref W11541) and in the ground-floor apartment of a part-14th century chateau, **sleeping 6**, near Châteaubriant (Ref W11942).

In a pretty valley at Wimille, near Boulogne, we found an exceptional property **sleeping 12**. Most recently the building housed a tavern but painted lettering on the outside wall advertises its initial incarnation as a mill. Reflecting the property's long history, authentic original features abound, with exposed wooden beams throughout and an open fireplace in the sitting room. The grounds are enchanting, containing a beautiful little waterfall just metres from the house and a huge pond, ideal for fishing. Ref W10769.

At Vérargues, a short distance from the elegant and ancient town of Nîmes – one of those southerly cities easily and cheaply accessible via Ryanair – and within comfortable travelling distance (about 25km) of the fascinating semi-wild country of the Carmargue, there is a detached house in three hectares of forest with private use of a swimming pool and a toddlers' pool. Excellent sandy beaches are also easily accessible.

Some impressive, sensibly priced properties, a skilful geographical spread.

Included in the portfolio are places we'll see for ourselves during 2006.

There's an open fire, a barbecue, a poolside bar, a large-screen TV, a dishwasher, a restaurant nearby and other good things. Ref W11146.

In Normandy is a single-storey house **sleeping 2 to 4** and close to historic Coutances. The property's lounge and bedroom open on to a private pool, and a sandy beach is a short walk away. Nearby Coutainville has tennis, horse riding and an 18-hole golf course. Ref W10429.

France Directory (Welcome Cottages), Spring Bank Mill, Earby, Barnoldswick, Lancashire BB94 0AA. Telephone (bookings) 0870 336 2232; brochures 0870 608 4754. See also Page 278.

www.francedirectory.co.uk

France – countrywide
'Chez Nous'

'Getting to know France is always a pleasure. Whether you are a regular visitor or still getting acquainted, she will always take your breathaway, delight you and refresh your soul' says the editor of Chez Nous which offers over 4000 privately-owned properties spread across the country.

Since Chez Nous first appeared in this guide three years ago, we have heard from several UK cottage owners and readers who have booked with them. You simply contact the owners direct. This not only saves money but also enables you to pick their brains and get a real feel of the place. Then, having made your booking, you can use the Chez Nous travel service to arrange your journey. Channel crossings start from only £109 return.

The colourful 508-page brochure begins each section with an interesting description of the region and a temperature chart. There is also a useful map on every double-page showing the relevant area. And the Chez Nous website has extra photos of most properties.

Among properties within an hour's drive of the Channel Tunnel and ferries at Calais is a pretty six-bedroom country house (**sleeping 11**) at Doudeauville. South-facing with a wealth of exposed beams, it overlooks a garden with its own stream, a source of the River Course. An unspoilt beach is half-an-hour away and Crecy, Agincourt and Le Touquet only a little further. Ref 12161.

The range of possibilities is amazing. You deal, exclusively, direct with owners...   *...which brings cost advantages as well as the chance to 'get chapter and verse'.*

Another recommended property is *La Boursaie*, a former cider farmstead south-east of Caen, in Normandy. Five 16th-century half-timbered cottages have been lovingly restored to provide accommodation **sleeping between 2 and 7**. The 100-acre estate includes magical woodland, wildflower meadows and apple orchards, with extensive views over a beautiful valley. And the D-Day beaches and museums are all within easy reach. Ref 4485.

On the Côte d'Azur, three miles south of Cannes, a large villa (**sleeping 8**) occupies one of the most exquisite locations on the French Riviera, above the Bay of Theoule. The building matches the setting, as it has a terrace and pool, all the rooms have panoramic sea views and there are three bathrooms to serve the four double bedrooms. The accommodation is spread over three floors, but carrying luggage or shopping is no problem, as there is an eight-person internal lift. This is probably a first for us! Ref 11182.

The Chez Nous range also extends to Corsica where we have enjoyed several very happy holidays. Still largely untouched by mass tourism despite its many sandy beaches, the island has some superb scenery and there is a breathtaking train ride through the mountains.

Among several interesting properties there, *A Pinarella* is a massively-beamed stone house at Monticello, about 15 miles up the coast from Calvi, in the north-west part of the island. **Sleeping 10**, it enjoys magnificent sea and mountain views, and the grounds include a pool, covered terraces for outdoor living and over an acre of walled garden with oak, pine, citrus, olive, aromatic shrubs and sculptural boulders. There's a village shop within ten minutes' walk, and the sea is under three miles away. Ref 15505.

In the Hautes-Pyrenées, at Gerde, a small village near the elegant little spa town of Bagneres de Bigorre, there are stunning mountain views from the balcony of a neatly restored house **sleeping 8**. One of the three bedrooms has four single beds – an arrangement which would delight many children. Ref 2028.

A large private south-facing terrace with stunning views of the Mediterranean, harbour and mountains is one of the delights of a sump-

All the honeypot regions and towns of France are represented...

... but it's nice to use the brochure for a 'virtual tour' of out-of-the-way places.

tuous new first-floor air-conditioned apartment in the fishing community of Port Vendre, a few miles north of the border with Spain. Only five minutes walk from the beach, it **sleeps 2/6**. Just a mile north beyond a headland, another charming port, Collioure, has been a magnet for artists since Matisse settled there in 1905. Ref 10307.

Brochure request number: 0870 607 5395

www.cheznous.com   email: enquiries@cheznous.com

Chez Nous travel service: 0870 192 1045

France
Quality Villas

For the last 20 years Quality Villas has been the leading UK specialist in French Villas rentals, and today it boasts an unrivalled portfolio of the finest collection of luxury villas, farmhouses and chateaux with private pools in coastal and rural France. All their sumptuously comfortable villas are hand picked and personally visited to ensure that only the highest standards are featured in this outstanding portfolio. This year is of course one for them to celebrate (twenty years in business), and they are proud of their position as being still a small, family owned business.

Beginning on the Côte D'Azur, there is a remarkable amount of choice. For example, the two astonishing 1860-built moorish villas called *Les Symphonies*, which can be rented as a whole to accommodate 31 people or separately for smaller groups. They are in individual lush gardens along the sea front between Cannes and St Tropez. Inside each, high

Les Mesanges, on the Riviera, is the stuff of family dreams: it sleeps ten. Ref PR304.

It's real, and you can actually stay here! It's the Château de la Rivière.

ceilings and grand windows create a wonderfully light, airy ambience. These stunning villas also offer jacuzzi, haman, solarium, private port and boathouse, with splendid sea views! **Sleep 10 to 31**. Ref PR 632, PR 631, PR 630.

Perched above the sea at Cap d'Ail, near Monaco, you will find the aptly named *Villa Elegant*. This classically furnished and sumptuously decorated villa in the *Belle Epoque* style is the last word in refinement, its marbled terraces with gleaming white pillars and balustrades overlooking the sea in a beautiful landscaped private garden. It is perfectly located to enjoy either complete seclusion and relaxation or the glamour and glitz of the Riviera. **Sleeps 8 to 9**. Ref PR 286.

Built in 1840, *Domaine des Anges* is arranged around a wonderful garden courtyard amid vineyards and fields of wheat and sunflowers, also a short drive from the dramatic mountains and canyons of the Cavernes. It has been carefully renovated by local craftsmen and decorated in a comfortable, traditional style to ensure it retains its original splendour. **Sleeps 18**. Ref PR 557.

Sleeping 12, *Les Fleurs D'Eté*, under an hour from Nîmes and Avignon, and just half an hour from the famous, Roman Pont du Gard, is notable for its unusual blend of modern and antique furniture. On the edge of the small village of Vallabrix, this visitor-friendly house is in extensive-grounds, safely enclosed and with a lawn for children to play on. Ref PR 531.

Le Vieux Four, once the old bakehouse, is in the 13th century fortified village of Montjoi, next to the village church. It has been cleverly restored to a particularly comfortable villa that retains original 'character' features such as the original bread oven. You can book Le Vieux Four in three different versions, **sleeping 6, 4 or 2**. Ref PR 555, PR 554, PR 556.

For an out of this world experience, consider a stay at *Château de la Rivière*, which due to its dominant position on a hill has stunning views of the Dordogne river. You can enjoy sports and strolling around local markets, but also cosy winter evenings by the huge stone fireplace: this stunning château is available all year. **Sleeps 12**. Ref PR 596.

This is one of Les Symphonies, dating from 1860, each in lush gardens.

Villa Elegant, near Monte Carlo, is amazing even in Quality Villas terms.

To best enjoy Biarritz, a very smart, upmarket town with fine shops and a casino, an aquarium and sea museum, and only a short drive from Spain, one could stay in a traditional Basque villa called *Brise Marine*. This beautiful property has a truly stunning location on the Cliffside overlooking the beach and the Atlantic ocean at Bidart, a delightful coastal town between Biarritz and St. Jean de Luz. It has been fully renovated to provide the utmost in modern living. Each room enjoys a magnificent sea view. **Sleeps 4 to 5**. Ref PR 569.

Further details and a copy of the quite superb brochure, perhaps the best you will find in a very competitive field, from Quality Villas, 46 Lower Kings Road, Berkhamsted, Hertfordshire HP4 2AB.

Telephone: 01442 870055

www. quality-villas.co.uk   email: info@quality-villas.co.uk

Note: Quality Villas now has separate portfolios of properties throughout Italy and Morocco.

See their respective websites:

www.qualityvillasitaly.co.uk

or www.qualityvillasmorocco.co.uk

Haut-Jura
Les Rousses Farmhouse Apartment

Roger Jones's Welsh properties (see Pages 164-166) have featured in this guide for many years, and he has brought the same energy and concern for his guests' comfort to his properties in mainland France and in Corsica – see below. Les Rousses, very close to the Swiss border, is compact but comfortable, at one end of a farmhouse now divided into five apartments. Charmingly, there is access via a wooden staircase to a garden area,

We see some fabulous locations in this job, but this really is something. And it's pretty nice in summer too!

and there are uninterrupted panoramic views across a wide valley to Les Rousses Lake, in a location known for its Alpine wild flowers. There's lots to do, including walking nature trails into Switzerland, golf (two 18-hole courses within sight of the apartment), exceptional ski-ing, fishing and sailing on the lake. And Les Rousses itself has restaurants, bars and shops. **Sleeps up to 4** in a double and a twin. Linen/towels not provided. TV/video. Bathroom with shower only. Cost: from about £195. Accessible by train and taxi, or about eight hours' drive from Calais. Details from Roger Jones, Flat B, The Old Granary, Tremadog, Gwynedd LL49 9RH. Telephone (01766) 513555.

Corsica
Calvi – La Reginella

If a picture's worth a thousand words, we can relax for a moment: the view on the right is what you see from the balcony of this town centre apartment, which is on the third (top) floor of a building overlooking the bay and mountains beyond. Calvi is a chic place, with shops, restaurants and boutiques in

Just add a glass of local wine, sit back and relax: this is the view from the balcony.

walking distance of the apartment. Most appealingly, you can pick up a train here on a narrow-gauge railway that links coastal villages and beaches, with connections to Ajaccio, in the south, and you are just ten minutes' walk from the ferry point from where there are connections to Marseilles, Nice, Toulon and the Italian sea-ports.

Specifically, the apartment **sleeps 4** in a double and a twin, with a combined sitting room/diner and a balcony with a table and chairs, and those marvellous views. TV/video. Bathroom with bath and shower. Very well equipped kitchen: oven, microwave, fridge, freezer, washing machine, dishwasher. Cost: from about £195. Further details from Roger Jones, Flat B, The Old Granary, Tremadog, Gwynedd LL49 9RH. Telephone (01766) 513555.

France – countrywide
Dominique's Villas

Dominique's Villas is a medium-sized agency created 20 years ago by Dominique Wells. The agency is notable for its stylish and beautifully illustrated brochure that's highly professional but also has some charming personal touches. Its great strengths in the Dordogne, Provence and the Côte d'Azur – so much loved by Brits – help towards its popularity.

During a 2004 visit to a number of houses in the Lot et Garonne region, we were much taken with two that are somewhat different in character and location. First, we saw an isolated, utterly quiet, rambling, many roomed and beautifully restored house being spruced up, as it happened, for the owners due down for their own holiday. Gorgeous! **Sleeps 10**. Ref DL72. Then, in a busier location, in an extraordinary situation beside an ancient bridge and a dramatic weir, we visited an exceptional property that use to be a well known rural restaurant and hotel (there's a huge 'professional' kitchen'). **Sleeps – yes – 13.** Ref DL34.

We also stayed in a handsome traditional house (that is, not a conversion) **sleeping 10**. See Page 292.

During a 2004 visit we were much taken with 'Property No DL72', near Nérac.

Open the wine and get the cook-books out! This is the kitchen in 'Property No NR21'.

We remember a house in a hamlet on a hill that overlooks the Lot Valley – a comparatively little-known part of the country. There's a pleasant pool and 'country' furniture, along with antiques. Ref DL60. **Sleeps 6**. Just across the Channel, within easy reach of the ferry ports at Caen and Le Havre, we came across a gem. It's a beautifully renovated 18th-century farmhouse (**sleeping 9/10**) with idyllic views. Sandy beaches at Deauville and Trouville are within fifteen minutes' drive. Ref NR21. And, handy for the Cherbourg ferries, there's an enchanting 17th-century chateau (**sleeping 15**) in the village of Yvetôt-Bocage, just outside Valognes. It's perfect for children, as the grounds include a child-size manor house, a games room, swings and sandpit. A heated pool is a recent addition. Ref NR18.

Details/brochure from Dominique's Villas, The Plough Brewery, 516 Wandsworth Road. London SW8 3JX. Telephone 020 7738 8772.

www.dominiquesvillasco.uk
email: dominique@www.dominiquesvillas.co.uk

France – countrywide
Country Cottages in France

With over 1200 of the finest cottages, villas and farmhouses throughout France, each selected for its own special character and charm, French Country Cottages aims to meet everyone's holiday requirements.

Typically it is the rustic farmhouses in the Loire Valley and 'last word' villas on the Côte d'Azur that one notices first in a remarkable brochure that bursts with colour. Each property gets a detailed write-up and is illustrated with uniformly excellent photos. Plenty of local information highlighting nearby beaches, towns and attractions is included with each entry. Also, the brochure is helpfully split into thirteen regional sections, each prefaced with a short description of the area.

French Country Cottages also has an excellent website, which allows for hassle-free online browsing. You can use it to view additional photos and information, find a property on a map, check availability and even make your booking online, all at your own pace. It also helps you find properties with swimming pools or that accept pets.

For its situation alone, *Le Cortal* is unmissable. Perched on a Pyreneean mountainside at a height of a 1000 feet, in the peaceful 12th-century village of Nohedes, near Prades, it is surrounded by spectacular scenery. 'It was absolutely incredible to wake up to that view every day. I wish we could have stayed longer,' said a Mr Williams of Colchester. The apart-

Le Pressoir is a most interesting conversion in the 'private and silent' grounds of a chateau. Surrounding the property itself are well kept lawns, a dovecote and a lake...

ment, **sleeping up to 4**, is part of an old dry-stone house which was originally a sheep barn. It has its own private terrace and a pool (shared with the owners), with a shallow section ideal for young children. The coast, which curves down towards Spain in an almost continuous strip of sand, is about 40 miles away. Ref F66107.

In a peaceful corner of Normandy, *La Londe* is a carefully renovated old stone cottage (**sleeping 4**) which cleverly combines French rural character with modern comforts. South-facing in the village of La Bazoque, it has a terraced garden overlooking a wooded valley and stream. For days out, Bayeux, with its famous tapestry and museums, is nine miles away, and the D-day beaches are only a little further. It's also handily-placed for the ferry port of Caen. Ref F14172.

Chinon is a lovely one-bedroom apartment (**sleeping 2/3**) in the Loire Valley, named after the historic town nearby. It's on the upper two floors in a group of ecclesiastical buildings dating from the 15th century. Great care has been taken to preserve the authentic atmosphere, with old beams and an open fireplace. Outside, there is a private terrace and shared courtyard garden with swimming pool. Ref F37121.

Although the Dordogne is first and foremost a river, the area has some of the most enchanting rural architecture in France. *La Pèch* is a modern but attractive house (**sleeping 10**) built in the traditional style with steep tiled roof, beamed ceilings, extensive stonework and tiled floors. It stands on a wooded hillside high above the river at the village of Badefols, near Bergerac, and enjoys panoramic views of the surrounding countryside. The garden includes a good-size swimming pool with feature waterfall and summer kitchen/barbecue. Sailing, windsurfing and tennis are all available at the international watersports centre at Tremolat, a short drive away. Ref F24204.

In the Vendée, a region where we have had several sun-blessed holidays, there are five top quality properties (**sleeping between 2 and 8/10**) in the grounds of the beautiful *Château du Breuil*, near La Roche-sur-Yon. They have been cleverly created by the owners from the estate's old hunting lodge, stables and forge. Each has its own terrace or garden, but guests also have access to the château's grounds, which include gardens, woodland, swimming pool and 18-hole golf course. Ref 85137.

Chinon is a first-floor apartment in what was a 15th century ecclesiastical enclave.

Les Cerisiers, Charente Maritime (not featured) is a beauty. Sleeps 8. Ref F17154.

Le Pressoir, a beautifully converted cider mill in the grounds of a private château, lies in the lush countryside of Picardy so is well-placed for >sampling and buying champagne straight from its makers. The building's original ancient wooden beams remain, set off by tasteful decor and modern home comforts. The château's tranquil grounds feature well-tended lawns, a lake and a stone dovecote. **Sleeps 4**. Ref F 80103.

For a brochure etc by post: French Country Cottages, Stoney Bank, >Earby, Barnoldswick BB94 0AA.

Booking 0870 192 1148; brochure request 0870 608 3791.

www.French-country-cottages2006.co.uk

Tuscany
Tuscan Holidays

This agency is run by the people behind Heart of the Lakes/Cottage Life, the much-admired Cumbrian organisation which has featured in every edition of the Good Holiday Cottage Guide since it first appeared in 1983.

Tuscany is a region of outstanding beauty and a treasure trove of history and culture. The superb landscape embraces vineyards, olive groves and medieval villages, while a visit to the ancient cities of Florence, Pisa, Lucca and Siena is an essential part of any holiday. Altogether Tuscan Holidays offer over 120 villas in prime locations, each hand-picked. A good number are either in, or on the fringes of Chianti, perhaps the region's most beautiful area.

There are two apartments in the beautiful Casa Leopoldo, 20 miles from Pisa.

Part of La Sughera: a very flexible arrangement of apartments, a super pool.

Among places readers have enthused about are a beautiful 18th century manor house called *Palazzo Rosardi*. **Sleeping up to 12**, it has fabulous panoramic views and a super swimming pool. Ref 490. Also, *La Villetta*, **sleeping 6**, near Castelfiorentino. They epecially loved the blissful peace and quiet. Ref 270.

Among those we ourselves have seen is *Casa Fabia*, at Palaia, a delightfully restored old farmhouse on a hillside which has lovely views and plenty of scenic walks all around. It's on a 20-acre farm estate covered with vineyards and olives, so few guests leave without purchasing some of the owner's wine and olive oil to bring home. With two bedrooms (**sleeping 4**), it's not huge but has lots in its favour, like the pretty sitting-room, a convivial dining room/kitchen, a most inviting sunny terrace and a good size garden with fruit trees. Ref 240.

Down a quiet lane, though less hidden away than Casa Fabia, the lovingly restored 19th-century *Podere Le Murelle* cottage (**sleeping 2**) is on the outskirts of Palaia. Very comfortably furnished, it has superb views of the surrounding hills. Altogether it is a perfect romantic retreat as the sole bedroom is particularly pretty, with its king-size double bed – ideal for honeymooners! Unusually the owners, who occasionally live next door, are happy to prepare a 'traditional Tuscan dinner' for guests. You can also buy the estate wine, olive oil and honey from them. Ref 140.

A simpler property, **sleeping 2 'plus 2'**, is *Casa Leopoldo* at Perignano, in the hills about 20 miles from Pisa. It's a spacious apartment with high beamed ceilings and terracotta floors in an old farmhouse. A comfortable double sofa bed and huge Tuscan fireplace occupy one end, with a fully fitted dining/kitchen area through a high archway at the other end. A pretty archway leads to the double bedroom, which has an iron bed, and a door to the garden. Ref 150. Another one-bedroomed property is also located at Casa Leopoldo. Ref 151.

We met two Australian families travelling together and staying at *San Angiola*, a big restored farmhouse (**sleeping 12/14**) near Terricciola. We arrived on a baking afternoon to find almost all of them soaking up the sun at the pleasant 15-metre long pool. Indoors in the cool interior of the rambling house, we admired spacious high-ceilinged rooms and very comfortable furniture of the old fashioned kind, especially several grand

Le Ginestruzze is one of the most-loved properties in this company's collection.

La Murelle is on the outskirts of the most attractive small town of Palaia.

extra-large beds. There are six en-suite bedrooms, including one on the ground floor, and a seventh sleeping area (with its own shower room) on a galleried landing behind a screen. Ref 440.

Uphill from there, we discovered one of Tuscan Holidays' most popular properties, *La Sughera*. Converted from two old farmhouses on an estate famed for its wines, it contains five apartments. Three of the apartments most usefully **sleep 6 'plus'** and two **sleep 4 'plus'**. The rambling nature of the buildings and their thick walls make each one nicely private and self-contained. Ref 90-94.

Another property (**sleeping 10**) that has many fans is *Le Ginestruzze,* at Montespertoli, just 18 miles from Florence and 20 from San Gimignano. The large private swimming pool in the olive grove is always very well maintained. Guests also love the spacious old Tuscan kitchen, which has access to a terrace for eating outdoors. There are beamed ceilings, cool terracotta floors and, particularly in the bedrooms, some lovely old country furniture. Wine and eggs are available. Ref 100.

Details and a top-class brochure that gives admirably full details of every property is available from Tuscan Holidays, Fisherbeck Mill, Old Lake Road, Ambleside, Cumbria LA22 0DH. Telephone 015394 31120.

www.tuscanholidays.co.uk

Southern Italy, Sicily, Sardinia
Long Travel

Fellow travel writers speak and write in glowing terms about this small family business, known for its friendly service, and about the vast local knowledge and attention to detail that helps clients get much more out of their holiday than is often the case.

As specialists in the south of Italy, Sicily and Sardinia, the company features a selection of characterful hotels, 'masserie' (fortified farmhouses), castles and palaces up to five stars, 'agritourist estates' and self-catering accommodation that includes a unique range of 'trulli houses'(conical shaped stone buildings), cottages, farms and apartments. The company can tailor-make holidays to include flights and car hire or accommodation-only. Each property is visited yearly. Many self-catering apartments are on working farms or country estates, where they produce their own food and wine. Others are close to the coast or characterful towns and villages, and most are in the more undiscovered and unspoilt areas.

Top left. In Sardinia, this delightful detached house is in a peaceful spot surrounded by olive groves, near the historic town of Alghero and the sea. Sleeps 2 to 4. Cost is from £595 per week, including car hire with air-conditioning.

Top right: in Puglia, this spacious 'trullo' in the Itria Valley was renovated to a high standard, using traditional materials. A 15 minute drive from super beaches. Sleeps up to 6. From £660 per week, inc car hire with air-conditioning.

Above right. There are wonderful apartments in this castle in the heart of the Monti Madonie National Park. Sleeps 2. Costs are from £645 per week per apartment, including car hire with air-conditioning. Note: Long Travel can also arrange flights.

* Regions covered are Puglia, Calabria, Basilicata and the Pollino National Park, Campania and the Cilento National Park, Naples, Sorrento and the Amalfi Coast, Abruzzo, Sicily and the Aeolian Islands, 01694 722367/722193. **www.long-travel.co.uk**

Italy
Sunvil

Knowing our readers, we are not surprised they've responded to previous features about 'Sunvil Discovery', a company that arranges 'unpackaged holidays'. With 34 years' experience in a number of European countries, Sunvil has a wide range of holidays for the independently minded, with destinations slightly off the beaten track. Cottages, villas and apartments in Portugal, Greece, Cyprus and Madeira are also available, many of them all year round.

In Italy, for example, the lure of the medieval university town of Perugia is a strong one for many travellers. The smaller towns of Assisi, Gubbio, Todi, Spoleto and Orvieto are also worth exploring, and the surrounding Umbrian countryside of olive groves, vineyards and woods shelters lovingly restored farmhouses converted into cottages and apartments.

Not far away is one such farm; *Le Due Torri*, between Spello and Assisi, has two separate stone-built country houses, offering both self-catering apartments and 'b and b'. The main house, *Torre Quadrano*, has a

The Ospitalita Rurale and La Fattoria apartments are in tiny Montemelino...

The main house at Le Due Torri is proud of its 900-year-old watchtower!

medieval watchtower about 900 years old, a restaurant serving local cuisine, a swimming pool, and an apartment, *Il Fienile* (**sleeping 2 'plus 2'**), with a double bedroom, bathroom with shower, living room with double sofa bed and corner kitchenette. The second house, *Ponte Pazienza*, about 2km away, has two studios, a three one-bedroom apartments and a swimming pool. Both houses are beautifully furnished with fine antique pieces. Although the farm is mainly devoted to cattle breeding, it does produce its own virgin olive oil, honey and wine. Another farm property, *Ospitalita Rurale* and *La Fattoria di Montemelino*, in the ancient hill-top hamlet of Montemelino, 14km from Perugia, has been restored and converted to provide several apartments of various sizes. The old buildings, their wooden beamed ceilings, thick stone walls and open fireplaces have all been retained, and all apartments have outdoor furniture, well-equipped kitchens and enjoy access to the swimming pool.

Sunvil Discovery, Sunvil House, Upper Square, Old Isleworth, Middlesex TW7 7BJ. Telephone 020 8758 4722; Fax 020 8568 8330. **www.sunvil.co.uk   email: discovery@sunvil.co.uk**

Italy: nationwide
Interhome

More than half a million clients annually, a good percentage of them regulars, surely 'can't be wrong'. Interhome offers over 20,000 properties, each carefully graded from one to five stars.

We've been especially impressed by the company's superb new 'Prestige' brochure, featuring nothing but the very best four and five star holiday accommodation in grand castles and chateaux, fabulous houses, luxurious villas and top notch apartments, all in sought-after European locations (plus Florida). We haven't the space to do more than scratch the surface, so here's just a flavour of what the company offers in Italy.

Villa Renate is 'both grand and intimate': it sleeps just six people in great style'.

The splendid entrance hall at Villa Il Borro is indicative of the place's style.

Villa Il Borro, for example, is an amazing property. About 20 miles from Florence, built in 1850 and renovated in 2000, it has retained its character while matching 21st century expectations. There's a superb entrance hall and main staircase, a sleek indoor swimming pool, an open fire in the drawing room and even a lift. **Sleeps 20**. Ref I5493/860.

Another 19th century property, sympathetically renovated a few years ago, is *Villa Renate*, in Lombardy. This exquisite house is both grand and intimate (it **sleeps just 6 people**), with fine antiques as well as 21st century comforts. It is quietly situated, in a cul de sac. Ref I2325/100.

For a taste of grand country-house living without the demands of taking on a complete house, the elegant *Villa Maria*, also in Lombardy, contains an apartment, on two levels, **for 4** (there are five other apartments in the house). Ref I2412/800B.

All the Interhome properties are available for viewing on a CD rom, available from Interhome Limited, 383 Richmond Road, Twickenham TW1 2EF. Write to that address for brochures for any of Interhome's destinations (eg Austria, Switzerland, France, Germany, Portugal, Spain, Poland, Croatia) or, particularly, their new brochures: 'Solemar' and (as featured above!) 'Prestige', 'featuring top quality Four and Five star properties and City Apartments'.

Telephone 020 8891 1294. Fax 020 8891 5331.

www.interhome.co.uk   email: info@interhome.co.uk

Tuscany: Casentino
Canova

This spacious farmhouse, recommended by a previous printer of this book, is close to the pretty town of Casentino. In spacious grounds among peaceful wooded and olive tree clad hillsides, and with its own secluded swimming pool, it **sleeps up to 12** – either as a whole or via two separate apartments **sleeping 4 and 8** people respectively. Specifically, there are two separate living rooms, six bedrooms and two bathrooms.

Though very pretty, this part of Tuscany, remarkable for its mountain scenery, is comparatively little known. But there is easy access to all the Tuscan 'favourites' such as Florence and Siena.

Details from Rebecca Rawlings. Telephone 020-7482 1663.

email: rebeccarawlings@hotmail.com

Tuscany/Umbria
Vintage Travel

Vintage Travel's Italian portfolio is concentrated in two popular regions, with access too to some famous places.

In Tuscany and Umbria there are about a dozen properties. In the former, Vintage Travel have taken the extraordinary medieval hilltop town of San Gimignano as their focal point. In the latter, most properties are within easy access of Perugia. We know these parts of Italy quite well, and 'Vintage' have the essence of them: almost without exception each property fits prettily into its surroundings, and panoramic views from the properties themselves are quite common.

As noted on other pages, the company's quite outstandingly good brochure is more like a coffee table book than a conventional brochure: quite inspiring. Though there is one modern house (25km from Perugia) that **can sleep up to 22**, most properties tend to be rustic and family-sized rather than palatial. Several have swimming pools – but this is the sort of villa/cottage collection in which the pool serves the property rather than the other way round. Altogether, very impressive.

Further details and a superb are brochure available from Vintage Spain Ltd, Milkmaid House, Willingham, Cambridge CB4 5JB. Telephone 01954 261431. Fax 260819.

www.vintagetravel.co.uk
email: holidays@vintagetravel.co.uk

Tuscany: Versilia
Il Castoro

Readers have recommended this, a rare chance for people who want to be in Tuscany to have a base by the sea. *Il Castoro* is situated on a small development just outside the village of Torre-del-Lago. It is one of the most appealing seaside resorts along the coast of Versilia – not a sleepy hideaway, but a lively resort likely to appeal most to youngish people. And if the occasionally frenetic atmosphere gets you down you can always escape into the hills or take a trip to easily accessible Florence, Lucca, San Gimignano and Siena.

The house **sleeps up to 7** in three double bedrooms and there is shared access for all residents on this complex to a swimming pool and tennis courts. (Music lovers should note that Torre-del-Lago is the place where Puccini wrote all his operas, which are performed every summer in an open air theatre.)

Cost: £350 to £700. Details from Mr N Castoro. Telephone 07979 528955. For a brochure: fax 020 8458 1394.

Tuscany: Posara
Watermill

Somewhat off the beaten track, only just outside the walled medieval town of Fivizzano in the district of Lunigiana, this privately owned watermill (it really is picture postcard stuff) stands beside the River Rosaro, in the small village of Posara. It's almost too good to be true: in a peaceful wooded valley

Five separate apartments in a very sympathetic conversion of this old mill.

with a background of rolling hills and mountain peaks, it has the big advantage of being within easy access of the sea – don't forget that inland Tuscany can get very hot in high summer – and the principal tourist attractions of this much loved region.

Specifically there are five self-contained apartments within the mill and it's possible to rent more than one at a time, so a group of **up to 16** can take the whole place.

There are secluded gardens extending for about a quarter of a mile beyond the millstream and around the mill there are grapes and vegetables for the use of guests. Add to this sunny terraces and millstone tables under the vines for eating outside.

Please note: during May and September there are painting courses based here. Further details of those or simply the accommodation from Bill Breckon or Lois Love. Telephone/fax 01466 751111.

Costa Blanca/Javea

It will be interesting to see whether our increasingly hot and dry summers will have any effect on the British love of 'the Costas', which is mainly driven by the weather. It has been reported that 60% of people in the UK would like to live all or part of the year abroad, and something like 50% of that number said they would choose to be on Spain's Costa Brava or Costa Blanca.

'Cottage guide' readers Eileen Robinson and Sally Martin have recommended a number of properties in this inescapably popular 'honeypot'. Not a place to get away from it all but as a colleague put it 'quite a good place to start getting to know holiday-Spain'.

1. Villa Alicia

Just five minutes' drive from Javea – shops, restaurants, discos and fine, sandy beaches – this is detached, comfortable and quietly situated among orange groves and its own well cared for gardens. There is a small but private swimming pool, a sitting room with satellite TV, a separate dining area and a very smart kitchen. **Sleeps 7**. Cost: £400 to £750.

Details from Mr Thomas McConkey. Telephone 0034 965 79 59 70.
email: tjmcconkey@yahoo.com

2. Villa Torre Wombata

This elegant stylish and extremely comfortable villa has been described as having the best view on the whole of the south coast. Though it looks

Villa Torre Wombata has been said to have the best view on the south coast...

...and they've said some pretty nice things about the interior too!

huge, it does in fact only **sleep 6**, so it has the advantage of a degree of intimacy as well. South facing, with several terraces, a large floodlit swimming pool, a solar heated jacuzzi and sauna (all with the view of fishing port, the marina, Javea bay and mountains beyond), it has been furnished with great care and is, not surprisingly, unavailable to children under 12. Cost: about £625 to £1250.

Details from Liane Webster. Telephone 01273 833072.

Among other property recommendations that have come our way are:

*Casa Tranquila and Casa Barranca (Javea)

Both in the same ownership, these excellent properties have a big following among Brits wanting to be close to this popular resort but with a good degree of privacy as well. The former is in spacious gardens in very peaceful surroundings, just 1km from Javea. **Sleeping up to 7** in a double and two twins, it has a particularly charming and shaded good sized swimming pool. The latter is most impressive, **sleeping up to 11** in three doubles and two twins with a particularly appealing sitting room with satellite TV, a dining room just made for convivial get-togethers and a 'last word' kitchen.

Cost: (Casa Tranquila) £400 to £1050: Casa Barranca £600 to £2400. Details from Brian or Angela Liddy. Telephone 0115 989 9118.

*Casa Gisela (Jesus Pobre/Javea)

This is superbly well situated in the foothills of the Montgo mountains among pinewoods, vineyards and almond groves. Just ten minutes' walk from the famous but still very attractive classically Spanish village of Jesus Pobre, it is also just 8km from Javea. **Sleeping up to 10** in two doubles and three twins (and, note, three bathrooms), it has a pool side patio and terraces. Babysitting possible by arrangement; satellite TV; barbecue. Cost about £435 to £1150.

Details from Sheelagh Massey. Telephone 01904 468777.

*Villa Babar/Casa Felix (Benitachell)

Here are two absolute charmers, the first in a quiet new development, with fabulous views and with the advantage for wheelchair users of being all on one level. There's a south facing terrace and a private pool (which the master bedroom gives straight on to). **Sleeps 4**. Details from 01346 515262. The latter also has great views, and the advantage of a feature open fireplace. **Sleeps 4**. Details from 0034 96 6493074.

Casa Barranca sleeps up to eleven. There are manicured gardens and memorable views...

Casa Gisela is just ten minutes' walk from Jesus Pobre, but it's private too. It sleeps up to ten people...

Andalucia
Spain at Heart

This is a spectacular region of the country, with a huge variety of land-scapes: sandy beaches, stark mountains, green valleys, clusters of white-washed villages and rolling green hills. The Moorish and Roman legacy is everywhere, and music, dance and food are among many attractions.

Seville, Cordoba, Granada and Jerez add to the attractions of this vast region. The Spain at Heart brochure suggests properties to enjoy in winter: look for the *Winter Sun* coding. The Axarquia region, bounded by the coast and the Sierra de Tejeda, is getting more accessible, but remains suitably rural for walks, wildlife and uncrowded beaches.

The beaches of the Costa de la Luz really are among Spain's 'best kept secrets'...

La Teja: a cool, spacious interior, with a number of original features retained...

Casa Azul, near Competa (**sleeps 5/6**), for example, home of a sculptress, exudes a particularly welcoming atmosphere. It delights in a circular tower sitting room, a shaded pergola, terraces and private pool.

South of Antequera are remote villages and the impressive El Chorro Gorge. On the edge of El Torcal Natural Park stands *La Teja* (**sleeps 4-8/9**), a country farmhouse retaining many traditional features, while the bathrooms and the kitchen have been updated.

La Saucedilla, near Antequera (**sleeps 6**), also turns heads, with its baronial-style dining room decorated with antiques and the mantelpiece collection of wooden decoy ducks. *El Tornero,* near Aracena (**sleeps 6**) is remarkable for its lovingly tended gardens and the cottage overflows with character: beamed rooms, wooden floors, an open fire, antique bedsteads, a country-style kitchen and a terrace overlooking orchards and pastures below. *El Chopo,* near Cortes de la Frontera (**sleeps 8**), is a restored 17th-century farmhouse, hidden away in a tiny country hamlet. Sympathetically restored, comfortably furnished, El Chopo is also endowed with a large cobbled terrace shaded by a vine-covered pergola, and a pool offset by lawned gardens.

Spain at Heart, The Barns, Woodlands End, Mells, Frome, Somerset BA11 3QD. Telephone 01373 814222 (bookings); 01373 814224 (admin). Fax 01373 813444.

www.spainatheart.co.uk email: spainatheart@spainatheart.co.uk

Mallorca, Menorca and Javea
Villa Select

As travel writers we've long had a high regard for Villa Select, which has a fine reputation for holiday villas in Mallorca, Menorca and Javea (plus Cyprus – see Page 336 – and also Portugal). Every villa has its own pool. We also have a special affinity with the organisation, as it was set up in the same year (1983) as The Good Holiday Cottage Guide! Standards can be depended upon: beyond that it's really a question of whether one looks for something grand or on a smaller scale.

There are a number of properties big enough for two families to join together or one big extended family, such as the highly recommended *Es Pujol,* on Mallorca, just outside a picturesque village, handy for Cala D'or and just ten minutes' drive from beautiful beaches. It is a moneyed area, so be prepared for stylish living in this property. Among good things there is a covered terrace with spectacular views, a lovely beamed sitting room with an open fire for cooler evenings. **Sleeps up to 8**.

Other very large properties on Mallorca include *Casa Nova,* looking from its fine position across attractive countryside towards the Bay of Pollença. **Sleeping 10**, it has masses of space, and an excellent swimming pool. On a smaller scale, *La Serelleta*, **sleeping 4**, has absolute privacy, fabulous views and a open fire. *C'an Lloberina*, **sleeping 8**, is a traditional *finca* in the Colonya Valley, at least 200 years old, private and full of character.

Menorca is slightly more sophisticated, slightly more private, with some really stylish properties, outstanding among which is C'an Xaloc. This stunning property is in millionaire country. **Sleeping 12,** it has fabulous views, total privacy, peace and quiet.

In brief, much-loved Javea, on the Costa Blanca is a favourite destination, with some quite beautiful villas. We love their style: generally rather elegant, shaded by trees, shrubs and climbing flowers, often full of character and, of course, reliably comfortable.

Villa Select, Arden Court, Alcester, Warwickshire B49 6HN. For a copy of a stunning brochure, telephone 01789 764909. Fax 400355.

www.villaselect.com   email: holidays@villaselect.com

Son Cisterna (not featured) is simply (or not so simply) an amazing property.

C'an Xaloc is 'a stunning property in millionaire country'. It sleeps twelve.

Cyprus: 'island in the sun' – and how!

A recent mid-winter visit to Cyprus brought us into Larnaca airport on one of those tension-relieving, golden-glow Mediterranean evenings.

We checked our watches ('exactly four hours from London – not bad'), but might also have checked our pocket calendars. The temperature was 20°C: was this *really* January? We thought of the dusting of snow at Heathrow, the upturned collars in our local high street.

Though we were mainly there to check out self catering properties for later editions of this guide we also luxuriated in sumptuous seafront hotels where reception areas are measured in acres rather than square feet. These were the Amathus Beach Hotel at Limassol, and the Coral Beach Hotel at Paphos, where we loved watching the sun go down – always more quickly than we are used to in northern Europe – from our sea-view rooms.

Some of our party were first-timers in Cyprus. They loved the balmy winter weather but cringed at the thought of the much-vaunted 42°C at the height of summer. We were all bowled over by Paphos's Roman mosaics of circa 250-450AD, impressed by the surprisingly modern faces at our feet, one dark-haired beauty a spit of Alma Cogan ('Who she?' Ed). We were also awed by our guide Louisa's fluency in *five* languages: maybe Latin too – we forgot to check.

She was from the north of the island. As far as the south is concerned that's not so much a 'no-go' place for tourists as a 'we'd rather you didn't go'. But British travellers are famously curious. In rather sad tones Louisa reminded us to order 'Cypriot' or 'Greek' coffee if we wanted to avoid the ubiquitous Nescafe, never 'Turkish'.

We exclaimed over the rich, sweet Commandaria dessert wine we tasted at the winery in Omodos (it's used as communion wine: no wonder the orthodox priests look so contented). As we pottered around the village, we paid high prices for jars of honey that did however taste like the nectar of the gods. And the jars were pretty, and some of them contained almonds along with the honey.

Via olive groves, almond trees in early blossom, with sudden glimpses of the all-embracing sea far below, we drove on blissfully empty switch-back roads. From a point overlooking 'Aphrodite's Birthplace' among an outcrop of rocks in the sea we rememebered that in Cyprus, disbelief in legends must be suspended

We travelled via Episkopi's RAF base – a bit of Basingstoke under the sun – to Kourion's Greco-Roman theatre, seating 12500. We half-expected graffiti: 'If Zeus had wanted us all to sit here for hours he'd have given us smaller bottoms and bigger cushions'.

Then to 'the best seafood restaurant in Larnaka' for an array of hot and cold fish dishes. Every time we looked up a waiter swam into view with more. So fresh, I bet the chips on the children's menu arrive wriggling.

Tochni, Troodos, Pafos/Akamas
'Cyprus Villages'

The aim of this most interesting concept is to revive rural communities and preserve their traditional houses. Once-deserted or ruined houses have been converted for visitors seeking an alternative to purpose-built tourist facilities, and the villages are able to keep more of the

A typical Cyprus Villages summer scene...

younger generations in their communities, with new sources of income. Cyprus Villages' traditional accommodation is dispersed around several locations. Guests can experience the tranquillity of village life in an authentic Cypriot house. (There's a choice of studios, one-bedroom apartments, two-bedroom apartments and three-bedroom houses.) Swimming pools are provided for the exclusive use of guests, the majority of whom take advantage of low restaurant prices and eat out. Car hire is highly recommended, as local bus services are extremely sparse.

The Tochni Region is ideal for first time visitors to Cyprus or for guests who want to explore this beautiful island. Centrally located between Larnaka and Limassol and not far from the sea, this is the ideal region to combine exploring the countryside with relaxation on the beach.

Also featured are the Troodos Region (traditional, tranquil wine villages among the mountains) and the Pafos/Akamas Region (the rugged beauty of the Akamas peninsula, notably the massive mountainous pine forests).

Details/brochures from 01202 485012. Or **www.cyprusvillages.com.cy**

Latchi/Coral Bay
Villa Select

Cyprus has never lost its longstanding popularity among British people. It seems immune to the fads and fancies that affect other tourist destinations. Villa Select (see Page 000), have some gorgeous villas notable for their pools, their spaciousness and reliable standards of comfort.

Mircini, in the Coral Bay area, is exceptional even in Villa Select terms!

Among others in two main locations are the sumptuous *Olive Grove*, notable for its rather stone archways and super pool and – yes! – hot tub. Air conditioning in most rooms. **Sleeps 8**. Another remarkable property among so many is the imposing *Mircini*, also **sleeping 8**, surrounded by banana trees and offering peace and quiet. All the bedrooms are air-conditioned at no extra charge. The excellent Coral Bay beach is close by, and there are sea views from the house. Contact details as on Page 314.

Ruhpolding (Upper Bavaria)

Here's a useful base for discovering much of the best of Bavaria. (Berchtesgaden and Chiemsee, for example, are less than an hour's drive.). But families especially love the farm itself: archery, sunbathing on the lawn, or going on long walks with the llamas. There's a barbecue and the tepee has room for up to 20 people, is equipped with an open campfire, and in terms of visitors is ideal for informal socialising. Children, of course, feel particularly at ease on the farm. The playground with the big tepee offers lots of fun and excitement. Or let your children hunt around in the nearby wood, play with the animals, build a dam in the stream, play table-tennis or simply let them use their own imagination.

Vacation Villas International property number 2616.

Telephone: 49 (0) 8663 2762. Also 01438 869489.

Rothenburg
(recommended by readers)

Apartments at Haus Benji, Wiesenstrasse. 10 Adelshofen,

Rothenburg o.d.Tauber. Germany 91587

Telephone 49 (0) 9865 941 97 91

In a rural situation, close to Rothenburg, on 'The Romantic Road', there are suites and apartments with **Four tourist board Stars**.

Garmisch-Partenkirchen
(Upper Bavaria)

Here's a convenient holiday flat near the base of the 'Zugspitze' (the highest mountain in Germany), with impressive mountain views. The centre of Garmisch is just eight minutes away from the house, which is surrounded by a beautiful garden – the holiday flat is on the first floor, and is suitable for **2 to 4** people 'sleeping comfortably'. Light and sunny, it has a big living room, an open kitchen and dining area. Cable TV, radio, CD player. There are two bedrooms, and a bathroom with bath and shower, and there are three balconies.

A garage is available for a small charge. The flat is also handy for mountain railways and hiking paths ice-skating in the ice stadium nearby and tobogganing,

Cost: from about 50 Euros per day for two; 60 Euros per day for four.

Details from Familie Huff, Hubertusstrasse 46, D82131 Gauting. Telephone 49 (0) 89-85 06 293. Fax 49 (0) 89-85 06 293

Bavaria: 'We got a little high'....

We thought we'd died and gone to brochure-heaven (*writes Bryn Frank*). Jagged snow-capped peaks against a sapphire sky, toffee-coloured cows watching us lugubriously across wild-flowery meadows, a sudden glimpse near Berchtesgaden of the Königssee below: scrubby cliffs sheering into the still, dark waters of the lake, famously so pure that sightseeing launches are electrically operated so as to keep it that way, with the added bonus of almost no engine noise.

As we cable-car'd it up to about 4000 feet, via summer pastures where the scent of new mown hay mingles with pine, we were surrounded by the rich local dialect. Bavarian is to formal 'High German' as clotted-cream-rich Devonian is to 'BBC English'.

After just a few days in Bavaria we began to feel quite light headed, and it wasn't just the height. There's something about the combination of high mountain air and chilled wine from small vineyards unknown outside Germany that hones the holiday mood. And the taste of local beer that beats the mass produced exports. I'm thinking about all those foaming *steins* we drained at a pint-sized beer festival in Ruhpolding. Litres come automatically: it's really not manly to whisper to the *dirndled* waitress 'Mine's just a small one'.

There was general agreement among us that the *Dirndl* is the most fetching national dress after the sari, though there were some who spoke up for the kimono.

In one mountain watering hole we got the best of both worlds – panoramic views, air good enough to bottle *and* good food and drink. For in Bavaria, at the beginning of time, God created great mountains, secret valleys, rushing streams and picture-windowed restaurants with log fires, antique decorative ceramic stoves, stags' heads, sepia hunting prints and home cooking.

Of course they were created for the view, but I like them when the mist closes in: eerie and beautiful. As people linger over a drink they tend to glance at the menu: 'Well, as we'll be here for a while, let's at least try a plate of *Bratkartoffeln* and *Spiegeleier'*. Which is fried eggs and fried potatoes. Sounds routine, but at its best, *haute cuisine*. Or perhaps something more substantial, like *Eisbein* (pigs' trotter) and sauerkraut, or wild venison with wild berries and potato dumplings .

Most south-easterly of all Germany's semi-independent States, bordered by Austria and the Czech Republic, dissected by great rivers, Bavaria likes to play the part of the simple peasant, but it is a prosperous place

As well as those lakes and mountains it suggests the lush green parks and the Baroque architecture of Munich, 'The Merry Widow' at the opera house, cycling in the English Garden: more an English parkland, a bit of 'Capability Brown' a long way from home. It's the weekend exodus, summer and winter, of Munich's sleek Mercedes, BMWs and Porsches to the Bavarian Alps, where against a backdrop of mountains and brochure-blue skies, the cobbled squares of medieval towns and villages are more like Ruritanian stage sets than the real thing. At night ghosts steal between shadows cast by ancient street lamps, and the striking of elaborately decorated clocks emphasises the silence. The fondness for nostalgic, moody lighting in the depths of winter, sudden gales of laughter from a snug bar in some 400 year old tavern, perhaps a snatch of music from a 'squeeze box', an intense pride in community is all very Bavarian.

A good tourist map will mark 'The Romantic Road', threading its way mostly in Bavaria, roughly on a north-south axis to the west of Munich. It takes in Nördlingen, where you can walk all the way round a town of red and orange roofs, and Dinkelsbühl, as pretty as its name and best known for its annual children's pageant. Also, the sweetest tourist honeypot of them all, Rothenburg, like a set of wood-cuts from a well thumbed book of fairy tales brought to life.

If there is one 'must-see' on the Romantic Road it's near the southern end. Neuschwanstein Castle is a cross between a wedding cake of the embarrassingly elaborate variety and a five year child's idea of the sort of castle in which Rapunzel would choose to let her hair down. Though she'd have the luxury of a different tall turret for each week of the year. This was 'Mad', though actually just very, very eccentric, King Ludwig III's greatest fantasy.

But he had taste, as we discovered at Chiemsee, where on one of the wooded islands in the lake another of his three castles is a partial recreation of Versailles. It was a bonus to stumble across another island, the Fraueninsel – the name comes from the pretty convent, an oasis of peace and simplicity, never more so than when the day boats have left and the picture postcard village is left to its own devices.

Storm clouds came over (contrasting with an elaborate rainbow) as we sailed back to the shore: 20 minutes' worth of pure calm, with the bonus of a final glimpse of Ludwig's palace through an avenue of tall trees.

Due south of Munich the serious ski resort of Garmisch-Partenkirchen, is close to the foot of Germany's highest peak, the Zugspitze. From a little station near the main line from Munich the partly rack and pinion route climbs to the top of the dramatic mountain. One draws a veil over the fact that the peak is technically just inside Austria.

On an early summer Sunday evening Garmisch was all very genteel: Franz Lehar from the bandstand in the park, elderly ladies with pugs and poodles on the lead. And, of course, gooey-cake shops, which in southern Germany have an almost religious significance.

British eurosceptics suggest that greater federalism in Europe will lead to a loss of national identity. They have probably not been to Bavaria. A Texan once told me, 'We are Texans first, Americans second'. In this not-to-be-missed corner of Germany – in some ways it contains the essence of the country – they go one better: they are Bavarians first, Germans second, Europeans third.

Kaprun, near Zell am See
'Haus Fischer' (Interhome)

After a false start, when we found ourselves in the wrong apartment in the heart of this famous ski resort (all round skiing on the fabulous, dramatic Grossglockner, but lots to see and do hereabouts in the summer), we detoured 'up the hill' to the correct building. Excellent! It's always nice to be a bit 'out of town', to have your own space. With good views of the mountains and easy access to the village, this was a spacious, reasonably priced delight.

With Zell am See just ten minutes by car, cable cars within three minutes and the one that transports you to the peak of the Grossglockner just ten, it was a good find. We walked for many miles on mountain paths, cycled on hired bikes round the lake at Zell, went on a round-the-lake boat tour.

Specifically, our first floor apartment had a spacious double-aspect double-bedded sitting room, a good sized twin room, the option of a further twin, a kitchen-diner and – yes – a bathroom. For some people this is important, and it's not automatic. Soakers must check the small print: only a minority of holiday properties in Austria (and Bavaria) have a bath rather than or as well as a shower. Not that there's any shortage of water around! There's a shared balcony, use of a garden, with some outside seating, and, at the back of the property – which contains other apartments, though all with a good degree of privacy – there's easy access to a charming country lane that, with rural views all around and a panoramic one of most of Kaprun, takes one down into the (large) village centre. **Sleeps up to 6.** Ref A5710/222B

In the same ownership, and in the main street of the village, a newly and smartly renovated apartment house is better suited to people who don't want to trek up the hill. There are two apartments, each **sleeping 6**. Refs A5710/230B and A5710/230C.

All the Interhome properties are available for viewing on a CD rom, available from Interhome Limited, 383 Richmond Road, Twickenham TW1 2EF.

Telephone 020 8891 1294. Fax 020 8891 5331.

www.interhome.co.uk   email: info@interhome.co.uk

Summer and winter, Austria is a playground for 'bon viveurs' and outdoor types alike...

Special Categories (UK/Ireland)

A quick reference

We're pleased when readers call us for extra information about cottages we feature. They ask all sorts of intriguing questions, but mostly it's things like 'This cottage looks nice, but can you confirm it has a swimming pool?' ... 'How far away is it from the sea?' ... 'There seems to be a railway station quite near, but are there taxis or will the cottage owners pick us up and take us back?' Listing such items as this is not, however, a value judgement, as many of our very best cottages scarcely score at all in these lists. **Please note that agencies are not included, as it is assumed that most of them can offer properties that include some or even most of the facilities featured.**

1.	*In or on the outskirts of a village or town.*
2.	*Beside a lake, a loch, a lough, a river, the sea.*
3.	*Within about five miles of the sea.*
4.	*Deeply rural and/or fairly remote.*
5.	*Home cooked food available (including freezer food).*
6.	*Access by rail or owner will collect from train.*
7.	*Owner/manager living on site or immediately adjacent.*
8.	*On working farm.*
9.	*Suitable for people with limited mobility.*
10.	*Suitable for the disabled (using ETC or RADAR criteria).*
11.	*Big houses, suitable for two or more families (say, 9/10).*
12.	*Swimming pool on site or immediately adjacent.*
13.	*Open fires/coal or woodburning stoves.*
14.	*Tennis court on site.*
15.	*Special play/entertainment facilities for children.*

* Asterisks mean the facility applies to some properties only.

NB: Some readers ask us to indicate cottages that are available for short breaks, but our records show that four out of five owners or agents offer this facility. It is worth phoning about short breaks even at the height of the season.

East Anglia/E Midlands/Shires	1	2	3	4	5	6	7	8	9	10	11	12	13	14	15
Blue Barn Cottage				✓	✓		✓	✓			✓		✓		
Bones Cottage	✓		✓				✓								
Box End	✓	✓				✓									
Bramble & Hawthorn				✓			✓		✓				✓		
Brancaster Farms Cottages			✓				✓	✓		✓•	✓•		✓	✓	
Carpenters Cottages, No.6	✓		✓												
Chantry	✓	✓													
Clippesby Holiday Cottages			✓		✓		✓		✓•	✓•		✓	✓•	✓	✓
Corner Pightle			✓										✓		
Danish House Gardens, No 17	✓	✓	✓						✓						
Dowagers Cottage, The	✓					✓	✓				✓				
Gladwins Farm				✓	✓	✓	✓		✓			✓	✓	✓	
Grove Cottages, The			✓				✓								
Highland House		✓									✓				
Holly Farm	✓			✓			✓		✓		✓				
Ivy House Farm				✓		✓	✓	✓	✓	✓•	✓	✓	✓		✓
Jenny's Cottage	✓		✓										✓		
Little River View	✓	✓					✓								
Margaret's Cottage				✓	✓		✓					✓	✓		✓
Moorings, The	✓	✓									✓		✓		✓
Northernhay		✓									✓				
Orchard Cottage	✓												✓		
Peartree Cottage	✓	✓											✓		
Peddars Cottage	✓						✓						✓		
Potash Barns				✓	✓		✓		✓		✓		✓		✓
Premiere Marina Cottages	✓	✓							✓•		✓	✓			
Riverside Rentals	✓		✓												
Stubbs Cottages				✓•	✓		✓	✓	✓•				✓•		
Sunnyside Cottage	✓		✓												
Vere Lodge				✓	✓		✓		✓		✓	✓	✓•	✓	✓
Vista/Carpenters Cottages	✓	✓											✓		
Willow Fen	✓	✓				✓									
Willow Lodge	✓	✓				✓			✓		✓				
Wood Lodge				✓							✓		✓		
Yorkshire and The Peaks															
Ashwall House									✓		✓		✓		✓
Beech Farm Cottages	✓						✓		✓•		✓	✓			✓
Billy's Bothy				✓	✓	✓	✓		✓		✓				
Cherry Tree/The Old House	✓•												✓•		
Cliff House	✓					✓						✓	✓•	✓	✓
Cotterill Farm Cottages						✓	✓						✓•		
Cressbrook Hall Cottages		✓		✓	✓		✓		✓	✓	✓				✓
Dalegarth & The Ghyll Cottages	✓					✓	✓		✓	✓		✓			
Dalehead Court	✓			✓		✓	✓								
Darwin Lake Properties		✓		✓			✓								
Dinmore Cottages							✓		✓	✓	✓		✓		
Farsyde Mews Cottages		✓	✓		✓•		✓	✓				✓•	✓•		
Fold Farm Cottages	✓			✓			✓	✓					✓		
Hartington/Courtyard Cottages	✓												✓		

	1	2	3	4	5	6	7	8	9	10	11	12	13	14	15
Hayloft, The				✓			✓						✓		
Headon Farm Cottages				✓			✓						✓		
Hillside Croft	✓			✓	✓	✓			✓		✓		✓		
Knockerdown Farm Cottages	✓			✓			✓		✓		✓	✓	✓•		✓
Layhead Farm Cottages				✓		✓		✓	✓•		✓•		✓		
Sarahs Cottage	✓					✓	✓								
Shatton Hall Farm Cottages				✓			✓						✓	✓	
Shepherd's Cottage				✓									✓		
Swaledale Cottages	✓•			✓•			✓•				✓•		✓•		
Thiemswood Cottage	✓			✓•			✓•		✓		✓•		✓•		
Townend Cottage	✓						✓						✓		
White Rose Holiday Cottages	✓		✓•			✓	✓•		✓•				✓•		
Wraycroft Cottages	✓•	✓					✓		✓•				✓•		
Wrea Head House Cottages			✓			✓	✓		✓	✓	✓	✓			✓
York Lakeside Lodges		✓					✓			✓•					✓
Northumberland and Durham															
Akeld Manor & Cottages				✓	✓		✓				✓•				
Blue Bell Farm Cottages	✓	✓	✓			✓	✓	✓•							✓
Boot & Shoe Cottage		✓		✓	✓		✓						✓		
Cresswell Wing				✓			✓				✓			✓	
Holmhead Cottage	✓	✓				✓	✓	✓		✓					✓
Old Smithy, The				✓			✓	✓	✓				✓		
Outchester & Ross Farm Cottages			✓	✓	✓		✓	✓	✓•				✓		
Pele Tower, The							✓						✓		
Shepherd's Cottage			✓	✓		✓	✓	✓	✓				✓		
Shilbottle Town Foot Farm	✓•		✓			✓	✓	✓	✓		✓	✓	✓	✓	✓
Stables, The & The Byre				✓	✓	✓	✓	✓	✓				✓		
West Lodge/Stables/Coachhouse/Bee Cott			✓	✓	✓		✓				✓		✓		
Scotland															
Ardblair Castle Cottages							✓•	✓•	✓•		✓•				
Arduaine Cottages		✓		✓			✓								
Ardverikie Estate Cottages		✓•		✓			✓	✓•			✓•		✓•		
Arisaig House Cottages		✓	✓	✓		✓	✓		✓•					✓	✓
Attadale				✓		✓	✓	✓			✓		✓		
Balnakilly Log Cabins/Cottages		✓		✓			✓	✓	✓•	✓•	✓	✓	✓	✓	
Blairquhan		✓		✓			✓	✓	✓•		✓•		✓		
Bothy, The		✓		✓			✓						✓		
Captain's House, The	✓	✓		✓									✓		
Culligran Cottages		✓		✓			✓	✓							
Druimarbin Farmhouse			✓	✓		✓			✓		✓		✓		
Drumblair	✓								✓						
Duinnish Chalets			✓	✓			✓		✓						
Duncrub Holidays				✓	✓	✓	✓	✓•	✓•				✓•		
Duns Castle Cottages		✓		✓	✓		✓				✓		✓•	✓	
Easter Dalziel Cottages			✓			✓	✓	✓	✓						
Ellary Estate Cottages		✓	✓	✓			✓	✓					✓		
Glen Coe Cottages		✓	✓	✓					✓						
Isle of Carna Cottage		✓	✓	✓									✓		

	1	2	3	4	5	6	7	8	9	10	11	12	13	14	15
Lorgba Holiday Cottages	✓	✓	✓		✓	✓	✓	✓					✓		
Machrie Hotel Lodges		✓		✓	✓		✓		✓						✓
Millstone Cottage		✓		✓			✓								
No 3 Dalfaber Park	✓	✓				✓					✓		✓		
Penmore Mill		✓		✓			✓				✓				✓
Pier Cottage/The Library		✓		✓									✓		
Rhuveag		✓		✓							✓		✓		
Seaview Grazings		✓													
Shore Croft		✓	✓	✓					✓				✓		
Speyside Holiday Houses	✓	✓							✓		✓		✓		
Tomich Holidays				✓			✓	✓				✓			
Torrisdale Castle Cottages		✓	✓	✓			✓	✓	✓•		✓•		✓•		
Cumbria/Lancashire															
Bailey Mill Cottage		✓		✓	✓	✓	✓	✓	✓	✓	✓	✓			✓
Bank End Farm Cottages		✓		✓	✓		✓	✓					✓•		
Bassenthwaite Lakeside Lodges		✓										✓			
Bowderbeck		✓		✓											
Croft House Holidays	✓•						✓•		✓•				✓•		✓•
Field End Barns		✓•		✓			✓		✓		✓		✓		
Howscales				✓		✓	✓		✓	✓					
Kirkland Hall Cottages				✓			✓				✓		✓		
Land Ends		✓		✓			✓		✓						
Long Byres				✓	✓	✓	✓	✓							
Loweswater Holiday Cottages	✓•	✓•		✓			✓		✓•				✓•		
Matson Ground Estate Cottages				✓•			✓•				✓•		✓•		
Meadowbank/Garden Chalet	✓								✓•		✓		✓		
Monkhouse Hill Cottages					✓		✓		✓•	✓•	✓•		✓•		✓
Mossgill Loft & Chapel	✓						✓						✓	✓	
No 4 Green Cross Cottages	✓					✓									
Old Coach House, The	✓								✓						
Wheelwrights	✓						✓		✓•			✓	✓•	✓	✓
Wales															
Aberdovey Hillside Village	✓	✓					✓	✓							
Beth Ruach		✓					✓		✓		✓				✓
Blackmoor Farm Holiday Cottages			✓				✓	✓							
Bryn Bras Castle			✓				✓								
Bryn-y-Mor		✓		✓					✓		✓		✓		
Carreg Coetan	✓		✓												
Clydey Country Cottages															
Cnewr Estate		✓•		✓				✓			✓•		✓		
Fron Fawr		✓					✓								
Gwynfryn Farm		✓			✓		✓	✓				✓	✓•		✓
Nantcol			✓	✓							✓		✓		
Pant Farm & Sanctuary Cottage		✓	✓•	✓			✓	✓					✓•		
Penbryn Bach Cottage			✓	✓			✓						✓		
Portmeirion Cottages	✓	✓										✓		✓	
Quality Cottages. Cerbid				✓	✓•		✓•	✓•	✓•				✓•		
Rhos-Ddu			✓	✓			✓	✓					✓•		✓

	1	2	3	4	5	6	7	8	9	10	11	12	13	14	15
Rhyd-yr-Eirin		✓	✓	✓									✓		✓
Rosemoor			✓		✓	✓	✓		✓	✓	✓				
Showman's Trailer		✓		✓			✓	✓					✓		
Talcen Foel			✓	✓									✓		
Trallwm Forest Cottages				✓	✓	✓	✓	✓			✓•		✓		
Trenewydd Farm Cottages			✓	✓			✓		✓	✓	✓	✓			✓
Victorian Barn		✓		✓			✓					✓	✓	✓	
Y Bwthwn		✓		✓			✓					✓	✓	✓	
Y Llaethdy		✓		✓			✓		✓			✓	✓	✓	
West Country															
Badham Farm Holiday Cottages		✓	✓	✓		✓	✓		✓•		✓•			✓	✓
Bosinver Cottages			✓			✓		✓	✓•		✓•	✓	✓•	✓	✓
Braddon Cottages		✓		✓			✓				✓		✓	✓	✓
Butler's Cottage			✓	✓			✓	✓					✓		
Chapel & Hockadays Cottages	✓•		✓•	✓•		✓	✓•						✓•		
Chew Hill Farm Holidays				✓			✓	✓							
Cider Room Cottage				✓			✓								
Coach House Cottages				✓	✓	✓	✓				✓	✓	✓	✓	✓
Compton Pool	✓	✓	✓	✓			✓		✓			✓		✓	✓
Dairy Cottages				✓	✓		✓	✓	✓•	✓•		✓			✓
Draydon Cottages				✓											
Duddings Holiday Cottages			✓	✓			✓		✓		✓	✓	✓	✓	✓
Fourwinds				✓		✓	✓		✓•			✓•	✓		✓
Fursdon				✓			✓	✓					✓	✓	
Glebe House Cottages	✓		✓		✓		✓								✓
Gullrock		✓	✓	✓			✓		✓						
Harbour View		✓	✓				✓								
Horry Mill Cottage				✓			✓	✓					✓		
Kirk House	✓	✓	✓								✓		✓		✓
Knowle Farm		✓•					✓•	✓•			✓•	✓•	✓•	✓•	✓
Manor Cottage				✓	✓	✓	✓						✓		
Marigold/Penny	✓	✓	✓				✓								
Mill Field Cottage	✓	✓	✓										✓		
Mineshop Holiday Cottages		✓•	✓	✓			✓				✓•				
Mudgeon Vean			✓	✓			✓	✓	✓				✓		
Old School Cottages, The		✓		✓									✓		
Oldaport Farm Cottages			✓	✓	✓		✓	✓	✓•						
Otter Falls		✓		✓			✓		✓•		✓•	✓	✓•	✓	✓
Pettigrew Cottage	✓	✓					✓						✓		
Pollaughan Cottages		✓	✓	✓	✓		✓	✓	✓•	✓•			✓•	✓	✓
Red Doors Farm Cottages				✓	✓	✓	✓					✓	✓		
Rockford Lodge	✓	✓	✓												
Scoles Manor			✓	✓			✓		✓	✓	✓				✓
Sea Meads Holiday Homes		✓	✓				✓				✓				
St Aubyn Estates Cottages	✓•	✓•	✓•	✓•			✓•	✓•			✓•		✓•		✓•
Stowford Lodge Holiday Cottages				✓	✓		✓		✓			✓	✓		
Tides Reach	✓	✓				✓	✓								
Trefanny Hill			✓	✓	✓		✓		✓			✓	✓		✓
Tregeath			✓					✓					✓		
Trevarrow Cottage	✓	✓	✓										✓		

	1	2	3	4	5	6	7	8	9	10	11	12	13	14	15
Trevorrick Farm Cottages			✓				✓		✓	✓		✓	✓		✓
Treworgey Cottages			✓	✓	✓	✓	✓		✓•		✓•	✓	✓		✓
Wheel Farm Country Cottages			✓		✓		✓		✓•		✓	✓	✓•		✓
Wooder Manor				✓			✓	✓	✓•		✓•		✓•		
South and South East															
Ashby Farms Cottages	✓•	✓•		✓•									✓•		
Coach House, The				✓		✓	✓						✓		
Eastwell Mews		✓			✓	✓	✓		✓•	✓•		✓		✓	
Pekes				✓	✓		✓		✓•		✓•	✓	✓•	✓	
Three Chimneys Farm		✓		✓			✓	✓	✓•		✓•		✓	✓	
Cotswolds/Heart of England															
Barn, The				✓		✓	✓						✓		
Bruern Stable Cottages				✓	✓				✓•	✓•	✓•		✓	✓	✓
Cotswold Water Park		✓					✓					✓		✓•	✓
Docklow Manor							✓		✓			✓	✓•	✓	
Foxes Reach	✓			✓			✓						✓		
Glebe Farm							✓		✓						
Hall Farm	✓					✓	✓	✓							
Heath Farm Cottages				✓			✓						✓		
Hillside Cottage/The Bothy	✓			✓			✓	✓				✓	✓		
Little Cottage, The	✓					✓	✓						✓		
Log House		✓					✓						✓		
Mainoaks Farm				✓									✓		
Oast House, The/Manor Farm	✓					✓	✓		✓				✓		
Old Cottage, The	✓												✓		
Old Dairy, The						✓	✓				✓		✓		
Orangery, The	✓					✓					✓				
Orangery, The							✓		✓			✓	✓		✓
Owlpen Manor Cottages				✓	✓		✓	✓	✓		✓		✓•		
Stanton Court Cottages							✓		✓			✓		✓	✓
Sudeley Castle Country Cottages	✓						✓						✓•		
Sutton Court Farm Cottages				✓	✓		✓		✓•				✓•		
Swiss Chalet, The		✓		✓		✓	✓		✓						
Vanilla Cottage		✓											✓		
Ireland															
Delphi Cottages		✓		✓	✓		✓						✓		
Holiday House, Ballina	✓	✓											✓		
Killarney Lakeland Cottages	✓					✓	✓	✓	✓		✓	✓	✓	✓	✓
Village and Country Holiday Homes	✓•	✓•	✓				✓		✓•				✓•		

326

East Anglia/ East Midlands/ The Shires

Numbers underlined on maps denote agencies (which in the main text are marked with an asterisk). With only a few exceptions the location marked on the map is the letting agency's headquarters, and it is normal for the agency to be strongly or even exclusively represented in that particular region. In the case of the larger regional and the main national agencies, no location reference is given.

Gainsborough · Caistor ·
58
56 Mablethorpe
63
60 · Lincoln · Skegness
Notts Lincolnshire
Nottingham · Grantham
Hunstanton 24 23
26 37 28
42 47 38 40 Cromer
46 25 41 31
20 43
Kings Lynn · 21 29 Fakenham 34
22 44 30
48 32 35
19 36 33 Great Yarmouth
Norfolk Norwich Lowestoft
Leicestershire/Rutland
· Leicester · Peterborough Diss
49 Thetford · Southwold
Cambs 18 5
Northants Newmarket · 4 9
Northampton Bury Suffolk 10
Milton Bedford Cambridge · St Edmunds 8
Keynes · Beds 3 Ipswich 7 Aldeburgh
Bucks 6
1 2 Harwich
Herts Essex Colchester
· Oxford St. Albans Clacton-on-Sea
Oxfordshire High Chelmsford
Wycombe
Map 1 Greater London

South & South East

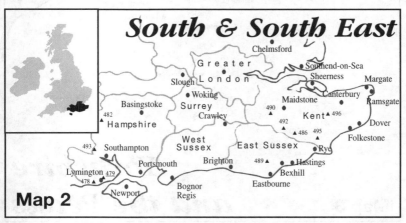

Chelmsford
Greater Southend-on-Sea
London Sheerness Margate
Slough Canterbury Ramsgate
· Woking Maidstone 496
Basingstoke Surrey 490 Dover
482 Crawley 492 Kent 486 495 Folkestone
Hampshire West East Sussex Rye
493 Southampton Sussex 489 Hastings
Portsmouth Brighton Bexhill
Lymington 479 Eastbourne
478 Bognor
Map 2 Newport Regis

327

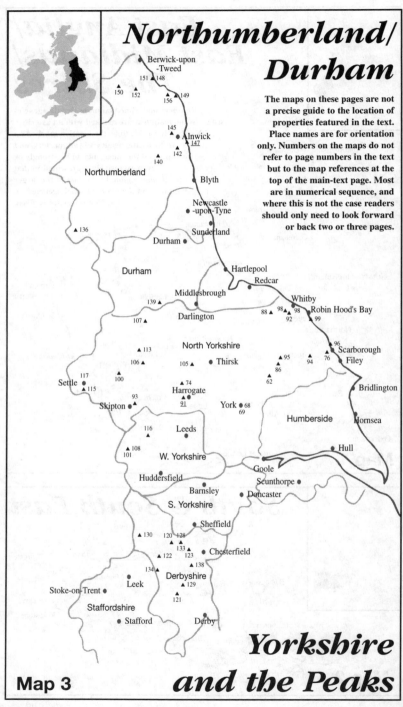

Northumberland/ Durham

The maps on these pages are not a precise guide to the location of properties featured in the text. Place names are for orientation only. Numbers on the maps do not refer to page numbers in the text but to the map references at the top of the main-text page. Most are in numerical sequence, and where this is not the case readers should only need to look forward or back two or three pages.

Berwick-upon-Tweed
151 148
150 152
156 149

145
Alnwick
147
142
140

Northumberland

Blyth

Newcastle-upon-Tyne

136

Sunderland

Durham

Hartlepool
Redcar

Durham

Middlesbrough
Whitby
139
107
Darlington
88 98 98 Robin Hood's Bay
92 99

North Yorkshire
113
106
105 Thirsk
95
86
94 76 Scarborough
Filey
62
117 100
Settle 115
74
Harrogate
91
93
Skipton
York 68
69
Bridlington

Humberside
Hornsea

116
Leeds
Hull

108
101
W. Yorkshire
Goole
Huddersfield
Scunthorpe
Barnsley
Doncaster
S. Yorkshire

Sheffield
130 120 128
133 123
122
Chesterfield
134 138
Leek
Derbyshire
129
Stoke-on-Trent
121
Staffordshire
Stafford
Derby

Yorkshire and the Peaks

Map 3

328

Scotland

John o'Groats
Durness
Thurso
Tongue
Wick
Unapool
Kinbrace
Lybster
Highland
Lochinver
Ullapool
Laird
Brora
Inveran
Dornoch
Gairloch
▲204
Invergordon
▲205
Lossiemouth
Macduff
203
Cromarty
Achnasheen
Nairn
Elgin
Buckie
Banff
Fraserburgh
Isle of Skye
▲207
189
Rothes
Peterhead
▲199
▲195
185
Inverness
Kyle
168 ▲
Huntly
Grantown-on-Spey
Invermoriston
181 ▲
Aviemore
Grampian
Mallaig
Invergarry
Kingussie
Banchory
Aberdeen
▲201
▲196
Stonehaven
Fort William
Pitlochry ▲166
Brechin
211
▲198
▲202
Montrose
Tobermory
212
Glencoe
Tayside
▲183
▲197
Aberfeldy
▲164
Mull
Dundee
Arbroath
200
Oban
165
Perth
▲209
Argyll
Callander
167 ▲
St Andrews
Stirling
Fife
Central
▲206
North Berwick
▲210
Dunoon
Dumbarton
Dunbar
Greenock
Glasgow
155
217
Lothian ▲
Edinburgh
Islay
Paisley
154 ▲
Eyemouth
▲215
Galashiels ●
153
▲218
Arran
Irvine
Kilmarnock
Melrose
Kelso
Prestwick
Campbeltown
Ayr
Strathclyde
Borders
▲162
Girvan
Dumfries
and
Dumfries ●
Galloway
Stranraer
Kirkcudbright
Whithorn

Map 4

329

Wales

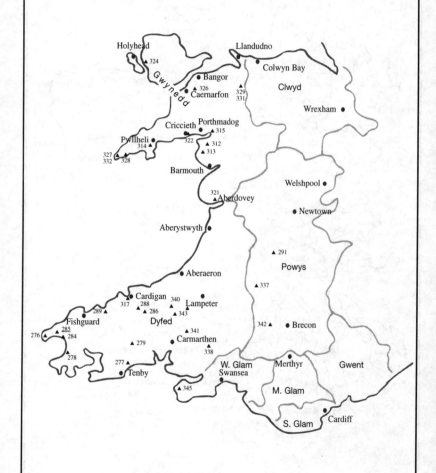

Holyhead
▲ 324

Gwynedd

Llandudno

Colwyn Bay

● Bangor
▲ 326
Caernarfon

329
331

Clwyd

Wrexham ●

Criccieth
● Porthmadog
▲ 315
Pwllheli ●
314
322
▲ 312
▲ 313

327
332
328

Barmouth

321
▲ Aberdovey

Welshpool ●

● Newtown

Aberystwyth ●

▲ 291

● Aberaeron

Powys

▲ 337

Cardigan
340
317
288
● Lampeter
286
343
▲ 341
Dyfed

342 ▲ ● Brecon

Fishguard
285
289 ▲
▲ 341
338
276 ▲
284
● Carmarthen

278

277 ▲ 279
● Tenby

W. Glam
Swansea
Merthyr
Gwent

M. Glam

▲ 345

S. Glam Cardiff

Map 5

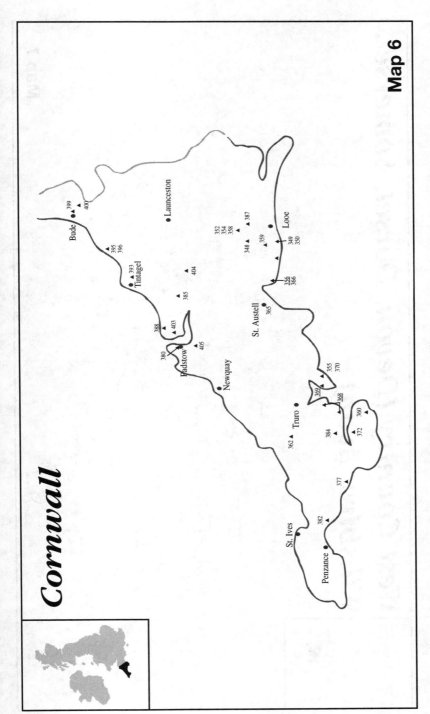

Map 6

Cornwall

Bude
399
400
395
396
Tintagel
393
404
385
388
403
405
Padstow
380
Newquay
Launceston
352
354
358
387
Looe
348
359
349
350
356
366
St. Austell
365
355
370
369
368
360
Truro
362
384
372
377
St. Ives
382
Penzance

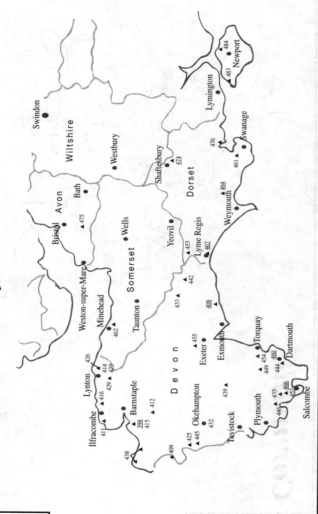

West Country (Devon, Dorset, Somerset, Wiltshire, Avon)

Map 7

332

Cumbria/Lakes/ Lancashire

▲ 222

▲ 221

Carlisle
●

▲ 226

▲ 262

C u m b r i a

232
▲

Penrith
●

▲ 220

259
▲

256
▲

269 ▲

▲ 236

Keswick
●

▲ 252

246 ▲

▲ 248

▲ 265

243 ▲ 258

Whitehaven
●

● Windermere
▲
250

253
▲

244
▲

273 ▲   ▲ 274

● Kendal

▲ 268

Barrow-in-
Furness
●

● Carnforth

L a n c a s h i r e

● Blackpool

Map 8

Cotswolds/ Heart of England

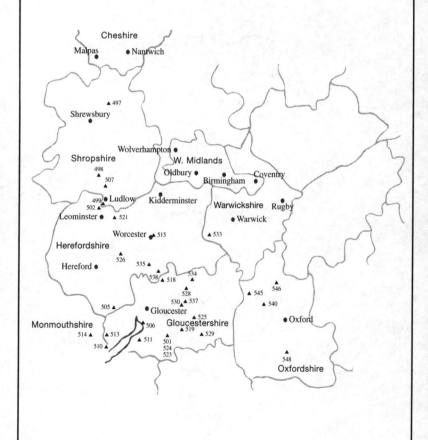

Cheshire

Malpas ● ● Nantwich

▲ 497

Shrewsbury

Wolverhampton ●

Shropshire   W. Midlands

498 ▲   Oldbury ●

507 ▲   Birmingham ●   Coventry ●

499 ● Ludlow   Kidderminster ●

502 ▲   Warwickshire   Rugby ●

Leominster ●   ▲ 521   Warwick ●

Worcester ● ▲ 515   ▲ 533

Herefordshire

▲ 526

Hereford ●   535 ▲

538 ▲ ▲ 518   ▲ 534

528 ▲   ▲ 545   ▲ 546

530 ▲▲ 537   ▲ 540

505 ▲   ● Gluocester

Monmouthshire   ▲ 525   ● Oxford

514 ▲ ▲ 513   ▲ 506   Gloucestershire

510 ▲   ▲ 511   ▲ 519   ▲ 529

501   ▲
524   548
523   Oxfordshire

Map 9

Ireland

Londonderry
Letterkenny
Belfast
Donegal
Killyleagh
Enniskillen
Armagh
Sligo

Ballina
563
Dundalk
Navan
Castlebar
Westport
580
Clifden
Athlone
Dublin
Dun Laoghaire
Galway
585
573
Port Laoise
Wicklow
Carlow
Arklow
Ennis
Limerick
Wexford
Tipperary
Waterford
581
Clonmel
582
588
Tralee
Killarney
562
Dingle
Cork
Bantry
572

Map 10

335

Listed below are brief details of cottages that appear on our associated website, www.goodcottageguide.com, but not in the guide itself. Enquiries can be directed to frank@cottageguide.demon.co.uk where an owner does not have their own email.

Walnut Tree Barn, Swanton Abbott, Norfolk. Barn conversion on village outskirts. Well placed for the Norfolk Broads and the coast. Sleeps 4. Telephone (01692) 538888, email: mark@citibuild.co.uk

Bosun's Rest, Blakeney, Norfolk. Fisherman's flint cottage; stone's throw from quay, log burning stove, modern appliances, sleeps 4. Telephone (02088) 662683, email: deborah.fitzpatrick1@btinternet.com

Plunketts Cottage in sought after Brancaster. Comfortable and well equipped sleeping up to 8. Close to stunning beaches, golf club and much more. Telephone (01485) 210892. email: roger.raisbury@btinternet.com www.brancasterstaithe.co.uk

Flagstaff House, Burnham Overy Staithe, Norfolk. Several properties with memorable coastal views. Sleep 2-11. Telephone (01278) 638637, email: admin@flagstaff-holidays.co.uk www.flagstaff-holidays.co.uk

Lower Wood Farm Country Cottages, Mautby. Bordering Broads and National Park. Indoor heated pool and facilities ideal for families. Sleep 4-9. Telephone (01493) 722523. email: info@lowerwoodfarm.co.uk www.lowerwoodfarm.co.uk

The Grove Cottages, Cromer, Norfolk. (1/2 mile Cromer). Converted barns in 3 acre grounds. Heated indoor swimming pool. Sleep 2-6. Telephone (01263) 512412. email: thegrovecromer@btopenworld.com www.thegrovecromer.co.uk

Norfolk House & Courtyard Cottages, Docking (near Burnham Market and Brancaster), North Norfolk. Traditional properties in village. ETC 5 Stars. Telephone (01485) 525341, email: holidays@witleypress.co.uk

Wood Farm Cottages, near Holt, Norfolk. Converted barns and stables in secluded five acres. Children and dogs welcome. Telephone (01263) 587347, email: info@wood-farm.com www.wood-farm.com

Heron Cottage, Horning, Norfolk. Enviable position right on the Broads - rowing dinghy provided! ETC 5 Star. Sleeps 6. Telephone (07788) 853332. email: info@heron-cottage.com www.heron-cottage.com

Wensum View, Gt. Ryburgh, Norfolk. Spacious cottage for 8+2. Indoor heated pool. Magnificent scenery - a must for artists and anglers. Telephone (01328) 829288. email: wensumview@aol.com www.wensum-view.co.uk

4 The Courtyard, Snettisham. In conservation area 3 miles from Hunstanton and Sandringham. Close to countryside/beaches. Sleeps 4. Telephone (01406) 422569. email: jennifer.overson@ntlworld.com www.cottageguide.co.uk/4.thecourtyard

Old School Cottage, Norfolk/Suffolk/Cambs borders. Near Thetford Forest. Ideal for nature lovers, walkers and cyclists. Telephone (01953) 498277, email: oscott@clara.net www.4starcottage.co.uk

Whitensmere Farm Cottages, Ashdon. Cambs/Suffolk/Essex borders. 3 well equipped barn conversions, 1 for disabled. Sleep 4-10. Telephone (01799) 584244, email: gford@lineone.net www.holidaycottagescambridge.co.uk

Bolding Way Holiday Cottages, Weybourne, North Norfolk Heritage Coastline. Four cottages sleeping 2 -14 + cot + 2. Telephone (01263) 588666, freephone UK only 0800 0560996, email GHCG@boldingway.co.uk www.boldingway.co.uk

Countryside Cottages, North Norfolk. Wide selection of quality cottages in stunning coastal and countryside locations, all within 20 minutes of coast. Telephone (01263) 713133, email: cottages@dialstart.net www.luxury-norfolk-cottages.com

Thaxted Holiday Cottages, Essex. In beautiful countryside, two cottages, each sleep 4, plus B & B in converted stables. Telephone (01371) 830233, email: enquiries@thaxtedholidaycottages.co.uk www.thaxtedholidaycottages.co.uk

Elms Farm Cottage, Fleckney. Comfortable, fully equipped cottage on working farm in heart of rural Leicestershire, ETC 3 Star. Telephone (01162) 402238, email info@elms-farm.co.uk www.elms-farm.co.uk

Woodthorpe, Lincolnshire (near Alford). Attractive, well equipped cottages near superb sandy beaches. Sleep 2-6. Telephone (01507) 450294, email: enquiries@woodthorpehall.com www.woodthorpehall.com

Belleau Cottage, near Alford. Situated on the edge of the Lincolnshire Wolds, steeped in history and places of interest. Telephone (07984) 437517, email: dom@thepersuadersltd.co.uk www.belleaucottage.co.uk

Waingrove Farm Country Cottages, Fulstow, Louth. Award winning cottages offering a rural retreat in the heart of Lincolnshire countryside. Telephone (01507) 363704, email: ptinker-tinkernet@virgin.net www.lincolnshirecottages.com

Cliff Farm Cottage, North Carlton, Lincolnshire. Converted 19th century farm building with panoramic views across the Trent Valley. Telephone (01522) 730475, email: rae.marris@farming.co.uk www.cliff-farm-cottage.co.uk

Keld Head, Pickering. Nine cosy stone farm cottages, by North Yorkshire Moors. Four-poster beds. Sleep 2-8+cots. Telephone (01751) 473974. email: julian@keld-headcottages.com www.keldheadcottages.com

Burton, Turbine, Greystones, Charlie's Stables, Reeth. Stone-built cottages with views to the Pennines, ideal for the Yorkshire Dales. Sleep 2-5. Telephone (01748) 884273, email: cproctor@aol.com www.uk-cottages.com

Baille Hill House, York. Outstanding and sumptuously comfortable gem of a house, overlooking York's historic walls. Sleeps up to 10. Telephone (01845) 597660, email: enquiries@baillehillhouse.co.uk www.baillehillhouse.co.uk

Mel House Cottages, Pickering. 3 properties in extensive grounds. Perfect for York and Moors. Indoor pool. Suitable for mobility impaired. Telephone (01751) 475396. email: holiday@letsholiday.com www.letsholiday.com

Westwood Lodge, Ilkley - Yorkshire's original spa town. Superbly equipped cottages and apartments. M2 disability access award. Sleep 2-9. Telephone (01943) 433430. email: welcome@westwoodlodge.co.uk www.westwoodlodge.co.uk

Bottoms Farm Holiday Cottages, Oakworth. 3 olde worlde character cottages sleeping 4-6. Set in Bronte Country with spectacular views and walks. Telephone (01535) 607720. email: bottomsfarm@btinternet.com

Lilac Cottage, Aldbrough, East Yorkshire. Small charming cottage close to coast. Sleeps 4. Telephone (01964) 527645, email: nick@seasideroad.freeserve.com www.dialspace.dial.pipex.com/town/walk/aer96/lilac-cottage

Rudstone Walk Farm Cottages, South Cave. Eleven cottages close to East Yorkshire sandy beaches. Sleep 2-6. Telephone (01430) 422230, email: office@rudstone-walk.co.uk www.rudstone-walk.co.uk

2 Mouldgreave Cottages, Oxenhope. 18th century Grade II listed rural cottage close to historic Haworth and York. Sleeps 5. Telephone (01535) 642325, email: 2mouldgreave@lineone.net

Orchard Cottage, Goathland, North Yorkshire. Quiet location in popular moorland village. Sleeps up to 6. Telephone (01947) 896391, email: enquiries@theorchard-cottages.co.uk www.theorchardcottages.co.uk

Cam Beck Cottage, Kettlewell, North Yorkshire. Idyllic 300 year old stone cottage with trout stream running alongside. Many walks from the door. Sleeps 4. Telephone (01132) 589833.

Dales Holiday Cottages offer cosy cottages for 2 to a splendid 16th Century building for 19. Telephone (01756) 799821, email: info@dales-holiday-cottages.com www.dales-holiday-cottages.com

Country Hideaways. 40 carefully selected properties in stunning locations in the heart of the Yorkshire Dales. Sleep up to 10. Telephone (01969) 663559. email: cottageguide@countryhideaways.co.uk www.countryhideaways.co.uk

Holiday Cottages in Yorkshire, Lancashire, Derbyshire and Cumbria. Over 200 properties from cosy cottages for 2 to spacious barns for 14. Telephone (01756) 700510. email: info@holidaycotts.co.uk www.holidaycotts.co.uk

Three traditional Dales stone cottages in beautiful Peak District National Park. Sleep 1 x 2 and 2 x 2+2. Telephone (07817) 900841, email: halleyr@aol.com www.thimble-cottage.co.uk

Bradley Hall, near Ashbourne, Derbyshire. Highly individual, converted apartments with original features in rural surroundings. Sleep 4-9. Telephone (01335) 370222. email: michelle@pmwproperty.com www.ashbourneselfcatering.com

Badger, Butterfield and Bluebell Cottages, near Buxton. Comfortable stone cottages in heart of Peak District National Park. Sleep 6-8. Children & pets welcome. Telephone (01298) 872927. email: jan@cosycotts.com www.cosycotts.com

Byanna Hall, Eccleshall, Staffordshire. 17th century manor house and butler's annexe close to Eccleshall Castle. Sleeps 20. Telephone (01785) 850518, email: byannanivas@aol.com www.holiday-rentals.com/index.cfm/property/6416.cfm

Rushop Hall, Castleton. Three historic cottages sleeping 2, 4 and 6 in the Peak District National Park on the Pennine Bridleway. Telephone (01298) 813323, email: neil@rushophall.com www.rushophall.com

Ollerbrook Cottages, Edale Valley. Two 17th century cottages yards from the Pennine Way. Original features and furnished to high standard. Sleep 3 or 5. Telephone (01433) 670083. email: greenlees@ollerbookcottages.fsnet.co.uk www.ollerbrook-cottages.co.uk

Breamish Valley Cottages, Branton. Beautifully situated at foot of Cheviot Hills; half hour from Northumberland coast. Telephone (01665) 578253, email: peter@breamishvalley.co.uk www.breamishvalley.co.uk

Burradon Farm Cottages, Cramlington, Northumberland. Cottages sleep 2-4. Fine views and ample parking. Good area for walking/cycling. Telephone: (01912) 683203, email: judy@burradonfarm.co.uk www.burradonfarm.co.uk

Beacon Hill Farm Holidays, Morpeth. Twelve superbly comfortable cottages on Northumberland farm with gym and other indoor and outdoor facilities. Telephone (01670) 780900. email: alun@beaconhill.co.uk www.beaconhill.co.uk

Britannia House and Cottage, Lindisfarne. Experience the magic of Holy Island; sandy beaches, castle and abbey. Sleep 6 and 4. Telephone (01289) 309826, email: ktiernan@onetel.net.uk www.lindisfarne-cottages.co.uk

Sandpiper Cottage, Low Newton, Northumberland. Delightful 18th century fisherman's cottage in outstanding coastal location. Sleeps 4+2. Telephone: (01665) 830783, email: sandpiper@nccc.demon.co.uk www.northumbria-cottages.co.uk

The Old Byre, Northumberland (near Hexham). Traditionally built farmsteading in 30 acres, panoramic views. Sleeps 6-9. Telephone (01434) 673259, email: enquiries@consult-courage.co.uk www.ryehillfarm.co.uk

Laneside Cottage, Barnard Castle, Durham. A haven of tranquillity; former farm-house with modern facilities and stunning views. Sleeps 8. Telephone (01833) 640209, email: teesdaleestate@rabycastle.com www.rabycastle.com

Kinlochlaich House, Appin, Argyll. Apartments/cottages within period house and grounds in spectacular Highlands. Telephone (01631) 730342, email: enquiries@kinlochlaich-house.co.uk www.kinlochlaich-house.co.uk

Achaglachgach Estate, South Knapsdale. Baronial mansion/cottages in secluded farm estate on shores of West Loch Tarbert. Sleep 4-14. Telephone (07770) 530249, email: Macleanh71@aol.com www.achahouse.com

Harrietfield Cottage, Roxburghshire. Two miles north of picturesque Kelso. Sleeps 2-5. Floors and Mellerstain Castles within easy reach. Telephone (01896) 831052, email: ncunnin640@aol.com

Crailloch Croft Cottages,Wigtownshire. 3 cosy cottages in peaceful countryside. Ideal base for local amenities and day trips to Ireland. Telephone (01776) 703092, email: viv@craillochcroft.freeserve.co.uk www.craillochcroftcottages.co.uk

The Pavilion, Ross-shire. Luxury apartment within historic and romantic Foulis Castle. Sleeps 4. Short breaks. Sitting room with open fire. Telephone (01349) 830212.

Alvie Holiday Cottages, Kincraig. Traditional cottages with superb views of the Cairngorms combining tranquillity and sports activities. Telephone (01540) 651255, email: info@alvie-estate.co.uk www.alvie-estate.co.uk

Lochinver Holiday Lodges, Sutherland. Seven lodges by the sea, each sleeping 4. STB 4 Stars. Telephone (01571) 844282. www.watersidehomes@bushinternet.com

Tigh-a-Chladaich, Sutherland. Split level house on rocky promontory with spectacular coastal views. Sleeps up to 8 people. Telephone (01571) 844282. email: enquire@by-sea.co.uk www.by-sea.co.uk

Coillabus Cottage, Isle of Islay. Comfortable cottage on working hill farm on beautiful Mull of Oa. Open fire. Sleeps 2-6. Telephone (01315) 531911, email: holiday@islay-cottage.co.uk www.islay-cottage.co.uk

Armadale Castle, Isle of Skye. Six comfortable log cottages plus suite with sea/mountain views. Sleep 4-6. Telephone (01471) 844305, email: office@cland.demon.co.uk www.clandonald.demon.co.uk

Pirate Gows Chalets, Eday, Orkney. Five self-catering chalets virtually on the seashore. Beautiful surroundings and views. Telephone (01857) 622285, email: jan.crichton@btinternet.com www.takeabreak.com.au/pirategowschalets.htm

Crosswoodhill Farm Cottages, West Calder. Four exceptional homes on West Lothian hill farm. Visit their award-winning website for a wealth of details and photos. email: gchg@crosswoodhill.co.uk www.crosswoodhill.co.uk

Auchtermuchty Holiday Homes. Two warm and comfortable homes in small historic town of Auchtermuchty in the Kingdom of Fife. Sleep 5 and 6. Telephone (01337) 828496. email: elizabeth@auchtermuchty.com www.auchtermuchty.com

Binnilidh Mhor, Glenmoriston. Large and luxurious cottage for 2-6 near shores of Loch Ness with spectacular views. Suitable for guests with mobility disabilities. Telephone (01320) 340258. email: sheila@binmhor.co.uk www.binmhor.co.uk

Duirinish Holiday Lodges, Ross-shire. Nine lodges offering excellent self catering facilities for up to 4 or 6 on North West coast of Scottish Highlands. Telephone (01599) 544268. email: sales@duirinishlodges.com www.duirinishlodges.com

Strathconon, Isle of Arran. Luxurious villa in sunny, secluded spot on outskirts of beautiful Whiting Bay. Sleeps 2-8. STB 4 stars. Telephone (01586) 830323. email: enquiries@arranselfcatering.com www.arranselfcatering.com

Dalhougal House Apartments, Croftamie. 200 year old refurbished apartments maintaining cosy Scottish atmosphere in Loch Lomond village. Sleep up to 4. Telephone (01360) 660558. email: dalhougal@croftamie.com www.dalhougal.com

Westloch House, Coldingham, Berwickshire. Ten character cottages sleeping 2 to 6. Coldingham Loch, known for its trout, is a stunning feature. Telephone (01890) 771270, email: westloch@hotmail.com

Leckmelm Holiday Cottages, near Loch Broom. Close to Ullapool, a lively fishing village on Scotland's scenic north west coast. Sleep 2 to 10. Dogs welcome. Telephone (01854) 612471.

Holiday Houses in Scotland. Some of the best self-catering houses and cottages in the most beautiful parts of Scotland. Tel. (01556) 504030, email: lettings@scothols.co.uk www.scothols.co.uk www.discoverscotland.net

The Association of Scotland's Self Caterers. A comprehensive choice of carefully vetted properties throughout Scotland. www.assc.co.uk

Brook House, near Keswick. Four 17th century stream-side properties in the delightful village of Bassenthwaite. Sleep 2-10. Telephone (01768) 776393, email: a.m.trafford@amserve.net www.holidaycottageslakedistrict.co.uk

Loft Holiday Cottages. 2 cottages between Skiddaw Mountain and Bassenthwaite Lake. Close to Keswick and Cockermouth. Telephone (01768) 776828, email: info@loftholidaycottages.co.uk www.loftholidaycottages.co.uk

Setrah Cottage, near Bassenthwaite. Charming cottage in quiet lane at the heart of Bothel Village. Excellent leisure facilities nearby. Telephone (01697) 320919, email: office@skiddawview.com www.skiddawview.co.uk

Barn House, Braithwaite. Traditional Lakeland Cottage, sleeps 2-6. Superb fells walks from the door and forest mountain bike trails. Telephone (01768) 778411, email: info@braithwaitefarm.wanadoo.co.uk www.barnhouseholidays.co.uk

Bridge End, Eskdale, Cumbria. Award-winning, characterful, Grade II listed cottages in small hamlet in valley beneath Scafell Pike. Telephone (08700) 735328, email: greg@selectcottages.com www.selectcottages.com

The Orchards Apartment and Coach House, Eskdale. Ideal base to explore the Lake District; wonderful views over fells. Sleep 2-4. Telephone (01946) 723374, email: selfcatering@orchards-eskdale.com www.orchards-eskdale.com

Ashness Apartment, Keswick town centre. Beautiful apartment with views of Keswick and Derwent Water. Sleeps 6. Telephone (01768) 780855, email: info@ashness.net www.ashness.net

Acorn Self Catering, Keswick. Three comfortable properties within five minutes of the town centre, sleep 6, 5 and 5. Telephone (01768) 480310, email: info@acornselfcatering.co.uk www.acornselfcatering.co.uk

Richmond Cottage, Orton Hall. Peaceful relaxation in elegant wing of 17th century mansion in unspoilt Cumbrian countryside. Telephone (01539) 624330, email: info@stayinortonhall.com www.stayinortonhall.com

Stonefold Cottages, Penrith. 3 cottages within tastefully furnished 18th century stone building next to the Lake District. Telephone (01768) 866383, email: email@stonefold.co.uk www.stonefold.co.uk

Fell View, Cumbria. Cottages/apartments in peaceful grounds close to Lake Ullswater, half a mile from Helvellyn. Pets welcome. Telephone (01768) 482342, email: enquiries@fellviewholidays.com www.fellviewholidays.com

Green View Lodges, Welton. On northern edge of Lake District National Park, close to Scottish Borders, Scandinavian lodges sleeping 4 or 7. Telephone (01697) 476230. email: ghcg@green-view-lodges.com www.green-view-lodges.com

Staffield Hall, Kirkoswald, near Penrith. Seven elegant apartments in a magnificent mansion. Sleep 2 to 5 all with four poster beds. Telephone (01768) 898656, email: goodcotguid@staffieldhall.co.uk www.staffieldhall.co.uk

Cumbrian Cottages. Cottages, apartments and houses in superb locations throughout the Lake District and Cumbria. www.cumbrian-cottages.co.uk

Traditional Lakeland Cottages. An unrivalled selection of self catering holiday retreats within this beautiful corner of England. www.lakelovers.co.uk

Sir Johns Hill Farm Cottages, Laugharne, Carmarthenshire. Three cottages in secluded location with views. Grazing for visiting horses. Telephone (01994) 427667, email: liz.handford@sirjohnshillfarm.co.uk www.sirjohnshillfarm.co.uk

Penffynnon, Aberporth. Characterful well-equipped properties by sandy beaches. Sea views. Dogs welcome by arrangement. Telephone (01239) 810387, email: tt@lineone.net www.aberporth.com

Melin Llecheiddior, near Criccieth. 2 self catering cottages between the mountains of Snowdonia and the beaches of the Lleyn Peninsula. Telephone (01766) 530635, email: elen@whevans.freeserve.co.uk www.cottages-in-snowdonia.co.uk

Ystumgwern Hall Farm, Dyffryn Ardudwy. 14th century farmhouse and barn conversions in heart of Snowdonia National Park. Telephone (01341) 247249, email: ynys@ystumgwern.co.uk www.ystumgwern.co.uk

Ffynnonofi Farm. Secluded farmhouse in North Pembrokeshire National Park with private beach. Sleeps 7-8 people. Telephone (01179) 268554 email: info@ffynnonofi.co.uk www.ffynnonofi.co.uk

Carno Farmhouse and Little Barn, Libanus. WTB Grade 5/Disabled Access 2, sleeping 4/5 in the heart of the Brecon Beacons National Park. Telephone (01874) 625630. email: june.scarborough@lineone.net www.brecon.co.uk/local/carno

Wales Holidays. Around 550 properties throughout all areas of Wales, many in the Pembrokeshire and Snowdonia National Parks. Telephone (01686) 628200. email: info@wales-holidays.co.uk www.wales-holidays.co.uk

Sea Front Holiday Cottages, Coverack, Cornwall with thatched roof and original shipwreck beams was once a smuggler's hideaway. Telephone (01736) 850549, email: ray@good-holidays.demon.co.uk www.good-holidays.demon.co.uk

Broomhill Manor, Cornwall (near Bude). 17 cottages and wing of manor house in beautiful 9-acre gardens. Sleep 2-6. Telephone (01288) 352940, email: chris@broomhillmanor.co.uk www.broomhillmanor.co.uk

Houndapitt, Bude, Cornwall. Traditional farm cottages set in 100 acre estate overlooking Sandymouth Bay. Sleeps 2-9. Telephone (01288) 355455, email: info@houndapitt.co.uk www.houndapitt.co.uk

The Old Farmhouse and Buttermill Cottage. Grade II listed farmhouse and barn conversion sleep 6/2. Telephone (01288) 341622, email: helebarton@hotmail.com www.helebarton.co.uk

Fresh Breaks, Cornwall. High quality self catering accommodation with extremely comfortable furnishings, all in idyllic locations. Telephone (02089) 932628, email: bookings@freshbreaks.co.uk www.freshbreaks.co.uk

Barclay House, East Looe, Cornwall. Luxury cottages ETC 5 star. Restaurant, lounge/bar, heated swimming pool. Telephone (01503) 262929, email: info@barclayhouse.co.uk www.barclayhouse.co.uk

Kennacott Court, Bude. Overlooking Widemouth Bay a variety of outstanding award winning cottages with excellent leisure centre sleeping 2-10. Telephone (01288) 362000. email: phil@kennacottcourt.co.uk www.kennacottcourt.co.uk

Treworgie Barton Holiday Cottages, St. Genny's. Nine superb character cottages in 36 acres of farmland and woodland setting within North Cornwall Heritage Coast area. Telephone (01840) 230233. email: info@treworgie.co.uk
www.treworgie.co.uk

West Tremabe Cottages, Liskeard. Two beautifully converted and well equipped traditional Cornish stone barns, ideal for couples. Telephone (01579) 321863. email: christine.j.foster@btopenworld.com www.west-tremabe-cottages.co.uk

Trenant Park Cottages, near Looe. Four spacious cottages in a country park setting. Sleep 2-5. Five minutes from South Cornwall's superb beaches. Telephone (01503) 263639/262241. email: liz@holiday-cottage.com www.trenantcottages.com

Trevigue Wildlife Conservation, Crackington Haven. Luxurious coastal cottages surrounded by National Trust farmland in North Cornwall. Telephone (01840) 230418 www.wild-trevigue.co.uk

Cant Cove Cottages, Rock. Six exceptional 5 Key Deluxe cottages sleeping 5-8 in private 70 acre setting overlooking the Camel Estuary in North Cornwall. Telephone (01208) 862841. email: info@cantcove.co.uk www.cantcove.co.uk

Penrose Burden, St. Breward. Nine character cottages in peaceful, rural setting, sleeping 2-6 close to Bodmin Moor. Especially suitable for disabled people. Telephone (01208) 850277/850617. www.penroseburden.co.uk

Best Leisure. Superb accommodation in magnificent settings in Devon and Cornwall. Family owned properties highly graded by the ETC. Telephone (01271) 850611. www.bestleisure.co.uk

Northleigh Farm Holiday Cottages, near Colyton. Three ETC 4 Star barn conversions in the beautiful rolling countryside of the Coly Valley. Telephone (01404) 871217, email: simon@northleighfarm.co.uk www.northleighfarm.co.uk

Halcyon Cottage, near Honiton. Attractive cottage within easy reach of East Devon Heritage Coast. Telephone (01404) 549196,
email anne_biddle@lineone.net web.pncl.co.uk/molehayes/

Hill Cottage, Clawton, Devon. Large, private gardens, spectacular countryside views. 20 mins drive from beach. Sleeps 8, children welcome. Telephone (01409) 253093, email: lgsg@supanet.com www.selfcateringcottagesdevon.co.uk

Nature's Watch, Honiton. Two high quality cottages on the edge of the Blackdown Hills in Devon. Panoramic views and wildlife. Telephone (01404) 891949, email: enquiries@natureswatch.com www.natureswatch.com

Kingston Estate, near Totnes. Beautiful cottages in glorious setting; easy reach of Dartmoor, sea and many Devon/Cornish attractions. Telephone (01803) 762235, email: info@kingston-estate.co.uk www.kingston-estate.co.uk

Beachcomber Cottage, Beer. Period stone cottage close to the beach and South Devon coastal footpath. Sleeps 6+cot. Children and pets welcome. Telephone (01298) 872927. email: jan@cosycotts.com www.cosycotts.com

Chalkway, Cricket St. Thomas. 19th century woodman's cottage sleeping 4 with panoramic valley views. Ideal for exploring Lyme Regis, East Devon and West Dorset. Telephone 0208 444 4296. email: elisabeth@thebuttonfamily.co.uk www.westcountryhideaway.co.uk

Lancombe Country Cottages, near Dorchester. Five flint and brick cottages with breathtaking views. Indoor heated pool with sauna. Telephone (01300) 320562, email: info@lancombe.co.uk

The Quarterdeck, Dorset. Spacious family property with sea views close to splendid Swanage beaches. Sleeps 10. Telephone (01929) 553443,
email: leanne@purbeckholidays.co.uk www.purbeckholidays.co.uk

Country Ways, High Bickington, North Devon. Beautifully converted stone barns on small farm. Five cottages sleeping up to 21/28. Lovely gardens. Telephone (01769) 560503, email: country-ways@virgin.net www.country-ways.net

Thorne Manor, Holsworthy. 10 cottages on working farm with games facilities. Ideal for families. Telephone (01409) 253342, email: thornemanor@ex227jd.freeserve.co.uk www.thorne-manor-holiday-cottages.co.uk

Widmouth Farm Cottages, North Devon. Nine cottages (sleeping 2-6) with spectacular views in secluded valley with private beach. Telephone (01271) 863743. email: holiday@widmouthfarmcottages.co.uk www.widmouthfarmcottages.co.uk

Stable/Blackspur Cottages, Norton-sub-Hamdon. Excellent cottages sleeping 2-4 in peaceful Somerset village nestling beside Ham Hill Countryside Park. Telephone (01935) 881789.

The Old Stables and Barley Cottage, Chichester. Cottages on working family farm. Both sleep 4. Telephone (02392) 631382, email: carole.edney@btopenworld.com www.theoldstables.net and www.barleycottage.co.uk

The Thatched Barn, Broadwater, near Andover. Self catering or B & B. Sleeps up to 3 in peaceful village setting. Telephone (01264) 772240, email: carolyn@dmac.co.uk www.dmac.co.uk/carolyn

The Barn at Bombers, Westerham. High quality 16th century barn conversions situated in open countryside. ETC 5 star. Sleep 6. Telephone (01959) 573471, email: roy@bombers-farm-co.uk www.bombers-farm-co.uk

Fairhaven Holiday Cottages. Specialists in Kent and Sussex plus 2 Wiltshire farm cottages. Almost 100 properties. Sleep from 2-14. Telephone (01208) 821255. www.fairhaven-holidays.co.uk www.scottscastles.com

Westley Farm, Chalford. Five cottages on old-fashioned Cotswold hill farm. Views over the Golden Valley. Cirencester/Stroud 6 miles. Telephone (01285) 760262, email: cottages@westleyfarm.co.uk www.westleyfarm.co.uk

Folly Farm Cottages, Tetbury. Twelve stone cottages nestling on 200 acre estate in the Rural South Cotswold. Sleep 2 - 8. Telephone (01666) 502475, email info@gtb.co.uk www.gtb.co.uk

Grove House Holidays near Ledbury. Four holiday homes sleeping 2 -5 in country setting within easy reach of the Malvern Hills. Telephone (01531) 650584, email: ross@the-grovehouse.co.uk www.the-grovehouse.com

Combermere Abbey, Whitchurch. 11 cottages in stable block of 12th century Cistercian monastery on 1000 acre estate. Sleep 4-8. Telephone (01948) 662876. email: cottages@combermereabbey.co.uk www.combermereabbey.co.uk

Oatfield Country Cottages, Blakeney. Six cottages converted from Grade II listed 17th century farm buildings overlooking Gloucestershire's Severn Estuary. Ideal touring location. Telephone (01594) 510372. www.oatfieldfarm.co.uk

Wye Lea Country Manor, Ross-on-Wye. 5 Star accommodation with excellent facilities for the whole family in an area of outstanding beauty. Sleep 2-54. Telephone (01989) 562880. email: enquire@wyelea.co.uk www.wyelea.co.uk

Cotswold Property Lettings. Find the perfect holiday home from cosy cottages to large period properties. All personally inspected. Telephone (01386) 858147, email: gill@cotswoldpropertylettings.com www.cotswoldpropertylettings.com

Largy Coastal Apartments. Five star accommodation on beautiful Antrim coast with spectacular views of Irish Sea. Telephone 0 2828 885635, email: gladyssmith@btopenworld.com www.ireland4you.freeservers.com

Index (UK/Ireland)

W

Y